ENGLISH SATIRE
AND SATIRISTS

ENGLISH SATIRE AND SATIRISTS

BY

HUGH WALKER

1 9 6 5

OCTAGON BOOKS, INC.

NEW YORK

Originally published 1925, by J. M. Dent & Sons Ltd.

Reprinted 1965
by special arrangement with J. M. Dent & Sons Ltd.

OCTAGON BOOKS, INC.
175 FIFTH AVENUE
NEW YORK, N. Y. 10010

LIBRARY OF CONGRESS CATALOG CARD NUMBER: 65-16780

Printed in U.S.A. by
NOBLE OFFSET PRINTERS, INC.
NEW YORK 3, N. Y.

INTRODUCTION

It is never easy to frame precise definitions of literary genera, and the attempt to do so is rarely profitable; for one form shades off into another. We know well enough what we mean by a lyric, but we are sometimes puzzled to determine whether a given poem should be called a lyric or not. Still more is this the case with satire. The Romans claimed to have invented satire, and in the sense in which they meant it the claim was justified. Most of their literary forms they borrowed from the Greeks, but not the satire. For satire the Greeks had no specialised form. Yet of course the thing itself, the spirit, is present in Greek literature. There is satire in Homer, and there have been few, if any, satirists greater than Aristophanes. There is satire even in the Bible: " No doubt ye are the people, and wisdom will die with you," is satirical. In short, satire is almost as old as literature; and each people in turn that develops a literature develops a satire also.

According to a view recently prevalent, it ought to follow from this that the true nature of satire is to be found by searching back to the beginnings of literature. Freeman saw practically the whole of the English constitution in the primitive laws and customs of the Teutons. The same spirit dominated Rousseau when he thought to find the natural state of man in his primeval condition. But another view is possible, and has been held by a man greater than either Freeman or Rousseau—Aristotle. He taught that we must look to the end of a process of development, and interpret the beginning by the end, rather than the end by the beginning. We do not get the true "natural man" until we arrive at the perfect political form—the city state. The Athenian of the age of Pericles is more "natural" than the naked savage, for "Nature implies complete development." The view which will be taken in this book is that this is as true of literature as it is of politics. Homer is an excellent exemplar of the epic, just because he is far from being

v

the earliest of poets. No amount of study of the first stumblings of satire will teach what satire really is: that is to be learnt from a consideration of the acknowledged masters—such masters as Aristophanes, Horace and Juvenal, Voltaire and Cervantes, and in English, Dryden, Pope and Swift, Burns and Byron. The oak reflects light upon the acorn, but from the acorn alone we could never divine the oak.

The word satire, then, has more than one meaning. As there is a Comic Spirit, so there is a Satiric Spirit; and as there is a form of the drama we call Comedy, so there is a form of verse we call Satire. But as the Comic Spirit may manifest itself in the novel or the poem no less than in the comedy, so the Satiric Spirit may appear in prose as well as in verse, and both in verse and in prose it assumes manifold shapes. There are satirical novels and tales, essays and allegories. There are satirical lyrics and even satirical odes; and *Paradise Lost* itself contains fragments of satire. What may be called the classical satire of England is derived from the satire of the Latin poets; and as the Latin satirists adopted the hexameter, so their English imitators used the English equivalent, the heroic couplet. When Hall wrote the often-quoted lines,

" I first adventure: follow me who list,
    And be the second English satirist,"

he must have had it in his mind that this was the only form of satire worthy of recognition; for except on that supposition his claim was not even plausible.

In dealing with English satire it is clearly impossible to take so narrow a view as this. We must regard the Satiric Spirit in all its breadth. Even if we were tempted to limit ourselves to verse, it would be necessary to include many forms of verse. Swift was one of the greatest of satirists; but when he wrote satire in verse he chose the octosyllabic line. *Don Juan* is one of the greatest of satires; but its structure is stanzaic. The idea, however, of dealing only with satire in verse must be rejected the moment it is seriously examined. Swift's greatest satires are in prose. Indeed, a little reflection shows that the Satiric Spirit is prosaic rather than poetical. There must, it is clear, be certain qualities of verse which are valuable to the satirist, or Latin, French, and English satirists

would not have resorted to it so frequently. Verse tends to neatness and concision; and the more concisely and neatly he can make
his points, the better for the satirist. It would hardly be possible
to draw the character of Atticus as perfectly in prose as Pope
drew it in verse. Neatness and concision are valuable to the poet
too, but they are only a small part of the soul of poetry; and it is
significant that the great age of the classical satire in English is
just the age in which the men of the romantic revival could scarcely
find poetry at all. And for the advantage he gains the satirist in verse
certainly pays a price. *Quicquid agunt homines* one of the greatest
of them has declared to be his theme; but not everything that men
do can be naturally expressed in verse. Swift would have been
shorn of his power if he had been forced to write his *Gulliver* in
verse, and Thackeray could never have uttered his criticism of the
world in a metrical *Vanity Fair* or *Barry Lyndon*.

The range of the Satiric Spirit, therefore, is extraordinarily wide.
It is found in every form of literature, and in English it does not
begin with Joseph Hall. We must seek it through all literature, and
from the beginnings of literature. But not earlier, and not outside
the bounds of literature. The first thing from which we must distinguish satire is mere scolding. Billingsgate is not, though the
language of the London cabman frequently is, or was, satire.
Billingsgate is simply abusive, but the cabman expressed himself
with a skill which was in essence literary, though he might never
have read a book. Where this skill begins to be shown in a critical
and negative way we have the beginnings of satire. The Satiric
Spirit is akin to "der Geist der stets verneint." Not that every
negation is satirical: there is plenty of negation in the Decalogue,
as well as in Mephistopheles.

Yet, omnipresent as the Satiric Spirit is, satire is in truth a
"channel" of English literature, and not something co-extensive
with it. We do not think of Milton as a satirist because he described
the Limbo of Fools, nor for certain passages in *Samson Agonistes*,
nor even for what may be culled from his prose. There are very
effective satirical passages in the dramas of Shakespeare, yet so
completely is satire lost in the larger mass of his thought that to
treat him as a satirist would be merely to distort him. Precision
is unattainable; the edges of the "channel" blend imperceptibly

with its containing banks. All are agreed that one swallow does not make a summer, but no one has ever yet defined how many swallows *do* make a summer. So too it is impossible to say how much of the Satiric Spirit it needs to make a satirist or a satire. But it is clear in the first place that regard must be paid to proportion. Where the satiric element is subordinate, it will usually be best simply to omit; and for this reason only a few dramas and novels will be dealt with. In the second place, while it is impossible to limit the view to formal satire alone, it seems reasonable to give special prominence to such satire. Finally, on the principle laid down above, the early rude attempts at satire before the rise of satire will be passed over lightly; for they bear to the work of an artist such as Pope a relation similar to that which the scrawlings of the cave-men bear to the paintings of Turner.

To

THE MEMORY OF

MY DEAR WIFE

CONTENTS

ENGLISH SATIRE AND SATIRISTS

CHAPTER I

THE BEGINNINGS OF SATIRE

ENGLISH satire was born in the twelfth century. The remains of Old English literature are as void of the satiric spirit as it is possible for literature to be, and it is not till some time after the Norman Conquest that we find whole compositions which may reasonably be called satires. The earliest of these compositions are not written in the English language. They are either Latin pieces of what we may call the classical tradition, or Goliardic Latin verses, or *sirventes* written in French. Gradually, in satire as in all literature, and for every purpose of life, the native English prevailed over the foreign tongues; but only after the lapse of some generations. In Wright's *Political Songs of England*, covering the period from John to Edward II., it is not till the reign of Edward I. that pieces in the vernacular become frequent; and the conspicuous instance of Gower shows that this division of the literature of England between three languages continued till near the end of the fourteenth century.

Among writers of the more formal Latin verse, only two seem to require notice here. John of Salisbury and Alexander Neckham have both been spoken of as satirists, but they are rather serious-minded preachers and moralists, and their methods are too direct for true satire. It is otherwise with John de Hauteville and Nigel Wireker. The former is the author of *Architrenius*, a long poem in unusually good hexameters, lamenting the vices of the age. Architrenius, "the Master Weeper," sets out on a journey to seek Nature and beg her help against temptation. Visits on the way to the palace of Venus and the abode of Gluttony occasion moralising and satire

I

of a sort which may be inferred from the names. More interesting is the moving picture of the privations and toils of the scholars of Paris. The sight of the Mount of Ambition leads to a satire on the corruption of the court. Then follow the Hill of Presumption and the Monster Cupidity. Next Architrenius arrives at Thule, where he finds the Greek philosophers, who denounce vice through the whole of one book and parts of two others. Ultimately he reaches the beautiful lady Nature, who discourses to him at great length on the marvels and mysteries of that for which she stands, and in the end rewards him with a beautiful wife Moderation.

This poem is highly characteristic of the time, both in its allegorical form and in its didactic spirit. There are large parts of it which are not satirical at all, and the absence of humour greatly lowers its effect; but the general purpose is satirical, and the strokes are occasionally sharp and telling. As a satirist however the author of *Architrenius* is much inferior to Nigel Wireker, a writer of the latter part of the twelfth century, who embodied his views of the world, and especially of scholars and monks, in the *Speculum Stultorum*, or *Fools' Looking-Glass*. As he was a Benedictine monk of Canterbury, his is criticism of the Orders from within. It is a feature of the satires of the time that the strictures on the Church are pronounced by men who are either themselves ecclesiastics or at least in sympathy with the institution which they criticise. What they desire is the reform of abuses, not radical change, still less destruction; and they are hopeful that reform may be brought about by comparatively mild means. " Many are the diseases," says Nigel, " which yield more readily to unguents than to caustic." [1] We must suppose the same spirit to have inspired Walter Map. If he was the author of the *Queste del Saint Graal*, he was sympathetic towards the highest spiritual claims of the Church. So was the author of *Piers Plowman*. It is not until we draw near the Reformation that we observe an attitude more decidedly negative and more hostile to the Church as a whole.

Nigel, though forgotten now, was popular in the generations following his own, and Chaucer has given him a place in his delightful *Nun's Priest's Tale*. When the Fox tells Chanticleer that he has "read in daun Burnel the Asse" how a cock in revenge for a blow

[1] Quoted by S. M. Tucker, in *Verse Satire in England before the Restoration*.

upon the leg had caused a priest's son to lose a benefice, the allusion is to Nigel. The *Speculum Stultorum* is a satirical allegory which relates how Burnellus the Ass, who represents the monks, has become discontented and desirous of novelty. The special novelty on which he has set his heart is a longer tail. In vain he is assured that in the matter of a tail he is as well off as certain of the greatest personages; nothing will satisfy him but to try to get a longer one; and so his physician Galienus gives him a receipt to make the tail grow. But the ingredients can only be got at Salernum, the great medical school of the Middle Ages. Thither Burnellus sets out, and the incidents of his journey are prolific of satire. On the way home he meets with dire misfortune through the malignity of a Cistercian monk—Burnellus himself being a Benedictine. Dogs bite off half his tail, and his bottles of medicine are thrown down and broken. Foiled in the original purpose of his journey, he goes to Paris to study; and in the description of the English "nation" and other "nations" of that great gathering-place of students, there is matter to compare with the corresponding passages in de Hauteville, and to supplement them by. But the ass's head is ill fitted for learning; so Burnellus leaves the university and becomes a monk—a sly hint that the cloisters are the resort of the stupid. Then follows an effective satire on the various Orders—Hospitallers, Black Monks, White Monks, Carthusians, and various others—in particular the *Ordo de Simplingham*. The last is really the Order of Sempringham, or the Gilbertine Canons as they were called; and the peculiarity which exposed them to the satirist was that monks and nuns were lodged in the same house, though they were separated, and intercourse between them was forbidden. Envy and jealousy, ignorance and stupidity and vices manifold are represented as characterising the monks. The satire culminates in the proposal, as each Order in turn has been found unsatisfactory, to found a *novus ordo Burnelli*—the Order of the Ass. In its rules is to be embodied the best from all the other Orders, and the best is the peculiar indulgence of each. Thus by skilful selection all that the world can give is brought back for the benefit of those who have renounced the world and retired to the cloisters. The companionship of women is sanctioned by the example of Sempringham; and fine linen and soft seats and flesh and dainty food and wines being found already in one or other of the Orders, are also to be enjoyed by the brethren of the Order of the Ass. But the precious right to lie without restraint, which is the special characteristic of the Templars, Burnellus reserves for himself alone. All the other goods of life are common to the Order; this, in its full extent, is enjoyed by the founder and head only.

The *Speculum Stultorum* stands first in its class, and the passage describing the Order of the Ass is by far the finest in the whole poem. The writers of the time who aim at satirical effect are, as a rule, much too downright; they do not know how by indirections to "find directions out." They wield the bludgeon, not the satirist's proper weapon, the rapier. But Nigel understands the value of irony, and is sufficiently detached to look upon the monastic Orders humorously. Thus, though his elegiacs are less scholarly than the hexameters of John de Hauteville, they are far more effective. His superiority was appreciated, and the conception of the Order of the Ass became popular. Nigel's idea is borrowed and worked out at greater length in a keen and lively satire in French of the time of Edward I., *The Order of Fair Ease.*

The less regular Latin satires of the twelfth century are associated with a name of much greater importance in English literature than that of Nigel Wireker. How far Walter Map was really the author of the Goliardic poems traditionally ascribed to him cannot be determined. No doubt much is attributed to him that he never wrote. Somehow or other he came to be regarded as *the* Goliard of his time; and so nameless poems were naturally ascribed to him, just as in our own day stories of certain types are habitually associated with certain names. So far has this been carried in the case of Map that he has been himself identified with the imaginary, or at least unknown, Golias; and the most familiar lines in all this literature are those in which he has without real ground been supposed to paint his own portrait:—

> "Meum est propositum in taberna mori:
> Vinum sit appositum morientis ori,
> Ut dicant cum venerint angelorum chori,
> ' Deus sit propitius huic potatori.' "

But Golias, if he ever lived, lived three hundred years before Map; for Mr. Chambers in *The Mediæval Stage* has shown that as early as A.D. 913 the name was already a by-word for the *Clericus ribaldus.*

Map, therefore, was not Golias, nor did he invent either the name or the character; he only found it convenient for the expression of his detestation of the Cistercian monks. To doubt whether he wrote any of the Goliardic poems because he certainly did not write all that have been set down to him, would be to carry scepticism to an extreme point. By far the most rational explanation of the fact that he came to be regarded as the Goliard *par excellence* is to suppose that he wrote either a great many Goliardic poems, or at least a few of special excellence. And while we must recognise the doubt that hangs over the authorship of these poems, there is an obvious convenience in discussing the whole of them in connexion with the name of Map, the supposed author of so many.

Goliardic verse, then, is satirical verse in Latin which, unlike that of John de Hauteville and Nigel Wireker, has no relation to classical Latin satire. It is frankly medieval. The language is the language of men who have no desire to follow in the steps of Cicero or Horace or Ovid. The metres are far closer akin to modern English metres than to the Latin hexameter or elegiac; and the prevailing theme is the Church, which was as far outside the purview of the Latin satirists as was Goliardic rhyme. Much of this Goliardic verse was apparently the work of wandering scholars who from dissipation or other causes had sunk to playing the part of buffoons. *Goliardi* are conjoined in an ancient ecclesiastical statute with *jaculatores* and *bufones*. In those days there were few scholars who were not connected with the Church, and so at first the Goliards were all ecclesiastics. Chaucer's Miller, however, who was " a Ianglere and a goliardeys," is proof that in later times these words did not connote scholarship.

Goliardic verse had for its principal aim an exposure of the abuses which had crept into the Church. The attacks are severe and sometimes even virulent. They bear witness to the greatness of the abuses and to the wide range over which they prevailed. If we may trust the satirists, corruption reached from the highest to the lowest. Greed is the vice of the papal court itself as well as of the monastery. The Pope is the devouring lion; the clergy do not feed their sheep, but rather feed upon them; the flock is stripped of property and follows blind guides; the bishop twists the law to his own advantage, and sells the rights of the Church; the clergy are

drunken, gluttonous and lustful. Such are the charges embodied
in *Apocalypsis Goliae,* a powerful and trenchant satire in the form
of a vision. The Grey Friars in particular are the object of unsparing
invective, and in a piece specially devoted to them their character
is painted in the blackest colours:—

> " Nil nisi praesentia sitiunt aut quaerunt,
> Farciunt marsupia, metunt quae non serunt,
> Pauperum penuria sese ditaverunt;
> Satanae mancipia sunt et semper erunt."

A similar but more restrained dislike is shown in Map's prose
work, *De Nugis Curialium,* where the Cistercians are accused of
making a solitude in order that they may be alone, of scattering
the parishioners of others because they have none of their own,
of destroying because the rule of the Order does not permit them
to save.[1]

Next to the Church as a theme for Goliardic satire came the female
sex. Sometimes, as in *Golias de Conjuge non Ducenda,* the satire
is little better than coarse abuse of women; but in many cases this
second theme is merely a branch of the first. The medieval Church
saw in every woman a potential Eve, and deemed it safer to shun
the temptation than to fight against it with the probability of
defeat. But nature is strong, and there was no small difficulty in
enforcing the papal policy of celibacy of the clergy. *De Concubinis
Sacerdotum, Consultatio Sacerdotum* and *De Convocatione Sacerdotum* are Goliardic pieces bearing witness to the resistance which
was offered to the papal decree forbidding the marriage of the
clergy. It is obvious that the mere fact that there was such a controversy must have tended to scandal; and all through the Goliardic
verse there is evidence that here was one of the gravest vices of
ecclesiastics. Next perhaps to the charge of greed that of impurity
is most insisted upon.

The earliest vernacular satire is akin to these Goliardic rhymes,
and to the French *sirventes* rather than to the statelier hexameters
and elegiacs. The metres are of a lyric type, and some of the pieces
have the rollick of the Goliards. The skill of the vernacular writers,
however, is far inferior. There is a lively rhythmical swing in the

---

[1] Map's *De Nugis Curialium* has recently been translated by Professors
F. Tupper and M. B. Ogle.

Goliardic Latin, but with few exceptions the English pieces are faulty and halting in metre. The educated preferred Latin, and, generally speaking, those who wrote English were those who did not know enough to write anything else. This vernacular verse is for the most part poor in substance as well as in form. It would be easy to attach too much importance to and to spend too much time upon these early efforts. It is well to bear in mind Carlyle's vigorous and characteristic comment upon the modern tendency to admire the antique merely because it is antique: "Old trash and filth is not the less filth and trash because it is old."

As has been said already, vernacular pieces do not become common until the reign of Edward I. Among the themes of satire the Church, of course, still holds a prominent place. The consistory courts are charged with exaction, the "somnours" misjudge all alike, and herdsmen and servants hate them. By far the ablest of such pieces is the amusing though extremely coarse *Land of Cokaygne*, which ridicules the gluttony and licentiousness of the monks. They and the nuns live together, their very dwellings are made of food, and the streams carry to them abundance of liquors more palatable and less innocent than water. But although the Church is still a prominent it is no longer the all-absorbing theme. In the earliest English *fabliau*, *Dame Siriz*, we have satire on the Church combined with satire on women. Other pieces deal with subjects wholly secular—the pride of the ladies, the extravagant retinues of the nobles, the covetousness of the king's ministers, or the burden of taxation, which leads one rhymer to complain that "ever the furthe peni mot to the kynge." The frequency with which the political note is sounded is significant. One of the most interesting pieces in Wright's *Political Songs of England* is that *On the King's Breaking his Confirmation of Magna Charta*, which shows a pungency by no means common in these rude compositions. "The charter," says the writer, "was made of wax, I hear so and well believe it; it was held too near the fire and is all melted away." There is merit too in the fable of the fox, the wolf and the ass in one of the *Songs of the Times*. The fox and the wolf are arraigned before the lion as evil-doers. The ass is charged too—and it is the ass against whom the lion pronounces sentence. He is bound and torn to pieces. His unnatural habit of eating grass begets suspicion. And who could suspect the fox, who has given the lion geese and hens, or the wolf, who has given him goats and mutton? The ass, like an ass, has given nothing and has relied upon innocence alone. The application of the fable is not left in doubt; the general theme of the piece is that pride and covetousness rule and the king's ministers are corrupt. Thus early did the satirist intervene in the long battle for popular rights; and as that battle was fought with greater determination in England than elsewhere, it is natural that the prevalence of the political theme should be one of the characteristics of English satire. It is natural too that a disastrous reign like that of Edward II. should afford more matter for the satirist than a period of able government such as that of his great father. The complaint with respect to Magna Charta belongs to Edward II.'s time, and so probably does the fable of the lion and the ass. So too does the long *Poem on the Times of Edward II.*, which sweeps the whole gamut of abuses, condemning not only the Church, but each section of the upper and middle classes in turn for oppression of the poor. Sometimes the point is neatly made. The friars care little for the poor, whether living or dead, but they will fight all day over the body of a rich man—not wholly for love of the rich man:—

> "Hyt is not al for the calf
> That the cow loweth,
> But it is for the gode gras
> That in the mede groweth,
> By my hod!"

CHAPTER II

ON such flimsy foundations did English satire still rest at the
beginning of the reign of Edward III.; nor was there any noteworthy change until that reign was approaching its close. The
brilliancy of Edward's victories dazzled Laurence Minot, and he
sang the triumphs of his country, like a ruder Campbell of an earlier
day. Minot is too happy in the victories to be satirical: only now
and then do we detect the note of satire on the enemy, not on
Edward or his England; and, as the quarrels of relations are more
bitter than those of strangers, it rings clearest in the celebration
of triumphs over the Scots. It is unmistakable in the song of the
Battle of Neville's Cross:—

> " When Sir Dauid þe Bruse · satt on his stede,
> He said of all Ingland · haued he no drede;
> Bot hende John of Coupland · a wight man in wede,
> Talked to Dauid · and kend him his crede.
> Þare was Sir Dauid · so dughty in his dede,
> Þe faire toure of London · haued he to mede."

The glories of Edward were, however, superficial; and though
Cressy and Poitiers and Halidon Hill and Neville's Cross threw their
glamour over the people as well as the minstrels, the real state of
the country was wretched. The wars were costly and the bills had
to be met; and when it was found that one of the consequences
was crushingly heavy taxation, poverty soon made the glories
dim. Neither had the victories over France and Scotland any power
to cure those vices of the Church which had been the theme of the
Speculum Stultorum and of the *Land of Cokaygne*. Naturally,
therefore, towards the end of the reign verse takes a tone widely
different from that of Minot. There needed only the seeing eye
and the gifted pen, and the two were conjoined in the person of
the author of *Piers Plowman*, who at once raised satire to a height
it had never before reached in England. It is true that *Piers Plowman* is a good deal more than a satire. There is pure poetic beauty

in the passage in which the author tells how in the summer season
he dreamed his dream on the Malvern Hills, and in many a passage
all through the poem there is the moral earnestness of the preacher
and reformer. But much of the teaching is conveyed through the
medium of satire, and the poem is the first satirical composition
in English which has any claim to be called great.

It is unnecessary here to discuss the vexed and difficult question
of the authorship of *Piers Plowman*. Whoever he may have been,
whether Langland, or some other man (or some group of men),
he was a man of high principle, profoundly in earnest, keenly
conscious of the evils of the time, and zealous, if he could, to remedy
them; a lover of the Church as she should be; an unsparing critic
of the Church as, in too many respects, she was. To avoid clumsy
periphrases it will be convenient to call this unknown man by
the name which has been for generations assigned to the author
of *Piers Plowman*—William Langland. Langland, then, chose a
dream for the framework of his poem, and made its substance
allegorical. In this he was by no means original. The Middle Ages
loved allegory, and a dream was among the commonest devices
from Dante downwards. The dream which most influenced Langland was that of Guillaume de Lorris and Jean de Meun, which was
translated into English under the title of *The Romaunt of the Rose*,
within a few years of the first appearance of Langland's work. For
there were no fewer than three versions of *Piers Plowman*, the first
appearing probably in 1362, soon after the Treaty of Bretigny, which
nominally ended the war with France; the second in 1376, the year
before the death of Edward III.; and the third in 1398, the year
before the tragic close of the reign of Richard II.

Langland falls asleep on the Malvern Hills, and in his dream
sees the fair field of the world full of folk. Eastward of it rises a
great tower, in which dwells Truth, and westward lies a deep valley,
the abode of Death and the Spirits of Evil. The scope of the poem
therefore is immense; it is a commentary upon life and death,
and it embodies a running satire on the world. Primarily it is a
satire on the fourteenth century, but incidentally it is also a satire
on that human nature which survives to the present day. Much
that is said in condemnation of the tricks of trade is still, it may be
feared, applicable with but trivial changes.

No class escapes the lash of Langland, but there are three subjects on which he specially enlarges, and by his treatment of which the quality of his satire may best be judged—the Church, the Law, and Trade.

Langland's satire of ecclesiastical corruptions is so unsparing that there is danger of forgetting that all the while he is a faithful son of the Church. What he detests is the abuse, not that which it deforms. The Lovely Lady who teaches him concerning Truth and Charity and shows him the character of Meed and Falsehood is Holy Church. Under her guidance he sees that churchmen are great friends of that questionable character Meed; not the Meed which God grants to those who do well on earth, but that Meed whom Conscience sees involved with Mahomet in a final destruction; not merited reward, but bribery. Clerks comfort Meed, and bid her be of good cheer, "for we are thine own to do thy will as long as thou mayest last." She is familiar with the Pope, provides parsons with prebends, and abets priests in having lovers and concubines. No wonder such men are blind guides. A thousand men cry out to Truth for guidance, but the exploration of all the holy places is all in vain. It is not undertaken in the proper spirit. The palmers in the prologue pledge themselves to make pilgrimage to Compostella and to Rome, and have "leave to lie all their life afterwards." No wonder then that later on we find the palmer helpless as a guide to Truth. He has the emblems of pilgrimage to Canterbury, to Rome, to St. James of Compostella, to Sinai and the Holy Land, and he has just come from our Lord's sepulchre. But when he is asked whether he knows aught of a saint called Truth, or can show the way to his dwelling, he can only reply helplessly that he never saw palmer with staff or with scrip ask before about him. It is the Plowman who knows Truth as well as the clerk knows his books, because he ditches and delves according to Truth's bidding, and is honest in all his life. When he is describing the way to Truth, it is the possibility of his being unknown that suggests hope to the Pardoner: "'By St. Paul,' said a pardoner, 'peradventure I be not known there; I will go fetch my box with my brevets, and a bull with bishops' letters.'" The ruling passion is strong to the end: he clings to his tricks even when searching for Truth.

From Langland to Lyndsay there is no abuse more vigorously denounced than this abuse of pardons. In Langland Truth has his bull of pardons as well as the Pope; but there is a difference, and the priest who interprets the Latin to Piers finds it to be no pardon at all. It is simply the assurance that those who have done good shall go to life eternal, and those who have done evil into everlasting fire. Clearly a dangerous doctrine, for it would make any system of theology superfluous. But the Pardoner's way is widely different. He "blears the eyes" of the people, instead of opening them to the light, and they give their gold to feed his vices. The whole ecclesiastical system is a system of trickery. The parish priest and the pardoner divide the silver which the poor folk of the parish ought to have, and on the plea that the parish is poor since the pestilence they get leave to live in London, where they sing the service for lucre. Bishops and bachelors too, who ought to be shriving their flock, live in London even in Lent. Ecclesiastics are ignorant and lazy in the extreme. It is significant that the allegorical figure of Sloth is a priest. He does not know his paternoster perfectly, but he knows rhymes of Robin Hood and Randolph, Earl of Chester. He makes vows and forgets them on the morrow. He never performs penance, and has never been truly sorry for his sins. If he tells his beads, what he utters with his tongue is two miles from his heart. He has been priest and parson more than thirty years, yet he can neither sing sol-fa, nor read saints' lives; but he can find a hare in field or furrow better than he can interpret *beatus vir* or *beati omnes*.

In his satire of ecclesiastical personages in *The Canterbury Tales* Chaucer spares the "povre persoun of a toun," and draws of him a most attractive picture. Langland makes no such exception. His parish priest is the ally of the pardoner, and his equal in greed and in indifference to the welfare of the poor. The greater kindliness of Chaucer is visible here, and the fundamental difference in outlook between him and Langland. Chaucer is humorous with a flavouring of satire; Langland is satirical with only a slight flavouring of humour; Chaucer is bright and hopeful, Langland is oppressed with a sense of evil; Chaucer is tolerant and sympathetic, Langland is indignant. Langland moves habitually in the region of abstractions, though it is true he humanises some of them;

Chaucer, after he had reached his full stature, deals invariably with the human, and nothing that is human can he believe to be wholly vile.

No other class fills nearly so great a place in *Piers Plowman* as the ecclesiastics; but the references to the men of law are sufficient to show that they were the objects of a special dislike on the part of Langland. For law, when it is not administered in the interest of justice, becomes an instrument of the most cruel oppression, and in no other place is corruption so dangerous to the community as upon the seat of justice. And very plainly Langland charges the men of law with corruption and want of conscience. It is the Justices at Westminster who comfort Meed and assure her that they will contrive that she may marry whom she pleases, "notwithstanding all the device and craft of Conscience"; and they have their reward: they take leave of her bearing "goblets of pure gold, and cups of silver; rings with rubies and many other rich things." Their conduct is remembered, and they fare worst of all when Truth issues his pardons. "The men of law, who had pleaded for Meed, had the least pardon, for the Psalter doth not save such as take gifts, and especially from innocents that know no evil." "When they come to die who take from poor men Meed for their pleading, and would have indulgences, their pardon is full small at their departure hence."

Somewhat akin to the men of law are the men who make the law—King and Parliament. Langland's political judgments are most enlightened. He is no believer in the unlimited and irresponsible power of kings, and M. Jusserand has pointed out that he is the only literary person of his time who understood the importance of Parliament. Yet he was penetrating enough to understand its limitations also, at least in his day, and he used the fable of belling the cat to satirise those who made excessive claims for it. A "raton of renon" proposes that the cat be belled, and the proposal is carried by acclamation. But there is none to hang the bell, and a mouse of wisdom stands out and says:—

> "Thauh we hadde ycullid the catte · ʒut sholde ther come another,
> To cracchen ous and al oure kynde · thouh we crepe vnder benches.
> For-thi ich consaile, for comune profit · lete the cat worthe,
> And neuere be we so bold · the belle hym to shewe.
> For ich hurde my syre sayn · seuen ʒer passed,
> 'Ther the cat nys bote a kyton · the court is ful elynge.'
> Witnesse of holy wryt · who so can rede—
> ' Ue terre ubi puer est rex: Salomon.' "

Still more interesting is Langland's judgment upon the traders of his time. The picture of Covetousness is a keen indictment of their morals. It is guile that enables Covetousness to sell his wares. Among the drapers, by trickery, he stretches out ten or twelve yards to thirteen, and his wife, a weaver, pays the spinners by a balance which makes them give a pound and a quarter for the price of a pound; and when she sells ale she measures it so as to give less than the proper quantity. Covetousness has a peculiar conception of restitution.

When asked if he had ever made restitution he replies cheerfully yes, once when he was lodged with a crowd of chapmen he rose when they were at rest and rifled their bags:—

" ' That was no restitucioun, quod Repentance · but a robberes thefte,
þow haddest be better worthy · be hanged þerfore
þan for al þat · þat þow hast here shewed.'
' I wende ryflynge were restitucioun, quod he · for I lerned neuere rede on boke,
And I can no Frenche in feith · but of þe ferthest ende of Norfolke ' "

—a district more remote from Paris than Stratford atte Bowe.

The popularity of Langland's poem is indicated by the adoption of the Plowman as the central character in more than one poem which appeared soon after the great Vision. *How the Plowman learned his Pater Noster* cannot be called an imitation, and indeed it is connected with Langland's poem only by the title. But the best and most interesting of the alliterative poems after Langland himself was a direct imitation. This was *Pierce the Plowman's Crede,* which seems to have been composed about the year 1394. It is a vigorous satire, and in every way an interesting piece. The author is as earnest as Langland himself, but, like Langland, he has a sense of humour and an eye for the ridiculous, which saves him from the pitfall of didacticism. His grotesque picture of the friar as big as a tun, with a face like a full bladder, calls up before the mind the image of an ecclesiastical Falstaff. The purpose of the piece is to satirise in succession the four orders of mendicants. An ignorant man is seeking for someone to teach him his creed. He goes first to the Franciscans, and is assured that he need not learn the creed—the friar will absolve him. All he has to do is to give money to the order; in return he will have a most tempting memorial, and a presentation by St. Francis himself to no less a personage than the Trinity:—

"And myȝtestou amenden vs · wiþ money of þyn owne,
þou shouldest cuely bifore Crist · in compas of gold
In þe wide windowe westwarde · wel niȝe in the myddele
And seynt Frances him-self · schall folden the in his cope,
And presente the to the Trynitie · and praie for thy synnes."

Unconvinced, the ignorant man goes to the Preaching Friars, and is amazed at the magnificence of the monastery of a body professing poverty:—

" þouȝ þe tax of ten ȝer · were trewly y-gadered,
Nold it nouȝt maken þat hous · half as y trowe."

But the poor friars have not yet enough:—

" And ȝet þise bilderes wiln beggen · a bagful of whete
Of a pure pore man · þat may oneþe paie
Half his rent in a ȝer · and half ben behynde!"

The Dominican is boastful, and the simple man, still dissatisfied, leaves him and goes to the Augustines. But among them he finds once more abuse of the other orders and greed for themselves. He begins to despair, but will leave nothing untried:—

" Here is no bote;
Heere pryde is þe *pater-noster* · in preyinge of synne;
Here Crede is coueytise; · now can y no ferþer,
ȝet will y fonden forþ · and fraynen the Karmes."

The Carmelites, like the rest, abuse their rivals, and lay claim to higher antiquity and greater sanctity. They might have spared their pains: they discover that the simple man has not a penny to pay, and their interest in him ends:—

" ' Trewlie,' quaþ þe frere · 'a fol y þe holde!
þou woldest not weten þy fote · and woldest fish kacchen!' "

With this unabashed expression of their spirit the search for instruction from the friars comes to an end. It is only when at last the plain man meets Piers the Plowman that he gets the teaching he longs for. Before he recites the creed Piers vigorously denounces the whole four orders. There was no health in them. Falsehood, ignorance, greed, luxury and lust are the sins of which they are specially accused.

A few years after *Pierce the Plowman's Crede* there appeared another remarkable alliterative poem of the same school—*Richard the Redeless*. Skeat had "not the slightest hesitation in ascribing this piece to the author of *Piers Plowman* himself"; but as the question who wrote *Piers Plowman* is still unsettled, it is obvious that a doubt at least as great must hang over the authorship of *Richard the Redeless*. It contains within itself evidence of date which fixes its composition to the closing days of the reign of Richard II.—a time too late for success in the well-meant purpose of reform. The poem is incomplete; possibly the pen dropped from the hand of the writer when the deposition of the king showed that the last hope of saving Richard from himself was gone. The whole piece breathes a spirit close akin to that of *Piers Plowman*; but whereas in that poem the main body of the satire is directed against the Church, the satire in *Richard the Redeless* is political. This powerful denunciation of the misgovernment of Richard and the misdoings of his courtiers begins with a profession, the sincerity of which may readily be accepted, of goodwill towards the king. But the friend who speaks is unsparingly candid. He condemns Richard for parting his power among his "paragals" (companions), for distributing his livery far too widely, for the crushing expense of the enormous royal household, which cannot be met even by oppressive taxation. An extravagant king makes an extravagant court, and the courtiers are not spared who squander their estates in their slavery to fantastic fashions. Their sleeves must sweep the ground even if the wearers are ruined. Parliament fares no better: it is denounced for subserviency and worthlessness.

There is scarcely any literary merit in the miscellaneous pieces of the time in which either the Lollards satirise the friars, or, occasionally, the friars retort upon the Lollards. An exception may be made in favour of the Lollard *Song against the Friars*, a highly effective popular piece, in which the author ironically laments the shameful fate of those virtuous men—the friars—who are compelled to beg their bread from door to door. But soon the disguise of irony is dropped, and the friars are charged with vice and greed. Their influence is fatal to the prosperity of a household:—

> " Thai dele with purses, pynnes, and knyves,
> With gyrdles, gloves, for wenches and wyves;
> Bot ever bacward the husband thryves
>   Ther thei are haunted tille."

It will be remembered that Chaucer's Friar is equipped with similar merchandise:—

> " His tipel was ay farsed ful of knyves
> And pinnes, for to yeven faire wyves."

Langland's was the keenest mind save one that studied the England of the latter part of the fourteenth century, and we have seen how sombre was the view he took of the condition of the country. Allowance must be made for the fact that the satirist—and the moralist of the type of Langland as well—looks habitually for the darker aspects of things. Why else should he cry, repent, repent? But after every allowance has been made it remains probable, or rather it is certain, that Langland's criticisms were substantially just. The sombreness was inevitable in the case of one whose sympathies were, like his, with the poor; it was only men like Froissart, who cared for nobody but knights and squires, to whom the medieval world could appear a satisfactory place. Yet it must be borne in mind that though every shadow seen by the denunciatory moralist or satirist may be real, that satirist is but a poor judge of the lights which fleck the shadows. The one mind still keener than Langland's saw those lights, and corrected what was amiss in the picture drawn in *Piers Plowman* by virtue of a wider humanity, and a morality less obtrusive, but really more subtle and profound. This was Geoffrey Chaucer. There was another, John Gower, who has all along rivalled Langland in fame, though he never rivalled him in real literary gift or in insight. Gower is a man who owes a great part of his fame to bulk rather than to merit: he wrote so much that he acquired a kind of false esteem by reason of his very quantity. But he is hardly at all a satirist; he is rather a sermoniser. The epithet "moral," which Chaucer applied to him, is not badly descriptive, and it is more polite than "dull."

Geoffrey Chaucer (1340?–1400) began his literary career within a few years of the appearance of the first version of *Piers Plowman*, and he died only two years after the appearance of the third. He and Langland were therefore strictly contemporary; yet nothing short of the inexorable testimony of dates would suffice to convince the reader of the fact. Chaucer is generally, and rightly, regarded as the earliest writer of modern English literature; Langland's is the last name in our older literature; and the reader feels as if, in moving from the one to the other, he had passed into another century. The wide difference of impression produced by the two writers is due partly to their different metrical systems. Chaucer's accentual verse and rhyming scheme survive to this day; Langland's alliterative system, inherited from the past, disappeared almost completely with himself. But the difference goes deeper than that. Langland's range of ideas is essentially medieval; Chaucer's is of all time. Langland's satire is indissolubly related to the medieval Church; but while some of Chaucer's most effective satire is directed against ecclesiastical personages, these are so thoroughly human that their profession becomes a secondary matter; it is the man who is satirised. These remarks however hold true only of Chaucer's satire in its fullest development. It is chiefly in *The House of Fame* and in *The Canterbury Tales* that satire is to be found; and though *The House of Fame* precedes *The Canterbury Tales* by only a few years, it still retains much of the medieval spirit. It is a dream, and it is allegorical. The allegory was a device ill adapted to bring out the strength of Chaucer, and the gulf between this poem and the later work is wide. He merely satirises the capriciousness of Fame. Her house is built upon a rock, not of steel or of glass, but of ice, and half the names that have been graven there are thawed away. And this unstable record is shown to be worthless from the start. Crowd after crowd of suppliants approach the throne of Fame, and their petitions are granted or refused for no reason better than the caprice of the goddess. By her decree good work is forgotten and bad remembered as good, and those who beg oblivion are doomed to remembrance. But there is no law in her decisions. Sometimes the wicked are driven away with railing and the good are honoured. The fickleness of Fame is the theme. If Chaucer had written no satire but this his place in the list would be low.

With respect to *The Canterbury Tales* it is necessary to say at once that while the satire that is to be found there is altogether admirable, the prevailing spirit is not at all satirical but humorous; and while humour is an invaluable ingredient in satire, only when it is combined with the spirit of criticism, with the desire to teach, or with ridicule, does it become satire. Now the very breadth of Chaucer's humanity, his almost universal tolerance, limits his satire, as the same characteristic limits still more that of Shakespeare. The majority of the tales which might seem to have an element of satire in them are really meant to amuse, or to illustrate quite dispassionately the workings of human nature. Even where men are shown in ridiculous situations, or doing things which the moralist must condemn, they are not necessarily satirised. The Miller and the Reeve try to besmirch each the trade of the other, but it is not by satire that they do so. The tales might be told, with merely a change of setting, of men of any other trades. Only two or three of the tales can be called satirical. Chaucer's own tale of *Sir Thopas* is a satirical burlesque, but it is not very interesting to us, nor was it to the company. Probably Chaucer meant before he began it to break it off, as he does; he must have known that whatever amusement a satire of that sort could give would be soon exhausted. *The Summoner's Tale*, however, and the prologue and epilogue to *The Pardoner's Tale* are satire of a far higher sort. The Somnour is stirred to anger by the tale told by the Friar, in which another Summoner is compared to the arch-thief Judas; and the character is branded upon the whole profession in the stinging lines:—

> " He was, if I shal yeven him his laude,
> A thief, and eek a Somnour, and a baude."

Roused by this insult to himself through his trade, the Somnour deliberately frames his tale so as to satirise the Friar's order. Their gluttony is slyly indicated by the words put into the mouth of the Friar, in the tale:—

> " Now, dame, quod he, '*je vous dy sanz doute*,
> Have I nat of a capon but the livere,
> And of your softe breed nat but a shivere,
> And after that a rosted pigges heed,
> (But that I nolde no beest for me were deed),
> Thanne hadde I with yow hoomly suffisaunce.' "

The same characteristic of the religious orders is shown both in the prologue to the whole poem, and in the prologue to *The Monk's Tale*. In the former the Monk is described as "a lord ful fat and in good point"; in the latter the Host slyly infers the quality of the pasture from the condition of the stock:—

> " It is a gentle pasture ther thou goost;
> Thou art nat lyk a penaunt or a goost.
> Upon my feith, thou art som officer,
> Som worthy sexteyn, or som cellerer,
> For by my fader soule, as to my doom,
> Thou art a maister whan thou art at hoom."

The vice of greed is satirised also in the prologue and epilogue to *The Pardoner's Tale*. In the former the Pardoner himself tells the company that the theme of his preaching is always that cupidity is the root of all evils, and proceeds with astonishing frankness to reveal his own greed and his own tricks to satisfy it. His preaching against avarice is meant

> " For to make hem free
> To yeven her pens, and namely un-to me.
> For my entente is nat but for to winne,
> And no-thing for correction of sinne."

Homer sometimes nods, and surely Chaucer nods in the epilogue when, after this open avowal, he makes the Pardoner angry with the Host for his scornful rejection of an appeal which, apparently, must be taken seriously:—

> " Now, goode men, god forgeve you your trespas,
> And ware you fro the synne of avarice.
> Myn holy pardoun may yow alle waryce,
> So that ye offre nobles or sterlinges,
> Or elles silver broches, spones, ringes.
> Boweth your heed under this holy bulle!
> Cometh up, ye wyves, offreth of your wolle!
> Your name I entre heer in my rolle anon;
> Into the blisse of hevene shul ye gon."

He who has spoken scornfully of the "longe cristal stones" he carries, "y crammed ful of cloutes and of bones," naturally appeals in vain to his audience to kneel and receive his pardon.

The Somnour goes on to expose the hypocrisy of the friars. When the dame tells the Friar of the tale that her child has lately died, he pretends that he saw it by revelation:—

> " And up I roos, and al our covent eke,
> With many a tere trikling on my cheke,
> Withouten noyse or clateringe of belles;
> *Te deum* was our song and no-thing elles."

And of course this revelation has been vouchsafed to the well-known virtues of the friars, their poverty, their chastity and their obedience:—

> " Who folweth Cristes gospel and his fore,
> But we that humble been and chast and pore,
> Werkers of Goddes word, not auditours?
> Therfore, right as an hauk up, at a sours,
> Up-springeth into their, right so prayeres
> Of charitable and chaste bisy freres
> Maken hir sours to goddes eres two."

These tales show that it was chiefly against the Church that Chaucer directed his satire. *The Canon's Yeoman's Tale*, that very humorous exposure of astrology, shows it too; for though the narrator disclaims the intention of satirising " worshipful chanouns religious," there is certainly a meaning in the choice of a canon as the astrologer and a priest as his dupe. But the fact is above all clear from the *Prologue*, where the spirit of satire is more prevalent than it is anywhere else in the poet's works. Few of the characters, it is true, wholly escape. The Doctor loves gold, because "gold in physic is a cordial"; the Reeve is cunning enough to lend his master

> " Of his owne good,
> And have a thank, and yet a cote and hood";

the Miller contrives to take his toll three times over; the Franklin is "Epicurus owne sone"; the Shipman has no regard for "nyce conscience"; the Somnour speaks Latin in his cups. But better than any of the rest, this last character illustrates the universal tolerance of Chaucer. He is depicted as a man ugly, ignorant and loose in principle. And yet

> " He was a gentle harlot and a kinde,
> A bettre felawe sholde men noght finde."

In a spirit so humane satire will as a rule be no more than incidental. And so it is in these masterly delineations of laymen in the *Prologue*. They are in essence pictorial rather than satirical. The purpose is to delineate the man in his habit as he lives, and satire enters only when it makes the picture more vivid.

But the most tolerant and humane of spirits may be roused by a sense of special evils; and Chaucer evidently was roused by a sense of the evils connected with the Church. The satire is still Chaucerian; that is to say, singularly free from bitterness. But the mere fact that he does so single out this institution is a severer condemnation than all the vituperation of the Goliardic poets, or than even the indignation of Langland. Chaucer's satire of churchmen is neither vindictive nor indiscriminating. He spares the nuns; the prioress is described with an amused smile, too gentle to be satirical. And of all the company of pilgrims the most attractive is the "poore Persoun of a toun." Nevertheless, besides *The Summoner's Tale* and the prologue and epilogue to *The Pardoner's Tale*, there are in the *Prologue* the portraits of the Monk, the Friar and the Pardoner to prove that the Church was the special object of

Chaucer's satire. These portraits are satirical to a degree far beyond any other in the *Prologue*. The edge of the satire is all the keener because of the contrast between conduct and profession. The Monk is one who

> " Leet olde thinges pace,
> And held after the newe world the space."

He sees not why he should study as Augustine bids, "and make him selven wood." If all did so, how should the world be served? "Lat Austin have his swink to him reserved"; the Monk for his part is a hard rider and a hunter. All this is harmless enough in itself; but it runs clean counter to the whole spirit of monasticism, and renders unjustifiable the existence of a class economically unproductive. There is still less to be said in favour of the Friar, whose success as a confessor is due to the fact that he proportions his penances to the amount he expects to receive, and who judges of penitence by gifts, rather than by prayers and tears:—

> " For if he yaf, he dorste make avaunt,
> He wiste that a man was repentaunt.
> For many a man so hard is of his herte,
> He may nat wepe al-thogh him sore smerte.
> Therfore, in stede of weping and preyeres,
> Men most yeve silver to the poore freres."

Worse still is the Pardoner, with his wallet "bret-ful of pardoun comen from Rome al hoot," his bit of Our Lady's veil, his fragment of the sail St. Peter had when he tried to walk upon the sea, his glass full of "pigges bones," his utter falsity.

> " With feyned flaterye and Iapes,
> He made the person and the peple his apes."

In only one other case does Chaucer resort to class-satire. Next to ecclesiastics, the Middle Ages loved most to satirise women; and in this too Chaucer follows the fashion. There is satire of women both in the prologue of *The Wife of Bath* and in *Lenvoy de Chaucer*, appended to *The Clerk's Tale*, to say nothing of slight touches elsewhere. There is no very sharp sting in *Lenvoy*, for the modern mind can hardly sympathise with the inane obedience of Griselda; but the satirical intent is obvious:—

> " O noble wyves, ful of heigh prudence,
> Lat noon humilitie your tonge naille,
> Ne lat no clerk have cause or diligence
> To write of yow a storie of swich mervaille
> As of Grisildis pacient and kinde;
> Lest Chichevache yow swelwe in hir entraille!"

The Wife of Bath's prologue is a much greater matter. Lounsbury strangely takes it as a satire on celibacy. Such satire is to be found in Chaucer, but it is to be found in the passage in which the Host banters the Monk and incites him to tell his tale; and it is part of the satire on the Church. As for the prologue of *The Wife of Bath*, most readers would rather interpret it as a warning against matrimony. Certainly, if all women were like her, the Church would have deserved well of her sons in saving them from the snare. It is in reality a satire upon the lascivious woman. But in this instance Chaucer is so mastered by his humour, so carried away by his realisation of the character, that the satire becomes a minor thing, and the picture is enjoyed just for what it is, irrespective of the vices of her who is delineated. Possibly Chaucer had some purpose of reading a lesson and playing the part of reformer when he began; but he forgot all that in the enjoyment of his own work, and the Wife of Bath stands out as one of the most amusing of the female figures in literature. She is no pattern of the virtues; she is certainly not the woman any sane man would choose for his wife. But she is eminently human, and for that reason Chaucer forgets all her sins and drops satire in order to be dramatic.

Limited as is the satiric element in Chaucer, the quotations make it plain how great a step he had taken. For the first time a great artist, wielding a weapon highly polished and finely tempered, devoted himself occasionally to a form of writing in which neatness and concision are especially telling. Hence such deft implications as that in the line already quoted, in which the Summoner, the thief and the bawd are placed all on a level. Hence that restraint which is shown in the Host's words to the Monk. Violence is common enough before Chaucer; but it would be hard to match from earlier writers such things as these.

CHAPTER III

THE ENGLISH AND SCOTTISH CHAUCERIANS; AND SKELTON

THE fifteenth century was destined to witness no summer of English literature: Chaucer was the single swallow, and he remained for many a day not only without an equal, but without a second. His immediate successors, John Lydgate (1370?–1451?) and Thomas Occleve (1370?–1450?), greatly admired him and proclaimed him their master; and in the stanzas in which he laments his "master dear and father reverent," Occleve is for a moment raised above himself. But, in spite of their discipleship, the difference between the master and the early fifteenth-century poets is amazing. They are almost as greatly inferior in technique as they are in respect of the soul of poetry, and the inferiority is as well marked in satire as in anything else. Some of the minor poems of Lydgate are satirical; but instead of such masterly touches as those quoted in the preceding chapter from *The Canterbury Tales*, we meet with crudities such as the "satirical ballad of the times," *So as the Crabbe gothe forwarde*, and *As straight as a Ram's Horn*. Both are to be read by contraries. In the former the poet in jolting verse assures the reader that "this world is full of stabilnesse," and a number of other desirable things, "so as the crabbe gothe forwarde." The latter simply repeats the same device, perhaps in slightly better style:—

> " Marchandyse of lucre takethe nowe none hede,
>   And usurye lyethe fetrede in dystresse,
>   And, for to speke and wryte of womanhede,
>   They banysshed have from hem newfanglenesse,
>   And labourers done trewlye here busynesse,
>   That of the daye they wolle none houre be lorne,
>   With swete and travayle avoydynge ydelnesse,
>   Conveyede by lyne ryght as a rammys horne."

Nothing could more vividly show the deplorable fall in the level of verse than the fact that this crude device would seem to have been the favourite form of satire, and to have remained so for several generations. It spread from England to Scotland, where, as is well known, the tradition of Chaucer and his successors took deeper root and produced better fruit than it did in England itself. The *Bannatyne MS.* contains a number of examples (of unknown date, but, at any rate, considerably later than these of Lydgate's) of satire based upon precisely the same principle. Most of these pieces are anonymous, but one bears the name of Stewart, who flourished a century after Occleve and Lydgate. Time and experience, aided perhaps by superior native gifts to begin with, have smoothed away much of the roughness which is seen in Lydgate, and greater ingenuity is shown in the invention of impossibilities. But the type is a poor one at the best, and soon becomes monotonous. One of these Bannatyne MS. pieces bears the title of *I yeid the Gait was nevir gane*:—

> " The air come hirpland to that town,
> The preistis to leir to spell;
> The hurchoun to the kirk maid boun
> To ring the commoun bell.
> The mowss grat that the cat was deid,
> That all hir kind mycht rew;
> Quhen all thir tales are trew in deid,
> All wemen will be trew."

Ane vther Ballat of Vnpossibilities also satirises female inconstancy, and shows very considerable skill in versification:—

> " Quhen that the schip may sicker saill but steir,
> Quhen men beis born to byid heir immortall
> Quhen glass and gold allyk are fundin deir,
> And every lord settis land but ferme or male,
> And quhen als swift as swallow beis the snale,
> Quhen Troy agane is biggit fair and new,
> Scho quhome I lufe sale steidfast be and trew."

If Lydgate was the author of *London Lickpenny*, which has been commonly attributed to him, but without evidence of his authorship, he deserves a higher place among satirists than it is possible otherwise to grant him. It is a rude piece enough, but shows considerable spirit, and paints with some humour a picture of the time. The theme is the omnipotence of money. The poet goes to London, and finds there that neither is justice to be got nor are goods to be bought without that money which he has not. So he returns into Kent, and resolves to meddle with the law no more.

He pays his penny for wine and goes away hungry, because he has no more to buy bread:—

> " The taverner took mee by the sleve,
> ' Sir,' sayth he, 'wyll you our wyne assay?'
> I answered, that can not mutch me greve,
> A peny can do no more then it may.
> I drank a pynt and for it dyd paye;
> Yet sone a hungerd from thence I yode,
> And wantyng mony I cold not spede."

Occleve too holds a very humble place in literature, but the autobiographical element which he frequently introduces gives his pieces an interest which their poetic merit alone would not confer. The reader can hardly help sympathising with the scribbler who is so very human, so very frank, and so very poor. He confesses to the sins of excessive eating and drinking, and even to cowardice. He has an annuity of twenty marks, and regular payment would make him happy. But beyond the annuity he has only six marks a year, and "paiement is hard to gete adayes." Occleve has a wider range in satire than Lydgate, though no greater skill. His *La Male Règle* has points of contact with *London Lickpenny*. In *A Dialogue with a Friend* he satirises women in verse harsh in itself, and deformed by his prevailing vice of inversion. In *A Letter of Cupid to Lovers, his Subjects*, the satire, which is conveyed under the form of a defence, is incomparably more effective. Unfortunately for Occleve it is only in a minor degree original; it is based on Christine de Pisan's *L'Epistre au Dieu d'Amours*. No acknowledgment of the debt is made: such matters sat light upon the conscience of our earlier writers. Besides women, Occleve satirises the Church. Churchmen, he tells us, neglect their duties; they do not preach and they absent themselves from their cures. But if they are neglectful of duties, they are keen for emoluments and pile benefice upon benefice. Fashions in dress are another object of his satire. In those days the spirit of the peacock obsessed the masculine at least as much as it obsessed the feminine mind. In the introductory part of *The Regiment of Princes* the Beggar denounces the wearing of costly garments by penniless men.

Commonplace as they were, these two poets were the best in England of the very barren century to which they belonged. And if the work which was good enough to make a reputation for its authors was of so poor a quality, it was not to be expected that the anonymous verse would be any better. In point of fact, it was neither copious nor good. There is still a sparse stream of verse by the Lollards and replies by their adversaries. *Jack Upland* declares that Rome is Antichrist, and the friars worst of all. Dan Topias replies and Jack rejoins. A song *Against the Lollards* exults over the defeat of the reformers:—

> " And, pardé, lolle thei never so longe,
>   Yut wol lawe make hem lowte;
> God wol not suffre hem be so stronge
> To bring her purpos so aboute,
>   With saunʒ faile and saunʒ doute,
> To rere riot and robberie;
>   By reson thei shal not long route,
> While the taile is docked of lollardie."

So too the satire upon women trickles on. An anonymous piece called *Ragman Roll* is believed to have been adapted to a sort of game, in which the player pulled a string and drew a character. It is in stanzas of eight lines, and each character is set over against its opposite. The beauty of one woman is praised, the plainness of another is ridiculed; one is virtuous, another goes like a snail to church, but runs to the temple of Bacchus; one is a miracle of patience, another inconstant as the moon; one speaks nothing but what tends to virtue, another has a tongue quick, sharp, loud and shrill. Thus the piece is half panegyric, half satire.

Not till the close of the fifteenth century was there any marked improvement in the literary state of England; but Scotland was more fortunate. James I., and not either Lydgate or Occleve, was the earliest writer who deserves to be called a successor of Chaucer; and if he were the author of *Peblis to the Play* and *Christ's Kirk on the Green*, he would have to be regarded as the earliest Scottish satirist. That conception of the authorship of the pieces can, however, no longer be seriously entertained; and in *The King's Quair* James is not satirical. In his successor, Robert Henryson (1430?–1506?), there is an element of satire, though it is subordinate. One or two of his *Fables of Æsop* are satirical. The moral appended to *The Taill of the Dog, the Scheip, and the Wolf* informs the reader, lest he should mistake the purpose, that it satirises the oppression of the poor under the forms of law; and with respect to *The Wolf and the Lamb*, we are similarly told that the lamb signifies poor people, and the Wolf "fals extortioneiris." Less hackneyed is *Sum Practysis of Medicine*, a piece which, though obscure and difficult, is clearly satirical in purpose. Chaucer, in the *Prologue* and in *The Nun's Priest's Tale*, aims a blow or two at the medical science of his time; but there is little in common here between him and Henryson. The ingredients of the latter's prescriptions are rather of the order of Burns's "sal alkali o' midge-tail clippins." Thus:—

> " Ye may clamp to this cure, and ye will mak cost,
> Bayth the bellox of ane brok,
> With three crawis of the cok,
> The schadow of ane Yule stok,
> Is gud for the host."

The appearance of Henryson's name in Dunbar's *Lament for the Makaris* proves that he died within the first decade of the sixteenth century, when his great successor in the roll of Scottish poets, William Dunbar (1465?–1530?), had reached middle life, and had probably written a large portion of his verse. With the exception of Chaucer no literary artist equal to Dunbar had hitherto written English, either in its northern or in its southern form. His satire has all that could be imparted to it by powerful imagination and by perfect mastery of poetic technique. For imagination, it is sufficient to appeal to the beautiful allegorical poems, *The Thrissill and the Rois* and *The Golden Terge*, and to the weirdly impressive *Dance of the Sevin Deidly Synnis*. As to his mastery of technique, he shows himself to be equally at home in alliterative measures like that of *Piers Plowman*, and in rhyming verse, such as that of Chaucer. That coarse but powerful satire, *The Twa Maryit Wemen and the Wedo*, is written in an alliterative metre, apparently based upon that of *Piers Plowman*. Whether or not Dunbar invented the modification of it here used, he certainly handled it with great skill. With respect to rhyming verse, few have equalled him in variety. If he was really the author of that admirable satiric tale, *The Freiris of Berwik*, he has almost, if not quite, equalled Chaucer himself in his handling of the five-foot iambic line. For the bulk of his poems he uses a great variety of stanzaic forms, all of which he manages skilfully.

In one respect however Dunbar was deficient as a satirist. He lacked moral earnestness, and there is seldom behind his satire that force of conviction of which we are sensible in *Piers Plowman.* Neither has he any prevailing theme; he flits from point to point as circumstance or the mood of the moment determines. He touches everything, but he dwells long on nothing. Though a Churchman himself, he is among the satirists of the men of religion, and even of his own order, the Franciscans. The fact that it is directed against the Franciscans has been used as an argument against the view that he was the author of *The Freiris of Berwik.* But he satirises them in *The Visitation of St. Francis,* the authorship of which is undisputed. In this piece, which furnished a hint long afterwards for George Buchanan's pungent *Sommium,* Dunbar shows but little respect for the order. To the saint's demand that he should don the "holy weid," he retorts:—

> " In haly legendis haif I hard allevin,
> Ma sanctis of bischoppis, nor freiris, be sic sevin";

and he throws a curious light upon his own life while he was a wearer of the garb:—

> "Als lang as I did beir the freiris style,
> In me, God wait, wes mony wrink and wyle;
> In me wes falset with every wicht to flatter,
> Quhilk mycht be flemit with na haly watter;
> I wes ay reddy all men to begyle."

Here, although the illustration is a personal one, the satire is directed against the order. In *The Fenzeit Freir of Tungland* it is pointed at an individual. This spirited piece is not unlike Burns's *Death and Dr. Hornbook,* though it is far inferior in humour. The sixteenth-century impostor of the court, like the eighteenth-century impostor of the village, pretended to skill in medicine:—

> " In leichecraft he was homecyd,
> He wald haif, for a nicht to byd,
> A haiknay aud the hurt mans hyd,
>   So meikle he was of myans.
> His irnis was rude as ony rauchtir,
> Quhair he leit blude it was no lauchtir,
> Full many instruments for slauchtir
>   Was in his gardyvians."

Just as Dunbar has satires against the clergy, so he has satires against women—another standard theme. The most elaborate is *The Twa Maryit Wemen,* which calls to mind *The Wife of Bath,* but is incomparably less human than that admirable piece. *The Twa Cummeris* pictures two women sitting drinking; one, who is described as "grit and fatt," lamenting that "this lang Lentern makes me lene"; while her friend assures her that she takes this meagreness from her mother. *Of the Ladyis Solistaris at Court* describes the power of such suitors, and hints that it is gained by questionable means. But Dunbar is no more disposed to dwell exclusively on the women than on the clerics. In *The Devil's Inquest* he satirises impartially every class of tradesmen. They all by false oaths deliver themselves into the hands of the devil, who calls upon them to come to him. *To the Merchantis of Edinburgh* gives an unsavoury account of the dirt and stench of the city, which Smollett nearly three centuries later found almost as offensive. And the admirable *Dance of the Sevin Deidly Synnis* bears witness, among other things, to that jealousy between Highlands and Lowlands which it proved so hard to root out:—

> " Than cryd Mahoun for a Heleand padȝane;
> Syne ran a feynd to feche Makfadȝane,
>   Ffar northwart in a nuke;
> Be he the correnoch had done schout,
> Ersche men so gadderit him about,
>   In Hell grit rowme thay take.
> Thay tarmegantis, with tag and tatter,
> Ffull lowd in Ersche begowth to clatter,
>   And rowp lyk revin and ruke:
> The Devill sa devit wes with thair yell,
> That in the depest pit of hell
>   He smorit thame with smoke."

While early Scottish poetry was culminating in Dunbar, the deplorable state of contemporary English verse received an illustration in the welcome given to that singularly dull and tedious production, *The Ship of Fools*. Not only was it welcomed at the time, it has been treated with great leniency ever since. Critics have doubtless been influenced chiefly by a sense of its historical importance. But the cunning author has set up a kind of scarecrow at the end which possibly has persuaded the censorious to take flight. One of the latest categories of fools is that "of backbiters of good men, and against them that shall dispraise this work." These put the cap of folly on their own head:—

> " To write playne trouth was my chefe mynde and wyll,
> But if any thynke that I lyt hym to nere
> Let him nat grutche but kepe hym coy and styll,
> And clawe were it itchyth so drawynge hym arere
> For if he be hasty, it playnly shall apere
> That he is fauty, gylty, and culpable
> So shall men repute hym worthy of a bable."

The author disdains all such dispraisers, and to remove all doubt returns to the point, and roundly declares that by their censure they write themselves down asses:—

> " I care not for folysshe bacbyters, let them passe
> The swete cymball is no pleasour to an asse."

The Ship of Fools was the work of Alexander Barclay (1475?–1552), probably a countryman of Dunbar's; certainly, like him, a churchman; and, it would seem, as much his superior in purity of life as he was his inferior in genius. Of genius, indeed, Barclay shows not a spark. His ponderous work, which runs to fourteen thousand lines, is not even original: it is a free translation of Sebastian Brandt's *Narrenschiff*; and Barclay's additions are of no great importance. The plan is indicated by the title. Fools of all sorts (and the vicious and the criminal as well as fools proper) are gathered for a voyage on a ship. But little or no use is made of the ship; the book is simply a collection of moral discourses on vices and failings of every kind, which are rather flung together than strung together. Rarely has a reputation so considerable and so enduring been so cheaply won. For literary merit *The Ship of Fools* will be searched in vain. Time however has given it a certain pleasing quaintness, and it has the merit—if it be not a vice—of being comprehensive. As all kinds of fools are passed in review, every phase of satire is inevitably touched. The medical profession is satirised in a section which deals with foolish physicians who pronounce the dying patient to be curable, go home to look up their books, and send the medicine to a man already dead. Comparatively little is said about women, but they are denounced for "ire immoderate," and for "wrath and great lewdness." The folly of unprofitable study is severely condemned. First in order of the fools comes he who gathers books he does not comprehend. "Styll am I besy bokes assemblynge . . . but what they mene do I nat understande." And the same theme is treated again:—

> " Many ar besy in Logyke and in lawe
> Whan all theyr gramer is skarsly worth a strawe."

> $\cdot$ $\cdot$ $\cdot$ $\cdot$ $\cdot$ $\cdot$

> " Nowe sortes currit. Nowe is in hand plato,
> Another comyth in with bokardo and pheryson
> And out goeth agayne a fole in conclusyon."

The vices of the clergy are touched upon several times. The root of all misgovernance is the ignorance of foolish priests, and the cause of that lies in the bishops who do not consider whom they ordain. The clergy are irreverent: priests and clerks "clatter and babble" in the choir:—

> " Goddes service is oft hyndred and let
> By suche iapes and dedys of farre and nere
> Whiche they as Folys recount within the quere."

The majority of ecclesiastics are either covetous or prodigal. They pile benefice upon benefice, and waste all in riot and pride. Barclay satirises waste and pride in other classes as well. It is shown in the fashions of garments:—

> " The garmentes ar gone that longed to honestye,
> And in newe sortes newe Foles ar arayede."

It is shown in the rearing of great buildings beyond the builders' means. "Nabugodosor, that worthy man," was punished for his pride and presumption in building Babylon; but the modern fool has failed to take the lesson to heart. Of all vices however Barclay would seem to have detested most that of usury. In the golden age poverty was of great laud and glory, but now the pursuit of riches causes it to be despised, and the rich alone are reputed wise. And yet

> " He that leuyth to haue reward or mede
> Or more than he lent, may of hell payne have drede
> And he that so borroweth gayne can haue none
> Therby in this lyfe, but hell whan he is gone."

Thus usury curseth him that gives and him that takes. "Usurers and okerers" are fools "wors than all other spoken of before."

Unlike Barclay, John Skelton (1460?–1529), laureate, can still be read with a certain pleasure, for rude as are his rhymes there is vigour in them. He was at once like and singularly unlike his Scottish contemporary, Dunbar. Both were clergymen, both were familiar with courts, both were masters in considerable measure of the learning of the time; but while Dunbar is among the most polished of poets, Skelton is among the most uncouth. He seems deliberately to go back to the rudeness of an earlier age. In *The Bowge of Court* he apparently aims at and in a modest degree attains polish; but the measure which has been named after him Skeltonian proclaims by its very appearance a preference for rudeness.

More than any contemporary or predecessor Skelton assumed the rôle of professional satirist, and with his caustic pen touched sores of all kinds. His position in the Church did not restrain him from criticising that institution. *The Boke of Colyn Clout* is a general satire of ecclesiastics, and *Why come ye not to Court ?* is directed against the greatest English member of the order; though he is treated less in his character of churchman than in that of statesman. *Colyn Clout* charges the clergy with idleness and greed: the sheep are unfed, but the wool is plucked from them. Ecclesiastics are unprincipled, turning monasteries into water - mills and abbeys into granges. They are proud; they are ignorant:—

> " Yet take they cures of soules,
> And woteth neuer what they rede,
> Pater noster nor Crede;
> Construe not worth a whystle
> Nether Gospel nor Pystle;
> Theyr Mattins madly sayde,
> Nothing deuoutly prayde;
> Their learning is so small,
> Their prymes and houres fal
> And lepe out of their lyppes
> Like sawdust or drye chippes."

Wolsey is satirised among the rest. He is satirised also in *Speke, Parrot*. But in *Why come ye not to Court ?* he is dealt with alone. This piece is obscure, probably in part because of imperfections in the text; but where it is intelligible it is Skelton's most powerful satire. It dwells upon the haughtiness of Wolsey, in contrast with his humble origin. It illustrates his enormous power by the terror in which all men stand of him, from the barons and the judges downwards. The barons' "hertes be in their hose"; judges he counts fools and daws; sergeants dare not speak but with his permission. Skelton evidently felt this awe himself, and he consigns Wolsey to hell in the conviction that he will keep the fiends too busy to attend to other mortals:—

> " God saue his noble grace,
> And graunt him a place
> Endlesse to dwell
> With the deuyll of hell!
> For, and he were there,
> We nede neuer feere
> Of the fendys blake:
> For I undertake
> He wold so brag and crake
> That he wolde than make

> The deuyls to quake,
> To shudder and to shake,
> Lyke a fyer drake,
> And with a cole rake
> Brose them on a brake,
> And bynde them to a stake,
> And set hell on fyer
> At his owne desyer."

Though he satirised the clergy Skelton seems to have been no reformer. His *Replycacion* is a piece of scurrilous abuse of the six Oxford readers of Tyndale who were made to join in burning the translation. He was a keen patriot, and the Battle of Flodden gave occasion for some coarse pieces against the Scots. The *Poems against Garneshe* show that he was " a good hater," and as much at home in abuse of an individual as in abuse of a nation. In *The Tunning of Elynour Rummynge* he paints a coarsely realistic picture of low life. Though not pleasant to read, it is instructive, and without reference to it the wide range of Skelton's satire could not be adequately appreciated. And even this does not exhibit the whole range: there is yet to be added *The Bowge of Court*. If Skelton can ever be called polished, it is here. The piece is a satire of the court under a number of allegorical figures of Disdain, Riot, Suspicion, etc. They are sketched with great vigour, as may be seen from one of the stanzas descriptive of Riot:—

> " Wyth that came Ryotte, russhynge all at ones,
> A rusty gallande, to-ragged and to-rente;
> And on the borde he whyrled a payre of bones,
> *Quater treye dews* he clatered as he wente;
> Now haue at all, by saynte Thomas of Kente!
> And euer he threwe and kyst I wote nere what:
> His here was growen thorowe oute his hat."

The seven-lined stanza, however, overstrains such metrical skill as Skelton possessed. His characteristic virtue is energy. He is rude, boisterous, uncouth, but sincere and strong.

Skelton is the only satirist of the time who remains more than the shadow of a name, but the fugitive pieces which still survive serve to show that others as well as he were impressed with a sense of the same and similar evils. *The Manner of the World Nowadays*, which satirises the extravagances of fashion, may have been by Skelton himself. Wynkyn de Worde's *Treatise of a Galaunt*, which belongs to the early part of Henry VIII.'s reign, handles the same subject in a manner rude enough, but vigorous and interesting.

Pride, extravagance and the imitation of French fashions and customs cause endless evils:—

> " Men arayed as women and woman as man,
> This causeth derth and that all thynge is so dere;
> Englande maye wayle that euer it came here."

The way to regain the old gladness is to return to the old "sadness" (sobriety) and to exile pride. *The Ruyn of a Ream*, a piece destitute of literary merit, takes a wider view. The nobles crowd to court and cease to keep great households. Archery is neglected for cards and dice. But the most baneful evil is the state of the clergy. They rule the land, and they are vicious, proud and gorgeous.

The satire of the extravagances of fashion could not fail to find pointed expression in relation to the court of Henry VIII. That court furnished abundant material for the satire against women also; and the result is seen in Hazlitt's *Early Popular Poetry of England*. The traditional complaints are repeated. Women are accused of pride and excessive love of fine raiment. In *A Merry Jeste of a Shrewde and Curste Wyfe lapped in Morrelles Skin*, the "curste wife" is tamed somewhat after the fashion of Shakespeare's shrew. *The Boke of Mayd Emlyn* is simply one of the stories, numerous from the time of *The Wife of Bath*, of women with many husbands, who betray and abuse them all. The general spirit of the piece is indicated by the lines which describe her after the death of her third husband:—

> " She was than stedfast and stronge,
> And kepte her a wydowe veraye longe,
> In faythe almoost two dayes."

In *The Proud Wyves Pater Noster*, the petitions are all turned into prayers for fine clothing:—

> " Adueniat regnum taum—thy kingdom come to vs
> After this lyfe, when we hens shall wende";

but in the meantime give me fine kerchiefs, caps and smocks. This the proud wife justifies by the desire to please her husband:—

> " Yet may I reioyce alway ywys,
> For my husbonde is glad, whan I go hyme,
> He wolde thynke I dyd full sore a mys
> If I wente not freshe, by swete sainte syme."

The Schole-house of Women traverses a much wider range, and maintains that there is a salve for every sore except marriage and the gout. Women will have the last word; they claim much and will give nothing in return; they are lazy and self-indulgent; their tongues move like the aspen leaf; they are unstable; they cannot keep counsel. There is safety neither in beauty nor in plainness:—

> " The fairer of face, the prouder of hart,
> The lother to wo, the sooner wun,
> The lesse of speech, the more ouerthwart,
> Not one so daungerous as is dame dun,
> The fowler she is, the sooner it is doon."

All the manifold vices are summed up in two venial sins—none of the seven deadly sins. Women can neither do well nor say well.

There is greater freshness in the beginnings of that satire of vagabondage which may be traced back to this period. It was due to economic causes which are summarised with great skill in Sir Thomas More's (1478–1535) *Utopia*. Though it was not till 1551 that Robinson's translation made the *Utopia* an English classic, in its Latin form it belongs to the early part of the reign of Henry VIII., having been published in 1516. Besides being a picture of an imaginary commonwealth, *Utopia* is a satire on the actual condition of England far too comprehensive and penetrating to be dismissed merely as a book which helps to start the satire of vagabondage. More had an observant eye, and, in spite of his kindliness of disposition, he had also a biting pen. The sanitary regulations of Utopia are an indirect criticism of the dirt and the smells of London. His ideal streets, of no less than twelve feet in width, remind us in what very narrow ways our fathers walked. More was present at the Field of the Cloth of Gold, and we may guess with what eyes he looked upon it from the sober garments in which he had clothed his Utopians, and the ridicule with which he had overwhelmed the Anemoleans, bedizened with gold chains and jewels in a land which valued both at their true worth. "Look what a great lubber goes there, mother," is the exclamation of a child who has been taught what their true worth is. It is the cardinal point in More's estimation, for he is convinced that "where money beareth all the sway" there can be no wholesome commonweal. Other passages of pungent satire deal with breaches of faith, with inhuman punishments, with mercenary soldiers and other matters of public importance. In those days, even as in these, treaties were apt to prove mere scraps of paper. In a passage of biting irony More pretends that such breaches of faith are common enough in the distant region of the Utopians, but, of course, unknown in lands where the light of Christianity shines. The policy of Henry VII., who procured subsidies for wars he never meant seriously to wage, is criticised under a very thin disguise. A most unflattering picture is drawn of the Swiss, the principal mercenaries of the time. In one of the most valuable and most enlightened passages of the book, merciless punishments are judged by their results. The case against indiscriminate severity is unanswerable; but three hundred years passed before England rose to the height which its wisest man had reached in the opening years of the sixteenth century.

The latter half of the eighteenth century was not the only period of industrial revolution in England; the time of Henry VIII. was another. More shows this too, though it is not clear that he understood the forces which brought it about, and, in consequence, his censure of individuals is, though not wholly undeserved, perhaps a little too severe. The great demand for wool, due to the development of the woollen industry of Flanders, had for a long time been gradually changing England from an agricultural to a pastoral country, and *Utopia* was written in the midst of the consequent crisis. Multitudes had been thrown out of employment. The policy of Henry VII. and Henry VIII., leading to the breaking up of the great households of the nobles, threw another class upon the roads. More points also to the wreckage of wars, civil and foreign, as another source of unemployment. Incidentally he aims shrewd strokes of satire at landowners, nobles, court, and all who are responsible. The general result of these various causes is the presence of a number of people incapable of earning their living, an economic wastage, a misery to themselves and a danger to the community. Hence the author of *Vox Populi, Vox Dei* appeals to the king to help the impoverished and oppressed people. Hence too the rising chorus of complaints against "sturdy beggars." It is the beginning of the evils which ultimately led to the passing of the great statute of Elizabeth which forms the foundation of the English Poor Law. Before that date these evils had produced a small literature of vagabondage. Only the beginnings of it are to be found in the reign of Henry VIII.; but beginnings are interesting.

In this case they are to be found in *The Ship of Fools*, among whose motley crowd of passengers are a few of the vagabond class. They play a larger part in *Cocke Lorelle's Bote*, the best of all the imitations of *The Ship of Fools*. *Cocke Lorelle's Bote* does not, indeed, limit itself to the vagabond class. It has the inevitable burlesque Pardoner, assuring the people in the name of the Pope of the blessings of

> "The coughe and the colyke, the gout and the flyxe,
> With the holsome tothe ache."

It has also numbers of tradesmen, "tailors, taverners and drapers, apothecaries, ale brewers and bakers." But along with these there embark upon the boat and sail through England all manner of vagrants, and incidentally some light is thrown upon their ways and character. So too that curious but most unpoetical piece, *The Hye Way to the Spyttel House*, passes in review the whole fraternity; for thither resort all those who live upon their neighbours, whether from unwillingness or from incapacity to live otherwise—spendthrifts of every kind, priests and clerks who live viciously, impostors, all the idle and all the worthless. Of course the lash of satire never reached this motley crew, but perhaps it gave some satisfaction to the better part of the population, and it may have been in some small degree useful in revealing the tricks of the vagabond fraternity. The systematic treatment of the subject for that purpose comes, however, at a later date.

CHAPTER IV

IT has been seen that from the first rise of satire the favourite theme was supplied by ecclesiastical abuses. But from the Goliards to *Piers Plowman* criticism is directed far less against doctrine than against abuses of life. The Lollards struck another note. The fragments of their work which remain criticise the teaching of the Church, and the pieces in which the orthodox attempt a reply defend it. The orthodox Lancastrian kings rooted out Lollardy, and the traces the reformers have left are scanty. But time, as it proved, was on the side of the Lollards, and in the fifteenth century the reforms were carried out which they had unsuccessfully tried to initiate in the thirteenth and fourteenth. When a movement succeeds, those writings which favour it naturally survive; and so from the reign of Henry VIII. we still possess a small but not insignificant body of satire bearing upon the burning questions of the faith. How little Henry VIII.'s action was inspired by the desire for doctrinal reform is notorious; but it is evident that a number of his subjects were eager to do more than substitute king for pope as head of the Church. The old complaints of greed of wealth and of evil life are repeated; but besides that, *Rede Me and be nott Wrothe,* the most notable of the poems of the English Reformation, bitterly attacks the doctrine of the Mass. So too *The Image of Ypocrasye,* a piece of about the same date, speaks in the most scurrilous language of the very centre and heart of the Romish organisation. The Pope is Antichrist, the Sire of Sin, the Whore of Babylon. As the head is, so are the members. The clergy of all sorts and ranks are denounced for their pride, trickery, avarice, ostentation and lust. Their fine garments rouse the ire of the critic:—

> " Your curtells be of sylke,
> With rochetis white as mylke;
> Your bootes of righte sattyne,
> Or velvett crymosyne;
> Your shoes wroughte with gold,
> To tread upon the mold."

The bishops are contrasted with St. Paul's bishop: the Scottish reformer distinguished three varieties — my Lord Bishop, my Lord's Bishop, and the Lord's Bishop. The cardinals are carnal and vicious, the preachers are Pharisees, the friars dwell in hell, and act as might be expected of the inhabitants of that region. An astonishing eloquence of vituperation is developed in the names which are hurled at them. The piece abounds in vigour, but shows an utter want of measure and balance. It is abuse rather than satire, Billingsgate rather than literary English.

The other side was not without its supporters too, and it is interesting to notice what they allege against their adversaries. Little can be gathered from Skelton's *Replycacion*, which is hardly better than meaningless railing; but in the ballad *Against the blaspheming English Lutherans and the poisonous Dragon Luther*, the charges advanced are the dividing of the Church, ridicule of fasting, the denial of confession, purgatory, and so on. That is to say, the offences are doctrinal; there is, as Furnivall points out, a notable absence of charges of personal vice. A similar difference may be observed in the earlier pieces on the Lollard controversy. The Lollards make the vices of the clergy one of the foremost subjects of complaint; in return they are rarely charged with anything grosser than hypocrisy. Among the defenders of the *status quo* were, no doubt, some of the best men; there was, for example, Sir Thomas More, who is satirised for his fidelity to the old faith; but there were also all or nearly all the worst. The prospect of faggots and tar barrels was deterrent to any but the most earnest.

The *Proper Dyalogue betweene a Gentillman and a Husbandman* approaches the subject from a different standpoint, but is as strongly anti-Romanist as *The Image of Ypocrasye*. The two interlocutors are roused by a sense of their economic ruin, and they trace that to the clergy. The Gentleman's ancestors have been induced by the clergy to alienate their lands in order to buy prayers for their souls, so that he has wife and children on his hands, and nothing to support them with. The Husbandman declares that his class are in a still worse condition. And the pretence of prayer, which has been bought so dear, is worthless; for the damned are beyond help, and there is no purgatory. The Husbandman has no doubt who is to blame. England was prosperous under temporal governors; it was when the clergy got rule that rents were raised. This charge is a useful reminder of the care that must be taken before we accept satire as well founded. The monks were notoriously easy landlords, and it cannot have been far from the date of this piece when the Pilgrimage of Grace bore emphatic testimony to the humanity which helped to redeem their vices. The satirist is on firmer ground when he goes on to accuse them of intolerance. If we assailed them with arguments of the Holy Scripture, he says, they could not resist. But then, they would persecute us as heretics, for it is forbidden to have the Scriptures in English, and the Testament was burned with shameful blasphemy in London—a blasphemy for which he fears the whole country will be plagued.

The "shameful blasphemy" here spoken of was the burning of Tyndale's Testament, to which reference has already been made in connexion with Skelton. It was a blunder on the part of the ecclesiastics, for the south and east were not so ready for a pilgrimage in their favour as was the north. The horror of the more serious minds is shown by contemporary references like that just quoted. In particular, it was probably this burning which gave occasion to the writing of *Rede Me and be nott Wrothe*. This remarkable piece, though it is far from being a great work of literary art, is deserving of close attention. It was written by William Roy and Jerome Barlow, two Franciscan friars who had been driven abroad by the persecution of the Lutherans. They settled in Strasburg, and there wrote their satire. Though earnest, sincere and intense, it is too long, and it is indiscriminating. Probably the writers believed the charges they made, and in many cases they were right in their belief; but still there is evidence of a strength of prejudice which makes them questionable witnesses. There is no white nor even grey to mitigate the deep black of Wolsey's character as they conceive him, and the admission of any merit among the monks is grudging and wholly inadequate. Like the *Proper Dialogue*, *Rede Me* charges those easy-going landlords with rack-renting; and that change from small husbandry to large sheep-farms, which was due to economic causes beyond the control of individuals or even of classes, is likewise set down to their account. The worst literary defect of the piece is that hopeless want of rhythm which blighted

English poetry after Chaucer. Artistic touches are only occasional, and the authors have no conception of the value of restraint.

Rede Me opens with a curious and instructive dialogue between the author and the "treatise." The author bids it go forth dedicated to the Cardinal of York. Wolsey was approaching his fall; but neither he nor his enemies knew that, and the "treatise" objects the danger of such a dedication. The answer is that the Cardinal is detested by the people. The "treatise" admits that it is so, but urges that they confide in the Mass and reverence priests —a noteworthy piece of evidence as coming from the party opposed to both. For, as will presently appear, Roy and Barlow, though friars, are unsparing critics of their own order and of all that was related to it. The author naturally has the last word, and urges the "treatise" to "lett antichrist crye and roare." Next a priest recites in stanzas of seven lines a lamentation on the death of the Mass.[1] The chief upholder of our liberties, cries the priest, that whereby our concubines and harlots were maintained, is gone:—

> " Our gay velvet gownis furred with sables
> Which were wont to kepe vs from colde
> The paulfreys and hackeneis in oure stables
> Now to make chevesaunce must be solde
> Adue forked mitres and crosses of golde
> Seynge that gone is the masse
> Now deceased alas alas."

Our fingers shining with precious stones, our effeminate flesh and tender bones must labour. We must go on foot. We shall lose our servants. Poor and noble will be against us. We devoured the substance of the poor. We shall lose our lordships and dominations. The Mass made us lords and kings over all. The Mass made us prevail against the gates of hell. The Mass made foul weather fair; procured rain, protected soldiers. What avails a shaven head now? The goods of the Church are taken away. Farewell the holy consecration with blessed *sanctus* and *agnus dei*.

Jeffray, a priest's servant, overhearing the lamentation of his master, asks another priest's servant, Watkyn, if it is indeed true that the Mass is dead. Watkyn assures him that it is true. Priests and monks and friars did their best and bribed liberally, but his adversaries slew him with the sharp two-edged sword of God's

[1] The idea, as Professor Herford indicates, is probably borrowed from Manuel's *Krankheit der Messe*.

word. What is to be done? In my country, says Jeffray, they resist the gospel openly, and their chief, whom some call "Carnall," while some say he is the devil, is one whose mule's trappings would ensure us a competent living for seven years. Where, then, did the Mass die? The answer is, in Strasburg. The clergy resist, and the bishop hangs, murders and burns; but in vain. They count him no better than a knave. Jeffray is somewhat shocked by this plain speech. Peace, he says, his skin is consecrated and anointed with holy ointment. The answer shows how little respect the reformers felt for such means of setting men apart from their fellows:—

> " Yee so many a knaves skinne
> Is gresyd with out and with in
> And yett they are not excellente."

When, it is asked, will be the burial? Some would have him carried to Rome, some to Paris, some to England. Jeffray thinks there can be no better place than England. There is the rich shrine of St. Thomas, there is the Cardinal in his pomp, there are clergy who in wealth and magnificence far surpass the nobles. But there the Bishop of London, with the Cardinal's authority, has set the gospel on fire in London. The Cardinal is the principal ruler. The king, though endued with all the gifts of nature, is governed by him "to the distayninge of his honoure." There never was such a tyrant in England as the Cardinal. The Commons are weary of their lives. The Cardinal "playeth the devill and his dame." Though he has founded a college, yet

> " Where pryde is the begynnynge
> The devill is commenly the endynge,"

and the college too will prove evil. He is so bad that Watkyn conjectures that the devils will be glad to let him go. It will be remembered that Skelton thought he would keep the devils so busy that other men would go free.

The other ecclesiastics are only a few degrees less bad. The bishops are incredibly rich. They have more skill of wines than of divinity; they care not for preaching, but love coursing and hunting; they play cards and dice. The secular priests have wealth incalculable. All these will labour against the burying, for it is only the Mass that supports their superfluity.

What of the men temporal? There will be difficulty at first, because they believe they will be saved through the Mass, and because of the great miracles daily wrought before our eyes. I never saw one, says the speaker, but the people reverence them a thousand times more than the gospel. Rogues and honest men alike expect salvation through the Mass:—

> " Crafty sorcerers and falce dyce players
> Pickeporses and prevy conveyers
>   By the masse hope to have socoure.
> Marchantis passyng viages on farre
> And soudiars goynge forthe to warre
>   By the masse are ofte preserved."

The nobles however are beginning to be suspicious of all this, and therefore they are forbidden to read the Scriptures in English.

Next comes a description of the life of the monks. They live in wealth and ease, neither sweating nor swinking, eating and drinking delicately. Their life is altogether abominable. Worst of all are the friars. They are intolerable beggars, "chickens of the devil's brood," "antichrist's godsons," "proctors of simony."

> " They are brokers heven to sell
> Fre coppy holders of hell
>   And fe fermers of purgatory."

But the Observants (to whom the authors belonged) are not so disposed? On the contrary, they are the very foundation of hypocrisy, worse than the scribes and Pharisees. Whereas the world is half beggared by the other orders, they rob it utterly. They live luxuriously. When they "walke their stacions" they fare well in gentlemen's houses, and murmur if by chance they fail to find such lodgings. They play upon the folly of the ladies:—

> " My lady not over wyse
> Is brought into foles paredyse
>   Thorough their wordes disceavable."

They are enormously rich. The Black Order alone has more than all the nobles. They exact excessive rents; they let a dozen farms to one tenant. The Cardinal has broken many monasteries, with consequences not altogether lovely:—

> " He plucketh downe the costly leades
> That it may rayne on sanctis heades
>   Not sparing god nor oure ladye.
> Where as they red servyce divyne
> There is grountynge of pigges and swyne
>   With lownge of oxen and kye.

The aulters of their celebracions
Are made pearches for henns and capons
    Defoylynge theym with their durt.
And though it be never so prophane
He is counted a good christiane
    No man doynge hym eny hurtt."

Had this vigorous piece obtained a footing in England it might have had considerable effect. But the exiled authors were afraid to return, and if it was ever proposed to them, English printers were afraid to meddle in the matter. It was printed at Strasburg. Wolsey's arm was long. He had the whole edition bought up and destroyed, and *Rede Me and be nott Wrothe* remained unknown. No other poet raised a voice more arresting than those which are heard in the fugitive pieces which have already been mentioned. More of these might be named were it worth while to do so; but they are artistically no better than the pieces already noticed, and their substance is just the same. Nothing else illustrates the deadness of English literature from Chaucer to the Elizabethan era so vividly as the fact that the greatest change in our history since the Norman Conquest has left such scanty traces of its opening stages.

The nascent drama, however, affords at this period two names specially worthy of note—John Heywood (1497?–1580?) and John Bale (1495–1563). Heywood has left two interludes in which various ecclesiastical figures are satirised with some freedom. These are *The Pardoner and the Frere, the Curate and Neighbour Pratte*, and *The Four P's*. Heywood resembled his Scottish contemporary Lyndsay in the fact that he was a privileged person. The freedom of Lyndsay's satire is supposed to have been due to the personal regard of James V. Heywood was a royal favourite also, though his relation to Henry VIII. was far less intimate than was Lyndsay's to James. There was however an important difference between the two. As his life went on Lyndsay became more and more closely associated with the reforming party, and it is probable that had he lived to see its triumph he would have broken definitively with the old Church. Heywood, on the contrary, was a favourite of Queen Mary as well as of her father. From such a man we should not expect such satire as that which we find in the writings of thorough-going supporters of the Reformation, like Roy and Barlow. While their *Rede Me and be nott Wrothe* attacks the central doctrine of the Romish Church, Heywood never does so. *The Pardoner and the Frere, the Curate and Neighbour Pratte* satirises the two first named, and arrays against them the parish priest and the parishioners. The piece is flimsy though amusing. The friar and pardoner assert each his own merits until they quarrel, and at last come to blows. The curate enters and bids them hold. Pratte follows and asks what the quarrel means. The curate explains that it is a case of one knave railing at another:—

> " Wherfore take ye the tone and I shall take the other,
> We shall bestow them there as is most convenient."

But the two prove to be tough antagonists. The curate presently calls upon Pratte for help; but Pratte has already more than he can do and in turn asks help which cannot be given:—

> " Nay by the mas felowe it wyll not be
> I have more tow on my dystaff than I can well spyn.
> The cursed frere doth the upper hande wyn."

The two champions of peace are glad to let both pardoner and friar go.

The Four P's is a far more noteworthy production, though here too the satire is in that burlesque vein which the interlude encouraged. The *dramatis personæ* are a Palmer, a Pardoner, a Potycary and a Pedlar. The Palmer recites a long catalogue of the holy places he has visited, and tells how he has seen Noah's ark. The Pardoner retorts that he has laboured in vain and come home as wise as he went, for pardons could have saved him without the trouble of all this pilgrimage. For a penny or twopence he will guarantee that

> " In halfe an houre or thre quarters at moste
> The soule is in heuen with the holy ghost."

The Potycary declares that they are both false knaves, but in the end admits that he is of the same company: they are "nought all thre." But there are grades in knavery, and in order to determine which of the three is the master-knave, it is resolved that the Pedlar shall be judge, and that the test shall be the telling of the greatest lie. The Pardoner makes a good beginning with a list of relics as spirited as it is absurd. He justly boasts that they are

> " Of suche a kynde
> As in this worlde no man can fynde";

for they include the blessed jaw-bone of All Hallows, a buttock bone of Pentecost, an eye-tooth of the great Turk, certain humble bees that stung Eve as she was eating the forbidden fruit, and, most wonderful of all, the great toe of the Trinity. The Potycary refuses to kiss this precious collection, with the tart remark:—

> ".These that stonge Eve shall nat stynge me."

It may be thought that here Heywood has passed the limits even of burlesque. But it must be remembered that the satirists from Chaucer and *Piers Plowman* downwards are of one consent as to the enormity of the abuse of pardons and relics. The crass ignorance of the bulk of the people made them ready victims to frauds almost incredibly gross. The "pigges bones" of Chaucer are grotesque enough, according to modern ideas; and we are helped towards the more extravagant grotesquerie of that "relic" of the Trinity by calling to mind the medieval piety which framed the petition: *Sancta Trinitas, ora pro nobis.* Men who could forget that when the Trinity was reached there was nothing else left to pray to, would not be so very much disturbed by the conception of a "relic" of the Trinity. Heywood unquestionably exaggerates; but exaggeration is a legitimate device in satire; and in order to judge whether the exaggeration is legitimate in degree or extravagant, we must first know the point from which we start.

When it comes to the actual lies by which the three rivals hope each to win the palm, the Potycary leads off with a tale of a wonderful cure. The Pardoner, following him, introduces the secondary subject of satire in the piece—the satire on woman. He tells how he descended into hell to rescue a woman, and finds his task unexpectedly easy, because Satan is so glad to get rid of her:—

> " For all we deuels within thys den
> Haue more to do with two women
> Then with all the charge we haue besyde."

But the prize is won by the Palmer, who tells how widely he has travelled, and how many women he has seen, and adds:—

> " I never sawe nor knewe in my consyens
> Any one woman out of paciens."

This, the Pedlar declares, is the most excellent lie of all.

As time passed it was to be expected that a more distinctively Protestant tone would prevail, and this we find to be the case in

John Bale's *Kynge Johan*, which was written towards the end of
the reign of Henry VIII. Bale does not rise to the level of either
Heywood or Lyndsay. He is not the equal of Heywood in brightness, nor of Lyndsay either in brightness or in force. His *Kynge
Johan* (the only one of his plays in which the satirical element is
strong) is a curious mixture of the morality with the historical
play, including among the *dramatis personæ* along with abstract
qualities historical characters, such as King John, Langton and
Pandulph. The mixture becomes peculiarly intimate when certain
of the characters are identified with certain of the qualities. Thus,
Langton is also Dissimulation. Dissimulation speaks with scanty
respect of Romish ceremonial:—

> " To wynne the peple I appoynt yche man his place,
> Sum to syng latyn, and sum to ducke at grace;
> Sum to go mummyng, and sum to beare the crosse;
> Sum to stowpe downeward as the beades were stopt with moose;
> Sum rede the epystle and gospell at hygh masse,
> Sum syng at the lectorne with long eares lyke an asse."

The principal part, however, is played by Sedition, who fills the
place of the Vice. He declares that he reigns in every religion and
monkish sect. He upholds the Pope and is always his ambassador.
Nobility is under his sway, and the lawyers are his secret friends.
He much prefers the present state of affairs to the old purity when
the most austere of churchmen ruled:—

> " Here is now gatheryd a full honest company.
> Here is nowther Awsten, Ambrose, Hierom nor Gregory,
> But here is a sort of companyons moch more mery.
> They of the church than were fower holy doctors,
> We of the church now ar the iiii generall proctors.
> Here ys fyrst of all good father Dyssymulacion,
> The fyrst begynner of this same congregacion;
> Here is Privat Welthe, which hath the chyrch infecte
> With all abusyons, and brought yt to a synfull secte:
> Here ys Usurpid Power that all kyngs doth subdwe,
> With such autoryte as is neyther good ner trewe,
> And I last of all am evyn sance pere Sedycyon."

When the King (Bale's very unworthy hero) is on the point of sur-
rendering his crown, Sedition is naturally overjoyed:—

> " Now shall we ruffle it in velvetts, gold and sylke,
> With shaven crowns, syde gownes, and rochettes whyte as mylke.
> By the messe, Pandulphus, now may we sing Cantate,
> And crown Confitebor with a joyfull Jubilate."

The Protestants, however, had it not all their own way. Mary
was no sooner on the throne than the anonymous Morality *Respub-*

lica appeared upon the opposite side. It deals by no means exclusively with religion; indeed, the satire is directed first against the misgovernment of Edward's reign; but as the Protestants had held sway, and were therefore responsible for that misgovernment, the criticism necessarily tells against them. Respublica is introduced, bewailing that she has fallen into decay "through default of policy." This puts her in the hands of Avarice, who has already entered and disclosed his desire to creep into the counsels of Respublica. He hopes to get from her all sorts of trifles which to her are nothing. But in order to succeed he requires two things—a more attractive name, and friends. He therefore proposes to call himself Policy, and to associate with himself Adulation, Insolence and Oppression, re-christened respectively Honesty, Authority and Reformation. This goodly company enter the service of the distressed Respublica, and for a time all goes as they desire. Oppression, helped by Insolence, wrings their wealth from the bishops:—

> " To some we lefte one howse, to some we left none.
> The beste had but his see place, that he might kepe home.
> We enfourmed them and we defourmed theym,
> We confourmed them, and we refourmed theym."

Avarice shows his bags filled by usury, perjury, bribes, but above all, by the robbery of Church goods:—

> " I have a good benefyce of an hundred markes:
> Yt is smale policie to give suche to greate clerkes—
> They will take no benefice but thei must have all;
> A bare clerke canne bee content with a lyving smale.
> Therefore, sir John Lacke Latten, my frende, shall have myne,
> And of hym maie I ferme yt for eyght powndes or nyne;
> The reste maie I reserve to myselfe for myne owne share,
> For we are good feeders of the poore, so wee are.
> And we patrones are bounde to see (I dooe youe tell)
> The church patrimonie to be bestowyd well."

In a dialogue towards the end between Oppression, Respublica and People, the Protestant claims and the Romanist answers to them are compendiously given:—

> " *Oppr.* Firste, your priestes or bisshops have not as thei have had.
> *Resp.* Whan they had theire lyvinges, men were bothe fedde and cladde.
> *Oppr.* Yea, but they ought not by scripture to be calde lordes.
> *Resp.* That thei rewle the churche, with scripture well accordes.
> *Oppr.* Thei were prowde and covetous and tooke muche vppon theim.
> *People.* But they were not covetous that tooke all from theym.
> *Oppr.* The coigne eke has chaunged. *Peop.*—Yea, from ʒilver to drosse;
> (Twas tolde vs) vor the beste; but poore wee bare the loose."

The closing lines pass from ecclesiastical matters to a notorious abuse of the time, the monstrous debasement of the currency. People's sarcastic remark that it had been changed from silver to dross was not far from the truth; for, in fact, at the close of Edward's reign the pound sterling only contained a small fraction of its value in silver. Other secular matters which are also touched upon are the destruction of woods and the establishment of great grazing farms, which, it is complained, has made meat dear. Such complaints had been current, as we have seen, from the beginning of the century. In the end, Veritas opens the eyes of Respublica, and shows her who her counsellors, Policy and his friends, really are.

The literary memorials left by the Reformation in Scotland were of a superior class. In the northern part of the island Dunbar and Gavin Douglas had raised poetry to a height far above that which it reached in those days in England; and though the Kirk was destined presently to lay a heavy hand upon verse, as well as upon other forms of art, in the days when the Reformers were struggling unequally against the ecclesiastical powers in possession, they received no small help from literary free-lances. The first and greatest of these was Sir David Lyndsay (1490–1555); for, of course, Dunbar was by no means in the ecclesiastical sense a Reformer, even while he was satirising his clerical brethren. The difference in age between the two men had something to do with this. Dunbar, born about 1460, was an old man before the tendency towards reform had gained any strength; while Lyndsay, nearly a generation younger, came under its influence in his susceptible youth. There was, besides, a fundamental and innate difference between them. Dunbar, by far the greater artist, was ethically the slighter character of the two. Lyndsay was essentially serious-minded.

It was not, so far as is known, till 1528, when he was about thirty-eight years of age, that Lyndsay appeared in the character of a poet. *The Dreme* is a composition essentially didactic, and mildly satirical. Both the Church and the State are criticised. The poet sinks beneath the earth into hell. There, alas, he finds multitudes of churchmen of all sorts. Covetousness, lust, ambition and neglect of their duty of instructing the ignorant are the vices which have brought them there. The corruption of which their presence in the place of torment is evidence has found its way into the Church through the acquisition of temporal wealth. This thought is repeated by Lyndsay over and over again. Of the fatal influence exercised by the gifts of the Emperor Constantine Lyndsay is no less convinced in *The Monarchie*, the last of his works, than he is in *The Dreme*, the first of them. The English satirists too lay stress on the corrupting influence of riches; and the Scottish poet had even more reason to do so than they had. Wealthy as the Church in England had become, it had not absorbed so enormous a proportion of the riches of the country as it had in Scotland.

The criticism is repeated with greater fulness and superior pungency in *The Testament and Complaynt of the Papyngo*. Round the dying parrot gather the Pie, the Raven, and the Gled (Kite), who propose to shrive her. The Pie declares that he is a canon regular, and points to his white rochet as the symbol of his pure life. But the Papyngo has seen that which suggests doubt:—

> " Father, be the rude,
> Howbeit your rayment be religious lyke,
> Your conscience, I suspect, be nocht gude;
> I did persauv, quhen preuelye ye did pyke
> Ane chekin from ane hen, vnder ane dyke.
> I grant, said he: that hen was my gude freind,
> And I that chekin tuke, bot for my teind."

The Papyngo however is still suspicious, because the Church has become wealthy, and wealth begets sensuality and drives out chastity and devotion.

A few years after the *Complaynt* came Lyndsay's greatest work, *The Satyre of the Thrie Estaitis*, which is certainly one of the best moralities in the language. It is a comprehensive criticism of the state of Scotland in matters both temporal and spiritual. The unruly nobles had taken advantage of the youth of James V., and oppression and misrule were prevalent everywhere. In the case of the king himself, a disposition naturally good had been corrupted by vicious advice and evil example, and Lyndsay shows him falling into the hands of Wantonness and Sensuality. The abstract qualities in the play are drawn with considerable skill. The virtues, indeed, are lifeless, but the vices are delineated with spirit. But it is above all in the ecclesiastical part that Lyndsay's satire tells. As the years passed, his sense of the grievousness of the abuses which the Church harboured grew keener. His condemnation is unsparing. Chastity

is driven from the doors of monk and nun alike, and finds refuge
with the Sowtar and the Tailor. "Auld use and wont" is the excuse
for every abomination and oppression:—

> " Wee will want nathing that wee have in use,
> Kirtil nor kow, tend lamb, teind gryse, nor guse."

The exactions of the parson reduce the poor to beggary. There is
probably only too much truth in the picture drawn in rude verse
by Pauper of the sinking of a decent family to misery:—

> " My father was ane auld man and ane hoir,
> And was of age fourscore of yeirs and moir.
> And Mald, my mother was fourscore and fyftene,
> And with my labour I did thame baith sustene.
> Wee had ane meir, that caryit salt, and coill,
> And everilk yeir, scho brocht us hame ane foill.
> We had thrie ky, that was baith fat, and fair,
> Nane tydier into the toun of Air.
> My father was so waik of blude and bane,
> That he deit, quharefor my mother maid gret maine;
> Then scho deit, within ane day or two;
> And thair began my povertie and wo.
> Our guid gray meir was baitand on the feild,
> And our land's laird tuke hir, for his hyreild.
> The vickar tuke the best cow be the heid,
> Incontinent, quhen my father was deid;
> And, quhen the vickar herd tel how that my mother
> Was deid, fra-hand, he tuke to him ane uther:
> Then Meg, my wife, did murne baith evin, and morrow,
> Till, at the last, scho deit, for verie sorrow:
> And quhen the vickar hard tell my wife was deid,
> The thrid cow he cleikit be the heid.
> Thair umest clayis, that was of raploch gray,
> The vickar gart his clark bere thame away.
> Quhen all was gane, I micht mak na debeat,
> Bot, with my bairns, past for till beg my meat."

The Pardoner too appears; and none has drawn a more lively
picture of him than Lyndsay. His name is Sir Robert Rome-Raker.
He consigns to the devil "this unsell wickit New-testament," and
he wishes St. Paul had never been born. We have a glimpse of the
gathering of his relics "from dame Flescher's midding," and a
most spirited account from the Pardoner himself of the relics
in question:—

> " My patent Pardouns ye ma se,
> Cum frae the Cane of Tartarie,
>   Weill seald with oster schellis.
> Thocht ye have na contritioun,
> Ye sall have full remissioun,
>   With help of buiks and bellis.
> Heir is ane relict, lang and braid,
> Of Fine Maccoull the richt chaft blaid
>   With teith and al togidder:

Of Colling's cow, heir is ane horne;
For eating of Makconnal's corne,
    Was slane into Balquhidder.
Heir is ane coird, baith great and lang,
Quhilk hangit Johne the Armistrang,—
    Of gude hemp, soft and sound:
Gude, halie peopill, I stand for'd,
Quha ever beis hangit with this cord
    Neids never to be dround.
The culum of Sanct Brydis kow,
The gruntill of Sanct Antonis sow,
    Quhilk buir his haly bell;
Quha ever he be heiris this bell clinck,—
Gif me ane ducat for till drink,—
    He sall never gang to hell,
Without he be of Baliell borne:
Maisters, trow ye that this be scorne?
    Cum, win this pardoun; cum."

The Monarchie, the last and longest of Lyndsay's works, denounces once more the same evils and abuses that are condemned in *The Satyre of the Thrie Estaitis*, but in a spirit which is didactic rather than satirical. There are however one or two minor poems which are wholly satirical. Though Lyndsay rarely stoops to lesser matters, in his *Supplication in Contemptioun of Syde Taillis*, he condescends to notice female luxury in dress, and in *Ane Descriptioun of Pedder Coffeis* he satirises pedlars. *Kittei's Confessioun* is a pungent satire on auricular confession. Some of the criticisms are hardly appropriate in the mouth of the imaginary speaker, but they show how Lyndsay himself regarded the subject:—

" He techit me nocht for till traist
The confort of the Haly Gaist;
He bad me nocht to Christ be kynd,
To keip his law with hart and mynd,
And lufe, and thank his greit mercie,
Fra sin, and hell, that savit me;
And lufe my nichtbour as my sell:
Of this na thing he could me tell;
Bot, gave me pennance, ilk ane day
Ane Ave Marie for to say:
And Frydayis fyve na fische to eit;
Bot butter and eggis ar better meit;
And with ane plack to by ane messe,
Frae drunkin schir Jhone Latynelesse."

Lyndsay was by no means the only writer who supported the Scottish Reformation with a satiric pen; neither was he the most accomplished; perhaps, though the best known, he was not even the most effective. The palm for literary skill must certainly be assigned to George Buchanan (1506–1582), whose satires on the Franciscans, though written in Latin, must be briefly mentioned,

because they are among the most telling satires in any language. They seem to have been written soon after Buchanan's return to Scotland in or about 1536, and therefore are nearly contemporary with *The Satyre of the Thrie Estaitis*. The earliest of the series, *Somnium*, an imitation of Dunbar's *Visitation of St. Francis*, is comparatively slight, but the *Palinodia* is an exquisitely severe and marvellously skilful piece of irony, and the *Franciscanus* is one of the most unsparing attacks ever directed against a great community. Burns was not more pungent when the reformed faith itself stood in need of reformation.

Even in those days however verses written in a learned language were understood by comparatively few: it was writings in the vernacular that were widely influential. Knox knew this well, and he himself in his *History of the Reformation* resorts occasionally to a grim kind of satire. He has also preserved in the *History* a very effective piece by Alexander, Earl of Glencairn, afterwards one of the foremost promoters of the Reformation, in which under the guise of a letter of warning from the Hermit of Loretto to his brethren, he rails in good set terms against the friars, their hypocrisy, their greed, their idleness:—

> " I dread this doctrine, if it last,
>   Shall either gar us work or fast."

Casual pieces such as this could not rival the influence of Lyndsay. There was however one collection which did rival, and, in the judgment of some, even surpass it. Among the means which furthered the Reformation, Professor Mitchell and Hume Brown rank next to the study of the Scriptures in the vernacular, the extraordinary volume known as the *Gude and Godly Ballates*. The earlier part, which is a serious exposition in metre of the Commandments, the Creed, the Lord's Prayer, etc., does not concern us here; but the astonishing collection at the end of popular lyrics and parodies of profane songs adapted to spiritual uses is full of interest and also of instruction. The greed, the ignorance and the corruption of the priesthood are exposed. Relics and pardons are denounced as vigorously as they had been denounced by Lyndsay. The piece which begins,

> " God send euerie Preist ane wyfe,
>   And euerie Nunne ane man,"

leaves no doubt as to the sentiment of the author upon one vexed question; and what follows makes the reason absolutely plain. So too the doctrine of purgatory is denounced with riotous delight:—

> " Of the fals fyre of Purgatorie
> Is nocht left in ane sponk;
> Thairfoir sayes Gedde, way is me,
> Gone is preist, freir, and monk.
>
> The reik, sa woundir deir, thay solde
> For money, gold, and landis;
> Quhile halfe the riches on the molde
> Is seasit in thair handis.
>
> Thay knew na thing bot couetice,
> And lufe of paramouris:
> And lat the soulis burn and bis
> Of al thair Foundatouris.
>
> At corps presence thay wold sing,
> For ryches to slokkin the fyre;
> Bot al pure folk that had na thing
> Was skaldit baine and lyre.
>
> Zit sat thay heich in Parliament,
> Lyke Lordis of greit renowne,
> Quhile now that the New Testament
> Hes it and thame brocht downe.
>
> And thocht thay fuffe at it, and blaw,
> Ay quhile thair bellyis ryue:
> The mair thay blaw, full weill thay knaw
> The mair it dois misthryue."

There is in this piece a ring of triumph won, which suggests that it is of late date. As a matter of fact, no edition of the *Ballates* is known earlier than 1567; but a collection such as this need be of no single date. It seems probable that the pieces were the work of the three brothers Wedderburn of Dundee, and that the date of composition was about twenty years before that of the earliest known edition. The *Ballates* are certainly a very singular and, in their way, a valuable record of the spirit of the Protestant party, and it can easily be believed that such lively and vigorous verse was helpful to the cause in support of which it was written. Some of the parodies are calculated to make the modern reader stare and gasp; but we must bear in mind that the contemporaries of the Wedderburns of Dundee were familiar with such adaptations. Perhaps they thought, like the evangelist Moody (and Wesley before Moody), that it was a pity the devil should have all the best tunes; and the Catholic Church herself had, in the days when her authority was supreme, sanctioned, or, at least, connived at the parodying of sacred pieces for secular use.

It was within the power of satire to injure the Romish party, but not to maintain unity within the ranks of the Reformers. Ere long we find one party of the Protestants turning the same weapon against the other; and a scurrilous but able picture of the head of the episcopal section of the Scottish clergy exists in Robert Sempill's *Legend of the Bishop of St. Androis Lyfe.* Patrick Adamson is one of those men who have been so unfortunate as to have their portraits painted by enemies. How far their charges against him were well founded can hardly be determined now; if Sempill may be believed, there were few vices from which he was free. The most interesting feature of the satire is the instinct it shows for the concrete. It is remarkable that the same instinct shows itself in all the other Scottish satirists from Dunbar to Burns; while the English satirists, from *Piers Plowman* to the close of the Elizabethan age, are, with few exceptions, far more abstract. The difference is all the more striking in view of the reputation of the northern people for metaphysical speculation, and that of the southern one for practicality and a belief in that which can be seen and handled, and, it seems to be thought, in that alone.

The most curious passage in Sempill's satire is that which recounts the charms and incantations of the hapless old woman who was charged with having cured Adamson with the help of the devil, and who was ultimately burned as a witch. There is a curious resemblance to the incantations in *Macbeth* on the one hand, and on the other to the passages in Chaucer, Heywood, Lyndsay and other satirists, ridiculing the relics hawked around by the pardoners:—

> " For Phetanissa hes he send,
>   With sorcerie and incantationes,
>   Reising the devill with invocationes,
>   With herbis, stanis, buikis and bellis,
>   Men's members, and south rinning wellis;
>   Palme croces, and knottis of strease,
>   The paring of a preistis auld tees;
>   And, *in principio*, sought out syne,
>   That vnder ane alter of stane had lyne,
>   Sanct Jhones nutt, and the fore levit claver,
>   With taill and mayn of a baxter aver.
>   Had careit hame hether to the oyne
>   Cuttit off in the cruik of the moone;
>   Halie water, and the lamber beidis,
>   Hyntworthe, and fourtie vther weidis:
>   Whairthrough the charming tuik sic force,
>   They laid it on his fatt whyte horse."

CHAPTER V

JUST as there were two phases of the great intellectual and spiritual movement which stirred the soul of the sixteenth century, so there are two phases of the satire in which its life is passed in review and criticised. That which has been surveyed in the preceding chapter is primarily concerned with religion, and the greater part of it gives expression to the feelings of the reforming party. But, somewhat paradoxically, the literary allies of the reformers are, in form at least, largely medieval. While the theologians are looking back to a past before corruption had crept in, or forward towards a future in which, as they hoped, it should be cast out, their literary allies contentedly use the forms which have been transmitted to them from the recent past, and write in rude stanzas, like the authors of *Rede Me and be nott Wrothe*, or compose moralities, like Lyndsay and Heywood. Yet the movement had already begun which gave rise to the regular drama, and so had that which settled the five-beat iambic line, and ultimately the heroic couplet, as the normal metre for satire. Wyatt wrote his satires only a few years after Barlow and Roy, and *Respublica* dates from the reign of Mary, when the regular comedy had already been born. In a word, the writers whose bias was theological were literary conservatives; innovations here came from the side of the humanists. And just as religious reform was inspired by a study of the ages of primitive purity, so was literary reform inspired by a study of classical antiquity, and specifically, in the case of the satire, by a study of the satires of Persius and Horace and Juvenal.

No precise line can be drawn, and there is no absolute breach with the past. The old forms lived on. A few years after Wyatt, Robert Crowley writes satire in his pleasant free doggerel verse, and later still Edward Hake uses a kind of ballad metre in his *News out of Paul's Churchyard*.

Robert Crowley (1518?–1588), to whom we are indebted for the earliest edition of *Piers Plowman*, is singularly infelicitous in the title of the little book which he published in 1550. He calls it *One and Thirty Epigrams*, wherein are briefly touched so many abuses. But the pieces are not epigrams, and they number thirty-three, not thirty-one. They are arranged alphabetically, according to their subjects, from Abbeys, Alehouses, Alleys and Almshouses, to Vain Writers, Unsatiable Purchasers and Usurers. He repeatedly touches upon matters connected with the Church and religion—perhaps an instance of the coming event casting its shadow before; for Crowley was ordained in 1551. He laments that alehouses are so placed in the country that they are in men's way when they go to church, and so those who do not like to be told their faults drink instead. London is better, for there the alehouses close during the time of service. He denounces "double-beneficed men," condemns as blasphemous oaths by God's blood, by cock and pie, and by the devil, laments that the occasion of the suppression of the abbeys was not used to provide for learning and for the poor, and ridicules obstinate Papists:—

> " An obstinate Papiste,
>   That was sometyme a frier
> Had of his friers cote
>   So great a desire,
> That he stale out of England,
>   And wente to Louayne,
> And gate his fryers coat
>   On his foles backe again."

Still, Crowley can hardly be described as a satirist of the Reformation, for in him the social outweighs the ecclesiastical interest. The Lord, he says, will judge without mercy merchants who take farms and let them again at higher rents, and who ruin young merchants by lending that which they are unable to repay. "Nice wives" are charged with following showy and immodest fashions and casting wanton looks. Drunkards, dicers, flatterers and fools all receive special treatment. So do forestallers; and here Crowley is touching upon an evil widely and deeply felt at that time:—

> " The fryses of Walis
>   To Bristowe are brought;
> But before thei were woven
>   In Walis they are bought;
> So that nowe we do paye
>   Foure grotes, or els more,
> For the fryse we have bought
>   For eyght pens heretofore."

This little book deserves to be better known; for, though it has only a modest share of literary merit, the light which it throws upon the manners and customs of the time is of considerable value.

There is less to be said in favour of Edward Hake's better-known *News out of Paul's Churchyard* (1567), a flat and prosy collection of eight satires, directed against each of the professions in turn, the Church, the law and medicine, and also against many who are of no profession. The author shows a decided bent towards the Puritans, and a corresponding dislike of the Papists. He complains that they "walk in Paul's," and is very bitter against them. They are

> " Bloody beasts
> And foul infected swine."

A marginal note, however, explains that such strong language as this refers only to "those of them that have been distained with the blood of the Lord's Saints."

Crowley and Hake were survivals from the past. It is in Sir Thomas Wyatt (1503?–1542) that we find the beginning of the new development; it is he who takes the first step in that evolution of satiric verse which culminates in Dryden and Pope. He is better known as a writer of sonnets than as a satirist; but in both he is a pioneer, and as such has an importance higher than the intrinsic merit of his work, great though it is, would give him. As a rule the conjunction of these two claims of priority and of merit raises an author to a position of prominence; and to such a position it has raised Wyatt as a sonneteer. But not as a satirist. Though Warton did him the justice to call him, in words faultlessly exact, "the first polished English satirist," and had penetration enough to discern that Wyatt's true gift was satirical rather than lyrical, Wyatt has never, except from a few students, secured that recognition as a great satirist which is his due. Compare the space devoted in any history of literature to the satires of Hall with that which is spared for those of Wyatt. It is true that Wyatt has left only three satires, while to Hall we owe six books. It is true also that Hall's satires are in heroic couplets, which became the orthodox measure for the satire, while Wyatt's are not. But on the other hand, there is nothing in Hall more effective than Wyatt's pieces, and nothing comparable to them in charm; for Wyatt is one of those rare satirists who, while censuring folly and denouncing vice, can convey the sense of a warm heart and a winning personality.

Wyatt's satires were first published in Tottel's *Miscellany* (1557), but their real date was much earlier. Until recently they were generally supposed to belong to the closing years of Wyatt's life, 1541 or 1542. Miss Foxwell however, the most successful and thorough of those who have studied his work, has found cause to conclude that they were written in 1536–37. In either case Wyatt was surprisingly in advance of his time, and many years passed before the mark he had reached was again touched. In two respects he stands in sharp contrast to his contemporaries; in respect of the model upon which he moulded himself, and in respect of the metre he adopted as the vehicle of his satire. Just as Wyatt was a pioneer in the introduction of the sonnet from Italy, so he, first among the English, went back to classical antiquity, and to the Italians, who were themselves following its tradition, for guidance in his satirical work. The second satire is a version of Horace's story of the town mouse and the country mouse; the third is an imitation of Horace, *Sat.* II. 5; while the first is founded upon a satire of Luigi Alamanni, himself an imitator of Horace. It is true that others before Wyatt had borrowed from the classics; Henryson, for example, had versified this very tale of the two mice. But no one before Wyatt had shown a set and steady purpose to make the classical spirit his own, and to follow its guidance. Henryson had no such set purpose: he is the author also of that satire, thoroughly medieval in its grotesquerie, *Sum Practysis of Medecyne*. In respect of metre too Wyatt found his inspiration in the classics; but fortunately not by way of direct imitation. The advocacy of the hexameter in English had not begun, and Wyatt had the good taste to feel that English metres were most suitable for the English tongue. He had also the good taste to feel that the rude measures prevalent among the medieval satirists were not adapted to classical polish. He was a student of Chaucer, yet for some reason he did not see fit to adopt the admirable five-beat iambic couplet which Chaucer had already used to good purpose in satire as in other things. For his satirical measure he uses the Italian *terza rima*. This choice, like his importation of the sonnet, shows the direction of Wyatt's studies; and though for that concision and antithesis

which are so important in the satire, the *terza rima* is by no means
equal to the heroic couplet, it is highly effective as Wyatt handles
it, and above all it has that polish which he felt to be necessary.

Wyatt was happy in the choice of Horace as his model. He has
little of the fierce indignation of a Juvenal, and the Juvenalian
model would have given no room for those personal touches which
are the most pleasing features of Wyatt's satire. There are, indeed,
echoes of Juvenal and of Persius in Wyatt, but they are of secondary importance: it is upon Horace and his Italian follower, Alamanni, that he leans. The main theme of his satire is the Court; and
the greater pungency and bitterness of the third satire, the last
in time of composition, may be accepted as evidence that the
iron had entered his soul. Shun truth, he says; so will both wealth
and ease be gained:—

> " Use Vertu as it goeth now a dayes so
>   In worde alone to make thy language swete;
>   And of the dede, yet do not as thou say so
>
> Elles be thou sure thou shalt be farr unmyt
>   To get thy bred, eche thing is now so skant;
>   Seke still thy proffet upon thy bare fete."

The fine personal touch at the close shows that Wyatt was by no
means inclined to take to himself this cynical advice:—

> " Laughst thou at me? Why, do I speke in vayne?
>   No not at thee, but at thy thrifty gest?
>   Would'st thou I should, for any losse or gayne,
>
> Chaunge that for gold that I have tan for best
>   Next godly thinges, to have an honest name?
>   Should I leve that? then take me fer a beest."

This third satire is addressed to Sir Francis Brian; the other two
are also in epistolary form, addressed to John Poyns, affection
for whom greatly increases their charm. "Mine own John Poyns,"
he calls him in the first line of the first satire,[1] which, after a
denunciation of the insincerity of the Court, closes on the same
note of personal affection:—

> " But here I ame in Kent and Christendome,
>   Emong the Muses, where I rede and ryme,
> Where if thou list, my Poynz, for to com,
>   Thou shalt be Judge how I do spende my tyme."

Such self-revelation humanises the satire; and it is characteristic

[1] In Miss Foxwell's edition: in the old order it was second.

of Wyatt. Though the Court was a favourite subject for satire in the sixteenth century, those who censured it rarely had much personal knowledge. Wyatt however knew it well, and we can hardly be wrong in reading his lines as the expression of his own feeling. Its insincerity offends him: he cannot

> " Praise him for counceill that is droncke of ale,
>   Grynne when he laugheth that bereth all the swaye,
>   Frowne when he frowneth and grone when [he] is pale."

Even when he is translating, the lines are at times so in harmony with his own character that it seems safe to attribute the sentiment to him:—

> " I cannot honour them that settes their part
>   With Venus and Bacchus all theire lyff long;
>   Nor hold my pece of them al tho I smart.
>
>   I cannot crowche nor knelle to do so grete a wrong,
>   To worship them, like Gode on erthe alone,
>   That ar as wollffes thes sely lambes among.
>
>   I cannot with wordes complayne and mone,
>   Nor suffer nought; nor smarte without complaint;
>   Nor torn the word that from my mouth is gone:
>
>   I cannot speke and loke lyke a saint;
>   Use wyles for witt, or make deceyt a pleasure;
>   And call craft counceill, for proffet styll to paint."

The words are the words of Alamanni, but the soul is the soul of Wyatt. His absolute sincerity, his love of friends, the truth and honour to which his whole life bears witness, remove these satires from the category of literary exercises to which satires too frequently belong, make them "documents" most eminently human, and impart to them a rare attractiveness.

Thirty years passed before there came a successor to Wyatt in the line of classical satire; and neither in form nor in substance was *The Steel Glass* (1576) of George Gascoigne (1525?–1577) equal to the pieces which have just been described. Gascoigne, like Wyatt, felt the need of a measure other than the measures which had been in current use, and he adopted the form of blank verse, which had been introduced only a few years before. As yet however no one understood how to handle it. The versification of *The Steel Glass* is stiff, the pause is monotonous, and alliteration is used to excess. The central conception of the mirror did not originate with Gascoigne; nor is there any great novelty in the things which it reflects.

The intention however is excellent: Gascoigne is a good moralist if he is no great poet:—

> "Art thou a craftsman? take thee to thine art,
> And cast off sloth, which loitreth in the campes.
> Art thou a ploughman pressed for a shift?
> Then learn to clout thine old cast cobbled shoes,
> And rather bide at home with barley bread
> Than learn to spoil, as thou hast seen some do."

Perhaps the most effective passage is one near the end, which tells the priest when he may leave off praying. It is when many impossibilities have come to pass:—

> "I tell thee (priest) when shoemakers make shoes
> That are well sewed, with never a stitch amiss,
> And use no craft in uttering of the same:
> When tailors steal no stuff from gentlemen,
> When tanners are with curriers well agreed,
> And both so dress their hides that we go dry:
> When cutlers learn to sell old rusty blades,
> And hide no cracks with solder nor deceit:
> When tinkers make no more holes than they found,
> When thatchers think their wages worth their work,
> When colliers put no dust into their sacks,
> When maltmen make us drink no fermenty,
> When Davie Diken diggs, and dallies not.
>
> .   .   .   .   .   .
>
> When all these things are ordred as they ought,
> And see themselves within my glass of steel,
> Even then (my priests) may you make holiday,
> And pray no more but ordinary prayers."

Specimens of satire based on the same principle have been quoted in Chapter III., so that Gascoigne is no more distinguished for originality of conception than for skill in execution. It is among the perversities of literary fame that his *Steel Glass* is known, at least by name, to thousands who have never heard that Wyatt wrote satires.

In respect of the use of blank verse for satire Gascoigne's example was not followed, either in his own day or in subsequent times, any more than was Wyatt's experiment in *terza rima*. Satirists were still groping for the right form; and the distinction of finding the best so far tried was reserved for Edmund Spenser (1552?-1599). Many touches and a number of passages in *The Shepherd's Calendar* had shown that Spenser knew how to look upon politics and social life with the eye of the satirist: in 1591 he produced a piece wholly satirical—*Prosopopoia: or Mother Hubberd's Tale.*

This piece is a blending of the old with the new. It belongs to the class of beast-fables, of which the great exemplar is the tale of Reynard the Fox. As such it is thoroughly medieval. On the other hand the measure, the five-beat iambic couplet, is new. In spite of Chaucer, it had fallen into disuse and been lost, and if Spenser did not invent it, he at least rediscovered it. To him therefore belongs the credit of establishing the metre of classical English satire, for the heroic couplet became, and remained for two centuries, the generally accepted measure for satire in verse. There were few who followed him in his revival of the beast-allegory, but Michael Drayton did so in his somewhat commonplace satirical tale of *The Owl* (1604).

The fluidity and ease of the verse of *Mother Hubberd's Tale* will surprise no one who has the least acquaintance with Spenser; but whoever thinks of him solely as the author of *The Fairy Queen*, and recalls its leisurely movement and meanderings and digressions, will be surprised by the lucidity and terseness of the narrative in the earlier piece. The story of the wanderings and adventures of the Fox and the Ape enables Spenser, in some 1300 or 1400 lines, to pass criticism successively upon soldiers, ecclesiastics, courtiers and kings. The pair set out upon their travels with the determination to get a living without working for it. In the guise of disabled soldiers, fit only for work

> "Which asks small pains but thriftiness to save,
> Or care to overlook, or trust to gather,"

they are set to watch sheep; but as they can show no lambs they are forced to flee when the day comes to render their account. Next the Fox attires himself in a gown and the Ape in a cassock, and they consult a priest as to the way in which they may get a benefice. His examination of their licence, which he pretends to read, gives scope for satire of the ignorance of the clergy:—

> "Of such deep learning little had he need,
> Ne yet of Latin, ne of Greek, that breed
> Doubts mongst Divines, and difference of texts,
> From whence arise diversity of sects,
> And hateful heresies, of God abhorr'd:
> But this good Sir did follow the plain word,
> Ne meddled with their controversies vain:
> All his care was, his service well to sain."

This pious person advises them that the name of clerks is enough to raise them to be deans and archdeacons and prebendaries. Even the lower station of curates is no longer so laborious as it was, for it now suffices to say services on the Sabbath. The coveted benefice may be gained either through the Court or by means of some nobleman. But the way of the Court is expensive, for the courtier must be recompensed with a benevolence or the primitias of the parsonage. The private patron will present the living on condition that his youngest son gets half of it: the other half is clear gain. When the adventurers find it necessary to abandon the Church in turn, they betake themselves to Court. On it Spenser pours his most pungent satire. The Ape clothes himself as a gentleman, and the Fox as his groom. If the Ape's garments are not quite according to fashion, it is all the better. He surpasses them all in "new-fangleness," and his behaviour is admired as altogether "alla Turchesca." He is surely "a noble Gentleman of high regard." He can play and dance and vault and spring, tell ladies' fortunes and juggle. This ape-like conduct is pleasing to the majority; but, says Spenser, "the right gentle mind would bite his lip"; and he proceeds to paint a fine picture of the true gentleman and rightful courtier.

The two conspirators live thus by trickery and fraud. The Ape's jugglery is dangerous, for

> "He so light was at legier demain
> That what he toucht came not to light again."

In particular they prey upon the hopes of poor suitors, whom the Fox persuades "to buy his master's frivolous goodwill." The poor suitor is powerfully delineated in colours mixed, it may be feared, with Spenser's tears:—

> "Full little knowest thou that hast not tried
> What hell it is in suing long to bide:
> To lose good days that might be better spent:
> To waste long nights in pensive discontent;
> To spend to-day, to be put back to-morrow;
> To feed on hope, to pine with fear and sorrow;
> To have thy Princess' grace, yet want her Peers'
> To have thy asking, yet wait many years;
> To fret thy soul with crosses and with cares;
> To eat thy heart through comfortless despairs;
> To fawn, to crouch, to wait, to ride, to run,
> To spend, to give, to want, to be undone.
> Unhappy wight, born to disastrous end,
> That doth his life in so long tendence spend."

Finally, the Ape, having stolen the crown and sceptre and skin of the sleeping Lion, assumes the rôle of king. In this part Spenser is clearly satirising the government of his own day. But there are passages which cannot be construed as applying to the politics of Elizabethan England. Whatever Spenser may have thought in his heart of the government of Queen Elizabeth, it would be going too far to read as a reference to her the lines in which he describes the means by which the Ape protects his power. It nevertheless is an admirable satire of the devices of arbitrary power:—

> "First to his gate he pointed a strong guard,
> That none might enter but with issue hard:
> Then, for the safeguard of his personage,
> He did appoint a warlike equipage
> Of foreign beasts, not in the forest bred,
> But part by land and part by water fed;
> For tyranny is with strange aid supported.
> Then unto him all monstrous beasts resorted
> Bred of two kinds, as Griffons, Minotaurs,
> Crocodiles, Dragons, Beavers, and Centaurs:
> With those himself he strengthened mightily,
> That fear he need no force of enemy."

The usurpation is at length ended by the interference of Jove; the Fox is "uncased," and the tail and half the ears of the Ape cut off.

The proper form had been discovered, a great poet had set the example, and the time was ripe. Satires, which hitherto had been separated from one another by wide intervals, might now be said to flow in a continuous stream from the press. In the last decade of the century there was probably more satirical writing than in the nine preceding decades. Much of it was in prose, but when verse was chosen it was usually the decasyllabic couplet. There were however fairly numerous exceptions. Stephen Gosson, in his *Pleasant Quips for upstart Gentlewomen* (1596), William Rankins, in his *Seven Satires applied to the Week* (1598), and Cyril Tourneur, in his obscure and inflated allegorical story, *The Transformed Metamorphosis,* used stanzas. So did Nicholas Breton (1545?-1626?), in his far more notable *Pasquil* series—*Pasquil's Madcap, Pasquil's Foolscap, Pasquil's Mistress and Pasquil's Pass and Passeth Not*— all entered in the Stationers' Hall register for 1600. Breton is at his best in his satires. A vein of poetry runs through them, the versification is good, the moral tone is admirable, and there is that mixture of approval with reproof which truth demands, and the

Elizabethan satirist generally forgot. *Pasquil's Madcap* in particular is an excellent satire. It shows that the rich man is praised,
however contemptible, and the poor is scorned, however good. The
rich woman, however ugly, shall be "woo'd and wedded, ere she be
aware," and the poor one, though beautiful, shall be held in scorn:—

> "The golden tale is ever soonest heard,
> The golden suitor soonest hath dispatch,
> The golden servant hath the best regard,
> And what such marriage as the golden match?
> And who so wise as is the golden patch?
>   Sweet music sounds it in a golden vein,
>   The sweetest stroke is in the golden strain."

But real values are different, and the rich man or rich woman may
be worthless. It is their mistaking their true value that provokes
the satiric muse.

Breton however by no means confines himself to this single point.
Pasquil's "Message" bids the Muse go abroad and tell the Court, the
lawyers, the Universities and men of all classes much that is true—
and some things that are not unflattering; for the principle is:—

> "Do no man wrong, give every man his right,
> For time will come that all will come to light."

Breton knew that apparent failure might really be high
achievement:—

> "Go tell the wretch that would and cannot thrive
> That his endeavour standeth for a deed;
> And bid the sick man in his soul revive,
> While angels' joys on sinners' tears do feed.
> And tell the soul that mourneth for her sin
> Heav'n's gates stand open for to let her in."

Breton has written much in this high moral strain. *Pasquil's
Foolscap*, which satirises every sort of folly, is, it is true, less earnest
and far less successful than *Pasquil's Madcap*; but *Pasquil's Pass*
in all its three divisions of the *Pass*, *Precession* and *Prognostication*,
is earnest moral advice rather than carping fault-finding, like so
much of the work of other satirists. The *Precession* is a prayer for
delivery from all sorts of evils, and its solemn close well illustrates
the profoundly moral character of Breton's work:—

> "When I am old, and sick, and lame and poor,
> And crucified a thousand sundry ways,
> And death begins to ope my fatal door,
> To call me home from my unhappy days,
> And all my passions then must end their plays,
>   Then from all evil, and both now and then,
>   The Lord of Heav'n deliver me, Amen."

The hand which is not callous with toil is easily pierced with thorns, and the moral skin which has not been exposed to rubbings is similarly tender. This probably is the explanation of the attempt which was made towards the end of the century not only to check satire, but to destroy some of the pieces which were already in existence, and to prohibit others for the future. Whitgift, Archbishop of Canterbury, and Bancroft, Bishop of London, issued an edict, which is entered in the Stationers' Hall register under date June 1st, 1599, directing that certain satires be burned, and that "no satires or epigrams be printed hereafter." Nash and Harvey were specially struck at; it was directed that all their books, wheresoever found, were to be seized, and that none of them was ever afterwards to be printed. Under this order Marston's *Pygmalion*, *The Scourge of Villany* and certain other books were burned. But the ecclesiastical authorities found it more difficult to deal with the future than with the past. Satire was certainly not stopped; and though for a few years the edict checked this kind of literary activity, it is amusing to notice that it was made the occasion of a satire against the satirists, and a reply to that. The former, *The Whipping of the Satire* (1601), was by a certain W. I., who, it is thought, may have been either John Weever or William Ingram. It attacks in particular Marston, Ben Jonson and Nicholas Breton; and it drew from Marston,[1] who was never disposed meekly to kiss the rod, a reply in the same year entitled *The Whipper of the Satire, his Penance in a White Sheet: or, The Beadle's Confutation*. Another piece, whose title shows it to be connected with the *Whipping*, is written in a different spirit. *No Whipping, nor Tripping : but a kind friendly Snipping* is a plea for moderation and practically an admission that there was some cause for the action of the ecclesiastics. It is believed to have been written by Nicholas Breton, and the tone is such as might be expected from him.

We cannot determine with certainty the precise chronological order of the satirists by whose work the decree of Whitgift and Bancroft was called forth. Of those who have not been submerged by time, perhaps the earliest was John Donne (1573–1631). By date of publication his satires are late; for, so far as is now known, it was not till 1633 that the first five of the seven appeared. They

---

[1] At least the reply is attributed to Marston.

are however among the works of Donne's youth. According to Professor Grierson, the earliest date that can be assigned to any of them is 1593, and he thinks 1594-5 more probable. They show the characteristics which mark Donne's works in general. They are weighty in thought and rich in wit, but almost intolerable in style. Ben Jonson, who, as is well known, declared Donne to be "the first poet in the world in some things," pronounces upon his versification a condemnation which, if allowance be made for its colloquial character, is hardly too strong—"that Donne, for not keeping of accent, deserved hanging." [1] Coleridge's assertion that if you read even the satires as Donne meant them to be read, "you will find in the lines a manly harmony" is puzzling. The manliness is unquestionable, but the harmony may be disputed. Coleridge was an admirable judge; but so was Jonson. Further, Jonson could not possibly be ignorant of the way in which English was spoken and read in Donne's time and his own. The inference is inevitable that if the lines are read so as to bring out that manly harmony, they must be read in a way which one of the foremost scholars and metrists of that time judged to be un-English. It would be another instance of that intellectual wilfulness which so seriously mars Donne's work. No man is great enough to be granted the right to take such liberties with his mother-tongue; and the taking of the liberties is an evidence not of greatness but of littleness.

The truth is that, in this matter, Donne's intellectual wilfulness found support in a mistaken principle, or rather a principle falsely interpreted, under which the Elizabethan satirists moulded their verse. Hall proclaims this principle in the postscript to his satires, where he speaks of the satire as being naturally "both hard of conceit and harsh of style," and therefore "unpleasing both to the unskilful and over-musical ear." In practice, as some of the lines which will presently be quoted from Donne show, the principle was often interpreted to mean that the lines need not obey any law of scansion at all. It is not hard to separate the element of truth in this conception from the erroneous interpretation which the Elizabethan satirists gave to it. If we look back at the Latin poets

---

[1] So too Dryden thought that Donne needed to be "translated into numbers." (Letter to the Earl of Dorset, quoted by Alden, *The Rise of Formal Satire in England*, p. 82.)

upon whom they fashioned themselves, it is clear that neither Persius nor Horace nor Juvenal gives to his hexameters the polish or the stately grace of the *Æneid*; and it is also clear that if they had done so they would have fallen into an error cognate to that of which the classical example is Gibbon's *Autobiography*. The style appropriate to the majestic decay of the Roman Empire is not appropriate to the private history of a scholarly but stout and not majestic nor even picturesque Englishman. Neither is that style which most fitly tells with what toil the state of Rome was founded, the appropriate one in which to criticise the trivialities of the daily life of Romans. So too in English, Miltonic sublimity is admirable for the purpose of delineating archangel ruined; but if the secret had been known when Hall wrote, it would still have been most unfitting for the task before him. So far the Elizabethan satirists were right. Where they went wrong and deserted the classical models whose example they were trying to follow was in writing verse which was not only plain, pedestrian, low in tone, adapted to the subject, but which was not really verse at all, which defied all rule and would not scan. The lines of Horace's satires, though they show occasional licences, scan; they are hexameters, homely though they may be in comparison with those which sing Arms and the Man. But all too frequently the lines of Donne, and sometimes those of other Elizabethan satirists, will not scan; they are not five-beat iambics, they have either to be "translated into numbers," as one great poet has said, or, according to another, read in a manner not understanded of the people. After a century we find Dryden and Pope complete masters of the art of writing heroic couplets highly polished, flawlessly correct, and yet well adapted to the purposes of satire. A century later still, Campbell uses the same measure, just when it is going out of fashion, in a rhetorical style which would have been ludicrous for the purposes aimed at in *The Dunciad*, and yet again with perfect correctness. That the tone must rise and fall according to the nature of the subject-matter is evident; but that the fundamental laws of verse have to be violated has never yet been shown.

In the first satire Donne depicts himself as a student dragged from his books by a "fondling motley humorist." Unwillingly he leaves his study and goes out; and the "humorist" "grins, smacks,

shrugs" to "every fine silken painted fool we meet," and darts
away after "a many-coloured peacock," in spite of the fact that
the student has stipulated not to be left in the street:—

> "Not though a captain do come in thy way
> Bright parcel gilt, with forty dead men's pay,
> Not though a brisk perfumed pert courtier
> Deign with a nod thy courtesy to answer."

The debt to Horace is obvious; but so is the vigour, and so is the
essential originality. The sins of lawyers form the subject of the
second satire, and in the third Donne passes to religion. Here he
rises, perhaps, to his highest point. He shows a noble disposition,
a noble love of truth, and a sense that she is difficult to discover
and manifold of aspect. Donne admires neither Mirreus, who seeks
religion at Rome, because he knows that "she was there a thousand
years ago"; nor Crantz, who

> "Loves her only who at Geneva is call'd
> Religion, plaine, simple, sullen, young,
> Contemptuous, yet unhandsome."

There is evidence elsewhere that Donne loved neither of these
extremes. In that brilliantly witty piece, *The Will*, he jibes at
both:—

> "My faith I give to Roman Catholics;
> All my good works unto the Schismatics
> Of Amsterdam."

It is the search for truth that Donne loves. To him, as to Leibnitz,
the search is more than the attainment; to him, as to Tennyson,
there is more faith in honest doubt than in half the creeds. The
search is itself a religion:—

> "He's not of none, nor worst, that seeks the best."

And the search leads him to a recognition that there is good in all
religions, and that the Truth, full and final, is very hard to find:—

> "To adore, or scorn an image, or protest,
> May all be bad; doubt wisely; in strange way
> To stand inquiring right, is not to stray;
> To sleep, or run wrong, is. On a huge hill,
> Cragged, and steep, Truth stands, and he that will
> Reach her, about must, and about must go;
> And when the hill's suddenness resists, win so;
> Yet strive so, that before age, death's twilight,
> Thy Soul rest, for none can work in that night."

The fourth satire, like the first, deals with a bore, Donne here
following Horace much more closely than he does in the other.

The vein is far less serious than that in which the third satire is written, yet it probably bears the impress of personal feeling. Donne disliked the Court, and here he depicts himself going to Court, though he has neither suit to urge nor new suit to show. *Noscitur a sociis :* he is judged to be as vain and witless and false as those who dwell there, and he falls a victim to a singular person clad in a jerkin which has once been violet, but is now "tum-taffaty." "This thing," as Donne contemptuously calls him, has travelled and speaks all tongues, yet speaks no language. He affects omniscience:—

> "He knows who loves; whom; and by what poison
> Hastes to an office's reversion;
> He knows who hath sold his land, and now doth beg
> A licence, old iron, boots, shoes, and egg-
> Shells to transport; shortly boys shall not play
> At span-counter, or blow-point, but they pay
> Toll to some courtier."

The impression of personal loathing of this character which the piece conveys would be deepened if we could be sure that Satire VII., which also treats it, was the work of Donne. The authorship is however doubtful; and Professor Grierson argues with considerable cogency that Satires VI. and VII. should rather be attributed to Sir John Roe. Whoever the author may have been, he treats Elizabeth and James I. with a frankness of speech rarely used with respect to such exalted personages.

The fifth satire, which deals specially with officers and courts of law and suitors and the wrongs they have to suffer, broadens out into greater generality and condemns the satirist's own age without measure. It illustrates Donne's habitual pessimism. He can find no name bad enough by which to call the time. The phrase "Iron Age," which sufficed for antiquity in its degeneracy, suffices no longer:—

> "O Age of rusty iron! some better wit
> Call it some worse name, if ought equal it;
> The Iron Age *that* was, when justice was sold; now
> Injustice is sold dearer far."

As early as Donne, or perhaps even earlier in the line of English satirists of the classical tradition, was Thomas Lodge (1558?–1625). *A Fig for Momus*, in which were embodied four satires in verse, appeared in 1595, and in the dedication, which is dated May 6th of that year, Lodge declares that if his satires "pass well, the whole

centon of them, already in my hands, shall suddenly be published."
Even therefore if we assign Donne's satires to 1593, the earliest
date suggested for them, it is not improbable that some
of Lodge's had been written before that date. Evidently
the satires did not "pass well," for the "centon" which
the author had ready was never published. Notwithstanding the
considerable merits of the four pieces we possess, there is little
cause to regret the fact that we do not possess more. If the pieces
published were representative, it is difficult to see how satires
of the same type could have been multiplied with much profit.
The satire is essentially moral, and most of the vices are already
dealt with in the four. The pleasantest piece is the last—a satire
on ambition, and a panegyric on moderation and contentment.
The picture of the lowly life is charming:—

> "An humble cot entapissed with moss,
> A lowly life that fears no sudden loss:
> A mind that dreads no fall, nor craves no crown,
> But makes his true-content his best renown.
> These are the choice contents, the goods, the gain,
> Which rightly can be ours: the rest are vain."

Here, clearly, is the pastoral spirit embedded in a satire. But
Lodge could be pungent when he chose. Thus the third satire,
"to a dear friend lately given over to covetousness," contains a
vigorous denunciation of the miserly spirit and an exposure of its
folly. The first satire still more pungently attacks flattery, and in
particular that form of flattery which most comes home to the
man of letters like Lodge:—

> "He is a gallant fit to serve my Lord
> Which claws, and soothes him up, at every word;
> That cries, when his lame poesy he hears,
> 'Tis rare (my Lord) 'twill pass the nicest ears.
>
> .   .   .   .   .   .
>
> Thus with the world, the world dissembles still,
> And to their own confusions follow will;
> Holding it true felicity to fly,
> Not from the sin, but from the seeing eye."

Compared with Donne, these passages show a superiority in metre
even more marked than is the inferiority in weight of thought.
Lodge had a good ear, he had behind him the example of Spenser

and long practice in the art of versification, and the result is lines which still retain the harmony he gave them.

Joseph Hall (1574–1656), who declares himself to be the earliest English satirist, came in reality later than Lodge, though not, so far as date of publication went, later than Donne. The first three books of his *Virgidemiarum* appeared in 1597. These he called "toothless" satires, a phrase which Milton, in the course of the *Smectymnuus* controversy, pronounced to be a bull nearly equivalent to toothless teeth.[1] The second three books, the "biting" satires, followed in 1598. Hall's satires therefore, like Donne's, were the work of his youth; for in 1597 he was only twenty-three. For extent and scope at least, if not for quality, Hall's work was by far the most remarkable hitherto attempted; and it was probably in part for this reason that it won attention. Wyatt's three satires had been forgotten; Lodge's four were disregarded; Spenser had written a tale in verse, and some readers perhaps did not realise that it was a satire as well. But in the first instalment of *Virgidemiarum* alone there were twenty-three satires; a number swelled to thirty-four by the addition of the biting satires. Lodge had made a mistake: had he published his whole "centon," probably Hall could not have made his much-discussed claim to priority. *Virgidemiarum* immediately became popular, and though afterwards it underwent a temporary eclipse, the editions through which it had passed before this occultation supplied the means of readily restoring its popularity.

In the third satire of Book V. Hall has expressed his own conception of satire, and the lines are worth quoting, together with those which compare the poet's own time with a robuster early age:—

> "The Satire should be like the Porcupine,
> That shoots sharp quills out in each angry line,
> And wounds the blushing cheek and fiery eye,
> Of him that hears and readeth guiltily.
> Ye antique Satires, how I bless your days,
> That brook'd your bolder style, their own dispraise;
> And well-near wish, yet joy my wish is vain,
> I had been then, or they were now again!
> For now our ears been of more brittle mould,
> Than those dull earthen ears that were of old:
> Sith theirs, like anvils, bore the hammer's head,
> Our glass can never touch unshivered."

[1] Quoted by Alden, *The Rise of Formal Satire in England*, p. 99.

The "staying" of Hall's satires within a year gives special point to these strictures on the sensitiveness of the time. The comparison of the satire to the porcupine seems applicable rather to the biting than to the toothless satires; but Milton was right: "toothless satire" is a contradiction in terms, and the difference between the two groups is only one of degree: there are biting teeth and fairly sharp quills in the earlier books too, though their point is rarely aimed at individuals. Hall describes the themes of these three books as "poetical, academical and moral." No one hitherto had given so prominent a place to literary subjects. Not only does the first book contain more satires than any of the others, but the first two satires of the second book are really misplaced and belong by subject to the first, where doubtless Hall was prevented from putting them by the consideration that if he had done so the balance of the books would have been utterly destroyed. Further, a large part of the long satire which forms Book VI. is also devoted to literature. If we take all these pieces together, the nine satires of Book I., the first (and longest) two out of the seven of Book II., and the passage in Book VI., in which the satirist returns to that unknown Labeo who had already been censured for his immorality in Book II., we have clearly something in the nature of a systematic criticism of English poetry. The criticism is partly ethical, partly æsthetic, and sometimes it is both at once. Thus the love-poetry of the time is censured on the æsthetic ground of its extravagance, as well as on the moral ground of its licentiousness; and Labeo, whether he was Chapman, as Warton conjectured, or someone else, is censured on both scores. As to licentiousness however the satire must be taken as general. Scarcely anyone, from Shakespeare downwards, was blameless, and in the face of this fact it seems idle to attempt to identify particular sinners. Again, the poets are condemned in the first satire of the first book for meanness of spirit. Hall feels the degradation of subservience to a patron, and condemns the "hungen-starven trencher poetry" of the poetical clients. No one who wishes to understand how well the satire was merited need search deeper than the dedications of Elizabethan books; and once more, unfortunately, the greatest must share the censure with the least. Shakespeare wrote phrases of adulation which we would rather he had never penned, Spenser sinned yet more grievously, while in prose Bacon outdid both. Others besides literary men sinned in the same way, and in Book II. vi., Hall pens a stinging rebuke to the clerical toady, lashing an abuse which Addison and Swift found still prevalent a century later:—

> "A gentle squire would gladly entertain
> Into his house some trencher-chapelain;
> Some willing man, that might instruct his sons,
> And that would stand to good conditions.
> First, that he lie upon the truckle-bed,
> Whiles his young master lieth o'er his head.
> Second, that he do, on no default
> Ever presume to sit above the salt.
> Third, that he never change his trencher twice.
> Fourth, that he use all common courtesies;
> Sit bare at meals, and one half rise and wait.
> Last that he never his young master beat,
> But he must ask his mother to define
> How many jerks she would his breech should line.
> All these observed, he could contented be,
> To give five marks and winter livery."

It is to the honour of Hall that he felt deeply the dignity, not only of the clerical profession which he entered upon not long after this passage was written, but that of other professions, and, in particular, the profession of letters, as well. The second satire of the second book expresses a rich man's scorn of the poor student, and adds the answer:—

> "Fond fool! six feet shall serve for all thy store;
> And he that cares for most shall find no more.
> We scorn that wealth should be the final end,
> Whereto the heavenly Muse her course doth bend;
> And rather had be pale with learned cares,
> Than paunched with thy choice of changed fares."

This sense of the moral dignity of poetry strengthens the impression caused by the elaboration of his satirical treatment of it that Hall must at one time have contemplated making letters the profession of his life. Either outward circumstances or a change of feeling, however, prevented this, and of the ten substantial volumes of his collected works there is only one in which the purely literary impulse is not secondary. The Bishop of Norwich's sermons are not literature in the full sense in which his satires are literature.

After a comparison between satires and other forms of verse, and a condemnation of the licentiousness which disgraced much of the poetry of his time, Hall proceeds in the first book to a consideration of various species of poetry. The prominence of the drama leads him first to turn his attention to tragedy. He condemns its extravagance and turgidity, especially as these faults are illustrated in Marlowe's *Tamburlaine*. Thence he passes to criticisms of heroic and of elegiac poetry. Next he deals with the pestilent attempt to saddle English poetry with the classical metres, and in particular with the hexameter. How narrowly that attempt missed doing irreparable harm to literature is well known, and it is to Hall's honour that he perceived that the English tongue had a genius of its own and was worthy of, and required, measures of its own. It would however be easy to exaggerate his services in this respect. The danger had passed before he wrote; Spenser, after a moment of hesitation, had seen the truth, and embodied it in verse far more convincing than any satire could be. After the metres the satirist deals in succession with erotic poetry and religious verse, and closes the first book with a renewed denunciation of licentiousness. There is, as has already been said, no real break here. The first satire of Book II. continues the condemnation of immoral verse, especially that of the unidentified Labeo, and the second contains that assertion of the superiority of the Muse to mere wealth which has already been quoted. Hall then had evidently thought deeply and thought justly upon the subject of poetry, and the soundness of his criticism, in its main principles, would now be generally admitted. The Elizabethans unquestionably allowed the romantic spirit excessive licence, and, as Matthew Arnold might have phrased it, lost the sense of the whole in eager quest of beautiful parts. They were curiously deaf and blind to incongruities, such as those which Hall ridicules in his satire of religious verse, where the Hebraic is unnaturally mingled with the classic. Milton afterwards showed that the mixture could be made, but those who attempted it in the reign of Elizabeth were not masters of Milton's secret. Hall is supposed to have had in his mind Markham's *Sion's Muse* and certain poems of Southwell:—

> "Parnassus is transform'd to Sion-hill
> And Jury-Palms her steep ascent done fill.
> Now good S. Peter weeps pure Helicon,
> And both the Maries make a music moan:
> Yea, and the prophet of the heavenly lyre,
> Great Solomon sings in the English Quire;
> And is become a new-found sonnetist,
> Singing his love, the holy spouse of Christ:
> Like as she were some light-skirts of the rest,
> In mightiest ink-hornisms he can thither wrest."

This last sarcasm about the "light-skirts" of the Song of Solomon might have been pointed with at least as much justice at the gravest commentators as at the poets, for in this point the "sonnetists" were but versifying the teaching of the commentators as expressed in sober prose.

The impression that Hall must at one time have contemplated following a literary career is deepened when we contrast the elaborate and quasi-systematic satire of poetry with the much slighter and more superficial treatment of the other professions in the "toothless satires." After the eleven literary satires, there follow four which pass in rapid review the lawyer, the physician and the clergyman. The lawyer is compared to a briar-bush sheltering the sheep from the storm, but also tearing the fleece from its back:—

> "Woe to the weal, where many lawyers be;
> For there is, sure, much store of malady."

Their costly protection is yielded only to those who can pay a large fee. The doctors are as eminent for folly as the lawyers for knavery and oppression. Book II. v. can hardly be described as a satire on the clergy, still less on the Church: it deals only with simony. Hall however returns to the clergy in the next satire, from which a passage dealing with the "trencher-chaplains" has already been quoted. These are what Hall named the "academical" satires. The "moral" satires of the third book are even less fit to balance the literary ones. They deal with nothing much deeper than the follies of fashion and of that vanity which seeks its gratification in splendid monuments. No doubt the young fop who puts all his estate on his back and goes hungry, is a fool; but he is neither very interesting nor dangerous. No doubt the man arrayed in the height of fashion is ridiculous:—

> "A French head joined to neck Italian:
> Thy thighs from Germany, and breast from Spain:
> An Englishman in none, a fool in all:
> Many in one, and one in several."

But here, too, we are still in the shallows of human nature.

This fact brings out Hall's real meaning in his not very happy distinction between the toothless and the biting satires. Variety in dress and bad taste in poetry are not among the major vices; and such things are the staple of Hall's first three books. In the latter half of his work there is some evidence of a design to deal systematically with the deadlier sins of the individual and the graver defects of society; but if the design was ever entertained it was not carried out, nor was any approximation made to it as close as that which is made in Book I. to a systematic treatment of literature. Book IV. i. condemns licentiousness in act as Book I. ii. and ix. condemn licentiousness in word. In IV. ii. we have Lolio drudging to make his son a gentleman; growing rich, acquiring lands and founding a family—and his reward is that he himself is blotted out by the son for whom he has toiled:—

> "His father dead! tush, no, it was not he,
> He finds records of his great pedigree,
> And tells how first his famous ancestor
> Did come in long since with the Conqueror."

The unscrupulous accumulation of wealth through the ruin of others, the exorbitant pretensions of the Pope, the oppression of the tenant by the landlord, the shameless stealing and enclosure of public lands—these are among the abuses against which Hall inveighs in these later books. He pictures Juvenal's disgust if he could see imperial Rome turned into papal Rome:—

> " How his enraged ghost would stamp and stare,
> That Cæsar's throne is turn'd to Peter's chair.
> To see an old shorn lozel perched high,
> Crossing beneath a golden canopy;
> The whiles a thousand hairless crowns crouch low
> To kiss the precious case of his proud toe:
> And, for the lordly fasces borne of old,
> To see two quiet crossed keys of gold;
> Or Cybele's shrine, the famous Pantheon's frame,
> Turn'd to the honour of our Lady's name."

In the last satire of all the author ironically retracts his censures, and professes to repent that he has written so harshly:—

> "Let me now repent me of my rage,
> For writing Satires, in so righteous age:
> Whereas I should have strok'd her towardly head,
> And cried Evöe in my Satires' stead."

In reality however his spirit has been oppressed by the contemplation of vice and corruption, and in Book IV. vi., after showing how empty and trivial are the ambitions for which men spend themselves and stain their souls, he ends with a panegyric of the quiet academic life, which he seems to have really loved:—

> " 'Mongst all these stirs of discontented strife,
> Oh let me lead an academic life!
> To know much, and to think we nothing know;
> Nothing to have, yet think we have enow:

In skill to want and wanting seek for more;
In weal, nor want nor wish for greater store.
Envy, ye monarchs, with your proud excess,
At our low sail, and our high happiness."

Long after these lines were written, Hall, looking backwards, declared that the years he had spent at Emmanuel were spent "with such contentment, as the rest of my life hath in vain striven to yield."

Hall was followed immediately by John Marston (1575?–1634), whose *Metamorphosis of Pygmalion's Image* and *The Scourge of Villany* were both entered in the Stationers' Hall register in the same year as Hall's second group of satires, though somewhat later in the year. It suited Marston to represent *Pygmalion* itself to be a satire; but in point of fact it is simply one of the most licentious poems of a period in which licentiousness was among the prevailing vices of verse; and the volume in which it appeared has a place here only because of the other pieces with which it is accompanied. That this is the case is apparent from the very title of the volume. It is: *The Metamorphosis of Pygmalion's Image. And certain Satires*—not *And other Satires*. The five satires which are appended deal with the hypocrisies of various classes and the complete reversal of values, the confusion of the mean with the great, virtue with vice, which must characterise any age so completely corrupt as Marston declares that in which he lives to be. The eleven pieces of *The Scourge of Villany* considerably extend Marston's range. Like Juvenal, he thinks it difficult to refrain from satire. He declares that vice is the way to success, while honesty leads to ruin, and that procrastination has taken away the hope of reform, for each man is resolved to abandon his vice— to-morrow. All this is expressed with the utmost violence of vituperation, in verse harsher than the harshest written by the other satirists, though adorned with the gems of a learning of which Marston seems to have been vain. The staggering compound "vizarded-bifronted-Janian" stares the reader in the face in the fourth line of the first satire of the *Pygmalion* volume, and he is expected to accept "what though dagger hack'd mouths of his blade swears" as an iambic line. Of course, this intolerable harshness is wilful: Marston is proud of his "rough-hew'd rime." No one else accepted quite so whole-heartedly—or at least, no one else pushed to such an extreme—the doctrine that the lines of the satire ought to jolt and bump along.

The violence of Marston is curious, because it is in glaring contradiction of the substance of the teaching conveyed in this 'Ercles vein. The easiness of excessive and indiscriminate satire is one of the points he makes in his attack upon Hall—in this matter an innocent babe in comparison with his censor:—

> "Who cannot rail, and with a blasting breath
> Scorch even the whitest lilies of the earth?
> Who cannot stumble in a stuttering style
> And shallow heads with seeming shades beguile?"

And yet it is Marston who pronounces a universal condemnation upon his kind, and declares that Circe's charm has turned all men to swine. He who is ever in extremes yet approves the mean. He satirises the High Churchman celebrating the Mass, but he also satirises the Puritan, charging him with carrying usury to a point beyond that reached by the Jews:—

> "With his bait of purity
> He bit me sore in deepest usury.
> No Jew, no Turk, would use a Christian
> So inhumanely as this Puritan."

Not the least curious point in connection with Marston is the quarrel which, in the satires, he fastens upon Hall. The view that Hall first attacked him is deficient in evidence; for Marston is not known to have published anything before his *Pygmalion*, which was later than Hall's satires, and it is improbable that Hall would have selected a wholly unknown man for attack.

There is neither evidence to show that *Pygmalion* had circulated in manuscript before it was printed, nor occasion to advance the conjecture; for both Marlowe and Shakespeare, to name no lesser men, had written what fully justified Hall's strictures on the licentiousness of contemporary verse. Probably Marston's attack was unprovoked, proceeding from that unamiable nature which involved him in the notorious quarrel with Jonson as well. Very likely the transparent pretence that *Pygmalion* had a satirical meaning was put forward from a sense of guilt brought home by Hall's satire. It is appended as a sort of postscript to *Pygmalion*, and may well have been written as an afterthought. We may reasonably suppose that Marston had written the poem, was too much in love with his own production, and too justly hopeful of its popularity to sacrifice it, yet felt the sting of Hall's lash, and tried by this means to defend himself in the eyes of the public, if not in the court of his own conscience. Here was the grievance. Hall had the assurance to denounce the vice of which Marston was afterwards guilty. The fact that he deliberately chose the worse way made Marston all the more venomous against him who had shown the better. Hence the violent attack in *Reactio*, the fourth satire of the *Pygmalion* volume, the parodies of Hall, the pretended scorn —"Ye lions tremble, for an ass doth bray." Hence the frequent recurrence to the theme in *The Scourge of Villany*, where an uneasy conscience brings Marston back to the question of the morality of *Pygmalion*. As he holds the pulpit, he is free to denounce those who have misunderstood that blameless poem. Hall is condemned as an envious detractor, and his style is ridiculed. In the tenth satire of *The Scourge of Villany* the cause of all this rancour is revealed. Hall had not only condemned Marston's sin before it was committed: he had acted like that very wicked animal which defends itself when it is attacked. He had written an epigram and attached it to all the copies of *Pygmalion* that came to Cambridge. Marston, in his indignation, quotes it, calling the author a "stinking scavenger"—a flower of rhetoric which shows that he had too completely lost his temper to be any longer literary.

The last-mentioned foul-mouthed satire is dedicated to the author's "Very friend, E. G."; and it has been conjectured that the person indicated by the initials may have been Edward Guilpin, the author of *Skialetheia* (1598), a collection of satires and epigrams. The satires, six in number, are preceded by a prelude, in which, and also in the sixth satire, the influence of Hall is probably to be traced. The prelude condemns lascivious poetry, and the sixth satire criticises Chaucer, Spenser, Drayton, Sidney and others. Guilpin however shows neither much force or originality in thought nor much skill in versification. Perhaps the most interesting passage is that in the second satire where he exposes the devices by which women seek to heighten their beauty—a crude anticipation of a passage in Pope's *Rape of the Lock*:—

> " They know your spirits and your distillations
> Which make your eyes turn diamonds to charm passions:
> Your ceruse now grown stale, your skein of silk,
> Your philter'd waters and your asses' milk.
> They were plain asses if they did not know
> Quicksilver, juice of lemons, boras too,
> Alum, oil Tartar, whites of eggs and gaules,
> Are made the bawds to morphew, scurfs and scauls."

Whether Guilpin was or was not the "very friend" of Marston, he shared his misfortune, for *Skialetheia* was burned along with *Pygmalion*. So was *Micro-Cynicon*, a collection of six "snarling satires" of very slight merit, which are commonly but doubtfully attributed to Thomas Middleton.

Of greater worth was the work of Samuel Rowlands (1570?–1630), the author of *The Letting of Humour's Blood in the Head-Vein* (1600), who wrote vigorously in verse, the smoothness of which stands in pleasant contrast to the harshness of most of the contemporary satirists. *The Letting of Humour's Blood* is a collection of epigrams, followed by seven satires. Rowlands ridicules the boaster who in his pretended travels has seen more wonders than Mandeville; draws an effective picture of Contempt, and deals skilfully with the boon companion who finds in liquor not only meat and drink, but clothing as well. The ecclesiastical prohibition had little effect upon Rowlands, for in 1602 he produced *'Tis Merry when Gossips Meet*, telling in six-line stanzas the carousal of a wife, a widow and a maid. It is a lively performance, somewhat coarse, but essentially good-natured, and not licentious like Dunbar's *Twa Mariet Wemen and the Wedo*. After a number of minor pieces Rowlands in 1609 opened the series of Knaves with *The Knave of Clubs*, finishing in 1613 with *The Knaves of Spades and Diamonds*. The first satirises various sorts of rogues and gulls, and among them, "Signieur word-monger the Ape of Eloquence," for his affected Latin diction. *The Knave of Hearts* deals with a dissembling knave, a hypocritical, a drunken, a swearing, a thieving knave, and many others. *A Lying Knave* is on Rowlands's favourite theme of satire, the lies of the braggart:—

> "He will your admiration entertain
> With secret things from Rome, from France, and Spain,
> Barbary, Turkey, Indies, East and West:
> He hath all kingdoms' business in his breast."

The picture of the prodigal is one of the best:—

> "Along the streets, as he doth jetting pass,
> His outside shows him for an inward ass.
> In a tobacco-shop (resembling hell,—
> Fire, stink and smoke must be where devils dwell)
> He sits, you cannot see his face for vapour,
> Offering to Pluto with a tallow taper."

No doubt Rowlands hoped by the condemnation of tobacco to win the favour of King James. He recurs to the subject more than once. He speaks of the nose of the smoker "stinking as loathsome as doth Hecla hill." Yet he sees the triumph of tobacco in spite of king and satirist combined:—

> "Like an ill weed that grows fast, 'tis come,
> To stink in nostrils throughout Christendom,
> So that of most it may be truly spoke,
> Their tongues yield idle breath, their noses smoke."

Not the least of Rowlands's merits is his variety. He is not, like Marston, for ever in extremes. He is ready to satirise practices like smoking, which, at the worst, are mere indulgences, or the graver vices; and equally ready to strike a note serious and even elevated, or to handle his theme lightly. The fine lines on the covetous man in *The Knave of Spades* are a good example of his more serious style:—

> "God he neglecteth for the bar of gold,
> His soul for money every day is sold,
> To scrape and get his care is night and day,
> And in a moment death takes all away."

Of the lighter style an excellent example is found in *The Melancholy Knight* (1615), an entertaining burlesque of the Arthurian romances. The knight has neither much courage nor much money. His wife is "a good rich grazier's daughter," and the grazier's death would cure the melancholy which results from impecuniousness and the disrespect consequent upon it. But unfortunately the grazier is hale and sound, and the knight is "sick to think upon his health." And in the meantime the necessity of enabling my Lady "to Lady it" lays a sore burden upon him. The volume ends with a group of poems by the Knight, mostly dealing with his own impecunious fortune, and ridiculing romantic verse. Thus the last of the satirists who carried on into the reign of James the Elizabethan tradition which had been partly broken by the ecclesiastical veto, in the end turns his wit against that which had given life and spirit to Elizabethan poetry. Romance was sometimes absurd, but when men became clearly conscious of the absurdities poetry either withered up, or, at best, lived upon a lower range of emotion and imagination.

In the lull caused by the ecclesiastical veto no new satirist appeared for some years; but in 1608 Richard Middleton published his unimportant *Epigrams and Satires*. Three years later came *The Scourge of Folly* by John Davies of Hereford (1565?–1618), a work of greater fame than merit. It is a collection of nearly three hundred epigrams, directed against all the vices—pride, lust, gluttony, greed, and so on. Davies's natural style was too wordy for the epigram, and his censure is generally pointless and commonplace. Sir John Harington's *Epigrams Pleasant and Serious* (1618) were better; but it needed a master of language like Ben Jonson to use this form with effect. Among even his *Epigrams* (1616) there are many in which the purpose seems to be no more serious than simply to display wit; but some, especially among the longer ones, are really telling satirical portraits. Thus the *English Monsieur*, who speaks French by means of his clothes, reiterates a complaint which, though familiar enough, had probably never before been so well expressed; *Don Surly* skilfully delineates a character who prides himself on his very vices, and conceives that they are proofs of greatness; and *The New Cry* ridicules the pretenders of the London streets who affect a knowledge of the affairs of every kingdom under heaven.

Soon after John Davies of Hereford, John Taylor (1580–1653), the Water Poet, began his long career as a writer. There are greater men whose names are less frequently mentioned in histories of literature than his; yet for generations he has been more often named than read, and his real merits are higher than they are supposed to be. It is true he is very unequal, often tiresome, and sometimes contemptible. In his satires on Coryat and his *Crudities* his puns surpass in vileness even the puns of his contemporaries. Often he is a preacher rather than a satirist. *Superbiae Flagellum, or the Whip of Pride*, is a very prosy moralising piece; and *Kicksey Winsey*, in which the author claims to have "satirically suited seven hundred and fifty of his bad debtors," is wearisome. Neither does *Taylor's Water-Work: or The Sculler's Travels from Tiber to Thames*, afford much that is to the purpose. It is described on the title-page as a "galli mawfrey of sonnets, satires and epigrams." The epigrams are of the usual sort on the usual subjects, and the two satires are mediocre. But the fourteen satires of *The Water-Cormorant, his Complaint: Against a Brood of Land Cormorants*, are a collection of satirical characters painted with real skill. The *Simoniacal Patron* is a grave condemnation of a grave abuse. The service of the Church is starved that the patron's wife may dress fine:—

> " She hath a preacher's living on her back,
> For which the souls of many go to wrack,
> And hires a mongrel cheaply by the year,
> To famish those, Christ's blood hath bought so dear."

The *Prodigal Country Gallant* is drawn with equal skill:—

> " This Fop late buried ere he came up hither
> His thrift and 's Father in one grave together.
>
> .   .   .   .   .   .
>
> His Father (a good house-keeper) being dead,
> He scorns his honest block should fit his head:
> And though he be not skill'd in magic art,
> Yet to a coach he turns his Father's cart,
> Four teams of horses to four Flanders mares,
> With which to London he in pomp repairs,
> Woos a she Gallant, and to wife he takes her:
> Then buys a knighthood, and a madam makes her."

A Separatist shows where Taylor's sympathies lay in that division on religion which was presently to produce such grave political consequences:—

> " Now enters next to play his oily part
> A Saint in tongue, but a rough devil in heart:
> One that so smoothly swallows his prey down,
> Without wrath shewn or any seeming frown,
> You'd think him when he does't, in a psalm,
> Or at his prayers, he's so mild and calm:
> No noise, no trouble to his conscience cries,
> For he devours his prey with heaved up eyes,
> Stands most demurely swallowing down his bit,
> And licks his lips with long grace after it."

Though the triumph of the Puritans made satire of this sort for a time unpopular, and occasionally even dangerous, in a collection published in 1651 Taylor again satirises the hypocrisy of Puritans. He detested the sectarians. In *The Praise of Hemp-Seed* he satirises the Brownists, while tracing the passage of hemp into paper, and jeers at their exaggerated regard for the Sunday:—

> " Suppose his cat on Sunday kill a rat,
> She on the Monday must be hanged for that."

More important in the history of satire is George Wither (1588–1667), the author of *Abuses Stript and Whipt* (1613). He writes pleasantly and leaves a pleasant impression of his own character, but his platitudinous verbosity sadly mars the effect of his writings. The moderation of his measured and sensible strictures makes his criticisms instructive, because we feel that they can be trusted. No age has ever been quite so bad as the professional satirist is apt to paint his own, but many periods have been little better than the England which Wither depicts. That a satirist so restrained should have suffered imprisonment for his writings is surprising —all the more because the claim he makes in the satire written in prison and appended to subsequent editions of the *Abuses* is justified:—

> " I have not sought to scandalise the State,
> Nor sown sedition, nor made public hate:
> I have not aim'd at any good man's fame,
> Nor taxt (directly) any one by name.
> I am not he that am grown discontent
> With the Religion, or the Government.
> I meant no ceremonies to protect,
> Nor do I favour any new-sprung sect;
> But to my satires gave this only warrant,
> To apprehend and punish vice apparent.
> Who aiming in particular at none,
> In general upbraided everyone:
> That each (unshamed of himself) might view
> That in himself which no man dares to shew."

It is true however that in the *Abuses* Wither had betrayed his knowledge that kings are not free from vice, and had spoken with force and plainness on the subject. It may be that, in spite of the generality of the passage, an uneasy conscience tempted James to think that the cap fitted his own head.

There is one other notable limitation of the scope of Wither's satire. In *The Scourge* he declares his resolution not to satirise women. While inciting himself to search for more subjects, he adds:—

> " But if thou hap to find
> Any among them of the female kind,
> Women or angels, bad or good, thine eyes
> Shall not look toward their infirmities.
> Whate'er some say, no woman will or can
> Wrong him (I'll warrant) that's an honest man,
> For they are good, and surely would be still
> Were't not that men did often make them ill:
> Those that are angry with them, let them show it,
> I'll say th' are virtuous, for because I know it."

He further declares his intention to confine himself to his own time and country:—

> " I am resolv'd to tie my rimes
> As much as may be to the present times."

But within these limits of politics, sex and time, Wither is extraordinarily comprehensive. Vices, manners and customs, classes and institutions, literature, education and religion, all pass under review. Clerical ambition and doctrinal excess, whether Romish or Puritanic, he detests. He is more original in his censure of the use made of the endowments of the universities:—

> "The Student poor
> For whom it was ordain'd, stands at the door
> And may not enter; whilst the golden ass
> Is quietly admitted in to pass."

Among literary characters he is particularly severe upon critics:—

> " They are but glow-worms that are brisk by night;
> And never can be seen when sun gives light;
> Ill-tongu'd and envious, ignorant of shame;
> And vile detractors of another's fame."

It is in the treatment of the moral qualities that Wither's weaknesses are most prominent. He is a sort of Elizabethan Martin Tupper, whose excellent intention and blameless morality are scarcely more exciting than the average sermon, to which much of his moral satire is close akin. The lines on beauty in the satire on Vanity read as if they might have been spoken from the pulpit:—

> " But why in beauty should men glory so;
> As well we may perceive there's many do;
> Sith 'tis no better than a fading flower,
> That flourishes, and withers in an hour?
> It could not save the good king David's son,
> From being justly by his foes undone:
> Nay, there's scarce any that enjoy the fame
> Can keep unto themselves an honest name."

A few other satirical works have come down to us from the latter part of the reign of James I., but none of importance or of great ability. *The Time's Whistle*, by R. C., who remains unidentified, appeared not before 1614, and probably between that year and 1616. The author was a moralist with a sincere desire for reform, but his skill was not great, and many passages are distinctly flat. He does not share Wither's virtue of moderation. This age, he says, has grown to an excess that was never known in Sodom. Avarice is unbounded. Justice is sold, simony is so common that it is no longer accounted a sin, the Universities sell fellowships, and "for double fees a dunce may turn a doctor" (an abuse condemned by Wither also); men apostatise for gold. The Scot is satirised; the Puritan, as usual, is charged with hypocrisy, while the Papist is denounced in unmeasured terms.

There is more vigour and greater originality in the work of Henry Fitzgeffrey, whose satires and epigrams were appended to *Certain Elegies, done by sundry excellent Wits* (1617). The epigrams call for little attention, for, as usual, they aim at smartness more than anything else. The satires of the first book follow the example set by Hall, and satirise literature, condemning the fulsome adulation of patrons by the poets, their unscrupulousness in plagiarism and their licentiousness. Above all, the satirist calls satire to account, condemning its excess and the spirit of prying into minute points of life and conduct. But by far the best and most interesting part of Fitzgeffrey's work is the third book, *Notes from Blackfriars.* It is based upon Jonson and the character-writers, and is, in fact, practically a book of characters in verse, much like those which Hall and Earle wrote in prose. The conception of the spectator watching the throng at the Blackfriars theatre and noting down his observations, supplies a certain unity and affords a natural introduction to an endless variety of types. The sketches are pungent and amusing. They are also instructive, for the plan compels him to be a realist and to delineate types which would recall to his readers figures they themselves had seen about the theatre. He thus escapes that vice of unreality and of insincere denunciation which was the bane of Elizabethan satire. It is this that marks him out as the last satirist worthy of note before the temporary eclipse of satire in the reign of Charles I. Henry Hutton, author of *Folly's Anatomy* (1619), and Richard Brathwaite, author of *Nature's Embassy* (1621), came after him, it is true. But they had little to add to what had been reiterated over and over again by their predecessors, and small skill in presentation or charm of style to atone for the lack of freshness. Hutton however did one thing that deserves to be remembered. His grammar is faulty, and his pictures of the bravado, the poetaster, the glutton and

the licentious woman commonplace. But not so that of the
lady-killer:—

> " See how, Narcissus like, the fool doth doat,
> Viewing his picture and his guarded coat;
> And with what grace, bold actor like he speaks,
> Having his beard precisely cut i' th' peak;
> Now neat 's moustaches do a distance stand,
> Lest they disturb his lips, or saffron band:
> How expert he 's; with what attentive care
> Doth he in method place each straggling hair.
> This idle idol doth bestow his wit
> In being spruce, in making 's ruff to sit:
> His day's endeavours are to be complete,
> To use his vestures nitid and facete:
> For vulgar oaths he raps forth blood and heart,
> As coadjutors in the wenching art.
> In 's frizzled periwig, with bended brow,
> Swears at each word for to confirm his vow."

CHAPTER VI

As it was only in the sixteenth century that the art of writing English prose passed out of its infancy, there is no history of satire in prose prior to the Elizabethan age, there are only a few scattered pieces of satirical prose. In the early part of the century however two remarkable works had appeared, which must have suggested to some minds the question whether verse was the true and natural vehicle for satire, and so must have prepared for the development of satire in prose when at length men knew how to write it. The works. in question were the *Epistolae Obscurorum Virorum* and Erasmus's *Moriae Encomium*. But these books were written neither by Englishmen nor in the English language. The only connexion of the *Epistolae* with England was the fact that the matter—satire of ecclesiastics—was familiar wherever the Catholic Church was planted, and was of vital moment in every country where the corruptions of that Church were rousing men to indignation, and were gradually awakening them to a sense of the need of reformation. That this was the condition in England the satire in verse which has already been passed in review sufficiently proves. With regard to *Moriae Encomium*, that was written in England, at the house of Sir Thomas More, upon whose name the author puns; and it is possible that talks between the two scholars may have suggested or given point to some of the satirical passages in *Utopia*.

In *Utopia* the satire is incidental, and it is not till a generation or more after Robinson's translation that we begin to come upon works in prose of which the main purpose is throughout satirical. In the interval appeared two or three tiny volumes dealing with vagabondage, in which there is a certain amount of satire. The most noteworthy of them is Thomas Harman's *Caveat or Warning for Common Cursetors* (1566), which ranks among the sources of the essay, and anticipates the character sketches which in the early years of the seventeenth century became a favourite vehicle for satire. But what Harman set out to do was to record and classify the facts with regard to a class whose existence was recognised as a grave social evil; in him too the satire is incidental. The same may be said with regard to the critical controversy which was occasioned by Stephen Gosson's *School of Abuse* (1579). It is in the polemical pamphlet that we first find satire raised to the foremost place, and at the head of the polemical pamphleteers stands the famous name of Martin Marprelate.

Though there is some lively reading in the Marprelate tracts, it is not to the lover of the beautiful that they appeal. To the historian of literature they have the interest of an unsolved and almost certainly an insoluble problem. The question who was Martin Marprelate is a literary enigma almost as baffling as the question who was Junius. Arber came to the conclusion that the real Martinists were John Penry, who has been called the father of Welsh Nonconformity, and Job Throckmorton; and Mr. W. Pierce, in his *Historical Introduction to the Marprelate Tracts,* in the main guardedly concurs. But Mr. J. Dover Wilson [1] has given very strong reasons for believing that the sole author of three and part author of certain other of the seven Martinist tracts was a totally different person—Sir Roger Williams, who was reputed to be the foremost English soldier of the day, and who was third in command, after Drake and Norris, of the unfortunate expedition against Spain in retaliation for the Armada. If the argument is sound, Williams was a man of very unusual gifts, for it is rarely that the man of action, which Williams certainly was, is at the same time interested in such questions as are discussed by Martin, and possesses the power to handle them with such effect. For though the tracts are purposely unkempt in style, their rude vigour is telling.

The controversy raged in the years 1588 and 1589. It was opened by *The Epistle* of Martin, which seems to have occasioned widespread interest and excitement. Curiously enough, though *The Epistle* is a Puritan tract, those who most objected to it, as Martin himself tells us, were the Puritan preachers. *Non tali auxilio,* they seem to have felt; and though the charge of blasphemy which was brought against Martin is absurd, it is easy to understand why those who thought that grave matters ought to be gravely handled

[1] "Martin Marprelate and Shakespeare's Fluellen " in *The Library,* 1912.

were disquieted. But Martin makes his own very effective defence: "The Puritans are angry with me; I mean the Puritan preachers. And why? Because I am too open; because I jest. I jested because I dealt with a worshipful jester, Dr. Bridges, whose writings and sermons tend to no other end than to make men laugh." [1] *The Epistle* declares the English Lord Bishops to be petty popes and petty antichrists, on the ground that they claimed authority over those to whom, as they lived in distant shires, they could not possibly discharge the duty of pastors. Instances of the grossest abuse are quoted. One bishop presents himself to a living: "'I, John of Rochester, present John Young,' quoth the Bishop." And the fact that the defence is a mere quibble shows that the charge is true. Aylmer, Bishop of London, is another of the prelates who are personally attacked, and he too has but a weak defence: "Who made the porter of his gate a dumb minister? Dumb John of London." The porter in question was deaf and dumb, and the defence is not a denial of the fact, but an assertion of the bishop's right to do as he had done. The Archbishop of Canterbury is another dignitary whom Martin detests. He threatens the archbishop with the heaviest punishment. "Remember your brother Haman. Do you think there is never a Mordecai to step to our gracious Esther, for preserving the lives of her faithfullest and best subjects, whom you so mortally hate and persecute?" "His Gracelessness of Cant " is the elegant style by which Martin designates the primate. Phrases of this sort have scarcely more wit than politeness; but in mitigation of Martin's offence it must be remembered that they were the fashion of the time in controversy, and that even so great a man as Milton, when he entered the arena, proved himself no better than the rest. Further, Martin could plead provocation. He asserts that John Penry, when summoned to answer for one of his books, was called by the archbishop "boy," "knave," "varlet," "slanderer," "lewd boy," "lewd slanderer." "This," he adds emphatically, "is *true*, for I have seen notes of their conference."

The Epistle offers peace on certain conditions—that the bishops promote preaching, ordain only fit men, refrain from urging illegal subscription, and so on. On these terms Martin will write no more, but if they break the terms he will write. Of course they broke the

[1] *The Epitome*, p. 118.

terms, and *The Epitome* followed after a very short interval. It deals with the first book of Dr. Bridges's work on the other side, which is described as "a very portable book; a horse may carry it, if he be not too weak"; while the style in which it is written is "as smooth as a crab-tree cudgel." There is more theology in *The Epitome* than in *The Epistle*; but the theology is handled in this style of homely vigour, and it was more effective than the dignified writings of the learned doctors on either side. There is some literary finesse too; Martin shows considerable skill in wielding the weapon of irony.

The third of the Martinist tracts is merely a broadside, *The Mineral Conclusions*, presenting in brief abstract the main points of the Puritan contention. The fourth is the more important *Hay any Work for Cooper ?* in answer to the argument of Thomas Cooper, Bishop of Winchester. There had been no small commotion among the dignitaries in consequence of Martin's attack, and Martin himself and his coadjutors ran considerable risk. Penry was ultimately executed for his complicity. The tracts had to be printed in secret, and the utmost care was taken to hide the traces both of author and of printer. In the "Epistle to the terrible priests" prefixed to *Hay any Work for Cooper ?* there is some amusing raillery about the search that had been made: "O Brethren, there is such a deal of love grown of late, I perceive, between you and me that, although I would be negligent in sending my 'pistles unto you, yet I see you cannot forget me. I thought you to be very kind, when you sent your pursuivants about the country to seek for me. But now that you yourselves have taken the pains to write, this is out of all cry." They have done him a great service: they have made his books more widely known, and also their own doings.

There are good grounds for believing that up to this point the Martinist tracts, except, perhaps, the *Mineral Conclusions*, were written by one man; but after *Hay any Work for Cooper ?* two other writers profess, at least, to come in. The fifth and sixth tracts are known familiarly and shortly as *Martin Junior* and *Martin Senior*, and their writers represent themselves as sons of the original Martin. This may have been suggested by an expression in the epistle prefixed to *The Epitome*, where Martin says, "I have many sons abroad that will solicit my suit." The "sons" are not quite so vigorous as the "father," and the tracts differ so widely in tone that it seems reasonable to suppose them to have been written by different hands—the former perhaps, as Mr. Wilson supposes, by Penry, and the latter partly by Penry and partly by Throckmorton. The latest Martinist paper is *The Protestation*, which appeared in September, 1589, just a little less than a year after *The Epistle*. *More Work for the Cooper* had been written and was being set up in type, when the accidental discovery of the surreptitious press suddenly silenced the Martinists.

Though the Marprelate tracts are not great monuments of literary skill, they have yet the merits of vigour and raciness, and, as the first sustained satires in English prose, they have a place in literature higher than their intrinsic merits would have won. The desire to be understood of the people saved Martin (if he ever felt the temptation to yield to them) from the prevalent vices of style. His is simple and colloquial, so that he who runs may read. If he had learning, he does not wilfully set out to show it. He is free, for the most part, from the involutions and inversions and parentheses with which the writings of more pretentious authors are loaded; and thus, perhaps without either intending or knowing it, he takes a considerable step forward in the evolution of prose style. Compare the structure of sentence in the quotations above given with that which we find in Sidney's *Apology for Poetry*, and it will be plain how important was the example given by this simple type of sentence. Or better still, set against the quotations from Martin the following passage from *Martin's Month's Mind*, one of the best of the pamphlets on the opposite side. From the style it is plain that the tract was by someone who had no mean opinion of himself as a literary artist. All who have helped to deliver us from this sort of artistry deserve our thanks:—

" Touching his body (for it should seem he had forgotten his soul: for the party that heard it told me, he heard no word of it), he would, should not be buried in any church (especially cathedral, which ever he detested), chapel, nor churchyard; for that they had been profaned with superstition: but in some barn, outhouse or field (yea, rather than fail, dunghill), where their prime prophesyings had been used; without bell, pomp, or any solemnity; save that his friends should mourn for him in gowns and hoods of a bright yellow; the hoods made of a strange fashion, for no ordinary thing contented him (belike with a crest after Hoyden's cut), and minstrels going before him; wherein he would have a hornpipe at any hand, because he loved that instrument above measure: the rest he referred to their discretion; but a Rebuke and a Shame, in my opinion, were the fittest fiddles for him."

In *The Epitome* Martin boasts of his popularity. He will make
the bishops rue their rejection of his conditions of peace: "I can
do it; for you see how I am favoured of all estates (the Puritans
alone excepted). I have been entertained at the Court; every man
talks of my Worship. Many would gladly receive my books, if they
could tell where to find them." But if Martin was entertained at
the Court it was certainly not with whole-hearted approval. And
there were classes whom he does not mention who read and condemned. Though the Puritan preachers shook their heads, he was
nevertheless a Puritan; and the literary class as a whole was anti-
Puritan. The prelates for their part apparently felt the need of
something less ponderous than their own artillery to reply to the
lively sallies of Martin; and there would seem to have been some
sort of understanding between them and the wits who undertook
to answer satire with satire. Those who were thus enlisted in the
cause of the prelates far surpass the Martinists in literary fame;
for among them we find the dramatists, John Lyly (1554–1606?)
and Robert Greene (1560?–1592), and Thomas Nash (1567–1601),
dramatist and miscellaneous writer. Yet, strange to say, the honours,
literary as well as theological, rest with Martin and his sons.
There is however a good deal of doubt as to the authorship of the
anti-Martinist tracts. It has been customary to ascribe most of
them to Nash, and they are to be found in the editions of his
works; but his latest editor, Mr. McKerrow, declares that, so
far as he can see, "there is not a single tract produced by the anti-
Martinist group of writers which may safely, or even probably,
be attributed to Nashe." Certainly the quotation given above
from *Martin's Month's Mind* is written in a style far less direct
and virile than that of Nash's indubitable works. But while the
bulk of the anti-Martinist tracts must be treated as writings of
unknown authorship, there can be no reasonable doubt that they
were the work of some one or more of the literary wits.

The satirists who undertook to reply to the satire of Martin did
not, like him, limit themselves to the prose pamphlet. They set
Martin upon the stage, they wrote verse, and they showed their
learning in Latin. *Martin Junior* refers contemptuously to the
players who had ridiculed him. They are "poor, silly, hunger-
starved wretches," so base-minded that "for one poor penny they

will be glad on open stage to play the ignominious fools for an hour or two together." The feud with the stage had already begun, and, no doubt, the wits felt that they were fighting their own battle as well as the battle of the bishops. As the plays in which Martin was belaboured are lost, it is impossible to say what their worth or worthlessness may have been. There are however some remains of anti-Martinist verse. There is *Mar-Martin*, a trivial piece, and there is *A Whip for an Ape*, a poem by Lyly of twenty-six stanzas of six lines each. Though worthless as poetry it is cleverly adapted to the end in view. It appeals shrewdly to the fears of the governing classes, making capital of the tendency of the reformer to advance from point to point until everything is overthrown. So it has been elsewhere:—

> " The German boors with clergymen began,
> But never left till prince and peers were dead."

Let all princes and peers therefore beware, for Martin has already shown this spirit. He would tear everything in pieces—caps, tippets, rochets, communion books, homilies, even women's wimples:—

> " Thus tearing all, as all apes use to do,
> He tears withal the Church of Christ in two."

Lyly took part in the war of the prose tracts as well, but his *Pap with a Hatchet* is mere scurrilous abuse. The spirit in which it is written is plainly indicated in the very title-page, where it is intimated that the pamphlets "are to be sold at the sign of the crab-tree cudgel in Thwackcoat Lane." This is the secret of the inferiority of the anti-Martinists. There is no earnestness of purpose in them; their object is mere vituperation, and they care little for the cause. Martin, on the other hand, is often enough vulgar and abusive, but always he has at heart an end higher than his own advancement or gain.

Before the appearance of *Pap with a Hatchet* two of the Pasquil tracts of no great merit had been produced—*A Countercuff given to Martin Junior* and *The Return of the Renowned Cavaliero Pasquil of England*. The writer of the latter is distinguished even in that age for the fulsomeness of his flattery of the queen, protesting that when she dies "he shall do me a pleasure that cuts my throat." To show his zeal for pure religion he somewhat naïvely quotes

Machiavelli's condemnation of Savonarola, not perceiving that Machiavelli's being "a politick not much affected to any religion" casts a certain doubt upon his authority. Rather later came *Martin's Month's Mind*, of which a specimen has already been given. Heavy as is the style, some humour is shown in the story of Martin's death and burial and of his will; but the piece sinks to the lowest depth in puns: "'No cross in the brow at baptism,' but never so many at any time in the bag. 'No bells,' but libels and labels of their own. 'No homilies read,' but their own 'homelies' preached." Though however on their merits the anti-Martinists were beaten, they had authority on their side, and after Martin was suppressed they were still at liberty to go on. *An Almond for a Parrot* and *The First Part of Pasquil's Apology* (which is mainly devoted to other things) are both later than *The Protestation*. A quotation or two from the former will further illustrate this group of satires. Already the influence of *Euphues* is apparent: "The humours of my eyes are the habitations of fountains, and the circumference of my heart the enclosure of tearful contrition, when I think how many souls at that moment [the day of judgment] shall carry the name of Martin on their foreheads to the vale of confusion, in whose innocent blood thou swimming to hell, shalt have the torments of ten thousand thousand sinners at once, inflicted upon thee." This comes near the end; a passage from the beginning will illustrate at once the clumsiness of the wit and its incivility: "It was told me by the undaunted pursuants of your sons, and credibly believed in regard of your sins, that your grout-headed holiness had turned up your heels like a tired jade in a meadow, and snorted out your scornful soul, like a measled hog on a muckhill, which had it not been false, as the devil would have it, that long tongued doctress, Dame Law, must have been fain (in spite of inspiration) to have given over speaking in the congregation, and employ her parrot's tongue instead of a wind-clapper to scare the crows from thy carrion."

Whatever may have been Nash's part in the Marprelate controversy, he was certainly a protagonist in another celebrated controversy, or rather squabble, of the time—that with the brothers Harvey. This is a contemptible affair in itself; but if Nash was Pasquil, he improves in the later contest. The quarrel began soon after the Marprelate affair, with which it was in an obscure way connected. Richard Harvey first assailed Nash in his *Lamb of God* (1590); and two years later Greene retaliated on behalf of his friend by attacking all the three brothers in his *Quip for an Upstart Courtier*. But he seems speedily to have repented, the passage was excised, and no copy containing it is known to exist. In the same year however Nash satirised Richard Harvey in a passage in *Pierce Penniless, his Supplication to the Devil*, which provoked Gabriel Harvey to enter the contest by attacking both Greene and Nash in his *Four Letters, and certain Sonnets*. Nash replied in *Strange News of the intercepting certain Letters*, and Harvey retorted in *Pierce's Supererogation*. In *Christ's Tears over Jerusalem* (1593) Nash offered an apology, which however was withdrawn in the second edition, as Harvey had either neglected or refused to accept it. And so *Have with You to Saffron-Walden* (1596), the most sustained of the satires on Harvey, came to be written. This book is dedicated in a strain of rather heavy and forced humour to Richard Lichfield, the barber of Trinity College; and the dedication affords a hint to the final document in the controversy, *The Trimming of Thomas Nashe* (1597), which purports to be the work of Lichfield.

In his part of this controversy Nash shows a wit which would have been most effective if he could have mastered the great art of omission. His vices are want of capacity to arrange, and inability to resist the temptation to say everything that occurs to him. He is better in parts than in the whole. Thus *Have with You to Saffron-Walden* is amusing in such passages as the dedication and the letter from Harvey's college tutor to his father; but it is too long, and is so ill-arranged that the reader inevitably loses his way. The tutor's letter is a good specimen of Nash's wit. He ridicules the pedantry (real or supposed) of his antagonist. Harvey is described as prolific of "strange-traffiqu't phrases"—*incendiary* for fire, *illuminary* for candle, *induement* for cloak. In his compositions every sentence ends with *esse posse videatur*. He has observed that in logic *ergo* is "the deadly clap of the piece," and *ergo* is used at every turn. He is, above all, distinguished in poetry, "having writ verses in all kinds, as in form of a pair of gloves, a dozen of points, a pair of spectacles, a two-handed sword, a poynado, a colossus, a pyramid, a painter's easel, a market-cross, a trumpet, an anchor, a pair of pot-hooks; yet I can see no authors he hath, more than his own natural Genius or Minerva."

If Nash had confined himself to Harvey alone he would have become intolerably wearisome; but in point of fact *Have with You to Saffron-Walden* is the only one among the more important documents in which the controversy is the principal ingredient. Both in *Pierce Penniless* and in *Christ's Tears* it is merely incidental. In the former the author finds a messenger to deliver his supplication to the devil, to whom he appeals because he finds wit and learning slightly esteemed elsewhere. He petitions therefore that he may receive the fees he deserves, and proceeds to make an attack on all the graver sins and abuses, on greed and miserliness, on murder, anger, gluttony, drunkenness, sloth and lust. He distinguishes no fewer than eight kinds of drunkenness, ranging from "ape drunk" to "fox drunk." He touches upon certain lighter matters as well. He ridicules antiquaries:—

" Let a tinker take a piece of brass worth a halfpenny, and set strange stamps on it, and I warrant he may make it more worth to him of some fantastical fool, than all the kettles that ever he mended in his life. This is the disease of our new-fangled humourists, that know not what to do with their wealth. It argueth a very rusty wit, so to doat on worm-eaten eld."

He takes occasion to avenge himself and his fellow-wits in his satire of the enemies of poetry, and incidentally shows that the champion of the prelates was not altogether happy in his clerical company. No doubt however the Puritan divines were worse enemies of the poets than "Dumb John of London" or "his Gracelessness of Cant." The poets have been denounced from the pulpit as "babbling ballad makers, . . . fantastical fools that have wit, but cannot tell how to use it." Nash himself has been spoken of thus disrespectfully, and he proceeds to tell his reverend critics just what he thinks of *their* intellect:—

" I myself have been so censured among some dull-witted divines: who deem it no more cunning to write an exquisite poem than to preach pure Calvin, or distil the juice of a Commentary in a quarter sermon. Prove it when you will, you slow spirited Saturnists, that have nothing but the pilfries of your pen to polish an exhortation withal; no eloquence but tautologies to tie the ears of your auditory unto you: no invention, but here is to be noted, I stole this note out of Beza or Marlorat: no art to move, no passion to urge, but only an ordinary form of preaching, blown up by use of often hearing and speaking; and you shall find there goes more exquisite pains and purity of wit to the writing of such a rare poem as *Rosamond*, than to a hundred of your dunstical sermons."

In *Christ's Tears over Jerusalem* Nash sets forth first the sins of the Jews, and passes thence to the sins of London, showing that there is as much cause to weep over the modern city as ever there was to weep over the ancient one. The sons and daughters of Pride still flaunt it in the homes and in the streets. In the denunciation of gorgeous attire the satire of women, which had been for generations a feature of verse, finds a freer expression in prose:—

" Ever since Eva was tempted, and the Serpent prevailed with her, women have took upon them both the person of the tempted and the tempter: They tempt to be tempted, and not one of them, except she be tempted, but thinks herself contemptible. Unto the greatness of their great grandmother Eva they seek to aspire, in being tempted and tempting. If not to tempt, and be thought worthy to be tempted, why dye they and diet they their faces with so many drugs as they do, as it were to correct God's workmanship, and reprove Him as a bungler, and one that is not his craft's master? Why ensparkle they their eyes with spiritualised distillations? Why tip they their tongues with *aurum potabile*? Why fill they up age's frets with fresh colours? Even as roses and flowers in winter are preserved in close houses under earth, so preserve they their beauties by continual lying in bed. Just to dinner will they arise, and after dinner go to bed again, and lie until supper. Yea, sometimes (by no sickness occasioned) they will lie in bed three days together: provided every morning before four o'clock, they have their broths and their cullises, with pearl and gold sodden in them."

To the end the Elizabethans could no more refrain from torturing words, as Nash here tortures "tempt," than they could forgo the sport of baiting bears. But how much Nash had learnt, perhaps from his contact with Martin Marprelate, as to the value of simplicity and directness, will be plain from a comparison between these passages and one from *The Anatomy of Absurdity*, an early work, written evidently under the influence of *Euphues*:—

" I am not ignorant, that many times the covetous ignorant scrapeth that from the tail of the plough which maketh all his after posterity think scorn to look on the plough, they overseeing that by a servant, on which their father was as tilsman attendant, being translated by his wit from the parish, good man Webb in the country, to a pertly gentleman in the court, bestowing more at one time on the herald for arms, than his father all his life time gave in alms."

If Nash was the author of *A wonderful, strange and miraculous Astrological Prognostication of this Year of our Lord God* (1591), he may claim the credit, not of inventing, but probably of introducing into England, a new satirical device, one of which Swift afterwards made skilful use. By whomsoever written, the *Prognostication* is a very amusing burlesque of the pretensions of the astrologists. Whether it was by Nash or not, the subject at any rate was congenial to him. Richard Harvey was the author of an *Astrological Discourse*, and in the *Four Letters Confuted* Nash ridicules him for it: "I say and will make it good that the Astrological Discourse, thy brother (as if he had lately cast the heavens' water, or been at the anatomising of the sky's entrails in Surgeons' Hall), prophesieth of such strange wonders to ensue from the stars' distemperature, and the unusual adultery of planets, as none but he that is bawd to those celestial bodies could ever descry."

In the form in which we now know it, *A Quip for an Upstart Courtier* (1592) bears no trace of Greene's connexion with the Harvey-Nash controversy, which must have been a mere excrescence. It is the most finished of Greene's satirical writings. Though the beginning is somewhat too flowery (in a double sense), it nevertheless has the charm of a poet's imagination. The device of the dream is trite, and the fundamental conception—a dialogue between two pairs of breeches, not men, seen by the dreamer—is grotesque. The sub-title accurately describes it as "a dialogue between velvet-breeches and cloth-breeches." On this curious foundation Greene has constructed a very able satire on the abuses caused by pride, indicating in the course of it the belief, which he shared with many of his contemporaries, that these abuses are largely due to Italian influence. Velvet-breeches boasts that he was born in Italy, and Cloth-breeches denounces the sins and debauchery wherewith Velvet-breeches has "infected this glorious island." They are about to fight when the dreamer intervenes, and is accepted as judge in their controversy. Velvet-breeches declares that the end of all classes is "the wearing of me and winning of preferment." Cloth-breeches retorts: "It was a good and blessed time here in England when King Stephen wore a pair of cloth breeches of a noble a pair, and thought them passing costly." Endless evils are due to love of display: "Indeed, I cannot say," says Cloth-breeches, "but your worship hath brought in deceit as a journeyman into all companies, and made that a subtle craft, which when I was holden in esteem was but a simple mystery: now every trade hath his sleights to slubber up his work to the eye, and to make it good to the sale, howsoever it proves in the wearing. The shoemaker cares not if his shoes hold the drawing on; the tailor sews with hot needle and burnt thread. Tush, pride hath banished conscience, and Velvet-breeches honesty, and every servile drudge must ruffle in his silks, or else he is not suitable." But the same complaint was made by Piers Plowman, and, no doubt, by his predecessors, back to the idyllic days of King Stephen himself. In order to settle the quarrel it becomes necessary to impanel a jury, and the endless challenging of both Velvet-breeches and Cloth-breeches gives rise to much satire against various trades, occupations and classes of society. The decision is in favour of Cloth-breeches: "Velvet-breeches is an upstart come out of Italy, begot of Pride, nursed up by Self-love, and brought into this country by his companion Newfangleness." The whole satire is in favour of simplicity of life and honesty of conduct.

In the *Quip* Greene is following a well-trodden path, and, while he is superior to most of his predecessors in skill of movement, shows little originality, except in the fact that he uses prose instead of verse. In his cony-catching pamphlets however, though he had predecessors in Harman and in the other contributors to rogue-literature, he stands nearer the fountain-head. The *Notable Discovery of Cosenage* and the *Second Part of Cony-Catching* both appeared in 1591, and were followed after a very short interval by *The Defence of Cony-Catching*, and this in turn by *A Disputation between a He and a She Cony-Catcher*. These pamphlets are investigations in a satirical spirit of social conditions. The illustrative tales, which are a prominent feature, show the bent of Greene's genius: he was primarily a story-teller. By far the smartest and wittiest of the series is *The Defence of Cony-Catching*. It purports to be "a confutation of those two injurious pamphlets, published by R. G. against the practitioners of many nimble-witted and mystical sciences," and the author is Cuthbert Cony-Catcher, Licentiate in Whittington College. The disguise is transparent, yet it deceived Grosart. "Curiously enough," he says, "the dainty Morocco-bound Huth exemplar is lettered 'Greene: Defence of Conny-Catching.' The most superficial reading of the clever 'Defence' would have shown that it is against, not by Greene." [1] It certainly professes to be against Greene, and it charges Greene with having sold *Orlando Furioso* twice over, and so being a

[1] Grosart afterwards became less certain that the pamphlet was not by Greene.

Cony-Catcher himself. But probably, as Bullen suggests, this was in Greene's eyes a clever trick, of which he need not feel ashamed. In any case, the name Cuthbert Cony-catcher and the expression "nimble-witted and mystical sciences" are enough to show in what spirit it is to be taken. What the *Defence* really does is to extend the view of cony-catching from the ragged to the well-clothed. In the previous pamphlets Greene has dealt with those needy rogues who often depend upon their wits for their dinner. In the *Defence* Cuthbert asks R. G. why he should be so spiteful "to poor cony-catchers above all the rest, sith they are the simplest souls of all in shifting to live in this overwise world." It is of poverty in respect of worldly possessions that he is thinking, for he goes on: "But you play like the spider that makes her web to entrap and snare little flies, but weaves it so slenderly that the great ones break through without any damage. You strain gnats and pass over elephants. You scour the pond of a few croaking frogs, and leave behind an infinite number of most venomous scorpions. You decipher poor cony-catchers, that perhaps with a trick at cards win forty shillings from a churl that can spare it, and never talk of those caterpillars that undo the poor, ruin whole lordships, infect the commonwealth, and delight in nothing but in wrongful extorting and purloining of pelf, whereas such be the greatest cony-catchers of all, as by your leave, Master R. G., I will make manifest." This he proceeds to do much after Greene's fashion, with tales interspersed, just as in the *Disputation*. The usurer preys like a vulture on the poor, "sleeping with his neighbour's pledges all night in his bosom, and feeding upon forfeits and penalties, as the ravens do upon carrion"; and there are "setters" and "versers" in usury as well as in cony-catching. So too, "Mounser the Miller with the golden thumb" is a cony-catcher, and the butcher "that hath policies to puff up his meat to please the eye" is really in the same trade. So is the man who boasts of his travels, although "his only travel hath been to look on a fair day from Dover Cliffs to Calais, never having stepped a foot out of England, but surveyed the maps, and heard others talk what they know by experience"; for he gets money from the young simpleton who hopes to benefit by the experience which the pretender does not possess. In short, the simpleton exists in every class, and in every class there is a rogue to trick him. "I have proved to your maships," says Cuthbert, "how there is no estate, trade, occupation, nor mystery, but lives by cony-catching, and that our shift at cards compared to the rest is the simplest of all."

The cony-catching pamphlets therefore are a comprehensive survey of society, and an exposure of the roguery which pervades every part of it. Greene may not have intended this when he wrote the first two; but it was a happy inspiration to add the third to them, for it makes a rounded whole—one of the completest and most telling satires of the time.

Greene, like so many of his fellow-wits, seems to have lived too fast to live long. He was only thirty-two at his death, which took place soon after he had written his famous *Groat's Worth of Wit bought with a Million of Repentance*. The volume of work produced in this short time is astonishing: no doubt it would have been better had it been less voluminous; and perhaps a sense that he had not made the best of his gifts was rankling in his mind when he made his well-known attack upon Shakespeare.

The ecclesiastical interdict had less effect upon satire in prose than upon satire in verse. Greene was dead before the interdict was issued, and Nash died in the year following it; but Samuel Rowlands carried on the tradition with *Greene's Ghost* (1602) and *Martin Maskall* (1610); and within four years of the issue of the edict we find a much greater man, Thomas Dekker (1570?–1641?), starting his career as satirist with *The Bachelor's Banquet* (1603). The geniality of Dekker is manifest in everything he wrote. His satire is almost invariably general; and, in spite of the quarrel with Ben Jonson, it is rarely bitter. Notwithstanding, too, many points of resemblance between him and Nash, the atmosphere of controversy in which the latter lived was alien to Dekker. His favourite weapon is irony: he teaches the better way by a pretended commendation of the worse. But his range is wide: there is broad burlesque in *The Raven's Almanac*, which ridicules the claim of the almanac makers to foretell the future; and there is much straightforward description, which is not satire at all, in *The Bellman of London* (1608). He was ready to take hints from any source. His *News from Hell* (1606 is suggested by Nash's *Pierce Penniless*; *The Bachelor's Banquet* freely reproduces *Les Quinze Joyes de Mariage*; and *The Gull's Horn-book* (1609) is based upon Dedekind's *Grobianus*.

In *The Bachelor's Banquet* Dekker ranges himself in the long line of the satirists of women, but his satire is less concentrated and has more of the element of narrative than the preceding satire in verse. The piece is however wholly satirical in spirit. It describes the various humours of a woman,—the young wife newly married —pranked up in brave apparel—striving to master her husband —gadding about—and so on. She pretends that she is ill; she wheedles and flatters; her gossips come and help to eat and drink her husband into debt. A pitiful picture is drawn of him going upon a journey in cobbled boots, with broken spurs, and an old laced coat, clean out of fashion, followed by his man in garments that were not made for him.

There is greater originality in *The Seven Deadly Sins of London* (1606). The originality does not lie in the conception of the seven deadly sins as subjects for satire; for that is very old. But in the first place, the sins Dekker has in mind are not the seven recognised as deadly by the Catholic Church; and in the second place, they are the sins of a city of which Dekker had made a special and profound study. He did for the London of the seventeenth century the same kind of work that Dickens did for the London of the nineteenth century. The seven sins with which he deals are the vices which, in his judgment, specially beset the community he had studied with such loving care. Mustered in seven days' triumphs, they are: Politic Bankruptism; Lying; Candle-light, or the Nocturnal Triumph; Sloth; Apishness; Shaving; and Cruelty. "The politic bankrupt" is one of whom "all knew that though he himself was broken, yet the linings of his bags were whole; and though he had no conscience (but a cracked one), yet he had crowns that were sound." He belongs to a class which, it would seem, must always be found in a commercial community. Fielding satirised him in the eighteenth century, and the records of the law-courts show that he is not unknown at the present day. In "Apishness" we have again the satire on extravagance in dress, especially in the imitation of one sex by the other, so that if men get up French standing collars, women must have them too. This apishness begets pride; pride breeds prodigality; and prodigality results in beggary.

If the satirists may be believed, this kind of folly was especially English. "Witty was that painter therefore," says Dekker, "that when he had liveried one of every nation in their proper attire, and being at his wits' end to draw an Englishman, at the last (to give him a quip for his folly in apparel) drew him stark naked, with sheers in his hand, and cloth on his arm, because none could cut out his fashions but himself."

"Shaving" is a theme on which Dekker, needy like the majority of his profession, wrote with feeling. Landlords who spend 30s. in building up a chimney and raise the rent £3, are shavers; there are usurers who shave young gentlemen before ever a hair dare peep out of their chins; market-folks, bakers, brewers, "all that weigh their consciences in scales," are shavers. Among this mercantile class Dekker has a special dislike to brokers and usurers. Of brokers he tells us in *News from Hell* that "there's a longer lane of them in hell than there is in London." Against the usurers Dekker is still more bitter, and it is to be feared that the virulence, so little in harmony with his nature, sprang from personal causes. In *News from Hell* he narrates the journey of Nash's "Knight of the Post" to the lower regions and back. Having received the devil's message he sets out on his return; but before reaching the ferry he meets an old, lean, meagre fellow, Usury, who begs him to go back once more and be his guide. Failing in this, Usury next tries to get information as to the inhabitants of the region whither he is going: "Doctor Dives requests him (in a whining accent) to tell him if there were any rich men in hell, and if by any base drudgery which the devil shall put him to, and which he'll willingly moil in, he should scrape any muck together; whether he may set up his trade in hell, and whether there be any brokers there, that with picking straws out of poor thatched houses to build nests where his twelve pences should engender, might get feathers to his back, and their own too." Dekker takes up the subject once more in *Lanthorn and Candle-light* (1609), a continuation of *The Bellman of London*, which is a piece of rogue-literature, more descriptive than satirical. The Gull-groper here is another satirical description of the "money-monger," showing how he deludes and entraps and ruins by forfeiture the young spendthrift whom he knows to be heir to property.

The most interesting piece of satire however in *Lanthorn and*

Candle-light is directed against hangers-on and pretenders of the literary class who were accustomed to make profit out of the vanity of country gentlemen ambitious to play the part of Mæcenas. As Dekker calls the tricks of the usurer "gull-groping," so he christens this other form of deception "hawking." In this hawking "he that casts up the lure is called the Falconer. The lure that is cast up is an idle pamphlet. The Tercel Gentle that comes to the lure is some knight or some gentleman of like quality. The bird that is preyed upon is money. He that walks the horses and hunts dry foot [the accomplice] is called a Mongrel." There follows a full description of the tricks whereby the dedication-monger deludes a number of gentlemen into the belief that each is receiving the dedication of the pamphlet, whereas what he really gets is the dedication of a single copy:—

"The falconer, having scraped together certain small parings of wit, he first cuts them handsomely in pretty pieces, and of those pieces does he patch up a book. This book he prints at his own charge, the Mongrel running up and down to look to the workmen, and bearing likewise some part of the cost (for which he enters upon his half share). When it is fully finished, the Falconer and his Mongrel (or it may be two Falconers joined in one), but howsoever, it is by them dursed what shire in England it is best to forage next: that being set down, the Falconers deal either with a herald for a note of all the knights' and gentlemen's names of worth that dwell in that circuit, which they mean to ride, or else by inquiry get the chiefest of them, printing so many epistles as they have names; the epistles dedicatory being all one, and vary in nothing but in the titles of their patrons."

In *The Gull's Hornbook* there is a passage, perhaps the best known in Dekker, which also deals with the interests of the literary class, but looks at them from the opposite point of view. This is necessary from the plan of the piece, which ironically advises a gallant of doubtful standing as to his behaviour in various circumstances, and incidentally throws a flood of light on the manners and customs of the more worthless of the Jacobean dandies. The pupil is conducted to Paul's Walks, the great resort of the rich and idle, and instructed as to his deportment there. Clearly if he takes his tailor with him to make notes as to the garments of the true leaders of fashion, he will be able to wear his clothes "in print with the first edition." At the ordinary he can show them off and draw attention by the simple device of loud talking: "Discourse as loud as you can, no matter to what purpose, if you but make a noise, and laugh in fashion, and have a good sour face to promise quarrelling, you shall be much observed." And so the seventh heaven of the gallant is reached. But the play-house presents the best opportunities of all. Dekker's ironical commendation of the rudeness of the gallants sitting upon the stage is highly effective. He points out the great advantages which are to be got there. The conspicuous position sets off the graces of the gallant in person and attire. It is for himself to improve his advantages:—

" By talking and laughing (like a ploughman in a morris) you heap Pelion upon Ossa, glory upon glory: As first, all the eyes in the galleries will leave walking after the players, and only follow you: the simplest dolt in the house snatches up your name, and when he meets you in the streets, or that you fall into his hands in the middle of a watch, his word shall be taken for you; he'll cry, ' He's such a gallant,' and you pass. Secondly, you publish your temperance to the world, in that you seem not to resort thither to taste vain pleasures with a hungry appetite: but only as a gentleman to spend a foolish hour or two, because you can do nothing else: Thirdly, you mightily disrelish the audience and disgrace the author: marry, you take up (though it be at the worst hand) a strong opinion of your own judgment, and enforce the poet to take pity of your weakness, and, by some dedicated sonnet, to bring you into a better paradise, only to stop your mouth."

Such were among the difficulties under which the greatest of all dramas were produced; and thus effectively, by simple observation and a narrative of facts, does Dekker lash the abuses of his time. The advantage of the greater freedom of prose is apparent: there is something fresher here and more telling, because in closer accord with fact than in any of the verse satire of the age.

In more than one of his books Dekker approaches the verge of the fashion of character-writing, in which may be traced another strain of satire. The fashion was just beginning when Dekker was writing his satirical books; and though Fuller calls Sir Thomas Overbury (1581–1613) "the first writer of characters of our nation so far as I have observed," that place really belongs to Joseph Hall, whom we have already met as a writer of satire in verse; at least Hall's *Characters of Virtues and Vices* appeared in 1608, while the earliest known edition of Overbury's *Characters* is dated 1614. Of course the characters were written before that year, for Overbury had already met his tragic end when this edition appeared. Anthony Wood too expresses the belief that this 1614 edition was not the first but the fourth or fifth. It is therefore possible that Fuller knew of an edition earlier than the appearance of Hall's book. If so, Overbury's *Characters* are the work of a very young man; and the artificial style is consistent with that supposition.

The characters are not by any means always satirical; on the contrary, they may just as likely be panegyrics, as are some of the most delightful. The purpose is to embody as it were in flesh and blood single qualities, and to paint the portrait of a proud man or a humble one, a generous man or a mean one, as if the pride or humility, the generosity or the meanness, constituted the whole man. Thus the "character" is very closely related to the "humour" which, just a little before Hall wrote, gained a footing on the stage. Naturally however, though the purpose may not be primarily satirical, the deliberate attempt to depict vices and defects is apt to result in satirical treatment.

If Hall's *Characters of Virtues and Vices* were in any great degree satirical, it would be peculiarly interesting as affording grounds for comparison with the same writer's satire in verse. But it is not so. The passage of the momentous ten years which changed him from a youth in the early twenties to a man in the thirties had made a deep mark upon Hall; and, no doubt, his adoption of the clerical profession had made the mark deeper still. There are many phrases and occasional passages in the *Characters* which are satirical in spirit. Thus we read that the covetous man "never eats a good meal but on his neighbour's trencher; and there he makes amends to his complaining stomach for his former and future fasts"; that the vainglorious man "swears big at an ordinary; and talks of the Court with a sharp accent; neither vouchsafes to name any not honourable, nor those without some term of familiarity"; and that the slothful "is a religious man, and wears the time in his cloister; and, as the cloak of his doing nothing, pleads contemplation; yet is he no whit the leaner for his thoughts, no whit learneder." The character of the busybody affords an example of satire somewhat more sustained:—

"His tongue, like the tails of Samson's foxes, carries firebrands; and is enough to set the whole field of the world on a flame. Himself begins table-talk of his neighbour, at another's board; to whom he bears the first news, and adjures him to conceal the reporter; whose choleric answer he returns to his first host, enlarged with a second edition; so, as it uses to be done in the fight of unwilling mastiffs, he claps each on the side apart and provokes them to an eager conflict."

But notwithstanding phrases and passages such as these, Hall's habitual tone, even when he is dealing with the vices, is that of the grave moralist; he shows the spirit of the preacher rather than that of the satirist.

With Overbury it was otherwise. A man of the Court, he felt none of the restraints which Hall's clerical profession imposed upon him. The wits loved to be witty; character-writing by its very nature tended to sharpness; and so, notwithstanding the fact that his most famous and best character, that of the milkmaid, is a charming panegyric, a large proportion of Overbury's essays are collections of sentences each of which is the lash of a whip. The character-writers loved, in particular, to make their first sentence short and biting, and to put into it the substance of the essay that was to follow. Overbury follows this fashion sometimes with excellent effect. "*A Fine Gentleman*," he says, "is the cinnamon tree, whose bark is more worth than his body"; and he proceeds to illustrate the gorgeousness of the bark and the worthlessness of the body. But the wit is apt to over-reach himself in the effort to be witty, and these smart beginnings are often strained. Thus: "*A Tailor* is a creature made out of shreds that were pared off from Adam, when he was rough-cast." The whole essay illustrates this besetting sin of the character-writers.

In one or other of his essays Overbury touches upon most of the customary themes of satire. Extremes in religion are censured in the pictures of *A Jesuit* on the one hand, and *A Puritan* and *A Precisian* on the other. No doubt there is exaggeration in the picture of the last, but it is the exaggeration of caricature which yet resembles that from which it is drawn: "If at any time he fast, it is upon Sunday, and he is sure to feast upon Friday. He can better afford you ten lies than an oath; and dare commit any sin gilded with a pretence of sanctity." The Puritan fashion of indicating piety by Christian names is neatly satirised: "He hath nicknamed all the prophets and apostles with his sons, and begets nothing but virtues for daughters." *A Devilish Usurer* and *A Covetous Man* betray a dislike only less intense than that which Dekker showed for the same class. No one has satirised better than Overbury the affectations of travellers or the emptiness of courtiers. A courtier, he says, "moves by the upper spheres, and is the reflection of higher substances"; and as to the *Affected Traveller*:

"His attire speaks French or Italian, and his gait cries, *Behold Me*. He censures all things by countenances, and shrugs, and speaks his own language with shame and lisping: he will choke rather than confess beer a good drink, and his pick-tooth is a main part of his behaviour." He is a satirist of women too. *A Very Woman* is satirical throughout: "She thinks she is fair, though many times her opinion goes alone, and she loves her glass, and the Knight of the Sun for lying. . . . She travels to and among, and so becomes a woman of good entertainment, for all the folly in the country comes in clean linen to visit her; she breaks to them her grief in sugar cakes, and receives from their mouths in exchange many stories that conclude to no purpose." The character-writer has however the advantage over the pure satirist, that he is not committed to the unfavourable view; and Overbury, who thus ridicules the weaknesses of women, amply acknowledges their virtues in *A Good Woman*, to say nothing of his masterpiece, *A Fair and Happy Milk-Maid*.

The mixture of the sweet with the tart was achieved more perfectly by John Earle (1601?–1665), the prince of all the character writers. Like his predecessor Hall, he adopted the clerical profession, and ultimately became a bishop. His little book, *Microcosmography* (1628), is a gem of its kind. Like Overbury, Earle achieves his greatest triumph in praise rather than in censure: his character of a child is the most delicious of all the essays of the character-writers—an essay Lamb might have been proud of. Like Overbury too, he could be pungent, and with still greater effect; for he is almost wholly free from that taint of artificiality and affectation which sometimes mars Overbury. The themes are much the same as Overbury's. *A She Precise Hypocrite* is the feminine of *A Precisian*. *A Church-Papist* satirises with less skill the opposite extreme: "He loves popery well, but is loath to lose by it, and though he be something scared by the bulls of Rome, yet they are far off, and he is struck with more terror at the apparitor." We have also, rather exceptionally, a sort of "centre of indifference" in *A Mere Formal Man*: "His religion is a good quiet subject, and he prays as he swears, in the phrase of the land." There is a modern ring in the sarcasm on *An Alderman*, who must be considered "not as a Body, but a Corporation." No one has handled that butt of so many gibes, the Gallant, more skilfully than Earle: "His first care is his dress, the next his body, and in the uniting of these two lies his soul and his faculties. . . . He is one never serious, but with his tailor, when he is in conspiracy for the next device." Unless he marries an old lady, "himself and his clothes grow stale together, and he is buried commonly ere he dies in the gaol or the country." The professions too afford material for satire. *A Mere Dull Physician* can cure his own purse, if he can cure nothing else; and he carries his load of learning not quite as lightly as a flower: "He tells you your malady in Greek, though it be but a cold or headache; which by good endeavour and diligence he may bring to some moment indeed." Nor did Earle spare his own profession. *A Young Raw Preacher* is an admirable satirical portrait: "The pace of his sermon is a full career, and he runs wildly over hill and dale till the clock stops him. The labour of it is chiefly in his lungs. And the only thing he has made of it himself, is the faces. He takes on against the Pope without mercy, and has a jest still in lavender for Bellarmine. Yet he preaches heresy, if it comes his way, with a mind I must needs say very orthodox. His action is all passion, and his speech inter-jections. He has an excellent faculty in bemoaning the people, and spits with a very good grace. His style is compounded of some twenty several, only his body imitates someone extraordinary. He will not draw his handkercher out of his place, nor blow his nose without discretion. . . . He has more tricks with a sermon than a tailor with an old cloak, to turn it, to piece it, and at last quite disguise it with a new preface."

There is nothing in the verse satire of the period more severe and cutting than this. Yet there is much that leaves an impression of virulence, which this does not do at all. What is the secret of the difference? Partly, no doubt, the fact that there is no virulence in the man Earle; but partly also the fact that it is prose. In verse we instinctively expect beauty, and there is a reaction when we are disappointed and find instead censure; in prose the expectation is far less strong.

Mention has been made of the lost Marprelate plays, and in an earlier chapter the great part taken by the early drama in the satire of the Church was indicated. The spirit of satire is in truth close akin to the spirit of comedy. This kinship is illustrated through the whole of the Elizabethan drama, for there are few of the comedies in which a vein of satire cannot be detected; and it even intrudes occasionally into tragedy. But in the main the satiric element is merely incidental: it can hardly be more where the spirit of romance reigns. There is meaning in the fact that the period *par excellence* of English satire is that in which romance is most completely in abeyance. There is satire, as there is everything else, in Shakespeare. The pseudo-statesman is satirised in Polonius, the courtier in Osric. Both Touchstone and Feste have caustic tongues. Malvolio shows that Shakespeare had no more liking for the Puritans than his fellow-players. Yet for all this, and for all that might be added, it would be absurd to rank Shakespeare among the satirists; and the same is true of the dramatists in general. Except when they fall into feud with one another, or with some class peculiarly obnoxious to them, they rarely make satire the staple of their plays. But it is the staple in the *Satiromastix* controversy, and Ben Jonson made it the staple when he wished to express his dislike of the Puritans.

Neither men nor communities are willing, if they can help it, to be thought the aggressors in a quarrel. States covetous of a neighbour's territory or wealth have been known to complain that they were attacked or encircled. Men act on precisely the same principle; and light will be thrown upon the obscure story of the *Satiromastix* controversy if we suppose that Marston and Dekker, the protagonists on the one side, were so acting against Ben Jonson (1573?-1637) on the other. In 1600 appeared Jonson's play of *Cynthia's Revels*, and Marston and Dekker professed to feel sure that they were caricatured in the unflattering characters of Hedon and Anaides. As a rule a man does not wear a cap unless it fits him, and probably for this reason the legend of their identity with these two *dramatis personæ* has lived on through three centuries. But Swinburne's criticism is difficult to answer. Anaides, "a fashionable ruffian and ruffler," can hardly be identified with Dekker, "a humble hard-working and highly-gifted man of letters"; nor is it easy to see how Hedon, "a courtly and voluptuous coxcomb," can have been designed to cast ridicule on Marston, "a rude and rough-hewn man of genius." If however the two were determined to wear their ill-fitting caps, Jonson was not the man to deny them. He took up the quarrel in *The Poetaster* (1601), where Crispinus and Demetrius certainly do stand for his two fellow-craftsmen, and are represented with qualities suitable for the purpose.

Probably, then, Marston was no more attacked than Germany was attacked in 1914. Even if we accept the identification of Clove in *Every Man out of his Humour* (1599) with Marston, it is still probable that Jonson was not the aggressor. The origin of the quarrel must be sought elsewhere than in *Cynthia's Revels*, and earlier than *Every Man out of his Humour*. Jonson told Drummond of Hawthornden that the cause of it was that Marston represented him on the stage; and at the close of *The Poetaster* he dates it three years back:—

> " Three years
> They did provoke me with their petulant styles
> On every stage."

Further, Marston is commonly believed to have attacked Jonson in his satires, in 1598, under the names of Tubrio and Torquatus; though it must be confessed that the identification is not free from doubt. This of itself would furnish temptation to a renewed attack, without provocation from *Cynthia's Revels*; for it is a sound principle of psychology that the wrongdoer bears resentment against the person he has wantonly attacked. At any rate Marston repeated the attack on Jonson in *Jack Drum's Entertainment* (1600). How Dekker came into the quarrel remains a mystery; but as Jonson uses the plural in the passage quoted above, Dekker would seem to have been a party to it from an early stage, if not from the beginning, and he certainly bears his share of the castigation in *The Poetaster*. He is spoken of however in a vein of good-natured contempt, rather than of bitterness: "O sir," says Histrio of Demetrius, "his doublet's a little decayed; he is otherwise a very simple honest fellow, sir, one Demetrius, a dresser of plays about the town here." Dekker, now taking the foremost part, did his best in *Satiromastix* (1602) to requite the satirist. And not without effect. Horace (Jonson) is depicted in the agony of composition, trying to find a rhyme to *name*, and muttering *game, dame, tame, lame, shame, proclaim*. He is ridiculed for his profession that he had attacked no one, and urged to

> " Make damnation parcel of your oath,
> That when your lashing jests make all men bleed,
> Yet you whip none. Court, city, country, friends,
> Foes, all must smart alike; yet court, nor city,
> Nor foe, nor friend, dare wince at you; great pity."

Personalities three centuries old are insipid; satire is more legitimately used when it is directed against classes and tendencies of the time, or against foibles, frailties and vices common to all times. And this is the rule in Jonson. He is exceptional in his generation, inasmuch as the whole conception and framework of his comedy is satirical. He proclaims it in the Prologue to his earliest play, *Every Man in his Humour*, where, after ridiculing the inadequacy of stage devices to meet the demands of the romantic drama, he goes on to promise:—

> " Deeds, and language, such as men do use,
> And persons, such as comedy would choose,
> When she would shew an image of the times,
> And sport with human follies, not with crimes."

In the Induction to *Every Man out of his Humour* he repeats the promise:—

> " With an armed and resolved hand,
> I'll strip the ragged follies of the time
> Naked as at their birth, . . .
> . . . and with a whip of steel,
> Print wounding lashes in their iron ribs."

He is as good as his word, for each of the *dramatis personæ*, with the exception of Asper, represents one or other of those "ragged follies," and the play as a whole is the most comprehensive satire of the time that had yet been produced.

Clearly the very conception of the "humour" promises satire. A quality harmless or even laudable in its proper proportion and just relation to other qualities becomes a weakness, or worse, when it dominates the whole man. The miser, the prodigal, the voluptuary, the swashbuckler, the zealot, may each in turn be food for satire when the dominant characteristic overtops; while any one of the qualities indicated by these names may be so combined with other qualities as to make a portrait which is not satirical. Shakespeare made Shylock miserly, but he made him also a lover of his own race and his own religion, treasuring the memory of his dead wife, more faithful to the duty of father to daughter than was Jessica to that of daughter to father, justly resenting the treatment he had received at the hands of Christians with a resentment strong enough to conquer his love of money:—

> " If every ducat in six thousand ducts
> Were in six parts and every part a ducat,
> I would not draw them."

Though in this character the love of money is inordinate, far too many colours are on the pallet for the portrait to be a satire. But it is not so in Jonson. His very names proclaim the difference and suggest the satirical purpose—Sir Epicure Mammon, Subtle, Morose, Fastidious Brisk, Sir Diaphanous Silkworm. In other cases it is still a quality that walks on legs, though the name does not proclaim the fact. Bobadill is the braggart incarnate, who, after the loudest boasts, declines to fight and accepts a beating on the plea that he has had a warrant of the peace served upon him. We are back among the abstractions of the moralities, and the subtler art of a more advanced age ensures a satirical treatment rather than more downright moralising.

The vein of satire runs through most of Jonson's comedies. *Cynthia's Revels* (1600) satirises the Court, *Bartholomew Fair* (1614) the Puritans. *News from the New World* (1621) is a riot of satire. *Eastward Ho* (in which Jonson had a hand, or perhaps only a finger, with Marston and Chapman) can hardly be called a satire of the Scots, but it certainly does contain satire of them, quite in the vein of Jonson's sturdy namesake of the following century. It is complained that they go everywhere, and some of them are in Virginia. The retort is: "I would a hundred thousand of them were there, for we are all one countrymen, ye know, and we should find ten times more comfort of them there than here." But the wits found that the subject was a dangerous one to jest about in the reign of the first Stuart king of England. Marston and Chapman were imprisoned, and Jonson manfully shouldered his share of the responsibility by voluntarily joining them in their captivity.

The *Poetomachia* was not the only instance in which Jonson was charged with personal satire. On the contrary, numbers of his characters were identified with individuals. In particular, the character of Volpone has been taken to satirise Sutton, the founder of the Charterhouse, and Lanthorn Leatherhead in *Bartholomew Fair* has been identified with Inigo Jones. In both cases the grounds of the identification seem to be insufficient, and for the sake of Jonson's good name it may be hoped that it is mistaken. It is impossible at this distance of time to say in how many less conspicuous cases Jonson may have had individual men in view, but he makes clear enough his anticipation that individuals would, rightly or wrongly, apply his strictures to themselves.

For reasons of history special interest attaches to Jonson's satire of the Puritans. Hostility had for many years been deepening between them and the players, and each, undoubtedly, took a jaundiced view of the other. On the one hand the players, though they were not exemplars of all the virtues, were not the mere sinks of iniquity that many Puritans conceived them to be. On the other hand, the Puritans were very far indeed from being the mere incarnation of hypocrisy that their adversaries believed, or professed to believe, that they were. They succeeded with a success that mere hypocrisy could never have won. They not only closed the theatres, they overthrew the Crown, and, further still, they made the name of England feared and respected over Europe. Jonson takes the easier and the shallower view. The two notes of the character of Zeal-of-the-land Busy are hypocrisy and greed. He is the Stiggins of the seventeenth century. His gluttony combines with Win Littlewit's "longing" to lead the party to Bartholomew Fair, though that is "no better than one of the high places," so that they may eat a pig. There is much virtue in a name. The Scriptures warn us to beware of "the vanity of the eye." But the pig can offer itself through the smell, and "it were a sin of obstinacy, great obstinacy, high and horrible obstinacy, to decline or resist the good titillation of the famelic sense, which is the smell." It is lawful, then, to eat, guided by the nose, though it be unlawful to follow the guidance of the eye. There is however a condition which governs the manner of eating: "We may be religious in the midst of the prophane, so it be eaten with a reformed mouth, with sobriety and humbleness; not gorged in with gluttony and greediness." Busy has been discovered a little before, "fast by the teeth in the cold turkey-pie in the cupboard, with a great white loaf in his left hand, and a glass of malmsey in his right." Subordinate to hypocrisy and greed is ignorance. Zeal-of-the-land "derides all antiquity, defies any other learning than inspiration; and what discretion soever years should afford him, it is all prevented by his original ignorance." In short, he is the complete Puritan as the satire of his adversaries depicted that character for two generations. Lest there should be any doubt as to the fundamental characteristic, Jonson repeats it in the person of Dame Purecraft: "Our mother is a most elect hypocrite, and has maintained us all this seven years with it, like gentlefolks. . . . She is not a wise wilful widow for nothing, nor a sanctified sister for a song."

Though vigorous, Jonson's satire is somewhat crude. Zeal-of-the-land Busy cannot rival Thackeray's Honeyman in subtlety. Except in his exquisite lyrics, Jonson's work has something of the coarseness, as well as the massive strength, of his physical frame. It is a thing to be admired rather than loved. He remains nevertheless the great master in English of satirical comedy, and in his works as a whole he has left by far the completest satirical commentary we possess upon the Elizabethan age. If it were possible for satire to show "the very age and body of the time his form and pressure," then Jonson would hold the place of Shakespeare. But just there lies the weakness of satire. Every form of literature is valued ultimately in proportion to the truth it embodies. Now romance embodies a deeper truth than realism—as the realists understand it. There is something of the Yahoo in humanity, but there is also something that responds to the *Serious Call*. Law and Wesley and Whitfield pierce nearer to the root of the matter than Swift with all his superb intellectual strength. There is a profounder reality in the "golden world" of *As You Like It* than in the realism of the Jonsonian comedy, and Shakespeare is far more vitally felt to-day than Jonson, just because it was he rather than Jonson who showed "the very age and body of the time his form and pressure." Satire is a relatively low form of literature, just because it embodies a relatively small element of truth. Is it without significance that Shakespeare's Puritan, Malvolio, absurd, ridiculed, outwitted, outraged, is nevertheless endowed with higher qualities than they who work his overthrow?

CHAPTER VII

FROM THE ECLIPSE OF SATIRE TO BUTLER

THE eclipse of satire which marked the closing years of the reign of James I. lasted through the whole of that of his ill-fated son. For twenty years or more satire, both in prose and in verse, was merely incidental. A thread of satire runs through all the character-writers, and the finest product of that school, Earle's *Microcosmography,* which has been treated in the preceding chapter, was published in the reign of Charles I. Though the Theophrastic vein showed signs of exhaustion, "characters" continued to be produced all through the century, and a very witty specimen, *The Character of a Sneaker,* is dated 1705. Fugitive pieces now and then, but very rarely, show great ability. One such is *Tom Tell-Troath,* which is supposed to belong to the year 1622. There are pieces of an earlier date bearing the same title, but the one in question is a very witty satire of King James's government. He has made Great Britain a great deal less than Little England was wont to be. His subjects dare not doubt that he is head of the Church; "but of what Church they would gladly know; the *triumphant,* they say, it cannot be, because there are too many corruptions and vexations in it. And how far it is from the *militant,* they call heaven and earth to witness. Therefore, they conclude, it must either be the Church *dormant,* or none."

But in spite of occasional bright things like this, until the controversy of Cavalier and Roundhead comes to an issue there is no such sustained satire in prose as that of the Marprelate tracts, nor any such satiric criticism of social conditions as we find in Dekker. Neither is there in verse any equivalent to Hall or Donne. There are satiric touches scattered through the lyrists, and occasionally whole pieces are in the satiric vein. Suckling's *A Session of the Poets* shows the influence of the Italian Boccalini, an influence which may be traced both in prose and in verse for more than a

century. It is however more a critical than a satirical influence.
There are numerous satiric epigrams; but in the masters, Jonson
and Herrick, what we admire is not the satiric epigram, but the
epigram whose function is to express the sense of beauty with the
utmost concision. Women, dress, religion, manners, are here and
there touched with caustic; but no one seeks to play the part of
Juvenal. The general tone is not sufficiently serious. The careless-
ness, real or affected, of the Cavaliers was inconsistent with the
seriousness of the sustained satire; and the seriousness of the
Puritan, though more than sufficient, was of the sort which finds
expression rather in the pulpit. It is the final clash of the two which
starts satire anew. As a consequence it is essentially political; and
being by its nature a literature of protest, it is Roundhead at one
moment and Cavalier the next, now Whig and now Tory, according
as the one party or the other is up or down. Under Charles I.,
Laud is punningly satirised because his canons have made Scots
cannons roar. A taste of military rule in the Commonwealth makes
the satirist sing another tune:—

> " No gospel can guide it,
> No law can decide it,
> In Church or State, till the sword has sanctified it."

The news-sheets which multiplied after the abolition of the Star
Chamber played some part in the revival of satire. Each side
required its organ. *Diurnals* gave the news from the point of view
of the Parliamentarians and *Mercuries* from that of the Royalists,
and both from time to time essayed satire, but to little purpose.
It is merciful to draw a veil over the work of far greater men
than the writers of such sheets: even Milton's controversial writings hardly bear examination. Such skill as was shown was shown
mainly in the service of the Crown, not of the Parliament. Martin
Parker, Roger L'Estrange and Samuel Sheppard, with whom was
associated John Cleveland, were perhaps the most meritorious
writers; but except Cleveland, and L'Estrange in respect of his
Fables, no one has retained or deserves a name in literature. Still,
there are occasional pungent pieces to be found in such miscellanies as *Rump*, that "collection of the choicest poems and songs"
relating to the years between 1639 and 1661, and the *Political
Ballads of the Commonwealth*, published by the Percy Society; and

however modest may be the literary merit of such collections, they at least illustrate the scope and general character of the satire of the time. They show that, though a large majority of the satirists were Cavaliers, the Puritans could, and at times did, retort with effect. Thus, *A Total Rout*, one of the most effective pieces in the Percy Society's collection, shows up the swearing and debauchery which the Cavaliers not only indulged in, but boasted of:—

> " For he's not a gentleman that wears not a sword,
> And fears to swear damme at every word."

The Puritan balladist shows what a pitiable boast it is, for "an orange-tail'd slut" shall out-vapour the Cavalier; and what a poor sort of pride is that which does not pay its score to the ale-house-keeper or the tailor, or to persons still humbler and far less reputable.

Though the titles of these collections suggest politics as the subject, the character of the times is illustrated by the fact that the question of Church and Dissent is more prominent than the question of Crown and Parliament. *The Anarchy, or the blest Reformation since* 1640, combines both and satirises their endless confusions:—

> " ' Sure I have the truth,' says Numph;
> ' Nay, I ha' the truth,' says Clem;
> ' Nay, I ha' the truth,' says reverend Ruth;
> ' Nay, I ha' the truth,' says Nem."

And again:—

> " 'Then let's ha' King Charles,' says George;
> ' Nay, let's have his son,' says Hugh;
> ' Nay, let's have none,' says jabbering Joan;
> ' Nay, let's be all kings,' says Prue."

Pieces like *The Poor Committee-Man's Accompt*, which jeers at the heavy imposts of Parliament after such strenuous opposition to ship-money, are comparatively rare. The most common theme of the satires on religion is the excesses of the sectaries—"the dis-sidence of Dissent." Thus the ballad of *Hugh Peters' Last Will and Testament* has for its sub-title *The Haltering of the Devil*; and the text bears out the promise this carries. Old Nick himself, we learn, after lurking many a year "in Calvin's stool and Luther's chair," held a convocation at Amsterdam in '41,

> " And resolved to cross the brine,
> And enter a herd of English swine."

In swinging verse, which must have been roared out at many a
Cavalier drinking-bout, *The Holy Pedlar* traces the advance from
point to point:—

> " First surplices I took,
>   Next the Common-Prayer Book,
>   And made all those Papists that us'd 'um;
>   Then the bishops and deans
>   I stript of their means,
>   And gave it to those that abus'd 'um.
>   The clergymen next
>   I withdrew from their text,
>   And set up the gifted Brother;
>   Thus Religion I made
>   But a matter of trade,
>   And I car'd not for one or t'other."

The Puritan is, of course, charged with hypocrisy, and with opposition to all that is pleasant or liberal or beautiful. He is the foe of
learning and flourishes on its ruin:—

> " We'll down with all that smells of wit,
>   And hey then up go we."

But perhaps the most effective of all these pieces is *The Rump's
Hypocrisy*:—

> " Is there no God? let's put it to a vote;
>   Is there no Church? some fools say so by rote;
>   Is there no King, but Pym, for to assent
>   What shall be done by Act of Parliament?
>   No God, no Church, no King; then all were well,
>   If they could but enact there were no Hell."

The authors of most of these fugitive verses are no longer known,
but some of the pieces are to be found among the works of Alexander Brome (1620–1666), and among those of John Cleveland.
Brome, who was the author of *The Holy Pedlar* quoted above,
deserves to be remembered better than he is. He wrote with spirit
and effect, he was capable of learning from adversity, and he had
a power which few of the political satirists show, of detecting the
vices and weaknesses of his own side. One of his best pieces, *On Sir
G. B. his Defeat*, is full of a sad acid wisdom taught by the Civil
War. Nothing endures, all things rise and fall, might is right, it is
muskets and full bandoliers that legislate:—

> " Words are but wind, but blows come home;
>   A stout tongu'd lawyer's but a name,
>   Compar'd to a stout file-leader."

The Leveller's Rant, a piece written in a less serious spirit, is also effective. The Leveller cannot bear that anyone should stand higher than himself, but he sees no inconsistency in setting himself above those whom he pulls down and appropriating what had been theirs, for all things belong to the Saints:—

> " The carnal men's wives are for men of the spirit,
> Their wealth is our own by merit,
>   For we that have right
>   By the law called might,
> Are the saints that must judge and inherit."

But Brome's most remarkable characteristic is that rare balance of judgment which enables him to criticise his own friends. *The Good-Fellow*, which will be further noticed presently, is perhaps unique; for in it the Cavalier satirist plainly tells this typical boozing and swearing Cavalier that his vices have brought ruin on his cause.

Brome however is rarely mentioned in the text-books of literature; the first satirist after the eclipse who enjoys that twilight immortality is John Cleveland (1613–58), an ardent Royalist who at one or two points comes in contact with the great protagonist of Parliament, Milton; for he had entered Christ's College, Cambridge, before Milton left it, and afterwards he ridiculed *Smectymnuus*, for which Milton wrote his famous *Apology*. Cleveland wrote satire in prose as well as in verse. He holds a minor place among the character-writers; but the *Character of a Country Committee Man*, the *Character of a Diurnal-Maker* and the rest are of no great value. As a writer of verse however he has considerable merit. Though in the indecent *Vituperium Uxoris* he takes his place among the critics of women, his satire is nearly all political, and, of course, consistently anti-Parliamentarian, anti-Puritan and anti-Scottish. *The Definition of a Protector* leaves no doubt as to his feeling with regard to Cromwell:—

> " He is a counterfeited piece, that shows
> Charles his effigies, with a copper nose.
> In fine, he's one we must Protector call,
> From whom the King of kings protect us all."

On the May-Pole reveals through a veil of irony his view of the Puritan opposition to amusements. There is a holy noise produced by belabouring the pulpit, and a wicked one by sounding the tabor. But unfortunately,

> " Such is Unregenerate Man's folly,
> He loves the wicked noise, and hates the holy."

Cleveland's most memorable productions are *The Mixed Assembly* and, yet more, *The Rebel Scot*. The former is still interesting, though its effect on the modern reader is lessened by the obscurity which inevitably falls in the course of time upon pieces rich in allusions to contemporary persons and events. *The Rebel Scot* remains more easily understood. It is clear that Cleveland flung all his energy into it, and the reason is that all his prejudices, or principles, were involved. Racial feeling, political beliefs and religious faith, all combined to embitter Cleveland against the Scots. They find their expression in the two parts of *The Scots Apostasy* as well, but the highest point is reached in *The Rebel Scot*. It is a vigorous and telling satire, which would have been more telling still had Cleveland been better able to keep his temper. Here is his weakness: the concurrence in one subject of everything he most intensely dislikes tempts him to elevate excess into a principle. He is convinced that he does well to be angry, and not merely to be angry but to foam at the mouth:—

> " A poet should be fear'd
> When angry, like a comet's flaming beard."

The ordinary measure of language is inadequate to the subject:—

> " Before a Scot can properly be curst,
> I must like Hocus, swallow daggers first."

It is idle to expect the lineaments of humanity in a figure drawn by an artist in such a mood; and the consequence is that *The Rebel Scot*, for all its vigour, is still only a third-rate satire. It is notable that in one couplet we find an anticipation of one of the most famous of Johnson's gibes against the Scots:—

> " Had Cain been Scot, God would have chang'd his doom,
> Not forc'd him wander, but confin'd him home."

Possibly these lines were in Johnson's mind when he said that the finest sight a Scotsman ever saw was the road to England.

The pieces quoted are all in rhymed couplets, a measure which Cleveland handled roughly, it is true, as compared with the standard of the next generation, but yet with a skill which was creditable in the middle of the seventeenth century. Herein he was following the example set by Hall and Donne, and helping to establish the heroic couplet as the proper measure for satire. Notwithstanding the adoption of the four-foot iambic line by Butler, the heroic couplet was generally accepted for that purpose before the end of the century. In the middle of the century however custom was by no means so uniform. The influence of medieval licence still survived among the journalists and ballad-makers, as may be seen in such collections as the Percy Society's *Songs and Poems on Costume* and *Political Songs published in England during the Commonwealth*. Some of the men whose names have survived in literature wrote in these less regular metres. Cleveland himself did so. *A Lenten Litany* is an example of anapæstic verse, somewhat surprisingly good:—

> " From a vinegar priest on a crab-tree stock,
> From a foddering of prayer four hours by the clock,
> From a holy sister with a pitiful smock,
>   *Libera nos*, etc."

Sir John Denham also used irregular measures. *A Western Wonder* and *A Second Western Wonder* are somewhat unkempt ballads. *To the Five Members of the Honourable House of Commons* is an attempt, far less successful than Cleveland's, to handle the anapæst. *A Speech against Peace at the Close Committee* is a good example of the freer satire against the Roundheads:—

> " And shall we kindle all this flame,
> Only to put it out again,
>   And must we now give o'er,
> And only end where we begun?
> In vain this mischief we have done,
>   If we can do no more.
>
> .   .   .   .
>
> Either the cause at first was ill,
> Or being good, it is so still;
>   And thence they will infer,
> That either now or at the first
> They were deceived; or, which is worst,
>   That we ourselves may err."

The Puritan and the Papist, originally published in 1643 " by a scholar in Oxford," shows Abraham Cowley a combatant on the same side with Cleveland and Denham. Its thesis is that the opposite extremes are equally wrong: *in medio tutissimus ibis*. Religion is a circle, and those who go contrary ways meet:—

> " The Roman Catholic, to advance the cause,
> Allows a lie, and calls it *pia fraus*;
> The Puritan approves and does the same,
> Dislikes nought in it but its Latin name."

In the matter of prayers Cowley leaves the advantage on the side
of the Papists:—

> " They in a foreign and unknown tongue pray,
> You in an unknown sense your prayers say;
> So that this difference 'twixt you does ensue,—
> Fools understand not them, not wise men you."

So it is too in the matter of knowledge:—

> " They keep the people ignorant, and you
> Keep both the people and yourselves so too."

Thus had satire been revived and the ground somewhat feebly
cultivated during the period of civil strife: it was after the Restoration that the crop was reaped; and the reapers were Royalists.
In order to keep the balance between the two parties, it is necessary
to remind ourselves that by far the greatest man of the time was
faithful to his old belief in the Commonwealth, and that while
bells were pealing and trumpets blaring to welcome back Charles II.,
and on through the years when Whitehall was sinking ever deeper
in pleasures as stupid as they were vicious, he was, in the words of
Macaulay, "meditating a song so high and so holy that it might
not have misbeseemed the lips of those ethereal essences whom he
saw with that inner eye, which no calamity could darken, casting
down around the sea of crystal their crowns of amaranth and gold."
Rarely, in human disputes, is all the right on one side and all the
wrong on the other. But he who is in doubt as to the comparative
merits of the English Commonwealth and the English Restoration
would do well to compare, in the political sphere, the English navy
under Cromwell, with that which under Charles II. was powerless
to bar the Thames against the Dutch; and, in the sphere of literature, *Paradise Lost* with the Restoration drama. Whether the
standard adopted be ethical or purely literary, the question is
equally beyond dispute. In satire however, it must be repeated,
notwithstanding some shrewd blows struck incidentally by Bunyan
a little later, the honours rested with the Royalists. Until *Absalom
and Achitophel* appeared there was no satire that rivalled *Hudibras*.

Samuel Butler (1612–80) had the fortune, good for his work,
however unpleasant to himself, to be brought into very intimate
connexion with the party which he was destined to satirise so
severely; for not only did he find his hero in Sir Samuel Luke,

whom he served for a time in some unknown capacity, but in Luke's household he had numerous opportunities of observing other Puritans, and of making himself familiar with their thoughts and language. At what date he actually composed *Hudibras* cannot be determined. It is irregular and loosely strung, and there is evidence that, in part at least, it is made up of fragments jotted down from time to time as occasion supplied the material. Probably it is best regarded as the work of Butler's whole life, a sort of general receptacle into which his thoughts on almost any subject could be thrown. It is emphatically his *magnum opus*. Though the prose characters which were published among the *Genuine Remains*, and have been added to in recent years, cannot be denied the merit of pungency, we have but to compare them with those of Earle, who in some cases treats the same subject, to see that they are second-rate. Neither do the miscellaneous satires in verse add to Butler's fame. The satirical Pindaric odes are dull and the ballads worthless; and though in some of the pieces there are fine lines and striking expressions, there is nothing that would have kept the memory of Butler green. We acknowledge a palpable hit, memorable because of the subject, when he objects against Milton, the controversialist, that he

> " Counted breaking Priscian's head a thing
> More capital, than to behead a king ";

and we admire the good sense of the satire *On our ridiculous Imitation of the French*; for it is right to ridicule the folly of those who would

> " Be natives wheresoe'er they come,
> And only foreigners at home."

But there is no piece so rounded and complete as to live by its own merit, nor is there mass enough to preserve the vital warmth by mere quantity.

Upon these miscellaneous poems Dryden founded an opinion which *The Cambridge History of English Literature* quotes without comment. He thought that "Butler would have excelled in any other kind of metre." The opinion of so great a poet and so great a critic must be treated with respect. But even Homer sometimes nods; and surely Dryden was in the deepest sleep here. If ever there was an *instantia crucis*, clearly it is *The Elephant in the Moon*.

In this very clever and witty skit on the Royal Society, the *savants* mistake the flies and gnats which have got into the telescope for two kinds of inhabitants of the moon, the Privolvans and the Subvolvans; and an unlucky imprisoned mouse for an elephant. This piece exists in two versions. We are told that "after the author had finished this story in short verse, he took it into his head to attempt it in long." Compare the beginning of the original with the later version:—

> " A learn'd society of late,
> The glory of a foreign state,
> Agreed, upon a summer's night,
> To search the moon by her own light;
> To make an inventory of all
> Her real estate, and personal."

The corresponding lines in "long verse" run as follows:—

> " A virtuous, learned society, of late
> The pride and glory of a foreign state,
> Made an agreement, on a summer's night,
> To search the moon at full, by her own light;
> To take a perfect inventory of all
> Her real fortunes, or her personal."

The closing lines yield the same result, and those in the middle still the same. Butler's innocent conception of the way to pass from the four-foot to the five-foot iambic line was therefore just to introduce any convenient word or expression of two syllables; in other words, "long verse" is "short verse" and gas. Curiously enough, Scott had an idea of the same sort, and defended his own "short verse" by pointing out how often the long line may be reduced without appreciable change of meaning by mere omission. It is true the thing may be done when the long line has been constructed as unskilfully as are the long lines of Butler. But try the process on any passage of acknowledged mastery—on Dryden's character of Shaftesbury or Pope's of Atticus. "Short verse" is not to be made "long" so simply, nor is it easy to believe that he who could conceive such a plan could be a master of metre. Far from having the flexible genius and the varied gifts with which Dryden credits him, Butler would seem to have been a man who could do one thing in one way supremely well. Whether he could have done that one thing in any other way, or have done anything else in masterly fashion, is doubtful. "One-poem poets" are fairly numerous; but the one poem is usually a short lyric. Is there any other example of a man of Butler's eminence who, having lived the full span of life, is so emphatically as he the author of one work?

Scarcely any statement can be made that does not require some qualification; and he who affirms that Butler could do only one thing in one way supremely well lays himself open to criticism. The one thing is, of course, political (which here includes religious) satire, and the one way is the medieval way, with a strong infusion of the grotesque. It will be objected that Butler was capable of achieving pure poetic beauty. He was; but there is just one singularly beautiful passage which is inevitably quoted to prove it:—

> " The moon pull'd off her veil of light,
> That hides her face by day from sight,
> (Mysterious veil, of brightness made,
> That's both her lustre, and her shade)
> And in the night as freely shone
> As if the rays had been her own."

As *Paradise Lost* was not published when Part II. of *Hudibras* appeared, it is nearly certain that Butler was not merely borrowing Milton's glorious conception, "dark with excessive light." Butler therefore could rise to the peak of Parnassus; but a single passage is not sufficient to prove that he was native there, any more than the occasional visit of a migratory bird proves that it is indigenous. In the same way it may be urged that Butler could show the restraint and rival the finish of the satirists of the classical school. But again, there is just one passage which may be plausibly adduced to show it. This is the character of Shaftesbury, or Baron Ashley, as he was then:—

> " 'Mongst these there was a politician
> With more heads than a beast in vision,
> And more intrigues in every one
> Than all the whores of Babylon;
> So politic, as if one eye
> Upon the other were to spy,
> That, to trepan the one to think
> The other blind, both strove to blink;
> And in his dark pragmatic way
> As busy as a child at play."

And so on. The character is admirably drawn, and not altogether unworthy of being placed beside Dryden's lines on Shaftesbury. Yet a comparison of the two passages shows that when he came nearest Butler was still wide apart from the classical style and far inferior in finish.

On his own ground, that of satire in the grotesque vein written in doggerel verse, Butler is supreme in English. The wide distance at which his numerous imitators stand shows that his achievement was by no means an easy one; while their very number is among the proofs of his complete success. Another proof is that Charles II., no mean judge of wit, carried *Hudibras* about with him, and was constantly quoting it. Still more notable is what we learn about the poem from Pepys. That Pepys had a low opinion of *Hudibras* is easily explained. Though he is at least as amusing as Butler himself, he is so unintentionally; and he who is the cause why wit is in others, has never either understood or liked the man who is himself witty. The remarkable point for the present purpose is that Pepys, having sold his copy at a loss because the contents were so little to his taste, felt himself obliged to buy a second copy. No one who wished to swim with the current could afford to be ignorant of *Hudibras*. So again, when the second part appeared, the thrifty diarist thought it would suffice to borrow, but once more found that he must go to the expense of buying it. There is probably no more striking proof of popularity in our literary annals. Unfortunately, all this popularity brought small gain to the author. The poem was shamelessly pirated, and though Charles II. seems to have been less callous towards Butler than he was to many of the supporters of his cause, the royal bounty did not save the poet from an old age of poverty. According to his contemporary Oldham,

> " Of all his gains by verse he could not save
> Enough to purchase flannel and a grave."

In adopting the mock-heroic form Butler was, no doubt, influenced by his French contemporary Scarron's *Virgile Travesti*, which was destined to produce such a crop of imitations in England and on the Continent; and Courthope has shown that the Oxford poet James Smith had afforded useful hints for the verse. The choice was happy both for Butler's genius and in view of the circumstances of the time. Milton shows that even when the scene is laid in heaven the epic tends to be martial, and England had but recently been shaken by the tramp of armies. In the civil contest was involved everything that Butler cared for. It was religious as well as political; and Cavalier and Roundhead represented different types of character, no less than diverse views of Church and State.

Even manners and fashions were sharply opposed—on one side
the "long essenced hair," on the other close-cropped locks; on one
side gaiety, freedom of speech and round oaths, on the other a sour
asceticism, and restraint of word and look. Restraint won, and
the other side was forced to confess defeat. "God's nigs and
ne'er stir, sir, has vanquish'd God damn me," sings Alexander
Brome, and

> " No accents are so pleasing now as those
>   That are caesura'd through the pastor's nose."

Even in courage, the same poet admits, temperance proved superior
to intemperance. However the Good Fellow may brag, he cannot face
his conquerors: "You'd as lief see the devil as Fairfax or Cromwell." Further, restraint won *because* it was restraint. Once more
Brome tells us that "'twas the cup made the camp to miscarry."
But next, restraint, forgetting to restrain itself—like vaulting
ambition overleaping itself—brought about the inevitable reaction,
and the conquered became in turn the conqueror. The Puritans
forgot human nature, which has never for long consented to
renounce its cakes and ale, its ginger hot in the mouth, its merry
tabor luring to the dance the merry toes.

Indian hunting parties are in the habit of making a kind of broth,
the stock of which consists of parts of all the varied game the guns
have brought in during the day. To what is not consumed the first
night there is added the game of the second day, and so on as long
as the expedition lasts. Each fresh variety contributes a new
savour to the whole, which tastes neither of duck nor deer nor
snipe nor jungle-fowl, but of all these blended in rich confusion
with a dozen more, until the whole puts to shame—or so it appears
to palates stimulated by exercise and an outdoor life—the skill of
the *chef*. What we call luck or chance has led to a result beyond the
reach of art. Such a "hunter's pot" as this is *Hudibras*. The loose
design enabled Butler to throw into his pot whatever of wit or
wisdom he possessed. Hence it is that *Hudibras* is his one memorable work. Shakespeare could not express himself fully even in
Hamlet, nor Milton in *Paradise Lost*, because these works have a
beginning, middle and end. *Hudibras* has a sort of beginning, but
it has neither middle nor end. To say it is unfinished is merely to
say it is *Hudibras*; it never could have been finished in the artistic

sense, because that implies design. Butler took whatever he found in the past that suited his purpose, and he added all that was in his own mind. *Hudibras* contains suggestions borrowed from *Don Quixote*, from *The Fairy Queen* and from the Arthurian legends. When Hudibras rides out "a-colonelling," he is just a Don Quixote or an Arthurian knight-errant, and the fact that he

> " Never bent his stubborn knee
> To anything but chivalry,"

brings the sectaries' objection to kneeling at communion into grotesque contact with the chivalrous pride of the knights.

The main theme of *Hudibras* is the quarrel between Crown and Parliament, with which is inextricably blended the quarrel between Church and Dissent. Butler could not have separated these two aspects if he had wished; for they are as indissolubly united as the obverse and reverse of a coin. It is not worth while following the wanderings of the Knight and the Squire; they meander with as mazy motion as the dream-river of Coleridge. But wherever they go the underlying theme is the same. They fling themselves against the amusements dear to the people, such as bear-baiting, and they illustrate the quibbling casuistry of sectarian theology. One is Presbyterian, the other Independent; and there runs through all a criticism, now open and now implied, of the religious and political evils which flow from insistence upon differences as to the dotting of the i's and stroking of the t's in either. In a passage of unusual elevation Butler praises the Royalists' steadfastness, which is due to unity of principle:—

> " For loyalty is still the same
> Whether it win or lose the game;
> True as the dial to the sun,
> Although it be not shined upon."

And with this he contrasts the confusion due to multiplicity of sects, which dates back from before the Civil War, for

> " Ere the storm of war broke out,
> Religion spawned a various rout
> Of petulant capricious sects,
> The maggots of corrupted texts."

The reign of the Saints is obstructed by their numbers; for though many hands make light work, it is just the contrary with intellects.

In a contemptuous image Butler expresses his sense of the inefficiency which flows from unrestricted differences of opinion. Many heads, he says,

> " Obstruct intrigues,
> As slowest insects have most legs."

The Roundhead centipede was incapable of progress, because its various members were all for moving different ways.

Macaulay thought that the tap-root of the Civil War was ship-money; but Carlyle insisted that serious men must have something more important than money at stake before they will fight. *Hudibras* confirms Carlyle; for it shows that not only ship-money but every political question was subordinate to religion. The sects spawned from "the maggots of corrupted texts" are the cause rather than the effect of the quarrel with the Crown; and if Butler ever wished to make the political predominant over the religious aspect, he completely failed. It is Presbyterians and Independents who are satirised, and the faithful Churchman who is inferentially approved. It is from false religion; from a forced interpretation of texts; from an ethical perversion on the part of those who compounded

> " For sins they are inclined to,
> By damning those they have no mind to";

and, still worse, from the outrageous claims of those who held that the regenerate were incapable of sin, so that what is a sin in the wicked is pious in the saint—it is from these causes that all political errors, in the view of Butler, spring. His picture of the sects is admirable. He brings Presbyterian into contact with Independent—the learned Knight, profound in logic, a master of rhetoric and mathematics, a shrewd philosopher, with the Squire, unlearned indeed, but the Knight's equal or superior by virtue of what some call Gifts, and others the New Light:—

> " A liberal art that costs no pains
> Of study, industry, or brains."

Thus Butler is enabled to introduce anything and everything. Learned himself, he had yet a hearty contempt for the pedantry of learning; and the character of the Knight gives ample scope for his ridicule of such pedantry. Hudibras is learned enough not merely to make the worse appear the better reason, but to explain away the most obvious facts. He has been soundly beaten, but what of that?

> " This thing called pain,
> Is, as the learned stoics maintain,
> Not bad *simpliciter*, nor good,
> But merely as 'tis understood."

Neither is such a beating derogatory to the honour of a soldier; for

> " Some have been beaten till they know
> What wood a cudgel's of by the blow;
> Some kicked, until they can feel whether
> A shoe be Spanish or neat's leather ";

and yet after long running away have taught the same cunning to others. And Ralph is quite the equal of Hudibras as a casuist. As the latter finds excuse for the drubbing he suffers, so does the former argue that running away is a most soldierly act:—

> " Timely running's no mean part
> Of conduct, in the martial art,
> By which some glorious deeds achieve,
> As citizens by breaking thrive,
> And cannons conquer armies, while
> They seem to draw off and recoil."

But Hudibras's learning could be applied to many things besides his own case. Butler anticipates Swift's satire of Laputa; for the Knight

> " By geometric scale
> Could take the size of pots of ale;
> Resolve, by sines and tangents straight,
> If bread or butter wanted weight;
> And wisely tell what hour o' th' day
> The clock does strike, by algebra."

Still, the satirist is no prophet; and if time often exposes the folly of pedantic learning, it occasionally reveals the danger which besets criticism resting upon a foundation of common sense. Probably Butler conceived the satire which he aimed, as is supposed, at Dr. Robert Hooke, secretary and curator to the Royal Society, to be as sound as that which strikes at the application of geometry to pots of ale. Butler evidently held investigation into the minutest forms of life to be idle, for he represents the conjurer Sidrophel as enquiring

> " How many different specieses
> Of maggots breed in rotten cheese;
> And which are next of kin to those
> Engendered in a chandler's nose;
> Or those not seen, but understood,
> That live in vinegar or wood."

But modern bacteriology has shown that Hooke was right and Butler wrong.

Several of his fellow-satirists fell into this error after Butler. The antiquary is fair game, and Young's lines on Sir Hans Sloane, "the foremost toyman of his time," and on "Ashmole's baby-house" are laughable; but London is now justly proud of the one collection and Oxford of the other. Richard Cambridge in *The Scribleriad* ridicules archæology; but the whirligig of time has brought the virtuoso his revenges, and the society which the companions of Scriblerus founded wins the respect of the modern mind:—

> " Be yours the task, industrious, to recall
> The lost inscription to the ruin'd wall;
> Each Celtic character explain, and show
> How Britons ate a thousand years ago."

The massive sense of Johnson, however, saves him from making the same mistake. In *The Rambler* he shows that he can ridicule trivialities as well as any man, and introduces his virtuoso with a vial, "of which the water was formerly an icicle on the crags of Caucasus," and "a snail that has crawled upon the Wall of China." But, to his lasting honour, in the serious reflexions of the next paper he anticipates the experience of later ages:—

> " It is impossible to determine the limits of inquiry, or to foresee what consequences a new discovery may produce. He who suffers not his faculties to lie torpid, has a chance, whatever be his employment, of doing good to his fellow-creatures. The man that first ranged the woods in search of medicinal springs, or climbed the mountains for salutary plants, has undoubtedly merited the gratitude of posterity, how much soever his frequent miscarriages might excite the scorn of his contemporaries. If what appears little be universally despised, nothing greater can be attained, for all that is great was at first little, and rose to its present bulk by gradual accessions and accumulated labours."

As the character of the Knight makes the satire of pedantry apposite, so does that of the Squire naturally introduce and justify satire of superstition. Sheer Gifts have carried Ralph farther than all his learning could carry Hudibras. The latter does things by geometry that plain men can do without it; but to the former the New Light has revealed the innermost arcana of Nature:—

> " He had First Matter seen undressed:
> He took her naked, all alone,
> Before one rag of form was on."

A personage so privileged can easily prove or disprove anything whatsoever. The recreations of the unregererate, such as bear-baiting, are wrong:—

> " For certainly there's no such word
> In all the Scripture on record."

It might be supposed that this rule of Scripture imposed disabilities on the Saints also. Not at all: Ralph is able to prove that all things are lawful for them. The Knight has sworn to the Widow that he will undergo the penance of whipping. The unpleasantness of the prospect leads him to ponder whether it be really necessary to keep his oath; and Ralph proves his value as a squire by demonstrating that it is not. For the Saint is a peer of the heavenly realm, and, as such, he is only bound to swear, like a peer of the earthly realm, "on the gospel of his honour"—of which who can be so good a judge as he? It has all been done before; the Saints *have* perjured themselves, and therefore it is right:—

> " Was there an oath the godly took,
> But in due time and place they broke?
> Did we not bring our oaths in first,
> Before our plate, to have them burst,
> And cast in fittier models, for
> The present use of church and war?
> Did not our worthies of the house,
> Before they broke the peace, break vows?"

A clear case is made clearer still by a consideration of the person to whom the oath has been taken; for looks, language and dress reveal the Widow to be one of the wicked, and

> " All of us hold this for true,
> No faith is to the wicked due.
> The truth is precious and divine,
> Too rich a pearl for carnal swine."

Oaths therefore may be broken—by a Saint—when it is inconvenient to observe them; an opinion which might have been "made in Germany."

The Knight's intellect is convinced: he may do the thing that it is convenient for him to do. But a Saint may incur certain dangers by acting according to his rights; for the fraud may be discovered. The question therefore arises whether he may consult a sorcerer in order to discover whether he may break his oath with safety. The same line of reasoning is available here. Ralph proves that the Saints may consult sorcerers by showing that they have done so.

Not only is their freedom such that they may consult sorcerers when they need them; they may even go to the devil himself "if they have motives thereunto."

Plain as Butler makes his view of the New Light through the mouth of Ralph, he so detests it that he must express his opinion directly, in his introductory description of the character of the Squire:—

> " 'Tis a dark-lantern of the spirit,
> Which none can see but those that bear it;
> A light that falls down from on high,
> For spiritual trades to cozen by;
> An *ignis fatuus* that bewitches,
> And leads men into pools and ditches,
> To make them dip themselves, and sound
> For Christendom in dirty pond;
> To dive, like wild-fowl, for salvation,
> And fish to catch regeneration."

So great indeed is his dislike that he puts into the mouth of Hudibras some expressions of dubious propriety in the dramatic sense. We can understand the objection of the learned Knight to the cobbler who does not stick to his last; yet in his language about tinkers who patch church-discipline instead of kettles, oyster-women who cry "No Bishop," mouse-trap men who denounce evil counsellors, and botchers who fall to turn and patch the church instead of old clothes, there is an unsparing vigour which is hardly consistent with the fact that, after all, these Saints of Gifts and the New Light are just the other section of the party to which he himself belongs.

It is however part of Butler's purpose to show how little love is lost between these two sections. When Hudibras, distressed in mind with the thought of the distress in body with which he is threatened through his promise to submit to the penance of whipping, raises the question whether the punishment may be suffered by proxy, Ralph replies:—

> " That sinners may supply the place
> Of suffering saints is a plain case,"

and supports his opinion by an appeal to the practice of "our brethren of New England." But he does not enjoy the application to himself when the Knight demands that the Squire should be the vicarious sufferer. The account to which this proposal provokes him of the steps by which the Independents gained the mastery

over the Presbyterians is all the more pungent because it is
strictly accurate, and the anger it arouses in the Knight is the natural
effect of unwelcome truth. It is fitting that two such friends should
mutually play one another false. Each approaches the Widow
unknown to the other; the Squire, arriving first, informs her how
Hudibras has broken his oath; and so the perjury which the latter
afterwards commits, however permissible in a Saint, is unfortunate.
In the masquerade to which the lady treats him, he is not allowed
to forget the errors of his party. The Voice takes the side of the
other section, and declares that

> " All the Independents do,
> Is only what you forced 'em to;
> You who are not content alone
> With tricks to put the devil down,
> But must have armies raised to back
> The gospel-work you undertake;
> As if artillery and edge-tools
> Were th' only engines to save souls."

Ralph at an earlier stage had still more keenly criticised the tyranni-
cal spirit of the Presbyterians and their extravagant claims:—

> " Presbytery does but translate
> The papacy to a free state,
> A commonwealth of popery,
> Where every village is a see
> As well as Rome, and must maintain
> A tithe-pig metropolitan;
> Where every presbyter and deacon
> Commands the keys for cheese and bacon;
> And every hamlet's governed
> By 's holiness, the church's head,
> More haughty and severe in 's place
> Than Gregory and Boniface."

"New Presbyter is but old Priest writ large." Evidently the day
when these two species of Christians loved one another was past.

Hudibras is rich in satire of minor points, as well as of things
essential. There were "scribes, commissioners, and triers" appointed
to discriminate between the true Saints and those who were not
so true; and they did it partly by searching questions as to conversion, and partly by a study of appearance, complexion and
speech. It was their business

> " By cunning sleight
> To cast a figure for men's light;
> To find, in lines of beard and face,
> The physiognomy of grace;
> And by the sound and twang of nose
> If all be sound within disclose."

Other affectations are ridiculed in the description of the Knight when he finds that the Widow knows how he has forsworn himself:—

> " While thus the lady talked, the knight
> Turned th' inside of his eyes to white;
> As men of inward light are wont
> To turn their optics in upon 't;
> He wondered how she came to know
> What he had done, and meant to do;
> Held up his affidavit-hand,
> As if he 'ad been to be arraigned."

By far the greater part of the poem is taken up with this absorbing subject of the sects which had, when Butler wrote, so lately ruled the land; and most of what does not bear upon that directly is indirectly related to it.

There are however one or two of these subordinate points which require separate illustration. Thus, in a satire so comprehensive as Butler's, it would be strange if there were no place for the satire on woman, which had been so popular a theme with his medieval predecessors. It is indeed present. Trulla, the Widow, and the virago who figures in the procession of the cucking-stool, together fill a considerable part of *Hudibras*; but still the satire of sex is subordinate. There are keen strokes on the foibles of women, and there are here and there lines as wise as they are witty on their psychology. For example:—

> " Valour's a mouse-trap, wit a gin
> That women oft are taken in."

But what interests Butler most keenly is the part women had played in the rise of the sects. It is the fact that women were "our first apostles" that induces Hudibras to interfere on behalf of the heroine of the cucking-stool. They have left no stone unturned to aid the cause, they have poured in their wealth, drawn in recruits, ministered to and fed the teachers when these were

> " Tired and spent
> With holding forth for Parliament."

The hardest physical labour has not deterred them; they

> " Raised rampires with their own soft hands,
> To put the enemy in stands;
> From ladies down to oyster-wenches
> Laboured like pioneers in trenches,
> Fell to their pick-axes, and tools,
> And helped the men to dig like moles."

Even politics, as has already been said, are subordinate. Something is written and more implied about Parliament, as in the passage from which the last quotation is taken; and the discussion of the freedom of the Saints to break their oaths shows how indissolubly the two aspects are connected and how worthy Parliament is of Conventicle and Conventicle of Parliament. Both are radically false, and as the one corrupts the texts of the Bible, so the other falsifies the news of the kingdom. It is noticeable that Butler passes lightly over the Mercuries, the Royalist news-sheets; not much could be said in praise of them, but silence was possible. It is on the Parliamentary Diurnals that his lash falls. He depicts Fame flying through the air,

> " With letters hung, like eastern pigeons,
> And Mercuries of furthest regions;
> Diurnals, writ for regulation
> Of lying, to inform the nation,
> And by their public use to bring down
> The rate of whetstones in the kingdom." [1]

Perhaps the most important subjects of Butler's satire which neither are in themselves nor are rendered by his treatment (as are pedantry and superstition) integral parts of the main theme, are law and lawyers. He, like Shakespeare, shows a knowledge of legal terms so intimate that it has been conjectured that he may have been employed in a lawyer's office. He certainly acted for a time as clerk to Thomas Jefferies, a justice of the peace, and it was probably in the same capacity that he served Sir Samuel Luke. However his knowledge may have been acquired, it did not inspire in him a high opinion of those who followed the profession of the law. His *Character of a Lawyer* is by no means flattering, nor is that other character of a lawyer with which (except for the *Heroical Epistle* and the Lady's answer) *Hudibras* closes; while, by way of deeper insult, Whackum, the miserable half-starved drudge of the scoundrel Sidrophel, is described as one

> " Bred to dash and draw,
> Not wine, but more unwholesome law."

Hudibras himself, on whom Butler's ridicule is so copiously poured, is described as great on the bench as well as in the saddle. From the description which is given of his greatness in the latter, we may

[1] A silver whetstone was the strange prize for the victor in lying.

infer the nature of his greatness in the former. The source of Butler's dislike of the legal profession lay, no doubt, in the fact that law, which ought to be the shield of the poor and weak, may, especially in times of civil strife, be wrested to purposes of oppression.

Of satire on literature and writers there is little in Butler; for the satire of pedantry is a different matter, and so is the satire of the news-sheets. The wooing of the Widow however gives occasion for an excursion into this province. The Knight in his protestations rivals the hyperboles of the love-poets, and the lady ridicules him and them in an admirable passage. The poet is insincere, and thinks more of himself than of his mistress:—

> " She that with poetry is won,
> Is but a desk to write upon."

She lays bare the absurdity of the similes which profess to laud her lips, her teeth, her cheeks, her voice and all the items of her beauty:—

> " The sun and moon, by her bright eyes,
> Eclipsed and darkened in the skies,
> Are but the patches, that she wears,
> Cut into suns, and moons, and stars."

Butler was under no temptation to fall himself into absurdities of this sort; but they were common enough in the verses of the scribblers about the Court, and he did a service in penning this stinging ridicule.

More than once in the history of the human mind has the perfect expression of some phase been found just when that phase was about to pass away. Plato lived through the decay of the Greek state, and he may have heard the earlier of the eloquent appeals of Demosthenes to the Athenian democracy to be up and doing itself, and to trust no longer to mercenaries. Aristotle was tutor to the great conqueror who dealt the death-blow to that and the other democracies of the time. Yet it was Plato and Aristotle who enshrined in their political treatises the conception of what the city state might have been, and what, it would seem, they hoped it might still be, or, if the pattern was laid up in heaven, approach to being. Medieval Catholicism was already tottering towards the great disruption of the Reformation, when Dante saw the grand vision of every part of the gigantic scheme of the universe from hell through purgatory to heaven. Butler stands on a far lower plane than these demi-gods of philosophy and of poetry; his mind was feeble compared with theirs, and the pen he wielded impotent. Satire at its best is a second-rate type of literature. Nevertheless, in his own kind and degree and manner, Butler stands in a relation to the past similar to that of Dante and the great Greek philosophers. He, like them, sums up a period; and he, like them, surpasses all (at least in England) who had belonged to it. He is the last and greatest of the English satirists who shared the medieval spirit. The light of a classical type of satire had glimmered and gone out and glimmered again. It was about to gleam yet once more, and this time it was destined to shine permanently. Dryden's *Absalom and Achitophel* appeared only three years after the third part of *Hudibras*. Yet *Hudibras* rarely shows any trace of the classical influence. In spirit and effect Butler is wholly medieval. His whimsical and grotesque yet highly effective rhymes are medieval. So are all his irregularities. That looseness of plan which enabled him to find a place in *Hudibras* for almost anything that occurred to his mind—this, which is the very antithesis of the classical, is of the essence of the medieval mind.

The statement that Butler is the last as well as the greatest of the medieval satirists, seems to be in flagrant contradiction of the facts; for imitations of *Hudibras* and of Scarron abounded for more than half a century after the death of Butler. But the explanation is simple and the defence easy. Macbeth complained of Banquo, who, appearing as a ghost, seemed not to know that he was dead. The imitators of Butler were in similar case. It was not because he was too original that they failed. What he had done was not to lay a foundation-stone, but to build the turret to its roof. An inferior workman might have built above a foundation-stone; but Dryden himself could not have built above the turret, and he was far too wise to try. There could be one *Divina Commedia* when Medieval Christianity was growing old, but not a second. There could be one *Hudibras* before medieval satire flickered out, but never another.

It would be waste of time to linger over these imitations of *Hudibras*. The most notable man who attempted to follow in the footsteps of Butler was Matthew Prior (1664-1721), and the poverty of his *Alma* goes far to show that the task was hopeless. There was also a Dutch Hudibras, *Hogan-Moganides,* and there were at least two which described themselves as Irish. In *Butler's Ghost, or Hudibras, the Fourth Part,* Tom D'Urfey produced a worthless continuation of the great original. The names of both Edward Ward and Thomas Ward are likewise in the list of imitators. The vogue spread north across the Border, and the imitations of Samuel Colvil and William Meston achieved perhaps more success and a wider popularity than any of the southern imitations. Colvil's *Mock Poem, or Whig's Supplication,* which deals with the rising of the Covenanters, has a considerable measure of rude vigour; but *The Knight of the Kirk* by Meston owes a good deal of such merit as it possesses to the fact that the author took the liberty of transferring what suited his purpose from Butler's pages to his own. It was partly on *Hudibras* that Alexander Pitcairn also moulded his *Babel,* a satire on the General Assembly of the Scottish Kirk in 1692.

With the influence of Butler there was mingled in these men and their like the influence of the French Scarron, and a small library might be compiled of the productions of which he, or Butler, or both, are the source. It is incredibly nauseous. It is neither criticism nor satire; it is merely a deliberate degradation of the finest things in literature. Ignorance of it is best, for the mind is capable of receiving from it stains which can never be washed out. Not that any of it is as obscene as many better writings; but the whole aim and purpose of such things is the defilement of the beautiful. Whoever feels himself bound to learn what such things are, may perhaps do so with least injury to himself by reading Charles Cotton's *Scarronides, or Virgil Travestie,* and observing how it debases and befouls Virgil's beautiful story of Dido.

CHAPTER VIII

CLASSICAL SATIRE TO DRYDEN

THOUGH the enormous weight of Butler was thrown into the scale of grotesque and irregular satire, and though the various miscellanies and collections of *Poems on Affairs of State* and the like contained numerous pieces of satire in such lyrical measures as have been illustrated above, yet even before Dryden won his triumph the heroic couplet was becoming more and more the accepted measure for satire. In his *Instructions to a Painter* Waller had used it to lay on adulation with a trowel, and incidentally showed how astonishingly prosaic a poet can be. But Waller, writing in 1665, failed to foresee the course of the war. The painter is to depict the British admiral as master of the sea:—

> " Make him bestride the ocean, and mankind
> Ask his consent to use the sea and wind."

But in fact, before the end of the war the Dutch were burning English ships at Chatham. The contrast between the forecast and the fact was too sharp to be missed; and Waller's poem furnished a model for a whole group of poems satirically instructing painters how to delineate the glories of the reign of Charles II. Sir John Denham (1615–1669) led the way. He is responsible for four *Directions to a Painter*, of no great literary merit, but penetrating because of their truth. With far more skill Andrew Marvell (1621–1678) followed in the same track, and wrote several poems of "instructions." His *Last Instructions to a Painter* (which were not the last) is the best of all the group. Writing in 1667, when England was still smarting with the disgrace of the Dutch Wars, Marvell had abundant material for his satire; and he has produced an interesting work, vividly illustrating the corruption of the Court and the disgraceful position into which that corruption had brought England. The satire is severe; but severer than anything Marvell wrote, than anything Juvenal himself could have written, is the contrast,

145

brought about by the history of a few years, between this piece and the Horatian Ode on Cromwell; the contrast between an England shaken by the terror of the Dutch guns, and that whose chief the poet in prophetic mood saw as a Cæsar to Gaul and a Hannibal to Italy. Then, he could call upon the War's and Fortune's son to "march indefatigably on"; now, he has to tell a story of sorrow and shame. If the Cromwellians need justification, here it is. Whenever he writes on the corruption of the Court and the shame it had brought upon England, Marvell's ink turns gall. In *Britannia and Raleigh,* he calls Raleigh up to hear how much worse were the French who now thronged the Court than the detested Scots of Raleigh's own day. *An Historical Poem* is a terrible piece, and all the more terrible because it is true. Misfortune has taught Charles nothing—except to see to it that he does not go on his travels again:—

> " Twelve years complete he suffered in exile,
> And kept his father's asses all the while."

Dryden himself has no keener stroke. On the other hand, Marvell was capable of sinking into the abyss. In *The Character of Holland* he has perhaps the worst pun ever made—a worst pun which has none of the sort of merit which might turn it into the best. Hollanders are ridiculed as Half-anders.

Other events of the time served satirists who had other ends in view. Titus Oates and the Popish Plot supplied fuel to the satire of religion; and the proposal to bar the Duke of York from the succession could be used by the writers on either side. Nearly all the wits of the time tried their hand; Buckingham, Rochester and Dorset among the nobles; Shadwell, D'Urfey, Otway, Oldham and Settle among the humbler commons. In *The Rehearsal* (1671), Buckingham and others applied their wit to ridicule in heroic couplets the rant and fustian which frequently marred the rhymed heroic drama. The wit has now lost the keenness of its edge, but the satire struck home at the time, and the example was remembered for more than a century; for *The Rehearsal* was in the mind of Sheridan when he wrote *The Critic.* The Restoration nobles, for the most part, wrote like "men of quality," disdaining the toil which inferior authors had to bestow. The consequence was that, though they have left a few memorable lyrics, they rarely wrote what was worthy of their real talents. Some at least of the commoners were of inferior national ability. Shadwell's *The Medal of John Bayes* is memorable only for the terrible castigation it brought upon its author. D'Urfey owed his success chiefly to scurrility and indecency. Otway's fine genius was misused when he turned to satire. Shaftesbury tempted him, as he tempted so many others, but Antonio in *Venice Preserved* is an ineffective attack. *The Poet's Complaint to his Muse*, in which he denounces libels, carries satire into the inappropriate province of the ode, and is merely ingenious.

Of the men just named by far the most noteworthy as satirists were John Wilmot, Earl of Rochester (1647–80), and John Oldham (1653–83). The former wasted in the dissipations of a licentious Court talents which approached near, if indeed they did not reach, genius; and though the truth about him is perhaps not quite so bad as his reputation, there is little but shame and disgrace to be met with in the circle to which he belonged. His most notable piece, *A Satire against Mankind*, illustrates his great but perverted ability. The miserably low view of human nature which it embodies was probably in truth Rochester's. It is profoundly sceptical. Reason is depicted as "stumbling from thought to thought," until it falls into the boundless sea of doubt. Human virtues themselves proceed from vices; while animals bite and tear for hunger or for love, in man courage is the outcome of fear:—

> " For fear he arms, and is of arms afraid,
> From fear to fear successively betray'd;
> Base fear, the source whence his base passions came,
> His boasted honour, and his dear-bought fame."

"Most men are cowards, all men should be knaves." Such was the philosophy which its most brilliant intellect learnt at the Court of Charles II. This was among the consequences of the victory of the cause which Butler championed.

In Oldham we hear a higher strain; for, though far from an ideal character, Oldham had known the wholesome discipline of hardship, and in the school of adversity had learnt lessons which enabled him to accomplish more than the far more richly endowed Rochester. Oldham still further shortened his short career by making a false start. The example of Cowley tempted him to try the Pindaric ode, for which his wretched ear unfitted him. Soon however he discovered that his true bent was towards satire; and though the defective ear still betrays itself in execrable rhymes, in the heroic couplet the fault is, at any rate, less offensive than in the ode. Oldham's best-known work is the *Satires upon the Jesuits,* which were written in 1679, and published two years later. They are Juvenalian in violence and intensity. It is evident that Oldham's temperament inclined him to violence, and, confusing it with strength, he unfortunately cherished rather than checked the inclination. This is evident already in the earlier piece, *A Satire upon a Woman*:—

> " Vilest of that vile sex that damn'd us all!
> Ordain'd to cause, and plague us for our fall! "

An equally violent spirit animates the *Satires upon the Jesuits.* The Prologue speaks of them as "the vile brood of Loyola and Hell"; and the first satire is a wild outburst, opening with the words, "By Hell 'twas bravely done"—that is to say, Sir Edmund Berry Godfrey's murder,—and calling upon the Jesuits to surpass all past examples in wickedness and cruelty. This violence runs through the whole series, and is perhaps especially marked in the third satire, *Loyola's Will,* where the founder enjoins his disciples to admit all who have been ruined by debauchery, to learn "how small a dram" of religion makes the Jesuit compound, and instructs them in the wiles and deceits by which they may beguile the rabble.

It was the circumstances of the moment which caused Oldham's choice of subject. All England was ringing with the Popish Plot. But England had suffered not very long before from an opposite kind of religious excess, with which Oldham had as little sympathy as the majority of his fellow-poets. While they were determined not to fall under the rule of Rome, they were scarcely less determined to resist that of "the gifted Brother." In the second satire Oldham illustrates the cruelties and persecutions of the Jesuits by the example of their opposites:—

> " So the late Saints of blessed memory
> Cut throats in godly pure sincerity;
> So they with lifted hands, and eyes devout,
> Said grace and carv'd a slaughter'd Monarch out."

The *Satires upon the Jesuits* are by far the best-known of Oldham's writings, because they form the only connected group of his satires.

But in real merit they are inferior to two or three of the miscellaneous satires. The *Satire in Imitation of the Third of Juvenal*, exposing with much ingenuity the life of the town, is at least their equal; and there are two others which are clearly superior. These are *A Satire addressed to a Friend that is about to leave the University*, and another satire in which Spenser is made to warn the poet against the study of poetry. These pieces are superior to the rest because of the personal note in them. Oldham was a sincere writer; but the evils he complains of elsewhere did not come home to him so closely as did those which form the theme in these pieces. In the *Satires upon the Jesuits* the genuine indignation of the author is exaggerated for effect. But this, if true at all of the pieces just referred to, is true in far less measure. They embody Oldham's own experience. The advice he addresses to the friend about to leave the University is that the bitter truth of which he has been forced to discover in his own case. He, the son of a Nonconformist minister of narrow means, had been compelled at the same juncture in his life to ask himself what were the careers open to him. His analysis of the situation makes this satire one of the most interesting social documents of the time. His friend might choose to take orders. But there are hardly more porters than parsons in the street. Or he might think of teaching. But who would choose that vile drudgery,

> " Where you for recompense of all your pains
> Shall hardly reach a common fiddler's gains"?

The career of chaplain to a noble family has superficial attractions:—

> " Diet, an horse, and thirty pounds a year,
> Besides th' advantage of his Lordship's ear,
> The credit of the business, and the state,
> Are things that to a youngster's sense sound great! "

But the life is slavery. In silken scarf and cassock the chaplain only wears a gayer kind of livery. He must consecrate the meat at dinner, but is seldom asked to sit down, and at best must withdraw before the tarts appear. Oldham rates his freedom higher, and will not truck liberty for food and raiment. He goes on to depict his ambition. His utmost wish is

> " That Heaven would bless me with a small estate,
> Where I might find a close obscure retreat;
> There, free from noise, and all ambitious ends,
> Enjoy a few choice books, and fewer friends.

> Lord of myself, accountable to none,
> But to my conscience, and my God alone:
> There live unthought of, and unheard of die,
> And grudge mankind my very memory.
> But since the blessing is (I find) too great
> For me to wish for, or expect of Fate,
> Yet, maugre all the spite of Destiny,
> My thoughts and actions are and shall be free."

The poet is rarely so completely pleased with obscurity as he sometimes imagines he will be, and though these lines have the ring of sincerity, it would be dangerous to interpret them as expressing Oldham's constant desire. In the satire which conveys Spenser's warning against the study of poetry, the uncertainty of achieving immortality is among the reasons advanced to dissuade the aspirant. The poet may please for a while, and afterwards be thrown aside to mould with Silvester and Shirley in the shops of Duck Lane. There is no modern Scipio, or Mæcenas, or Sidney:—

> " A poet would be dear, and out o' th' way,
> Should he expect above a coachman's pay:
> For this will any dedicate, and lie,
> And daub the gaudy ass with flattery?
> For this will any prostitute his sense
> To coxcombs void of bounty, as of brains?
> Yet such is the hard fate of writers now,
> They're forc'd for alms to each great name to bow:
> Fawn, like her lap-dog on her tawdry Grace,
> Commend her beauty, and belie her glass,
> By which she every morning prunes her face:
> Sneak to his Honour, call him witty, brave,
> And just, tho' a known coward, fool and knave,
> And praise his lineage and nobility,
> Whose arms at first came from the Company."

Cowley, Waller and Butler are recent instances of neglected greatness. The effect upon genius is disastrous, for

> " What can we expect that's brave and great,
> From a poor needy wretch, that writes to eat? "

In the vigorous lines quoted above Oldham anticipates Johnson's struggle against the patron, and the honour due to him is none the less although, like Carlyle's heroes of letters, he "fought bravely and fell." For he was consistent. As Mr. Previté-Orton points out, in that age of fulsome flattery he published his *Satires upon the Jesuits* without a dedication.

In his elegiac lines to the memory of Oldham Dryden proclaims his kinship to his younger contemporary. Both alike abhorred knaves and fools, both sought the same goal. Both perhaps would have shown themselves more wise had they followed the apostolic injunction to "suffer fools gladly." "The gentle art of making enemies" is dangerous; and satirists were perhaps even less prosperous than other writers in that period. Dryden as well as Oldham laments the fate of Butler, making his Hind reproach the Panther thus:—

> " Unpitied Hudibras, your champion friend,
> Has shown how far your charities extend.
> This lasting verse shall on his tomb be read,
> ' He shamed you living, and upbraids you dead.' "

Oldham died young, poor and unhappy; and the last tasks of Dryden's own pen were the prologue and epilogue to Fletcher's play *The Pilgrim*, which was revived in 1700 in order to buttress the ex-laureate's failing fortune. The prologue begins significantly with the line, "How wretched is the fate of those who write"; while the epilogue makes the mournful defence against Jeremy Collier's attack upon the stage that the poets had but supplied the wares which a dissolute Court and a corrupted nation demanded. But whether Dryden's choice of satire as his vehicle was prudent or not, there can be no question that it was consonant with his literary genius. From the first the admirable fitness of the man to the form and the form to the man was evident.

John Dryden (1631–1700) had gone a considerable way in his literary career before he practised the formal satire. He had indeed, at an earlier date, embodied incidental satire in his plays and prologues and epilogues; and in a note to the third of the *Satires of Persius* (1693) he informed his readers that he remembered translating it when he was a king's scholar at Westminster; adding with a touch of pride that he believed this and many other of his exercises in English verse to be still in the possession of Dr. Busby. In one case at least his satire was deemed to be more than incidental; for *Limberham* (1679) had to be withdrawn, because it was interpreted as a libel on Lauderdale. Dryden therefore, long before *Absalom and Achitophel*, was a practised hand at satire both in verse and in prose, and doubtless knew his own power perfectly well. He had the further stimulus of attacks upon himself, some of which he was not unwilling to requite. Butler (who was dead, and whom he did not answer) had ridiculed the swelling style of "the modern heroic way" in *Repartees between Cat and Puss at a*

Caterwauling; and Buckingham, with the help of Butler and others, had done the like in *The Rehearsal*. Clever as is the satire of that celebrated skit, there certainly remained no balance to the credit of Buckingham, after the incomparable lines on Zimri, a satiric portrait probably unsurpassed not merely in English, but in either Latin or Greek, or the languages of Western Europe. No one ever challenged Dryden to a contest of this sort but he suffered for it, if, as he generally did, Dryden thought it worth while to take up the challenge. Shadwell, Settle and Burnet are other cases in point.

All the circumstances of the time were favourable to a great development of satire. That exacerbation of feeling which was the inevitable legacy of the recent civil strife, imparted the satiric spirit. Of the two parties, that which, being now dominant, enjoyed complete freedom of expression, was also that which had by far the greater aptitude and inclination for satire. Butler had already taken advantage of the situation; but, as has already been pointed out, Butler was the last of the medieval satirists. A place was still vacant; not indeed for the first modern satirist, for he is to be found in the age of Elizabeth, but for the first master in that style. Dryden was the man, and his earliest attempt remains still unsurpassed. Here at once is discarded that pestilent heresy of the metre, which had beset and so sorely damaged the Elizabethans. Dryden showed that it was possible to write satiric verse without being either inflated or harsh; and he was the first to convince the world of the possibility. Even when he is in the vein of panegyric, Dryden has to admit that his immediate predecessor knew not this secret. He asks what advancing age might have added to Oldham's "abundant store," and answers:—

> " It might (what nature never gives the young)
> Have taught the numbers of thy native tongue."

He once for all banishes the conceit which had so recently dominated verse through the example of Cowley, and he puts behind him (if he ever felt it) the temptation to torture language. He is equally free from that other error, conspicuous alike in Donne, in Cleveland, and in Oldham, which confounds violence with strength. He produces his effects through a wit too incisive to be called urbane, yet in which there is often an element of urbanity. It is this combination—smoothness of verse, lucidity of style, urbanity of manner

—which makes Dryden's satire so strikingly original. In English there had hitherto been nothing comparable to it.

All these qualities are seen in perfection in *Absalom and Achitophel* (1681). In the previous year a prose tract had appeared, which, as Scott noticed, apparently gave Dryden the hint. It was entitled *Absalom's Conspiracy: or, The Tragedy of Treason*. Dryden was now fifty years of age, and further development in his art was not to be expected; whatever changes there might be would probably be for the worse. It is the work of one who was an experienced man of the world as well as an accomplished man of letters. The man of the world is seen in the deft way in which Absalom's ambition is fed. He owns his ambition, but vanity whispers that it leans to virtue's side—"desire of greatness is a god-like sin." Achitophel feeds the flame, declaring that it is such qualities that become a throne:—

> " Not that your father's mildness I contemn;
> But manly force becomes the diadem."

Here Dryden has to face one of the greatest difficulties inherent in his theme. Achitophel must criticise the king; but royal ears are rarely willing to hear criticism, and possibly the royal memory might retain the fact that the words had been written by Dryden, though they were put into the mouth of Achitophel. The peril is evaded with masterly skill. The criticism of Charles is made into an imputation of virtues. He is mild, he is lavishly generous to his subjects. It is true he is charged with real vices as well; but they are vices he was proud of, not vices he was ashamed of. He thought the better of himself for his amours, and his courtiers thought the better of him too. Thus lightly did Dryden skim over the dangerous ice; thus skilfully did he frame criticism so as to be more welcome to the subject of it than panegyric. The man of the world is shown too in the whole series of portraits. Something more goes to the making of those portraits than mastery of style; something more even than long study of character for the purposes of the drama. These were indispensable; but indispensable likewise was the familiar knowledge which came from mingling for many years with the very men he drew, their friends, their equals in station, men who looked at life from the same angle and cherished the same ambitions. Only so could the perfect fitness of the phrase to the character have been assured.

Absalom and Achitophel is a political satire in a different way from *Hudibras*. Not only is the latter medieval and the former modern; but while religion predominates over politics in the latter, in the former politics predominate over religion. The difference is partly due to lapse of time: England was still interested in questions of sects, but the fervour of religion was gone or going. Partly it is due to difference of plan. Hudibras rides forth for adventures, and whatever he meets is the subject of the book. Dryden's poem has for its theme a definite political project, the plot to bar the succession of James and put in his place the Duke of Monmouth. Consequently the sects, which were Butler's main theme, fall into the background. But though no longer first they are still important. The Popish Plot is a thread in the fabric, and to that we owe the terrible portrait of Oates under the name of Corah. The "dreaming saints" are struck at, who employ their power "nothing to build, and all things to destroy." The doctrine of election provokes a jeer:—

" Born to be saved, even in their own despite,
  Because they cannot help believing right."

The multiplicity of sects is ridiculed in a characteristic couplet:—

" Gods they had tried of every shape and size
  That god-smiths could produce, or priests devise."

The scornful mention of priests is, as Johnson has noted (and as the satirists of Dryden's own day had noted too), characteristic of Dryden. The very first line is in this tone—" In pious times ere priestcraft did begin,"—and this dislike occasions the sweeping generalisation, "priests of all religions are the same." Either Dryden wrote the opening lines of the second part, or Nahum Tate would seem to have shared the dislike, for the first couplet refers to the time when "trade began, and priesthood grew a trade."

Important as all this is, however, the purely political element is more important still. The speeches of Achitophel and Absalom are political. They are full of reminiscences of past politics, as well as of schemes for the future. "They who possess the prince possess the laws" is clearly suggested by the experience of the Civil War; and the line "not only hating David, but the king," indicates with unsurpassed neatness that the conflict had been, and still was with many, a conflict of political theories, and not merely a question of persons. The theme is treated with greater amplitude in *The Medal*

(1682), which of all his writings throws the strangest light on Dryden's own political principles. It can hardly be doubted that he is expressing his own sentiment in the vigorous passage at the close, where he traces the advance from point to point along the path of revolution. Presbyter displaces noble; but his rigid yoke provokes the puny sects, and frogs and toads "croak to heaven for help from this devouring crane." Then "cut-throat sword" and "clamorous gown" quarrel about the spoils of war; there is universal division; property is attacked;

> " And our wild labours wearied into rest,
>   Reclined us on a rightful monarch's breast."

In all this Dryden has one eye on the past and another on the future. Such had been the course of events which led through the Commonwealth to the Restoration; such, he anticipates, will be the course if the nation is induced to follow Shaftesbury in a new career of revolution, and to tread the weary round once more. Dryden did not foresee the moderation of the new revolution towards which events were moving when he wrote. He believed there could be no half-way house between monarchy as he knew it and the rule of the multitude; and, like many of our greatest literary men from Shakespeare to Carlyle, he had a profound distrust of the multitude. In Shaftesbury he saw an unprincipled politician who, having tried in vain to seduce Charles to arbitrary government, had turned round, and now "drives down the current with a popular gale." This demagogue

> " Maintains the multitude can never err;
>   And sets the people in the papal chair."

But Dryden dreads the instability of the mob. "We loathe our manna, and we long for quails," is the singularly felicitous phrase by which he links on the fickleness of the English to the fickleness of the Israelitish crowd; and in lines of telling irony he reminds his readers that this same fickleness had characterised the Athenian populace as well:—

> " Athens no doubt did righteously decide
>   When Phocion and when Socrates were tried;
>   As righteously they did those dooms repent;
>   Still they were wise whatever way they went:
>   Crowds err not, though to both extremes they run;
>   To kill the father, and recall the son."

The supreme merit of *Absalom and Achitophel* is beyond doubt its superb gallery of portraits. Here Dryden has no competition to fear, except competition with himself. If Zimri has a rival, it is Achitophel; if Achitophel has one, it is Corah or Og. Pope, in his masterly portrait of Atticus, rose to the same level; but then Pope had Dryden to work upon; and in Dryden there is a vein of humour which Pope did not possess. The secret of success is Dryden's consummate mastery of style, his instinct for the apt word, his power to condense without *l*osing his pellucid clearness. The qualities of his verse are just the qualities which fitted him to lead the way towards a new prose, whose foremost characteristic was to be lucidity. There are gifts of the imagination with which he was ill endowed. The highest levels of poetry are beyond him; perhaps just because he sees so very clearly what he sees at all—sees it to the very end and all round. But the highest levels of poetry are not necessary to satire; for that Dryden had every endowment that man could possess. Perhaps one reservation ought to be made. Burns and Byron showed that a strain of pure poetry could be blended with satire, and that the result would be something not, perhaps, satirically more effective, but certainly more charming than satire undiluted and unmixed. In *The Holy Fair* we have a delightful picture of nature, in *Don Juan* passages of exquisite human tenderness, intermingled with the satire. Such was not Dryden's way; and he certainly could not have equalled the two later poets in this vein if he had tried.

There is more than mastery of word and phrase in Dryden's portraits. They are as remarkable for what they do not, as for what they do contain. First of his tribe, Dryden saw the superlative importance of moderation in detail as well as in tone. Not only is he never loud and violent, he is never exhaustive. He never tries to include everything; on the contrary, the inmost secret of his art is careful selection of that which is most effective. Not to tire the reader, but just to give enough to stimulate imagination—that is his aim. His satires are comparatively short, not merely because his style is condensed, but also because of this principle of selection. Herein he is the precise opposite of Butler; it is what most of all distinguishes the classical way from the medieval. The purple patch justifies itself in the eyes of the follower of the medieval style because it is purple; the classical writer considers how it harmonises with its surroundings: it must, in short, be something other than a patch, or be rejected. Though in *Absalom and Achitophel*, as in all works of human art, various passages are of varying quality, there are no patches. We rise naturally to the great character of Achitophel, and in the subtle speech which follows there is no such sinking as to jolt the mind of the reader. Naturally, again, we move to the character, even greater, of Zimri, and thence to the "monumental brass" of Corah, to the panegyric on Barzillai and the rest. The movement everywhere is like that of an accomplished skater on flawless ice.

Not the least admirable aspect of the art of Dryden is the variety he contrives to impart. It is one of the points in which he most strikingly differs from his predecessors, a reward accruing to him from the care with which he holds himself in. The older satirists know only the superlative degree; their instruments are the biggest drum and the loudest trumpet. Dryden is just the opposite of his own Zimri:—

> " So over violent, or over civil,
>   That every man with him was God or devil."

The only character of Dryden's painting which suggests the devil is Corah. There is something to admire in Achitophel:—

> " A fiery soul, which, working out its way,
>   Fretted the pigmy body to decay,
>   And o'er inform'd the tenement of clay."

The satirist has even so much of the spirit of justice that he does not withhold positive praise when he feels positive praise to be due. While denouncing Shaftesbury the politician, with a sense of fairness, for which it would be difficult to find any precedent except in Brome, he ungrudgingly praises Shaftesbury the judge:—

> " Yet fame deserv'd no enemy can grudge;
>   The statesman we abhor, but praise the judge.
>   In Israel's courts ne'er sat an Abethin
>   With more discerning eyes, or hands more clean,
>   Unbribed, unsought, the wretched to redress;
>   Swift of dispatch, and easy of access."

Dryden the artist reaped a reward from the fairness of Dryden the man; for this recognition of the good along with the bad gives to his work the added grace of variety. No effort to be fair was needed when he proceeded to write panegyrics on Ormond as Barzillai,

Halifax as Jotham, and Sir Edward Seymour as Amiel; but the presence of these laudatory passages contributes yet more to the variety of the poem.

Masterly as it is, *Absalom and Achitophel* is yet marred by one great flaw—its end. When the speech of David, by no means worthy of the preceding ones of Achitophel and Absalom, closes, and there is nothing to follow, we suddenly become conscious of the fact that from beginning to end there is no action. There are characters, and some of them speak; but nothing is done. Jove nods, Olympus trembles, the cloudy scene fades away. It has all been *vox et praeterea nihil*. Neither is the flaw mended in Part II.; for that is not really a continuation of Part I., but rather an independent piece, and moreover, one of which, so far as we know, not much more than one-sixth part is by Dryden. The characters of Doeg and Og are his—Doeg, who

> " Spurr'd boldly on, and dash'd through thick and thin,
> Through sense and nonsense, never out nor in ";

and Og, of whom "every inch that is not fool, is rogue." In these portraits Dryden took his revenge upon Elkanah Settle and Shadwell. The bulk of the second part, however, is by Nahum Tate (1652–1715), with what measure of help from Dryden it is impossible to determine. Unless Dryden himself did a good deal to it, Tate must be admitted to have acquitted himself very well, and to have justified the choice of Dryden, if it be true that he suggested the task to Tate, when he declined himself to undertake a second part. Though the second part is markedly inferior to the first, it has no small merit even in the passages which are not by Dryden, and the style of the original is far more successfully imitated than it is by those who, in the interval between the first part and the second, attacked Dryden with his own weapon.

Before the appearance of the second part, Dryden had followed up his great satire with another, *The Medal: A Satire against Sedition*. The subject was once more Shaftesbury, in whose honour a medal had been struck to celebrate his escape from a charge of treason. The satire which he wrote upon the popular hero Dryden in a prose epistle dedicated to the Whigs. The superiority of *Absalom and Achitophel* has led to an undue neglect of *The Medal*, which would have made the reputation of any satirist before

Dryden. Something has been said already about the light it throws upon the political views of Dryden. It throws a light no less interesting upon his attitude towards the sects in religion. He is especially severe upon their hypocrisy and their gloom. Their hypocrisy he had already touched upon in *Absalom and Achitophel*, in the character of Shimei, who made his wealth

> " By the most ready way
> Among the Jews, which was to cheat and pray."

In *The Medal* he further develops the theme of that "hypocritic zeal" which "allows no sins but those it can conceal." With such hypocrisy Shaftesbury himself is charged:—

> " He cast himself into the saint-like mould;
> Groan'd, sigh'd, and pray'd, while godliness was gain,
> The loudest bagpipe of the squeaking train."

Dryden's prologue to Southerne's play *The Loyal Prince* extends the charge to the whole Whig party. He has small faith in the sincerity of "the fawning Whig petitions":—

> " Five praying saints are by an act allow'd;
> But not the whole church-militant in crowd.
> Yet, should Heaven all the true petitions drain
> Of Presbyterians who would kings maintain,
> Of forty thousand scarce five would remain."

As to the gloom of the sectaries, it is seen even in their God and their heaven; for their God is a tyrant, and

> " The heaven their priesthood paints
> A conventicle of gloomy sullen saints;
> A heaven like Bedlam, slovenly and sad,
> Foredoom'd for souls, with false religion mad."

It is hardly necessary to suppose, as Todd does, that Dryden borrowed from *The Geneva Ballad* (1674), but that spirited piece, which he quotes, deserves to be remembered for its own merits. The fanatical preacher is skilfully ridiculed:—

> " To draw in proselytes like bees,
>   With pleasing twang he tones his prose,
> He gives his handkerchief a squeeze,
>   And draws John Calvin through his nose."

The political satirist seldom goes long unanswered. When Dryden attacked Shaftesbury, that statesman was making a vigorous effort to attain power, and the occasion which called forth *The Medal* shows how strong was the support he enjoyed among the people. It is true that he was soon compelled to take refuge in Holland; but meanwhile his partisans, however unwelcome they might be at Court, had no reason to shrink from speaking out. Unfortunately for Shaftesbury, so far as the literary war was concerned, there was but one Dryden in the country. Few remember, and none need lament that they have forgotten, if they ever knew, the answers to *Absalom and Achitophel* and *The Medal* by Elkanah Settle, Samuel Pordage and Thomas Shadwell. Nothing more strikingly demonstrates the greatness of Dryden than the dreary flatness here and the unmannerly virulence there of these imitations—in the original, every line memorable; in the imitations, something that constantly sounds like their prototype, yet for ever refuses to give up any meaning worth finding. Their productions are memorable only for the terrific castigation they provoked. Yet such is the uncertainty of contemporary opinion, or, more probably, the blinding influence of party prejudice, that both *Absalom Senior, or Achitophel Transposed*, Settle's answer to Dryden's earlier poem, and *The Medal Revers'd*, which was long attributed to him, but was really the work of Pordage, were by many thought to be equal or nearly equal to their originals. Settle received payment in full in the character of Doeg. Shadwell sat for the companion picture of Og. But with respect to him Dryden was not content to let the matter rest here. The malignity of Shadwell's *The Medal of John Bayes* caused Dryden to write a special satire on this literary sinner alone—*MacFlecnoe* (1682), the most severe of all personal satires in English—unless it be, perhaps, *Holy Willie's Prayer* or *The Vision of Judgment*.

In this almost miraculously witty piece Dryden breaks what is for him fresh ground: it is no longer political but literary satire. He had indeed touched this in passing — for example, in the prologue to his own *Œdipus* (1679); but no substantive work had hitherto been devoted to it. The poem is based upon the happy conception of an Empire of Dulness. What it was that induced Dryden to fix upon the obscure Irish writer Richard Flecnoe as the reigning monarch of that empire is unknown, and it seems impossible to advance any better conjecture than that Flecnoe may have been brought to his mind by a commonplace satire of

Marvell's, *Flecnoe, an English Priest at Rome*. That piece however could suggest no more than the name. The essential conception of Flecnoe as a monarch called to empire young, and reigning during a long life "through all the realms of Nonsense, absolute," is Dryden's own. The happy application of it gives an admirable setting to the satire on Shadwell. Pope, as is well known, borrowed the idea in *The Dunciad*; and Johnson seems to have thought that he had improved it by making it more extensive and more diversified in incidents. Rarely as Johnson went astray in his criticisms on the poets of that period, it is difficult to agree with him here. To the modern reader *MacFlecnoe* seems as nearly perfect in its kind as a poem can be, largely because the plan is not made too extensive, nor the incidents too diversified. The average reader constantly fails to grasp the point in *The Dunciad* without the aid of a commentary. He probably knows as little about Shadwell as about the minor Dunces; but all that is essential he can learn from Dryden himself. Nothing but intelligence is necessary to make *MacFlecnoe* a source of the keenest enjoyment. The plan reacted upon the writer. *MacFlecnoe* has been referred to above as one of the most severe of personal satires. So unquestionably it must have seemed to the victim. But Dryden sank the greater part of his rancour in the humour of the conception, and the reader enjoys the fun without thinking much of its application to an individual. He laughs in pure amusement, and only with an effort realises what it meant to the subject of the satire.

The development is masterly, from the opening in which the aged monarch is represented pondering

> " Which of all his sons was fit
> To reign, and make immortal war with wit,"

down to the closing speech, in which he enjoins the supreme dullard to "trust nature, do not labour to be dull," and to select as most suitable for his gifts "some peaceful province in Acrostic land." Shadwell is marked out for the succession by supremacy of endowment, both intellectual and physical. He alone is the perfect image of his father:—

> " The rest to some faint meaning make pretence,
> But Shadwell never deviates into sense."

And the body is worthy of the mind:—

> " His goodly fabric fills the eye,
> And seems design'd for thoughtless majesty;
> Thoughtless as monarch oaks, that shade the plain
> And, spread in solemn state, supinely reign.
> Heywood and Shirley were but types of thee,
> Thou last great prophet of tautology."

There is a notable difference in tone between this passage and the corresponding one in the character of Og, which appeared in the second part of *Absalom and Achitophel* only a few weeks after the publication of *MacFlecnoe*. Og is a tun, "round as a globe, and liquor'd every chink," against which the readers are warned to stop their noses. The description contains one of the most loathsomely coarse expressions to which Dryden ever sank. In *MacFlecnoe*, instead of virulence we have good-natured contempt. There is no more striking example of the humanising influence which humour exercises upon wit. For the two qualities are mingled in *MacFlecnoe*, while the character of Og is destitute of humour.

The allegorical accompaniments of Shadwell befit the character of his kingdom. His brows are graced by thick fogs instead of glories, "and lambent dulness play'd around his face." His oath is "ne'er to have peace with wit, nor truce with sense." Poppies are spread over his temples; and his reign is inaugurated with the omen of "twelve reverend owls," instead of the vultures which presaged the rule of Romulus. Finally,

> " The sire then shook the honours of his head,
> And from his brows damps of oblivion shed
> Full on the filial dulness."

The years 1681 and 1682 saw the culmination of Dryden's genius. The latter was especially fruitful, for it produced not only *The Medal, MacFlecnoe*, and the second part of *Absalom and Achitophel*, but *Religio Laici* as well. Neither this poem nor its successor *The Hind and the Panther* (1687), written after Dryden had changed his faith, can be classed without reserve as a satire; but both are in part satirical. And they exposed Dryden himself to keen and piercing satire. In *The Hind and the Panther* he used the beast-fable in an indefensible way, and exposed himself to the ridicule of Montague and Prior in *The Country Mouse and the City Mouse*; and his conversion from Protestantism to Romanism, at a time when the latter was in favour at Court, laid him open to suspicion as to his sincerity. This suspicion is expressed in a sharp satire entitled *Ecebolius Britannicus,* which is quoted by Todd:—

> " Since religions vary like the wind,
> Who would to one be *cursedly confin'd*?
> He that can servilely *creep after one*
> Is safe, but *ne'er shall reach* promotion."

The two poems show that, in whatever else Dryden might change, his dislike of the sectaries was permanent and unchangeable. In *Religio Laici* the distaste of the scholar for "the gifted Brother" is manifest. The demand that the laity should have access to the Bible leads to excess:—

> " The tender page with horny fists was gall'd;
> And he was gifted most that loudest bawl'd:
> The spirit gave the doctoral degree:
> And every member of a company
> Was of his trade, and of the Bible, free."

Study and pains are neglected; texts are explained by fasting and prayer; there is great zeal and little thought; crowds buzz and swarm about "the sacred viands"; and the fly-blown text turns to maggots what was meant for food. The doctrine of *Religio Laici* is that the middle way is best:—

> " Neither so rich a treasure to forego,
> Nor proudly seek beyond our power to know."

The spirit in which he satirises the sectaries in *The Hind and the Panther* is no less bitter. He detests the Independent bear and the Baptist boar, but more than either he hates the Presbyterian wolf:—

> " More haughty than the rest, the wolfish race
> Appear with belly gaunt, and famish'd face:
> Never was so deform'd a beast of grace.
> His ragged tail betwixt his legs he wears,
> Close clap'd for shame; but his rough crest he rears,
> And pricks up his predestinating ears."

So loathsome is he that the poet hesitates to charge the Deity with creating him; perhaps he was never made, but descended from some curs run wild.

The two poems differ widely with respect to the Church of Rome, *Religio Laici* being an argument in defence of the Anglican Church against both the extreme represented by Rome and the opposite extreme of Geneva; while *The Hind and the Panther* finds pure

Christianity in Rome only. In the former the Romish clergy are charged with self-seeking. In the Dark Ages they take up "a gainful trade":—

> " Then Mother Church did mightily prevail:
> She parcell'd out the Bible by retail:
> But still expounded what she sold or gave,
> To keep it in her power to damn or save.
> Scripture was scarce, and, as the market went,
> Poor laymen took salvation on content;
> As needy men take money good or bad;
> God's word they had not, but the priests' they had."

In *The Hind and the Panther* it is the sectaries who are charged with greed. England has become not only a breeding-ground for them at home, but a refuge for such as have been driven from their own homes on the Continent. The Hind asks the Panther to consider the motives of these foreign refugees:—

> " Think you your new French proselytes are come
> To starve abroad, because they starved at home?
> Your benefices twinkled from afar;
> They found the new Messiah by the star:
> These Swisses fight on any side for pay,
> And 'tis the living that conforms, not they."

If justification is needed for thus making the living conform rather than the incumbent, no doubt it can be found in the doctrine of Faith rather than Works:—

> " A lively faith will bear aloft the mind,
> And leave the baggage of good works behind."

The satire in these two poems is naturally confined in the main to questions of religion. But these questions reach out into everything else. Thus *Religio Laici* opens with an interesting satire on the schools of philosophy, the irreconcilable differences between which indicate how we must regard them. One school finds the *summum bonum* in Content, another in Virtue, a third in Pleasure:—

> " Thus anxious thoughts in endless circles roll,
> Without a centre where to fix the soul."

"The Deist thinks he stands on firmer ground"; but he has really borrowed unconsciously from revelation. The conclusion is that philosophy alone is insufficient. And just as on the one hand the questions at issue between sects may be broadened out into the universal questions of philosophy, so on the other they may be narrowed to an individual. Influenced, no doubt, by the sense he must have had of his special gift for the satiric character, Dryden does this in the apologues of the Swallow and the Pigeon and Buzzard in the third part of *The Hind and the Panther*; and inevitably he puts the best work into the latter, which conveys the criticism of the Hind. The character of the Buzzard (Bishop Burnet), though not quite equal to the characters in *Absalom and Achitophel*, deserves to be better known than it is:—

> " Prompt to assail, and careless of defence,
> Invulnerable in his impudence,
> He dares the world; and eager of a name,
> He thrusts about, and justles into fame.
> Frontless, and satire-proof, he scours the streets,
> And runs an Indian-muck at all he meets.
> So fond of loud report, that not to miss
> Of being known (his last and utmost bliss)
> He rather would be known for what he is."

The work of Dryden fixed for several generations the course of English satire. After its masterly handling in *Absalom and Achitophel* there could be no doubt as to the fitness of the heroic couplet as the vehicle, and the consummate sketches of character set an example which could not fail to be useful as long as political controversy endured.

CHAPTER IX

POPE

THE true successor to Dryden in the line of satirical verse was not
Thomas Shadwell, nor Elkanah Settle, nor Samuel Pordage, nor
Matthew Prior, nor any other of the writers who in Dryden's own
day imitated the poet and satirised the satirist; it was Alexander
Pope (1688–1744). For the ripe fruit of Dryden's work we must
look on to *The Dunciad* (1728), which, though neither Pope's
earliest nor his greatest satire, is that in which Dryden's influence
is most conspicuous—so conspicuous indeed that Pope seems to
have been a little uneasy as to his debt to *MacFlecnoe*. His acknowledgment is hardly adequate; for in plan *The Dunciad* is just
MacFlecnoe broadened out in scope from the individual to the
class. From the first, it is true, Pope's workmanship bears the
stamp of Dryden. He has himself singled out Waller and Dryden as
the two predecessors who had imparted smoothness, and then
variety, fulness of sound, majesty and energy to the verse which
he after them adopted as his chief instrument. But he used it
first to depict pastoral scenes, for which he cared little and of which
his knowledge was only superficial; next he used it as the vehicle
for critical principles which would have been more naturally
expressed in prose; and when, in 1712, he produced his earliest
satire, *The Rape of the Lock*, it was of a type for which there was
no model in Dryden. This "most exquisite specimen of filigree
work," as Hazlitt called it, "the most airy, the most ingenious,
the most delightful" of all Pope's compositions, as Johnson pronounced it to be, belongs to the class of mock-heroics, and among
pieces of that description we must look for its ancestry. Technically,
MacFlecnoe is of this class too, but in spirit it is simply a personal
satire. *Hudibras* belongs to another species of the genus, as do the
works of all the obscure imitators of Scarron and of Butler. But
the more immediate progenitor of *The Rape* was Boileau, who, in
turn, had borrowed from the Italian.

Before Pope however one or two other English writers had borrowed hints from *Lutrin*. One was Sir Samuel Garth (1661–1719), the amiable physician whose personal charm won him the praises of both parties in an age when party was apt to blind the keenest eyes to any merit shown on the opposite side. *The Dispensary* (1699) is no longer read, and, while it is still praised for its versification, rarely receives any other sort of commendation. It certainly did not deserve the panegyrics of contemporaries; but perhaps the reaction has gone a little too far the other way. We care nothing now about the quarrel between the physicians and the apothecaries, which is Garth's theme. The poem is much too long and becomes wearisome, yet it seems rather to cease than to end. The structure is extremely loose, and only a few passages have real merit. But such passages exist. There is more than a hint of Pope in the criticism of Sir Richard Blackmore:—

> " Dare not, for the future, once rehearse
> The dissonance of such untuneful verse;
> But in your lines let energy be found,
> And learn to rise in sense and sink in sound.
> Harsh words, though pertinent, uncouth appear;
> None please the fancy, who offend the ear."

And the character of Urim (Atterbury) is of a merit rare indeed until Dryden showed the way, and by no means common even after Dryden:—

> " Urim was civil, and not void of sense,
> Had humour, and a courteous confidence:
> So spruce he moves, so gracefully he cocks,
> The hallow'd rose declares him orthodox:
> He pass'd his easy hours, instead of prayer,
> In madrigals, and phillysing the fair;
> Constant at feasts, and each decorum knew,
> And, soon as the dessert appear'd, withdrew;
> Always obliging, and without offence,
> And fancy'd, for his gay impertinence."

Soon after Garth, John Philips (1676–1709) essayed the mock-heroic in a different vein and measure. He was throughout, both in serious verse and in burlesque, an imitator of Milton, and seems to have been the first poet after him to write blank verse, at least on a considerable scale. He did so both in a serious spirit and in the spirit of parody, and his contemporaries took him in either case according to his own intention. To the modern reader, however, it appears that while *The Splendid Shilling* (1701) is a very good intentional burlesque of Milton, *Blenheim* is a no less amusing burlesque written in all solemnity.

The Splendid Shilling is decisively what it sets out to be—a burlesque; not a burlesque in spite of the poet, or with consent of only half his mind. The travesty of the epic style is entertaining. The poet labouring with eternal drought and singing

> " Of groves and myrtle shades,
> Or desperate lady near a purling stream,
> Or lover pendent on a willow tree ";

and his galligaskins subdued by time "(what will not time subdue !)," are legitimate objects of raillery. The debtor, the dun and the catch-pole are material suitable for comic treatment, and the similes in which the catchpole is compared to the cat and the spider are an excellent burlesque of the epic simile. As he lies hid, watching for the debtor,

> " So (poets sing)
> Grimalkin, to domestic vermin sworn
> An everlasting foe, with watchful eye
> Lies nightly brooding o'er a chinky gap,
> Protruding her fell claws, to thoughtless mice
> Sure ruin."

Such were the predecessors of Pope in the mock-heroic style. *The Rape of the Lock*, even in its original form, left them far behind; but that itself was greatly surpassed by the revised version published in 1714, in which the poem is expanded to more than twice its original length, and, in particular, the whole delightful machinery of the sylphs and the gnomes is added. By inexhaustible resource and scintillating wit Pope raises the mock-heroic to another plane. The piece sparkles in every line. The touch is never too heavy, an air of gay good humour is preserved throughout. The nicest proportion is kept. On a mere lock of hair the powers of air, as well as of earth, are centred. But the sylphs are no more too great for their task than are Milton's archangels for theirs. They preside over fashions, and

> " Oft, in dreams, invention we bestow,
> To change a flounce, or add a furbelow."

They are the spirits of coquettes, and in a new generation reimpose the vanities they themselves have felt of old:—

> " With varying vanities, from ev'ry part,
> They shift the moving toyshop of their heart;
> Where wigs with wigs, with sword-knots sword-knots strive,
> Beaux banish beaux, and coaches coaches drive."

She over whom they preside is worthy of such spirits. Her eyes first open on a *billet-doux*. She adores the cosmetic powers and bends to the heavenly image in the glass; while "the inferior priestess"

" Trembling begins the sacred rites of Pride."

The objects that load the toilet-table make an exquisitely suggestive medley — "puffs, powders, patches, bibles, *billets-doux*." Pope is peculiarly skilful in thus mingling the great with the trivial. The scream when the lock is severed is as loud as the shrieks which rend the skies "when husbands, or when lapdogs breathe their last." But the most perfect example is the passage in which Ariel explains to the other sylphs that danger threatens the lady, while it remains doubtful

" Whether the nymph shall break Diana's law,
Or some frail china jar receive a flaw;
Or stain her honour, or her new brocade;
Forget her prayers, or miss a masquerade;
Or lose her heart, or necklace, at a ball;
Or whether Heaven has doom'd that Shock must fall."

Raillery of fashions and of the vanities of beaux and belles is the staple of *The Rape of the Lock*, but it is not quite the whole. Pope knew well the value of variety. In the midst of banter he rises to pure poetic beauty in the line, "and beauty draws us with a single hair." He strikes a keen stroke in passing in the couplet,

" The hungry judges soon the sentence sign,
And wretches hang that jury-men may dine."

There is excellent burlesque of the martial style in the description of the combat; and there is the essence of many sermons in the passage which asserts the need of good sense to "preserve what beauty gains":—

" Oh! if to dance all night, and dress all day,
Charm'd the small-pox, or chas'd old age away;
Who would not scorn what housewife's cares produce,
Or who would learn one earthly thing of use?
To patch, nay ogle, might become a saint,
Nor could it sure be such a sin to paint.
But since, alas! frail beauty must decay;
Curl'd or uncurl'd, since locks will turn to grey;
Since painted, or not painted, all must fade,
And she who scorns a man, must die a maid;
What then remains but well our pow'r to use,
And keep good-humour still whate'er we lose?"

The Rape of the Lock was the first notable satire of Pope, but its brilliant success gave assurance that it would not be the last. He had moreover already formed a connexion with Swift which could not fail to influence him in the same direction; and the two had collaborated in a volume of *Miscellanies* (1711). Nevertheless, Pope was so occupied with other work, in particular his translation of Homer and his edition of Shakespeare, that fourteen years passed without his writing anything more than incidental satire. But the satire, though incidental and in itself insignificant, helped to make the enmities which ultimately supplied material for *The Dunciad*. From that date onwards Pope devoted himself to original work, or to imitations which are largely original; and much of that work belongs to the domain of satire. To that domain belong, in particular, the *Satires and Epistles of Horace Imitated*, which may vie with *The Rape of the Lock* for the first place among Pope's works, and which, paradoxical as it seems to say so, are also among the most original. The separate poems which compose the collection were published between the years 1733 and 1738. In an intermediate position stands the collection called *Moral Essays* (1731–35): it mingles with satire a strain of the pure didacticism of the *Essay on Man*, which appeared during the years when Pope was composing the *Moral Essays*.

Of all the satires of Pope, *The Dunciad* is that which has worn worst; and the reason is not far to seek. It is the least dignified, for it is the least faithful to the poet's own higher conception of satire. In the advertisement to the epistle to Mr. Fortescue (the earliest of the imitations of Horace) he draws a broad line of distinction between the satirist and the libeller: "There is not in the world a greater error than that which fools are so apt to fall into, and knaves with good reason to encourage, the mistaking a satirist for a libeller; whereas to a true satirist nothing is so odious as a libeller, for the same reason as to a man truly virtuous nothing is so hateful as a hypocrite." In the text of the epistle the same doctrine is reiterated. It is the poet's pride to

> " Dash the proud gamester in his gilded car;
> Bare the mean heart that lurks beneath a star."

"Unplac'd, unpension'd, no man's heir or slave," he stands in a position of greater independence and of less danger than the pensioned Boileau or the laureate Dryden, and it is all the more incumbent upon him to lash vice and to foster virtue. This is the aim of his satire.

> " Yes, while I live, no rich or noble knave
> Shall walk the world, in credit, to his grave.
> To virtue only and her friends a friend,
> The world beside may murmur, or commend."

The same doctrine is reiterated in the epistle to Augustus, where satire is described as the mean between libel and flattery, which "heals with morals what it hurts with wit."

There were two Popes; one who occasionally bares his own heart, as in the fine compliment to Arbuthnot near the beginning of the epistle addressed to him, and in the pathetic lines about his own parents at the end of the same piece; and another in whom spite and malignity were the dominant qualities. Unfortunately it is the latter Pope who, on the whole, has the mastery in *The Dunciad*. A poem whose aim is to lash and scarify scores of the insignificant and dull—for such, according to Pope, they are—has clearly no very lofty moral aim. Here are no gilded cars, no stars decking the mean breast. On the contrary, the poet insists upon the poverty of his victims. Poetry and Poverty lodge in the same cave, and Poetic Justice weighs in her scale "solid pudding against empty praise." But Pope's sin has brought its own punishment: the fact that its strictures are essentially true has sapped the vitality of *The Dunciad*. Nobody cares any longer about the obscure authors whom Pope pillories. Not that they are all as obscure as he pretends. Defoe may not unreasonably be ranked in a class as high as Pope's own; and Theobald's real offence was not that he lacked genius, but that he had proved himself a better Shakespearean scholar and commentator than the satirist.

Pope however was far too skilful to make so long a poem merely on dullards, and to furnish no relief. He is not for ever girding at Blackmore or Settle or Cibber: he passes from the instance to the quality it illustrates. With the wide realms of Dulness he contrasts the meagre empire of Science, and shows the lamentable ease and speed with which it is overrun and conquered by the offspring of Chaos and old Night:—

> " See, the bold Ostrogoths on Latium fall;
> See, the fierce Visigoths on Spain and Gaul!
> See, where the morning gilds the palmy shore
> (The soil that arts and infant letters bore)

> His conqu'ring tribes th' Arabian prophet draws,
> And saving Ignorance enthrones by laws.
> See Christians, Jews, one heavy sabbath keep,
> And all the Western world believe and sleep."

Education too is ridiculed. The Geniuses of the schools aid Dulness by confining their teaching to words; and the result of this teaching is seen when the pupil has made the grand tour and

> " Dropt the dull lumber of the Latin store,
> Spoil'd his own language, and acquir'd no more;
> All classic learning lost on classic ground;
> And last turn'd air, the echo of a sound."

The trivialities and follies of learning are a favourite subject with Pope, and he recurs to them once and again:—

> " There, dim in clouds, the poring scholiast mark,
> Wits, who, like owls, see only in the dark,
> A lumberhouse of books in ev'ry head,
> For ever reading, never to be read."

In the same spirit he lashes the critics in the epistle to Arbuthnot:—

> " Pains, reading, study, are their just pretence,
> And all they want is spirit, taste, and sense.
> Commas and points they set exactly right,
> And 'twere a sin to rob them of their mite."

Carlyle himself had not a more supreme contempt for the literary Dryasdust. Triviality of this sort is the badge of all the tribe of Dulness, the aim and end of every son of the great Empress. To this they reduce the greatest victories won by character and by intellect:—

> " From priest-craft happily set free,
> Lo! ev'ry finish'd son returns to thee:
> First slave to words, then vassal to a name,
> Then dupe to party; child and man the same:
> Bounded by nature, narrow'd still by art,
> A trifling head, and a contracted heart."

Even in *The Dunciad* Pope once at least rises to a height where we almost forget the satire in the grandeur of the rhetoric. The passage at the close, describing the coming of Night and Chaos, is extremely fine:—

> " She comes! she comes! the sable throne behold
> Of Night primeval, and of Chaos old!
> Before her, fancy's gilded clouds decay,
> And all its varying rainbows die away.
> Wit shoots in vain its momentary fires,
> The meteor drops, and in a flash expires."

But in spite of the relief furnished by this passage and by passages of general utility, such as the ridicule of the follies of learning, the absurdities of the stage and the fulsome flattery of dedications, in spite even of the omnipresent wit, *The Dunciad* is not a poem which it is any longer possible to read either with much pleasure or with much profit.

The case is very different with the two groups of satires called *Moral Essays* and *Satires and Epistles*. The latter are Pope's masterpiece in one style, as *The Rape of the Lock* is in another. The former are, as has already been said, partly didactic; but the didacticism is close akin to satire. The principal themes are the characters of men and of women, and the use of riches. In the essay which deals with the first theme, the doctrine of the ruling passion is treated in the person of Wharton in a thoroughly satirical spirit; and it is the satirist who points out how the virtues vary in value with the rank of those who have them:—

> " 'Tis from high life high characters are drawn;
> A saint in crape is twice a saint in lawn;
> A judge is just, a chancellor juster still;
> A gownsman, learn'd; a bishop, what you will:
> Wise, if a minister; but, if a king,
> More wise, more learn'd, more just, more ev'ry thing.
> Court-virtues bear, like gems, the highest rate,
> Born where Heav'n's influence scarce can penetrate:
> In life's low vale the soil the virtues like,
> They please as beauties, here as wonders strike."

So too the picture of the moral Catius is drawn satirically. He cannot endure a knave—except at dinner, when, naturally, he prefers "a rogue with ven'son to a saint without."

Satirical portraits are a conspicuous feature of Pope's later writings. Specimens are to be found from the beginning; Sir Plume is a case in point. So is the hero Bays in *The Dunciad.* But that poem yields fewer than might be expected, the reason being that Pope's victims are usually too petty for more than a passing satiric stroke. When, however, he wrote the *Moral Essays* and the *Satires and Epistles,* and probably long before, Pope was fully conscious that his type of mind was peculiarly fitted for the satiric portrait. He had attained mastery in the art at least as early as 1716; for in that year, according to Spence, the character of Atticus, the most skilful of them all, was written. In the *Moral Essays* he drew Timon and Atossa as well as Wharton; in the *Satires and Epistles* Bufo as well as Atticus. In these portraits there is less breadth and force than in those with which Dryden enriched *Absalom and Achitophel,* but there is greater neatness. They show very precisely both the gifts and the limitations of Pope. Bays of *The Dunciad* is less familiarly known than the rest, but this portrait exhibits the same qualities. Bays

> " Gnaw'd his pen, then dash'd it on the ground,
> Sinking from thought to thought, a vast profound!
> Plung'd for his sense, but found no bottom there,
> Yet wrote and flounder'd on, in mere despair.
> Round him much embryo, much abortion lay,
> Much future ode, and abdicated play;
> Nonsense precipitate, like running lead,
> That slipp'd through cracks and zig-zags of the head;
> All that on Folly Frenzy could beget,
> Fruits of dull heat and sooterkins of wit."

If Bufo was Charles Montagu, Earl of Halifax, and it seems nearly certain that he was, then in this character Pope has paid back a large part of his debt to Dryden by avenging him for the ridicule poured upon him in *The Country Mouse and the City Mouse.* The justice of the portrait has been challenged, and readers of history will hardly take the satirist literally. But the skill of the satire is indubitable. And Pope's fellow-satirist Swift is in agreement with him. He had already charged Halifax with meanness as the "Mæcenas of the nation"; for he

> " For poets open table kept
> But ne'er considered where they slept;
> Himself as rich as fifty Jews,
> Was easy though they wanted shoes."

Perhaps the character looks less black than the satirist meant it to be. There must be a limit to the bounty even of a rich man, and the accuser admits that the English Mæcenas kept open-table. This, after all, is something. Pope's lash cuts deeper. A Mæcenas who has no relations with Horace needs defence; and defence becomes all the more difficult if he shows interest in the funeral of the man whom he has neglected during his life. Such is the position of Montague in relation to Dryden, and Pope with his unerring skill probes the weak point:—

> " Dryden alone (what wonder?) came not nigh,
> Dryden alone escap'd this judging eye:
> But still the great have kindness in reserve,
> He help'd to bury whom he help'd to starve."

The second essay is on a theme for his treatment of which Pope

has incurred severe censure—the characters of women. The censure
has been exaggerated. Pope clearly had no high opinion of the
characters of women, and in some respects he is highly reprehensible.
His treatment of the character of Lady Mary Wortley Montagu
under the name of Sappho is vile and unmanly. It goes beyond the
limit of legitimate satire, and by its excess defeats its own end.
Nowhere else does that spite which unfortunately was an ingredient in Pope's character show so loathsome. It is also clear that
many of his general dicta are false. When we read that " most
women have no characters at all," or that " every woman is at
heart a rake," we know that it is untrue. But it is surely idle to
become indignant over lines like these; the proper charge to bring
against them is that they are artistically poor. The satirist's censure
should be at least plausible. As to the general question, Pope, after
all, had a right to his opinion; and in his case it has been hardly
sufficiently remembered that the satirist's trade is censure. He is
there not to say smooth things, but to expose defects. The character
of Atossa, however severe, is legitimate satire. So is that of Cloe.
There is no better illustration in literature of "the little less, and
what worlds away." Cloe wants just one thing—a heart:—

> " She speaks, behaves, and acts just as she ought,
> But never, never, reach'd one gen'rous thought.
> Virtue she finds too painful an endeavour,
> Content to dwell in decencies for ever."

Fine as are the *Moral Essays*, the *Satires and Epistles* are still
richer. Bolingbroke's suggestion, which led immediately to the
production of the epistle to Mr. Fortescue, and ultimately to the
whole group of the imitations of Horace, was a singularly happy
one. Horace is the most imitable of great poets, because his easy
wisdom is cosmopolitan. Pope was able, by a sort of free para-
phrase, to run into the mould of the Roman poet the very thoughts
of his own heart. He addresses his epistles to personal friends, and
the satire is relieved and humanised by the expression of a friendship which is very warm and sincere. Pope's admiration of his
friend leads him in the beautiful epistle addressed to Bolingbroke
to paint the picture of the ideal man:—

> " Great without title, without fortune bless'd;
> Rich ev'n when plunder'd, honour'd while oppress'd;
> Lov'd without youth, and follow'd without pow'r;
> At home, tho' exil'd; free, tho' in the Tower;

> In short, that reas'ning, high, immortal thing,
> Just less than Jove, and much above a king;
> Nay, half in heav'n, except (what's mighty odd)
> A fit of vapours clouds this demy-god!"

There is a similar ring of true feeling in the epistle to Mr. Murray, afterwards Lord Mansfield.

Already in the *Essay on Criticism* Pope had used the materials of Horace as critic. He does so again in the epistle to Augustus; and here the imitation is enriched with a vein of irony which is not to be found in the epistle of Horace. It was a daring venture to apply to George II. the phrases which the Roman poet thought appropriate to Augustus. But Pope had no high opinion of either the character or the intelligence of the courtier, nor any better opinion of the Hanoverian sovereign whom the courtier fawned upon. He trusted to the stupidity of the king and to his known dislike of poetry, to which sarcastic reference is made in the course of the epistle. His view of the Court as a whole may be inferred from a telling passage on the courtiers in the first dialogue of the epilogue:—

> " Silent and soft, as saints remov'd to heav'n,
> All ties dissolv'd, and ev'ry sin forgiv'n,
> These may some gentle ministerial wing
> Receive, and place for ever near a king!
> There, where no passion, pride, or shame transport,
> Lull'd with the sweet nepenthe of a court;
> There, where no fathers', brothers', friends' disgrace
> Once break their rest, or stir them from their place:
> But past the sense of human miseries,
> All tears are wip'd for ever from all eyes;
> No cheek is known to blush, no heart to throb,
> Save when they lose a pension, or a job."

To a court inspired by such ambitions and headed by one of the stupidest of English sovereigns, Pope addressed the reflexions which Horace had offered to one of the ablest emperors in history. The daring irony of the address to the English Augustus is astonishing even now:—

> " Great friend of liberty! in kings a name
> Above all Greek, above all Roman fame:
> Whose word is truth, as sacred and rever'd,
> As heav'n's own oracles from altars heard.
> Wonder of kings! like whom, to mortal eyes
> None e'er has risen, and none e'er shall rise."

But irony is a weapon difficult to parry. King George could hardly complain without proclaiming how very far he was from meriting the pretended praise. The illiteracy of the king makes peculiarly

ludicrous the address to him of the argument, deftly expressed,
against valuing books merely by their age. What was it to him that
"Sidney's verse halts ill on Roman feet," or that Milton now soars
like an eagle into the empyrean, and now serpent-like sweeps the
ground? Pope's argument gains piquancy from the incongruity,
and the subject was one in which he as well as Horace had a keen
and personal interest. The author of the day has, through all ages,
had to struggle against the stupidity and the intellectual supine-
ness which prefer the reputation already made:—

> " Authors, like coins, grow dear as they grow old;
> It is the rust we value, not the gold."

Pope hits hard at this same stupidity in the fourth of the *Moral
Essays,* in the description of Timon's study:—

> " His study! with what authors is it stor'd?
> In books, not authors, curious is my lord;
> To all their dated backs he turns you round;
> These Aldus printed, those Du Sueil has bound!
> Lo some are vellum, and the rest as good
> For all his lordship knows, but they are wood.
> For Locke or Milton 'tis in vain to look;
> These shelves admit not any modern book."

Pope is generally, and justly, regarded as one of our greatest
masters of poetic technique. He aimed at "correctness," and few
men have come so near the complete attainment of the end they
have set before themselves. The quotations show how high he has
risen above the verse of even Dryden; how immeasurably above
that absurd view which spoilt the satire of the Elizabethans,
and led to such results that Pope deemed it necessary to "versify"
the satires of Donne. So great was his success in technique that
Ruskin called him and Virgil "the two most accomplished *Artists,*
merely as such, whom I know in literature." Elsewhere however
Ruskin declares that the classical spirit, the pursuit of which led
Pope to this perfection, "spoiled half his work," and implies that
it was only when he broke through it that he attained "true
enthusiasm and tender thought." Tennyson, as his biographer tells
us, admired single lines and couplets very much, but, after quoting
one particular line—"What dire events from amorous causes
spring,"—emphatically declared that he "would sooner die than
write such a line." It was the collocation of sibilants that hurt the
ear of Tennyson. After all, an occasional lapse like this is not very

surprising. Skilful as Pope was in metre, he neither aimed at, nor, probably, was capable of achieving, such enchantments as Coleridge and Keats could produce. Neither are things like the lines on Sappho or those on Sporus very surprising. They are lamentable; artistically as well as morally they are bad; but we can see how Pope has been led to misuse his own faculty. There is however one artistic lapse in Pope which is not merely surprising, but astounding, at which it is difficult to do more than stare and gasp. He, the careful artist, who has polished and refined more than any other English poet, yet has hardly ever altered without improving; the professed student of style, who in the Scriblerus papers has left a little treatise on the Bathos—he himself has exemplified the Art of Sinking as strikingly as any of the scribblers whom he ridicules. Mark Pattison justly says that Pope's lines in the epistle to Murray:—

> " Grac'd as thou art with all the power of words,
>   So known, so honour'd, at the House of Lords,"

are as ridiculous as those he quotes in the essay on the Art of Sinking:—

> " And thou, Dalhousie, the great God of war,
>   Lieutenant-Colonel to the Earl of Mar."

The lapse becomes all the more astonishing when we contrast with this absurdity the fine lines which follow:—

> " Conspicuous scene! another yet is nigh,
>   (More silent far) where kings and poets lie;
>   Where Murray (long enough his country's pride)
>   Shall be no more than Tully, or than Hyde."

It is a noble compliment, rendered all the finer because it is so well deserved, and because it is so skilfully conjoined with the suggestion of the triviality of all differences in the stature of men. Tully and Hyde and Murray, kings and poets, meet at last, and all alike are dust. If Pope could sink amazingly, he could also rise gloriously. There are much loftier heights of poetry than even these fine lines, and there may be lower depths than "So known, so honour'd, at the House of Lords." But is there another example in all literature of movement from the ridiculous to the borders of the sublime, without even the proverbial step between?

The epistle in which this remarkable lapse occurs is warm with the personal friendship of the writer for the man to whom it is addressed. So is Pope's masterpiece, the epistle to Arbuthnot. The same glow of feeling is manifest in the epistle to Bethel and in the reference to him in the *Essay on Man*. Pope has been so often—and with so much justice—stigmatised as waspish, venomous, malignant, that it is worth while calling attention once more to this other side of his character. If he was a bitter enemy, he was also a warm friend. What is peculiar in the case of Pope is the sharpness of the contrast. It is unfortunate for his reputation as a man that his literary work brings into prominence the less amiable features of his character. As a poet, it is his special praise that he carried his own particular style to perfection. Of his numerous imitators none ever equalled him. They could fashion smooth couplets, but the ineffable something which made the couplets worth remembering was wanting. For energy Dryden, and for polish Pope, are the culminating points of classical satire in English verse.

CHAPTER X

NOTICE has already been taken of the cessation of satire towards the end of the reign of King James I. It was even more complete in prose than in verse, and it continued almost without a break till near the close of the seventeenth century. Notwithstanding the fact that in the course of the Stuart period the principles of a sound prose style were gradually evolved, and that, in spite of the censorship, a great mass of material was produced in the shape of pamphlets and journals—Corantos, Mercuries, Newsletters and what not—only a small portion of it deserves to rank as literature at all, and a still smaller fraction as satire. A revival might have been expected after the Restoration; but the success of the new satire in verse, whether Hudibrastic or classical, delayed the development of satire in prose. Probably no man has read the whole of the vast mass, and it is conceivable that some literary gem may lie buried there. What is certain is that no one has yet found it, and that each enquirer in turn who has dipped into the mass has come away convinced that its literary value is trifling. In the great majority of cases it is the controversial rather than the literary purpose that stands foremost; and in spite of an occasional Junius the spirit of controversy does not seem to be very favourable to literary satire. In the seventeenth century it was very unfavourable; for the journalists and pamphleteers had not yet learnt the lesson that a certain command of temper is necessary in order to be effective. Even so great a man as Milton suffers himself to be abusive where a higher literary art would have made him satirical; and this weakness exposes him to the violence of so petty an antagonist as Sir Roger L'Estrange (1616–1704) in *No Blind Guides*. L'Estrange is worthy of remembrance rather for his antagonists than for his own satire. Not only did he cross swords with Milton, but, at a later date, he was the antagonist of James Howell

(1594?–1666) of the *Epistolae Ho-Elianae*. Howell was one of the few sufferers in the cause of the Crown who gained some recompense from the bounty of Charles II. This led him in *A Cordial for the Cavaliers* to express a view which most of the disappointed Royalists rejected; and L'Estrange answered him in *A Caveat to the Cavaliers*. Howell himself occasionally played the satirist. There is a vein of satire in some of the letters, and in the latter part of his career he figures as the satirist of two peoples. *A Perfect Description of the Country of Scotland* is an example of that vituperation which had been popular in England ever since the union of the crowns; and *A Brief Character of the Low Countries under the States* satirises the Dutch with more restraint, and therefore with more effect.

The flaw which disfigures *A Perfect Description* is to be seen everywhere in this period. Where even Milton failed such journalistic hacks as Marchamont Nedham, Henry Walker and Samuel Sheppard were not likely to succeed. But occasionally superior restraint wins the reward of greater success. Edward Sexby's celebrated *Killing no Murder* is a case in point—strangely enough, for the man was among the last of whom restraint would have been expected. In *Don Juan Lamberto*, which has been attributed to John Phillips the nephew of Milton, and also to Thomas Flatman, it was easier to observe moderation, for the piece is written in a far lighter spirit. It is a very clever imitation of the romances of chivalry, representing Cromwell as Soldan of Britain, and his son as the Meek Knight; while Sir Lambert, Knight of the Golden Tulip, is the chief knight, and Sir Vane is the knight of the Mystical Allegories. Generally it is causes or parties rather than individuals that are the subject of satire; but we must except Cromwell, who is so pre-eminent as to be a cause and a party and a person all in one. There were other exceptions too. Philip Herbert, fourth Earl of Pembroke, may not have been witty in himself, but he was certainly the cause that wit was in other men. Among the *Somers Tracts* there are several pieces which satirise him very cleverly. One, *The last Will and Testament of the Earl of Pembroke*, which is supposed to be by Sir Charles Sedley, though it has been ascribed also to Samuel Butler, is extremely witty. But it illustrates the characteristic defect of the time. The author could not persuade himself to forbear a quip, and the consequence is that the wit is not always in keeping with the character delineated. At the best, these fugitive prose satires are no more than tolerable; they hardly rank as literature at all. Nor are they much better when they aspire to be more than occasional. Andrew Marvell was a more highly gifted man than most of their writers, and in the two parts of *The Rehearsal Transprosed* he devoted a substantial volume to ecclesiastical satire. It is intolerably dreary. To the modern reader the contorted wit serves only to obscure the meaning; and very few and very weary are they who are in at the death—if there *is* a death at the end. In the ecclesiastical sphere the violence and virulence are even greater than in the region of politics; as may be seen in such works as *Scotch Presbyterian Eloquence Displayed* and the answer to it.

The political pieces, and the ecclesiastical ones as well (they are as a rule closely connected), generally date themselves by their subject, and collectively they supply a sort of running commentary on the history of the time. Thus, *The humble Address of the Atheists* satirises the addresses asked for by James II. on his Declaration of Indulgence. More than twenty years later we find another flood of addresses, both serious and satirical, on the question of the succession; of which probably the ablest was *The true genuine Tory Address* by Benjamin Hoadly, afterwards Bishop of Bangor.

None of the journalists deserves serious consideration as a satirist till we come to Daniel Defoe (1661?–1731); and though no man was ever more clearly designed by nature to eschew verse and write prose, he shows the influence of the time by starting his career with a satire in verse. The earliest piece that has been identified as his is *A New Discovery of an Old Intrigue* (1691); and for a number of years after 1701 he was proud to distinguish himself as the author of another satire in verse, *The True-Born Englishman*. Provoked by the abuse showered upon William III. and his Dutch followers, Defoe in rough but vigorous verse ridicules the English as the most mongrel of races. "Your Roman-Saxon-Danish-Norman English," he calls them; and Minto justly remarks on the good-humoured magnanimity of the English people, who received this satire with laughter and applause. The same engaging trait of

temper was still more strikingly illustrated in the Great War, when
Tommy Atkins astonished the Germans in the opposing trenches
by singing the Hymn of Hate with the utmost verve and vigour.
Defoe makes effective use of the ennobling of Charles II.'s bastards,
which threw a shadow upon the peerage; he paints an unflattering
picture of the temper and manners of the people; he touches upon
the unreasonable multiplication of sects:—

> " In their religion they are so unev'n
> That each man goes his own by-way to Heav'n."

And he makes a shrewd thrust at the clergy, who found themselves
in a difficult position between James II.'s popery and their own
doctrine of non-resistance. The clergy

> " Unpreach'd their non-resisting cant, and pray'd
> To Heav'n for help, and to the Dutch for aid."

Jure Divino (1706), a satire on a much larger scale, has far less
literary merit. It is surpassed both by *The Mock Mourners*, with
its severe comments on those who "never value merit till 'tis
dead"; and, still more, by *The Diet of Poland*, which, under a
transparent disguise, deals with English politics and politicians
in the reign of Anne. Perhaps the liveliest passage is that which
ridicules the book of travels by William Bromley, afterwards
Speaker and Secretary of State.

Not only was Defoe no poet, he was hardly even a tolerable
versifier. We naturally expect more from his prose; but even his
prose only shows that satire was in him a secondary gift. A vein of
satire runs through many of his essays; there is occasional satire in
The Political History of the Devil, and in *The Complete English
Tradesman*. Indeed it may be suspected in most of his writings;
for it is often difficult to determine in what spirit Defoe was writing.
But by far the most notable of his satires in prose is *The Shortest
Way with the Dissenters* (1702); and even that is interesting now
less for its intrinsic literary merit than for the light it throws upon
the spirit of the time. Only bigotry incarnate could have misunderstood the irony; yet at first the piece was taken as a straightforward
statement of the opinions of a High Churchman. It is skilfully
constructed, beginning quietly and gently leading the mind on to

stronger doctrine; and this, no doubt, is the reason why Defoe's true purpose was misunderstood. But one or two specimens of the argument will show how much is revealed by the misunderstanding. Thus, it is stated as a popular objection to their dealing with the Dissenters that the Queen has promised to continue them in their tolerated liberty. The answer is: "What her Majesty will do, we cannot help, but what, as the Head of the Church, she ought to do, is another case: Her Majesty has promised to protect and defend the Church of England, and if she cannot effectually do that without the destruction of the Dissenters, she must of course dispense with one promise to comply with another." Again, it is objected that the proposals amount to a revival of the Act *De Heretico Comburendo*, and are cruel: "I answer, 'Tis cruel to kill a snake or a toad in cold blood, but the poison of their natures makes it a charity to our neighbours to destroy those creatures, not for any personal injury received, but for prevention; not for the evil they have done, but the evil they may do." Moses slew 33,000 idolatrous Israelites, and to do so was mercy to the rest. Mulcts and fines are vain; just one severe law is needed, to banish all who are found at conventicles, and to hang the preachers.

The same spirit is shown in *The Secret History of the October Club* (1711), which reveals the disgust of the High Churchmen because "the toleration of Dissenters is continued, and they called in public *fellow Christians*, whom they always were made believe should be esteemed worse than Papists." And it affords food for thought that in the dialogue which follows the High Churchman Sir John laments to the High Churchman Sir Thomas that the powers that be give "to that abhorred generation of rebels whom we look upon to be worse than Papists, the titles of *Protestants* and Fellow Christians." Tolerance spreads, though slowly. The High Church of the present day would not begrudge the title of Protestant at least. Defoe makes no mystery of his contempt for the brains of the good knights, and even the dullest of his readers could hardly be in doubt as to the meaning of the speech which he puts into the mouth of one of them against *considering* what grounds they had for action, because "a true October man must be above *considering*, 'tis inconsistent with the name, and was ever inconsistent with the party." Defoe's own profession of letters is not spared, but naturally it is the writers on the opposite side who receive casti-gation. The two authors who are introduced into the service of the October Club are Mr. Post-boy, "for eminence in open, profest, hardened, barefaced lying"; and *The Examiner*, "for unintelligible jingle, fine-spun emptiness, and long-winded repetition, without truth, without evidence, and without meaning." No less a person than Jonathan Swift (1667-1745) was among the writers to the periodical which is thus severely handled, and indeed he wrote the whole of it from the fourteenth number to the forty-sixth, embracing the very period to which Defoe must be referring. We hardly recognise the characteristics of his mind in the phrases Defoe applies to his paper; but it is the nature of the partisan on one side to be blind to merit in the partisan on the other.

There is no other great English writer in whom the satiric ele-ment is so predominant as it is in Swift. His three principal works, *The Battle of the Books, A Tale of a Tub*, and *Gulliver's Travels*, are all satires; his verse is prevailingly satirical, and the best of his miscellaneous writings are also satirical. The satire is generally tinged with irony, and sometimes it is irony pure and simple. The general standpoint is revealed in a sentence which has been quoted again and again from a letter to Pope: "I hate and detest that animal called man, although I heartily love John, Peter, Thomas, and so forth." The hatred can hardly be disputed by any reader of the loathsome *Voyage to the Houyhnhnms*, and the love is attested by the history of Swift's relations with men like Pope and Arbuthnot, and by his charities as Dean of St. Patrick's—his secret pension to Mrs. Dingley, for example. There is not much personality in his satire. He "exposed the fool and lash'd the knave," not as individuals, but as types. In the main, he is justified in saying, as he does in the verses on his own death,

> " No individual could resent,
> Where thousands equally were meant."

He differed therefore very widely from Pope in spirit as well as in form.

Swift's octosyllabic lines are lucid and terse. He can effectively ridicule the flatteries of courtly rhymers, or expose the emptiness of the fine lady's mind. In the rhapsody *On Poetry* he satirises the would-be wits who rely upon the mechanical devices of italics, capitals and initials. In the death of the Duke of Marlborough he finds the text for a discourse on the vanity of human greatness:—

> " Come hither, all ye empty things!
> Ye bubbles, raised by breath of kings!
> Who float upon the tide of state;
> Come hither, and behold your fate!
> Let Pride be taught by this rebuke
> How very mean a thing's a duke;
> From all his ill-got honours flung,
> Turn'd to that dirt from whence he sprung."

But Defoe pointed the same moral with the same example still more impressively in prose, and Swift could have done so too.

The verse form brings him no gain; in all but a few cases it is a positive disadvantage. Its proper use is to show up beauty; but Swift's diseased love of filth turns it to the task of displaying ugliness, and makes it sometimes more loathsome, if that be possible, than the satire of the Yahoos.

Primarily and essentially Swift's satire is aimed at human nature. It is not satire of a party, or of a creed, or of a person, or of an age; though satire of all these is to be found in his writings. It is satire of the very nature of man. Further, it is eminently intellectual satire. Swift valued himself above all on the power of his understanding; and when, according to the familiar story, he was observed in his declining years turning over the leaves of *A Tale of a Tub* and muttering, "Good God, what a genius I had when I wrote that book!" it was the incisive power of its logic he was admiring. Other men have agreed with this judgment. Even those who have been least favourable to him have, like Thackeray, borne emphatic testimony to the sheer force of his mind. When Dryden told his cousin that he would never be a poet, we may be sure that his judgment was based on a sense of the absence, not of intellect, but of the something more ethereal without which verse cannot be poetry. We have to look upon Swift, then, as the embodiment of pure intellect, and his satire, both verse and prose, as intellectual satire. There is in it none of that atmosphere of poetry which we find in the satire of Dryden and Pope, and still more, at a later date, in that of Burns and Byron. It must be judged by the canons of the intellect; and, so judged, it is in detail singularly great. But one of the canons of the intellect is consistency. Given the premises of a syllogism in Barbara, there is only one conclusion. All men

are vile: John, Peter and Thomas are men: therefore——The conclusion is so obvious that it need not be stated. But the great
misanthrope heartily loves John, Peter and Thomas, and must therefore somehow have found that they are not vile. A famous logician
has asserted that the great business of life is drawing conclusions.
If it were so, life would be a very simple affair; for there is hardly
any fool so abject that he cannot be taught from given premises to
draw correct conclusions. But life is not simple, and the difficulty
lies not in drawing conclusions, but in framing right premises. Here
is the point where Swift has gone wrong. The hearty love of John,
Peter and Thomas was really the proof, if he had been wise
enough to see it, that the animal called man was not wholly hateful
and detestable. The fact that Swift never detected this glaring flaw in
his logic and never revised his premises may be taken as illustrating

> " How very weak the very wise
> And very small the very great are."

There is a larger wisdom than Swift's in the saying that to know all
is to pardon all. Intellectual humility will reach the truth before
intellectual arrogance.

The general opinion is that Swift's was the most powerful intellect
of his age, and one of the most powerful of any age; and no doubt
it is right. What, then, is the explanation of this glaring *non
sequitur*? Swift died insane, and some might be tempted to see in
this gross failure of logic a foreshadowing of the final collapse of
intellect. But such a view can hardly be maintained. The whole
gigantic blunder can be exposed in a single syllogism, and Swift
for many years showed far more power than the majority of men,
both in framing premises and in drawing conclusions. Is it the
Nemesis of an unbalanced and inharmonious development of
intellect at the cost of other phases of human nature? Does such a
development expose the sinner and victim to the risk of errors
that would shame the merest tyro? There is a familiar instance
in the nineteenth century which may be thought to point to such
a conclusion. Herbert Spencer based a whole philosophy, and a
very ambitious one, on the Unknowable, which is equivalent to
Nothing. Or was it simply that Swift was obsessed with the poor
ambition of posing as a very clever fellow?

Of the three principal works in which this misanthropic satire finds vent, two, *A Tale of a Tub* and *The Battle of the Books*, were published together in 1704. They had been written some years before—*A Tale of a Tub* probably in 1696, and *The Battle of the Books* in 1697. At that time the misanthropy had not yet developed. *The Battle of the Books* is a good-natured contribution to the celebrated controversy which raged over Boyle's edition of the letters of Phalaris. The question of the genuineness of the letters, on which Bentley pronounced the conclusive, though not the last word, broadened out into a dispute as to the comparative merits of ancient and modern literature. Swift took part because his relative and patron, Sir William Temple, had already declared his preference for the ancients. The satire therefore is mainly literary. It is fluent, witty and diverting; sometimes stinging, but rarely bitter. The moderns are the spider, fixed in one place and spinning his web out of his own entrails; the ancients are the bee, ranging over all nature, filling his hive with honey and wax, and so furnishing mankind with the two noblest of things, sweetness and light. But though he is not bitter, Swift does not forget those who have incurred his displeasure. He had not forgiven Dryden's contempt of his verse, and in the description of the tumultuary host of the moderns he places Tasso and Milton at the head of the horse and Dryden and Withers at the other extreme, though they claim the leadership. And last among the confused multitude "came infinite swarms of calones, a disorderly rout led by L'Estrange; rogues and ragamuffins, that follow the camp for nothing but the plunder, all without coats to cover them."

As Swift was a man of letters, it was natural that literature and learning should bulk large in his satire. Not only do we find it in *The Battle of the Books*, but in such pieces of verse as the rhapsody *On Poetry* and the *Directions for making a Birthday Song* already referred to. In *A Tale of a Tub* the fifth section is a digression upon the controversy which is more fully treated in *The Battle of the Books*, and the introduction contains a pungent satire on dedications, in which once more Dryden suffers; while another passage, still more pungent, scarifies those who "become scholars and wits, without the fatigue of reading or of thinking":—

" The most accomplished way of using books at present is two-fold; either, first, to serve them as some men do lords, learn their titles exactly, and then brag of their acquaintance. Or, secondly, which is indeed the choicer, the profounder, and politer method, to get a thorough insight into the index, by which the whole book is governed and turned, like fishes by the tail. For to enter the palace of learning at the great gate requires an expense of time and forms; therefore men of much haste and little ceremony are content to get in by the back door."

In the same work a whole section is devoted to a merciless criticism of critics; and in the preface Swift even satirises satire.

Just as Swift in other works diverges from his main theme to satirise literature and litterateurs, so in *The Battle of the Books* he mingles general satire with the satire of the modern writers. Not a few of his happiest touches are digressions. At the very start he points out that the passions involved are just the same as in any other sort of battle, and these passions are to be observed not only in the communities of men, but among animals: "We may observe in the republic of dogs, which in its original seems to be an institution of the many, that the whole state is ever in the profoundest peace after a full meal; and that civil broils arise among them when it happens for one great bone to be seized on by some leading dog, who either divides it among the few, and then it falls to an oligarchy, or keeps it to himself, and then it runs up to a tyranny."

In the introduction to *A Tale of a Tub* Swift shows again this power of clothing wisdom in the garb of wit:—

" Whoever has an ambition to be heard in a crowd, must press, and squeeze, and thrust, and climb, with indefatigable pains, till he has exalted himself to a certain degree of altitude above them. Now in all assemblies, though you wedge them ever so close, we may observe this peculiar property, that over their heads there is room enough, but how to reach it is the difficult point; it being as hard to get quit of number as of hell;

—— evadere ad auras,
Hoc opus, hic labor est."

Hence the value of those "wooden machines," the pulpit, the ladder and the stage itinerant.

A Tale of a Tub is altogether more massive and weighty than *The Battle of the Books*. In the latter piece Swift is as playful as it is given to such a nature to be. In *A Tale of a Tub* he is too much in earnest to be playful. He took part in the Boyle-Bentley controversy as a dutiful follower of Sir William Temple; but he was not absorbed in it, and probably in his heart cared little about the relative merits of ancients and moderns. At any rate it is clear that the question whether the greatest writers are living now or lived two thousand years ago, and whether they have written English or Greek and Latin, does not go to the root. But religion does; and religion is the principal theme of *A Tale of a Tub*—the principal theme, but by no means the only one. The digressions are about equal in bulk to the main apologue, and they are not inferior to it in wit. The general idea is well known. Swift takes for his subject Christianity as he saw it professed and followed—or not followed— in Western Europe. The great division between Roman Catholics and Protestants had governed politics as well as ecclesiastical systems since the sixteenth century. The divisions among Protestants had been suppressed so long as all were moved by fear of the common tyrant, but they had come into prominence as security was won. Thus there is a subordinate division between the moderate Protestants, represented as followers of Luther, and the extreme Protestants, who looked for guidance to Calvin. And so we have the story of the three brothers, Peter, Martin and Jack. It illustrates the petty vanity of human nature, which makes a deity of the tailor and takes the whole universe to be "a large suit of clothes, which invests everything," and similarly explains everything down to man, who is just "a micro-coat, or rather a complete suit of clothes with all its trimmings." The three brothers have inherited from their father each the coat of true religion, and the theme of the piece is their treatment of this coat. Peter is seduced by worldly ambition to add to the coat all sorts of bedizenments and trumpery ornaments. Martin and Jack at last awake to the errors into which they have been led, and proceed to remove the ornaments—Jack violently and with grave damage to the coat; Martin, after the first burst of anger, cautiously and judiciously.

This book was a barrier to Swift's promotion in the Church, and he felt aggrieved because many on account of it suspected the sincerity of his religion. The line of his defence is obvious from the foregoing sketch. He has represented Martin (the Church of England) as guilty of nothing worse than a little violence in the first heat of the Reformation; he pours his satire upon Peter, and he does not spare Jack, or Protestant Dissent. This is true; and it is also true that a fair review of Swift's life and writings shows that he sincerely held the creed he professed. And yet the defence is unconvincing. The fourth section is devoted to a satire of Romish errors. It is unsurpassed, perhaps it is unequalled, in force and scathing wit. But the author of the satire on transubstantiation, on the relics of the true cross, and on the stories of the milk of the Virgin, had no right to be surprised that people doubted his sincerity. Thousands who have no belief in the doctrine, nor any doubt that the relics are wholly fraudulent, must nevertheless have shivered at the manner in which they are ridiculed, even while they were amazed at the intellect of the writer. Swift's coarseness was not confined to matters of sex. He shows it here almost as offensively as he shows the sheer delight in foulness in the fourth part of *Gulliver*. The ridicule of the other extreme in religion, under the name of the Æolists, if less supremely witty, is also much less offensive. We learn with indifference that the originator of this sect, Jack, was mad; especially as the author goes on to demonstrate that all the greatest actions—the founding of empires, and the contriving of new schemes of philosophy and of new religions —have been done by "persons whose natural reason had admitted great revolutions, from their diet, their education, the prevalency of some certain temper, together with the particular influence of air and climate."

Many consider *A Tale of a Tub* to be the greatest of Swift's works. He certainly never surpassed it in style, and there are passages in it of irony and sarcasm as penetrating as anything he ever wrote; and though in that respect it does not surpass the masterly paper on *The Abolishing of Christianity in England*, the larger scope of the former work made the task more difficult and the triumph therefore greater. Severe as is the satire, and petty as human nature is made to appear, there is more *humanity* in it than there is in *Gulliver's Travels* (1726); and so far it is the better of the two. On the other hand, there is in *A Tale of a Tub* none of that admirable movement which makes the later work the delight of children, while the genius it displays excites the astonishment of men. Probably the sounder judgment is that which pronounces *Gulliver's Travels* to be the greatest, as it is the longest, of Swift's works. And this in spite of the loathsome blot of the concluding part. Except *Robinson Crusoe*, probably no English book is so widely known. Half a century ago *The Pilgrim's Progress* might have rivalled either, but it does so no longer. It is curious that all three appeared within one half-century, and that by no means the richest in our literature; while only seven years intervened between Defoe's work and *Gulliver's Travels*. It would be hard to imagine books more widely different in spirit and purport. But in one respect they are similar: they are books of adventure. And this goes far to explain their popularity.

It would be superfluous to describe the plan of *Gulliver's Travels*. All read it in childhood for the story, which is one of those that refuse to be forgotten. Some return to it in later years for the thought; and this is the theme with which we have now to deal. Measuring by dates of publication, twenty-two years divide *Gulliver's Travels* from the earlier satires; but the interval between the writing of it and the writing of the others is not far short of thirty years. We can easily trace the mark of the years in the later book. They had made Swift an unhappy and an embittered man, and the evidence is there to be read. Of the two qualities he calls the noblest he had always possessed in plenty the light of intellect. He possesses it still, but in no higher degree. Of sweetness he had never had much, and he now has none—none, at least, that he shows in *Gulliver's Travels*. His misanthropy is now fully developed, and his purpose is to belittle and contemn humanity. In the voyages to Lilliput and to Brobdingnag he does this by making Gulliver a sort of middle term between the extreme of littleness and the extreme of bigness. In each case human passions are made contemptible by the comparison. The intrigues, plots, cabals and factions of men, seen on the scale of a creature not half a foot in height, are absurd. Their officials attain honours by cutting capers on the tight-rope, risking their lives in doing so. And the honours they prize most highly are silken threads, blue and red and green. Men of a larger growth have heard of the leader who left his party "just for a ribbon to stick in his coat." The bitterest disputes of the Lilliputians concern the question whether the heels of shoes shall be high or low, whether an egg shall be cut at the big end or at the little end. Thousands of the Big-endians have suffered death and thousands more are in exile over this important question. Thus does Swift ridicule sects and factions in religion and politics.

But Swift would miss his aim if he failed to bring it home that the Lilliputians are just ordinary men with their passions and ambitions as seen by the eye of wisdom. We are left in no doubt that the intrigues in the Court of Lilliput are just the intrigues in the Court of George I., seen through the wrong end of the telescope. A personage about the Court visits Gulliver secretly in a close chair, and Gulliver puts him, chair and all, into his coat-pocket. The object of the visit is to reveal to Gulliver a design against his life, and the action of his friend at Court Reldresal, who appeals to the king to show the clemency for which he is justly celebrated and content himself with putting out the offender's eyes. This however is deemed too light a punishment, and it is finally determined gradually to starve Gulliver after his eyes have been put out. He could, it is true, probably have saved himself by destroying the Lilliputian nation. But he had not yet "learned the gratitude of courtiers, to persuade myself that his majesty's present severities acquitted me of all past obligations." The injury thus contemplated was likely to be followed by insult; for it was the custom that after the Court had decreed any cruel execution, the emperor always made a speech expressing his great lenity and tenderness. "This speech was immediately published throughout the kingdom; nor did anything terrify the people so much as those encomiums on his majesty's mercy; because it was observed, that the more these praises were enlarged and insisted on, the more inhuman was the punishment, and the sufferer more innocent."

This theme of the clemency of princes is handled again with bitter satire in the voyage to Laputa, where it was the etiquette to approach the king crawling upon the belly and licking the floor. The floor may be more or less dusty, according to the degree of favour or disfavour in which the courtier is held; and an offending noble may be put to death in a gentle indulgent manner by strewing a brown powder upon the floor. "But in justice to this prince's great clemency (wherein it were much to be wished that the monarchs of Europe would imitate him), it must be mentioned for his honour, that strict orders are given to have the infected parts of the floor well washed after every such execution; which, if his domestics neglect, they are in danger of incurring his royal displeasure."

That the passions of Lilliput and Blefuscu are much the same as those of England and France is shown clearly by the satire on ambition. After Gulliver has captured the navy, which threatened invasion, the Emperor of Lilliput immediately conceives the ambition of subjugating Blefuscu: "So unmeasurable is the ambition of princes, that he seemed to think of nothing less than reducing the whole empire of Blefuscu into a province, and governing it by a viceroy; of destroying the big-endian exiles, and compelling that people to break the smaller end of their eggs, by which he would remain the sole monarch of the whole world." It is a kind of ambition not unexampled in Europe. The contrasting conception of Brobdingnag gave Swift the opportunity of viewing the same thing from the opposite standpoint. How would such ambitions appear to beings twelve times taller than man? The answer is given in that chapter of the voyage to Brobdingnag in which Gulliver, on the invitation of the king, describes and eulogises the political and judicial system of England. It is the most comprehensive and telling piece of political satire Swift ever wrote. Gulliver is quite self-satisfied in his account, notwithstanding the fact that his best qualification for describing the courts of justice was that he had been formerly "almost ruined by a long suit in Chancery, which was decreed for [him] with costs." The king's questions raise misgivings as to the excellence of the system, and his final judgment is devastating: "My little friend Grildrig, you have made a most admirable panegyric upon your country; you have clearly proved, that ignorance, idleness, and vice are the proper ingredients for qualifying a legislator; that laws are best explained, interpreted, and applied by those whose interest and abilities lie in perverting, confounding, and eluding them." And so on to the final pronouncement: "I cannot but conclude the bulk of your nation to be the most pernicious race of little vermin that nature ever suffered to crawl upon the surface of the earth."

But though the Brobdingnagians are beings of a larger growth and have the kind of generosity we associate with real power, they are human, and Swift would be inconsistent if he failed to show that they share human infirmities. Among the means by which he does this the ridicule he throws upon the learned of Brobdingnag is the most amusing. They have to explain this phenomenon of a being apparently human, yet far too small to be classed as a dwarf; for the queen's favourite dwarf, the smallest ever known in that kingdom, was near thirty feet high. "After much debate, they concluded unanimously that I was only *relplum scalcath*, which is interpreted literally *lusus naturæ*; a determination exactly agreeable to the modern philosophy of Europe, whose professors, disdaining the old evasion of occult causes, whereby the followers of Aristotle endeavoured in vain to disguise their ignorance, have invented this wonderful solution of all difficulties, to the unspeakable advancement of human knowledge."

The remaining two parts of *Gulliver's Travels* reveal a deplorable falling off. The *Voyage to Laputa* shows very little, and the *Voyage to the Houyhnhnms* none at all of that playfulness with which, as in the passage quoted above, Swift relieves his trenchant satire in the earlier voyages. There are some telling passages in the *Voyage to Laputa*, such as the satire on the school of political projectors, who proposed schemes "of choosing for employment persons qualified to exercise them; with many other wild impossible chimeras, that never entered before into the heart of man to conceive; and confirmed in me the old observation, 'That there is nothing so extravagant and irrational, which some philosophers have not maintained for truth.'" This is in Swift's happiest manner. But in the main the *Voyage to Laputa* suggests a mind perverse and distorted; and the *Voyage to the Houyhnhnms* not only confirms but immensely deepens the impression. It is utterly inhuman, and the reader has difficulty in believing that the hatred of humanity is any longer accompanied by the love of individual men. But further, it is intellectually inferior. Not only does it exhibit that fundamental failure in logic which has already been pointed out, but, as Mr. G. A. Aitken, and Coleridge in a passage discovered by him, have shown, it is inconsistent in detail as well. The outrage on humanity has not even the merit of being coherent.

Apart from the three works which have now been noticed, Swift's numerous satires were sporadic and occasional. Some of them are familiar to all by name, and to many more intimately. Such are the playful skits on the almanack-maker Partridge, *Predictions for the Year* 1708; *A Meditation upon a Broomstick*, with its masterly exposure of the platitudinous moraliser: "Surely man is a Broomstick"; and the *Directions to Servants*, which, though it is disfigured by Swift's besetting sin of nastiness, is marvellous as an evidence of power of observation as well as of wit. Most famous of all, perhaps, is the *Modest Proposal*—a thing as grim and gruesome as the conception of the Struldbrugs of Laputa.

Two of Swift's occasional papers deserve somewhat fuller notice. One of them is *Mr. Collins's Discourse of Freethinking ; put into plain English, by way of abstract, for the use of the Poor*. Swift's abstract brings to light some striking conclusions. "There is not the least hurt in the wickedest thoughts, provided they be free." "If you are apt to be afraid of the devil, think freely of him, and you destroy him and his kingdom. . . . My meaning is that to think freely of the devil is to think there is no devil at all; and he that thinks so, the devil is in him if he be afraid of the devil." "Do not trust the priest, but think freely for yourself; and if you happen to think there is no hell, there certainly is none, and, consequently, you cannot be damned." "A perfect moral man must be a perfect atheist; every inch of religion he gets, loses him an inch of morality; for there is a certain quantum belongs to every man, of which there is nothing to spare."

The other paper referred to is that on *The Abolishing of Christianity in England*. There is nowhere, even in Swift, a more admirable and masterly example of irony. He gravely hopes that no reader will imagine him to stand up in defence of real Christianity, "such as used in primitive times (if we may believe the authors of those ages) to have an influence upon men's beliefs and actions." This, he goes on to show, would be "to dig up foundations; to destroy at one blow all the wit and half the learning of the kingdom." It would deprive the freethinkers of the best object of their wit, for "who would ever have suspected Asgil for a wit, or Toland for a philosopher, if the inexhaustible stock of Christianity had not been at hand to provide them with materials?" It is even possible that the abolition of Christianity may bring the Church into danger, and it "will be the readiest course we can take to introduce popery." At any rate, the abolition had better be deferred to a time of peace, for it might alienate our allies, who are bigoted Christians, and drive us into alliance with the Turks, who "are not only strict observers of religious worship, but, what is worse, believe a God; which is more than is required of us, even while we preserve the name of Christians." Swift therefore ranks the Christianity of the English no higher than that of the Dutch, which he satirises in *Gulliver's Travels*. For Gulliver, pretending to be Dutch on his arrival in Japan after the voyage to Laputa, begged to be excused the ceremony imposed upon his countrymen of trampling upon the crucifix. The emperor expressed surprise and said, "He believed I was the first of my countrymen who ever made any scruple in this point; and that he began to doubt whether I was a real Hollander or not; but rather suspected I must be a Christian."

Thackeray has been much criticised of late years for his treatment of Swift. But was he really wrong? He makes the amplest acknowledgment of Swift's tremendous strength of mind, but beyond that he finds little that is admirable in him. Leave aside the debated question of Swift's relations with the two women, Esther Johnson (or Stella) and Hester Vanhomrigh, and take only the indubitable evidence of his writings—how much is there that is amiable or attractive, except for that unquestionable intellectual strength? Is it easy to pardon the creator of the Yahoos? or the author of the verse satires on women? or the clergyman who failed to see the offensiveness of *A Tale of a Tub*? And which attitude is the greater and the wiser—Swift's scorn and hatred of mankind, or Wordsworth's love and reverence? On the plea that he was unsound in mind Swift may be pitied, but not praised or admired.

There is no "brother near the throne" of Jonathan Swift: he is unrivalled among English prose satirists. Yet there is one, a contemporary and friend, perhaps nearly equal to him in native gifts, and incomparably more amiable and attractive. This was John Arbuthnot (1667–1735), the foremost physician of his time, immortalised by Pope's famous epistle, a piece honourable alike to him who sent and to him who received. If Swift was in some respects almost inhuman, Arbuthnot was both eminently human and humane. No one was ever less troubled than he with the *cacoethes scribendi*, no one ever showed less of literary jealousy. His writings are of considerable volume, but they were penned because he had knowledge to convey or thoughts to express, not because he desired fame as an author. To that he was so indifferent as to leave the works for which he is now best remembered mixed up with those of Swift and Pope. These two may have made suggestions, but there is no doubt that Arbuthnot was the author, either sole or principal, of *The History of John Bull* (or, *Law is a Bottomless Pit*) (1712), *The Art of Political Lying* (1712), and the *Memoirs of Martinus Scriblerus*, which was not published till 1741. These are the works which concern us; the much inferior *Brief Account of Mr. John Ginglicutt's Treatise concerning the Altercation or Scolding of the Ancients* may be passed over; and Arbuthnot's professional and scholarly works and the *Sermon at the Mercat Cross* lie outside the scope of this book.

The History of John Bull originally appeared in the shape of a series of five pamphlets. The theme is the long war of the Spanish Succession, which was then drawing near its close, and the principal characters are Lord Strutt (Spain), Lewis Baboon (France), John Bull (England), and Nicholas Frog (Holland). The two latter are tradesmen who are anxious to retain the custom of Lord Strutt. They threaten to take action against him, and he promises that he will not change his draper; "but all to no purpose, for Bull and Frog saw clearly that old Lewis would have the cheating of him"— a very neat thrust at the moral standard of trade. An action is brought, and John Bull is assured that the suit will not last above a year or two. But "law is a bottomless pit; it is a cormorant— a harpy that devours everything." The attorney Hocus (Marlborough) steers the cause for ten years through all the meanders of the law. "John's ready-money, book-debts, bonds, mortgages, all went into the lawyers' pockets"; and Lewis Baboon is reduced to his last shift. But John wins every suit, and at last he who is only a plain tradesman is tempted to imagine himself a lawyer.

The allegory is broadened out by the introduction of Mrs. Bull (the Whig Parliament), who intrigues with Hocus, falls ill and dies; and is succeeded by a second Mrs. Bull (the Tory Parliament). John's mother (the Church of England) also appears, and the character assigned to her admirably represents the intermediate position of the Church between Romanism and Calvinism. John Bull's sister Peg (Scotland) is also skilfully portrayed, and her lover Jack (Calvinism) is satirised with great wit. In this section of the work Arbuthnot is indebted to *A Tale of a Tub*, and makes no attempt to conceal his debt. There is nothing better in the whole piece than the account of the reconciliation of John with Peg (the Union), and the quarrels after the reconciliation. It was a thing Arbuthnot had close at heart, and his *Sermon at the Mercat Cross in Edinburgh* aimed at promoting it. At last the long-drawn-out dispute is ended by meetings at the Salutation tavern (the Congress of Utrecht).

An immense amount of art and ingenuity goes to the work: there are few writings of the time, or of any time, that show greater talent. But it is largely thrown away; a plain straightforward statement would probably have been as effective. The truth is that the wits wrote more for their own satisfaction than for the purpose of converting others.

The success of Arbuthnot's satire is indicated by the number of answers and imitations. Whether he invented the name John Bull or not, it was certainly he who gave it a place in literature. A number of skits obviously suggested by Arbuthnot's followed within the next five years. An anonymous opponent embodied the arguments against peace in *Law not a Bottomless Pit*. *John Bull's Last Will and Testament* was published, and the state of his family was reviewed after probate of that will. From 1714 to 1717 various pamphlets dealt with the *History of the Crown-Inn*. Long afterwards, Adam Ferguson (1723–1816) carried on the satire in a pamphlet on the militia question entitled *The History of the Proceedings in the Case of Margaret, commonly called Peg, only lawful Sister to John Bull, Esq.* (1761). This very ingenious and diverting production is a worthy sequel to Arbuthnot's work, and fully deserves the compliment paid by Scott in *The Antiquary* in the last year of his old friend's life—that it flowed from a head that "though now old and somedele grey, has more sense and political intelligence than you find nowadays in a whole synod." In 1816 Demodocus Poplicola thought it worth while to review the whole history of England in *John Bull's Bible : or, Memories of the Stewardship and Stewards of John Bull's Manor of Great Britain*. And as late as 1851, Lord Lytton addressed *Letters to John Bull, Esq., on affairs connected with his landed property, and the persons who live thereon*.

The Art of Political Lying is every whit as good as *John Bull*, if it is not even better. At least it carries its justification more plainly upon the surface. We may doubt whether the cause advocated in *The History of John Bull* would not have been equally well served by a plain statement, but it is clear that the effect arrived at in *The Art of Political Lying* would have been missed had not Arbuthnot adopted the method of ironical satire. He has done it with extraordinary success: there is nothing better in Swift. It professes to be an abstract of the first volume of a treatise on ψευδολογία πολιτική. In the first chapter, we are told, the author "reasons philosophically concerning the nature of the soul of man, and those qualities which render it susceptible of lies. He supposes the soul to be of the nature of a plano-cylindrical speculum, or looking-glass; that the plain side was made by God Almighty, but that the devil afterwards wrought the other side into a cylindrical figure. The plain side represents objects just as they are; and the cylindrical side, by the rules of catoptrics, must needs represent true objects false, and false objects true; but the cylindrical side, being much the larger surface, takes in a greater compass of visual rays. That upon the cylindrical side of the soul of man depends the whole art and success of Political Lying." On this excellent foundation the superstructure of the treatise is built. The art of political lying is defined as "the art of convincing the people of salutary falsehoods for some good end." This is shown to be lawful; and then the question is discussed "whether the right of coinage of political lies be wholly in the government." It is decided not to be so confined for several good reasons, one being that "abundance of political lying is a sure sign of true English liberty." Political lies are next classified, and precepts are given for inventing, spreading and propagating them. Then the miraculous, terrifying and prodigious are discussed. As to the prodigious, "he has little to advise, but that their comets, whales, and dragons should be sizeable; their storms, tempests, and earthquakes, without the reach of a day's journey of a man and horse." Then the question is raised, which of the two parties are the greatest artists in political lying? It is not easy to settle, for "they have both very good geniuses among them." The ill success of either is due to their glutting the market: "when there is too great a quantity of worms, it is hard to catch gudgeons." Special praise, however, is bestowed upon the Whig party for the right understanding and use of proof-lies. "A proof-lie is like a proof-charge for a piece of ordnance, to try standard

credulity. Of such a nature he takes transubstantiation to be in
the Church of Rome, a proof-article, which, if anyone swallows,
they are sure he will digest everything else; therefore the Whig
party do wisely to try the credulity of the people sometimes by
swingers, that they may be able to judge to what height they may
charge them afterwards." Other chapters treat of the celerity and
duration of lies, and of their characteristics, distinguishing Dutch,
English and French ware. Finally, the question is raised whether
a lie is best contradicted by truth, or by another lie. "The author
says that, considering the large extent of the cylindrical surface of
the soul, and the great propensity to believe lies in the generality
of mankind of late years, he thinks the properest contradiction
to a lie is another lie."

Both *John Bull* and *Political Lying* belong to the class of political
satires. The *Memoirs of the Extraordinary Life, Works and Discoveries
of Martinus Scriblerus* is a satire on pedantry, from which Swift
borrowed in the *Voyage to Laputa*, just as Arbuthnot had borrowed
from him in *The History of John Bull*. Cornelius Scriblerus at the
birth of his son "was infinitely pleased that the child had the
wart of Cicero, the wry neck of Alexander, knots upon his legs
like Marius, and one of them shorter than the other like Agesilaus.
The good Cornelius also hoped he would come to stammer like
Demosthenes, in order to be eloquent, and in time arrive at many
other defects of famous men." The playthings of the young Martinus
are chosen on the score of their antiquity: "Neither cross and pile,
nor ducks and drakes, are quite so ancient as handy-dandy, though
Macrobius and St. Augustine take notice of the first, and Minucius
Foelix describes the latter; but handy-dandy is described by
Aristotle, Plato and Aristophanes." He acquires great skill in
physic, and can prescribe at a distance and cure by intuition. He is
great in projects and devices, one being "to relieve consumptive
or asthmatic persons by bringing fresh air out of the country to
towns, by pipes of the nature of the recipients of air-pumps: and
to introduce the native air of a man's country into any other in
which he should travel, with a seasonable intromission of such
steams as were most familiar to him; to the inexpressible comfort
of many Scotsmen, Laplanders, and white bears." The resemblance
to Laputa is manifest, but there is in *Scriblerus* a good-nature which

is foreign to Swift. No one in that age did his fooling either with a better grace or "more natural" than Arbuthnot.

Apart from the contributors to the periodical essay, perhaps the only other writer who still deserves serious consideration as a satirist is Thomas Edwards (1699–1757). His *Canons of Criticism* (1747) is satire of a comparatively rare type—satire on a critic. It is represented as a supplement to Warburton's *Shakespeare*, of which work it is really a very stinging exposure. The outrageous liberties taken by Warburton are ridiculed in twenty-one canons deduced—as a rule quite fairly—from the critic's practice and illustrated by examples chosen from him. The work has lost its utility, for Warburton's faults are not those to which modern editors and critics are prone, but it affords conclusive evidence that the author was a man of rare ability.

We have touched the border without as yet penetrating the territory of the most characteristic literary product of the age of Queen Anne—the Periodical Essay. It is needless to retell the familiar story of its rise. Defoe, the principal precursor of Steele, has been already dealt with. Richard Steele (1672–1729) created *The Tatler*. *The Tatler* is the earliest of the periodicals which are embraced within the classical canon, and in Steele and his coadjutor, Joseph Addison (1672–1719), we find the spirit of the Periodical Essay incarnate. None of the subsequent periodicals equalled *The Tatler* and *The Spectator*; and the two friends *were The Tatler* and *The Spectator*. Of the two hundred and seventy-one numbers of the former journal only some half-dozen, and of the *Spectators* only forty-five, were by other pens.

It is clear that Steele had the more originative mind of the two. He and not Addison created *The Tatler*, and after some experiments he had moulded it to the shape it kept to the end before Addison became a regular contributor. It is equally clear that Addison was the greater literary craftsman. There are qualities in *The Tatler*, a freshness, geniality and frankness, which have caused some excellent critics to prefer it to *The Spectator*; and in *The Tatler* Steele's papers are more than four times as numerous as Addison's. But if we seek for grace and finish of style we must turn to the paper in which Addison predominates. No one was more keenly conscious of this than Steele himself, and Goldsmith has acutely remarked that "Steele sank in his merit as an author," because his efforts to equal or eclipse Addison "destroyed that genuine flow of diction which is discoverable in all his former compositions."

There is the widest possible difference between satire as it was practised by Swift and satire as we find it in the two great essayists. Ferocious, virulent, merciless, are adjectives which have constantly to be applied to Swift. But in Addison and Steele there is of ferocity and virulence not a trace, and lack of mercy is extremely rare. Addison's dissection of a beau's head and its less successful companion piece, the dissection of a coquette's heart, may fairly be called merciless in their wit. The head is found to contain no brain, only something like it; the pineal gland smells very strong of essence and orange-flower water; the *musculi amatorii* or ogling muscles are very much worn and decayed with use, "whereas, on the contrary, the elevator, or the muscle which turns the eye towards heaven, does not appear to have been used at all." The satire could hardly be surpassed in pungency, but it is neither virulent nor ferocious. Even Steele, whose native kindliness is constantly peeping out, can on occasion be very severe, but virulence is wholly foreign to him. It is significant that the harshest thing, probably, he ever wrote, was written about the sex whose champion it is his glory to have been; for nothing so raised his anger as the corruption of that which ought to be good. "A coquette," he says, "is a chaste jilt, and differs from a common one, as a soldier, who is perfect in exercise, does from one that is actually in service." For the same reason there is an unusual sharpness of sting in his remark about "some impertinent young woman, who will talk sillily upon the strength of looking beautifully."

The difference between the satire of Swift and that of Steele and Addison is due mainly to two causes. The first and fundamental cause is the difference between the men in character. Swift's satire was savage because there was savagery in his own nature; whereas Steele was the most genial and kind-hearted of men, and though there may have been some taint of malice in Addison, he was essentially good-natured. The second and subsidiary cause was the difference of the circumstances in which the satires were produced. Swift's great satires were substantive works; and even the shorter occasional papers were for the most part independent of their surroundings. But the papers of Steele and Addison had to conform to the general tone of the periodicals to which they were contributed. We cannot imagine the Yahoos in *The Spectator*. It was partly circumstance that made the periodical essay the censor of the minor morals. But it was partly also the character of the men. Though Swift's contributions were few, they were sufficient to show how different would have been the destiny of the periodical essay if he rather than Steele and Addison had controlled it—how different, and how immeasurably worse. Imagine the spirit of the paper on Madonella spread over *The Tatler* and from it transmitted to *The Spectator*, in place of the raillery about puffs and patches and furbelows and hoops and Picts and Salamanders.

The periodical essay did not, indeed, wholly exclude the graver aspects of life and death: we find such things as the Vision of Mirza and the elaborate criticism of *Paradise Lost*. But in the main the theme is the minor morals. *Quicquid agunt homines nostri farrago libelli* was the motto of the early *Tatlers*. But the *homines* wore wigs and all the paraphernalia of the eighteenth - century courtier or wit or citizen. Swift's *homines* are stripped naked— there lies the difference. Moreover, Swift's *homines* are suffering from some incurable and usually loathsome disease, Steele's and Addison's from some malady which is rarely beyond hope of cure and never disgusting. Addison ridicules valetudinarians in one paper, virtuosi in another, and idols (that is, vain and silly women) in a third. In the proposal for a Newspaper of Whispers he lashes gossip in the persons of Peter Hush and Lady Blast, who "has such a peculiar malignity in her whisper, that it blights like an easterly wind, and withers every reputation that it breathes upon." Steele satirises the ill-timed waggery that ruins serious conversation, and especially that peculiarly objectionable wag called the biter (he who says what the listener has no reason to disbelieve, and laughs because it is believed). "A biter," says Steele, "is one who thinks you a fool, because you do not think him a knave." The fault is silly and the satire sharp, but it ends far from the fundamentals of human folly and guilt.

Of the two coadjutors, notwithstanding Steele's wider experience in the drama, Addison would seem to have had the greater gift for characterisation. Though the first conception of the Spectator

Club and the first draft of Sir Roger de Coverley were Steele's, in the main the development of Sir Roger was due to Addison, and it is with Addison that we associate Will Honeycomb and Will Wimble. His satires are also more apt than Steele's to have the names of individuals. One form of pedantry is incarnate in Tom Folio; the "very pretty poet" is called Ned Softly; and Sir Timothy Tittle is the "importunate, empty, and conceited animal, which is generally known by the name of a critic." In the case of Steele, on the other hand, the scold whose husband "knows every pain of life with her but jealousy" is not an individual but a class. So are the Picts (women who paint), who are "some of them so exquisitely skilful this way, that give them but a tolerable pair of eyes to set up with, and they will make bosom, lips, cheeks, and eye-brows, by their own industry."

In things of this sort the essayists found their material for satire; the fundamentals, when they were touched at all, were treated seriously. The satire is most commonly social, but occasionally literary. Even politics, as such, are left alone—necessarily, for the introduction of politics would have roused the party spirit and created a dangerous division, as it did at a later date. We have indeed in *The Spectator* ridicule of the lady's head-dress or patches as signs of party, but there are no consequences more serious than that Nigranilla, a Tory, is obliged by a pimple to patch on the Whig side. Or we are taught the mischief of party spirit by Sir Roger's story of the difficulty he had as a boy in finding St. Anne's Lane. If he asked for it by that title he offended the Roundhead, and if he omitted the "Saint" he roused the Cavalier to fury. Addison's ridicule of the coffee-house politician is political only by accident; it is a satire on pretentiousness, as Steele's of the poet who, when his panegyric had been half printed off, altered it to a satire upon the removal of the minister, is a satire on the time-serving spirit.

Sometimes, but rarely, either the tone of an essay or persistence in the same theme through a series of essays indicates a fixed purpose to deal with some graver fault. The best example is Steele's treatment of duelling, which runs through half a dozen essays in *The Spectator*. It is clear that he felt this to be a very serious social evil. He had dealt with it already in his play *The Lying Lover*, and in No. 25 of *The Tatler* he took it up again. He shows both scorn and indignation. The duel is "an illegitimate species of the ancient knight-errantry" satirised by Cervantes. Its code is "an imposture, made up of cowardice, falsehood, and want of understanding." Its uncertainties are such that it would be as sensible to "throw up cross or pile who should be shot." It perverts morality: "As the matter at present stands, it is not to do handsome actions denominates a man of honour; it is enough if he dares to defend ill ones." And how grotesque is the conception of *satisfaction*! The man who has done wrong offers it. "'This is fine doing,' says the plain fellow; 'last night he sent me away cursedly out of humour, and this morning he imagines it would be a *satisfaction* to be run through the body.'" All honour to Steele for the stand he made: he was a century before his time.

Still more in earnest and more rapidly successful in his purpose was he in his treatment of women. He did more than any other man to make the filth of the Restoration odious. Repeatedly he shows his loathing of anything that offends the modesty of women. He puts into the mouth of a Quaker an admirable rebuke of an impudent captain who had sinned in this way in a stage-coach. "To speak indiscreetly," says the Quaker, "what we are obliged to hear, by being hasped up with thee in this public vehicle, is in some degree assaulting on the high road." It is evident that Steele felt keenly this sort of violation of the personality, for in a later paper he uses even stronger language concerning a kindred offence: "To say a thing which perplexes the heart of him you speak to, or brings blushes into his face, is a degree of murder."

As we have already seen, Steele can be severe upon silly and bad women, but his severity is due to the high respect in which he holds good women. It is for this reason that he is scathing alike on the jilt, the prude and the coquette. His demonstration of the kinship between the two latter is admirable:—

"The Prude appears more virtuous, the Coquette more vicious, than she really is. The distant behaviour of the Prude tends to the same purpose as the advances of the Coquette; and you have as little reason to fall into despair from the severity of the one, as to conceive hope from the familiarity of the other. What leads you into a clear sense of their character is, that you may observe each of them has the distinction of sex in all her thoughts, words and actions."

Here we see the kinship between apparent opposites. In No. 168 of *The Tatler* Steele turns his method round about, and shows the contrast between impudence and absurdity, which are apparently akin.

So too sorrow over a fine thing misused inspires Steele's satire of the lady of quality. She who has none to withstand her may become petulant, and so we read of a lady who is "very seldom out of humour for a woman of her quality." Having none to criticise her openly, she may develop many faults and become censorious of others; and so we have the "lady of quality, who is one of those who are ever railing at the vices of the age, but mean only one vice, because it is the only one they are not guilty of." In a lighter spirit he ridicules the waste of time in paying meaningless calls. One lady writes: "I have several now with whom I keep a constant correspondence, and return visit for visit punctually every week, and yet we have not seen each other since last November was twelvemonth." But it took something greater than Steele to put a stop to this absurdity—the Great War. Both frivolity and affected gravity are struck at in the double-barrelled sarcasm on the devotee, who "never carries a white shock-dog on her arm or dormouse in her pocket, but always an abridged piece of morality, to steal out when she is sure of being observed."

Addison played his part in the moral cleansing which was effected by *The Tatler* and *The Spectator*, but, on the whole, he did it with a less hearty good-will to women. Not that there is anything very severe in his satire. Like Steele, he deals mainly with fashions in dress and with feminine trivialities, and probably nowhere does he pass a judgment so stern as that which has been quoted from Steele on the coquette. But neither does he show that warmth of admiration which is so conspicuous in Steele; for him the trivialities *are* the woman. What a satire on frivolity is Clarinda's journal, or the fuss over the sickness of a lap-dog! Patches, the towering head-dress, the hoop-petticoat, the fan—things of that sort subtend a far larger angle in Addison's treatment of women than in Steele's. An empty life directed by an empty head and a shallow heart—such is the impression he leaves. He is pungent on the loquacity of women: "It has been said in the praise of some men, that they could talk whole hours together upon anything; but it must be owned to the honour of the other sex, that there are many among them who can talk whole hours together upon nothing."

Addison was more apt than Steele to look abroad upon the general structure of society, apart from questions of sex. The servant question, which existed then as now, was, it is true, handled by Steele; but such treatment as politics and party-spirit receive is mainly Addison's. The Political Upholsterer is his creation. He too exposes in the character of Will Wimble the position of the younger brother. The character is a satire on the folly of a great family, "who had rather see their children starve like gentlemen, than thrive in a trade or profession that is beneath their quality." And so the unfortunate Will spends his life making or mending hunting and fishing tackle for the neighbours with whom he dines, or carving toys for their children. It is Addison too who satirises the treatment of private chaplains, who dine indeed at the table of the squire or lord who employs them, but are expected to rise from the table before dessert.

The province of literature is common to both the essayists, and Steele as well as Addison contributes serious critical papers on literature, as well as satirical ones. Still, in this province Addison preponderates. The best-known criticisms in *The Spectator* are those on *Paradise Lost* and on *Chevy Chase*, and both are Addison's. There is the same preponderance in the satire of literature. Steele ridicules the Critic and the Wit, and gives a satirical catalogue of poetic stock, including "about fifty similes, that were never yet applied, besides three-and-twenty descriptions of the sun rising, that might be of great use to an epic poet." Artificiality and insincerity are the faults that most readily rouse him. They rouse Addison too. His Ned Softly would find use for Steele's similes and sunrises. His Timothy Tittle is the pedantic critic who judges Homer and Virgil, "not from their own works, but from those of Rapin and Bossu," and who laughs or sheds tears by rule. Tom Folio, "an universal scholar, so far as the title-page of all authors," is a satire on another form of pedantry. He can find but two faults in Heinsius's Virgil: "One of them is in the *Æneid*, where there are two commas instead of a parenthesis; and another in the third Georgic, where you may find a semicolon turned upside down."

The Spectator expired in 1712 (to be revived for a short time in 1714), but *The Guardian* continued the tradition till October, 1713, when Steele suddenly brought it to an end, in order to turn to politics in *The Englishman*. In *The Guardian*, Steele and Addison increased the volume of their satires upon life, but developed nothing new. The philosopher Berkeley however showed a very pretty wit in his observations on the pineal gland of a freethinker, finding to his astonishment that the seat of the understanding was "narrower than ordinary, insomuch that there was not any room for a miracle, prophecy, or separate spirit." But the most remarkable of the recruits to the new periodical was Pope, who showed in his satire on dedications, in the celebrated ironical panegyric on the pastorals of Ambrose Philips, and in the receipt to make an epic poem that he could, had he chosen, have been supreme (if we bar Swift) in the prose satire of his time, as he was in verse. Of satire on literature the age produced nothing better than these three pieces, and perhaps nothing equal to them.

In *The Examiner, The Whig Examiner,* and other periodicals, the literary merit declines as the political purpose grows stronger; and it is only now and then that we meet with a sketch such as the Tory Foxhunter (in *The Freeholder*), which is worthy to be ranked with the best of the *Spectators*. *The Craftsman*, which ran from 1726 to 1735, is of more importance. It introduces the considerable figure of Bolingbroke, and presents some prose satire on the policy of Walpole. But in the main it is a quarry for the historian rather than for the man whose interest is centred in letters. More important still are *The Champion* (1739-10) and *The Covent-Garden Journal* (1752), for they bring before us no less a person than Henry Fielding (1707-54). But Fielding's most effective satire, outside the novels, is *A Journey from this World to the Next*, which admirably illustrates both his power to sting and his skill in compliment; the former in showing the miser compelled slowly to part with the money which lies before him in heaps, "every one of which would have purchased the honour of some patriots, and the chastity of some prudes"; and the latter in the visit to "his Most Mortal Majesty, Death." The only victories which are not represented on the walls of the great potentate's palace are those of Marlborough: "His Majesty hath no great respect for that duke, for he never sent him a subject he could keep from him, nor did he ever get a single subject by his means, but he lost a thousand others for him."

Among the other works of Fielding, we need notice as a satire only *Jonathan Wild the Great* (1743). The novels are something larger and finer, but *Jonathan Wild* is irony from start to finish. It proceeds upon the principle that "no two things can possibly be more distinct than greatness and goodness," and has for a hero one who "had only enough of that meanness [goodness] to make him partaker of the imperfection of humanity instead of the perfection of diabolism." With him is contrasted Heartfree, who is "so silly a fellow, that he never took the least advantage of the ignorance of his customers, and contented himself with very moderate gains on his goods"; and Mrs. Heartfree, "who, with an agreeable person, was a mean-spirited, poor, domestic, low-bred animal, who confined herself mostly to the care of her family." Fielding maintains the irony with a relentlessness that, truth to tell, makes the book extremely unpleasant reading; though he has sufficient mercy on his readers to drop hints of his real view from time to time, and in the end makes Wild die on the scaffold, while the simple and trusting Heartfree recovers his fortune and lives in love and happiness with his family. The closing chapters are the best in the book.

Two years before *The Covent-Garden Journal*, Samuel Johnson (1709–1784) had entered the ranks of the periodical essayists with *The Rambler*. It follows the tradition of *The Spectator*, eschewing politics and dealing with questions of morals or manners or literature. But it follows the tradition in a Johnsonian way, and is, in general, rather gravely ethical than bantering or satirical. Still, there are character-sketches, like those of Suspirius, the human screech-owl (the original of Goldsmith's Croker), and Mrs. Busy, who in her thrift neglects nothing but her children. There are exposures of specific vices or foibles, like the paper on the Detractors, subdivided into Roarers, Whisperers and Moderators; and that on Peevishness in the person of Tetrica. The education of a fop is satirised, and the misery of the man who makes it his business in life to win and maintain the reputation of a wit among ladies is depicted with powerful strokes. The relations of the sexes are discussed. Hymenæus and Tranquilla justify, from the two sides, the breaking-off of courtship. Literary themes are handled also. No. 27 shows Johnson's well-grounded hatred and scorn of patronage; and the loathsomeness of the flattering dedication is the subject of No. 136. Pope had treated the same subject in *The Guardian*, but the grave censure of Johnson was new. "Every other kind of adulteration," says he, "however shameful, however mischievous, is less detestable than the crime of counterfeiting characters, and fixing the stamp of literary sanction upon the dross and refuse of the world." The well-known picture of Dick Minim, the pseudo-critic, is in *The Idler*, and it is painted in much lighter colours. On the whole Johnson's touch is heavy, and in prose satire he is inferior to the founders of the periodical essay.

Few of the miscellaneous writers who flourished about the middle of the eighteenth century are worthy of more than a passing reference. The journals for which they wrote, even those of them which have been included in the canon of the British Essayists, are rarely read; and the few who do read them find them somewhat vapid. The influence of Johnson tended to make satire subordinate. His disciple Hawkesworth, in *The Adventurer*, cultivates chiefly the moral allegory and the apologue, and rarely uses the weapons of irony and satire. That he could use them to good purpose is shown by his ironical defence of the character of the gamester in No. 29, and, above all, in his admirable account in No. 100, of the progress of an innocent country-fellow from the stage of Greenhorn to that of Blood. In this progress the bumpkin is hindered by his virtues. He becomes more fashionable in his garb, but his manner does not keep pace with his dress; he is still "modest and diffident, temperate and sober, and consequently still subject to ridicule." It is when he has become "utterly insensible to shame, and lived upon the town as a beast of prey in the forest" that he acquires "the proud distinction of a Blood," and is thrown into prison. In the most palmy days of the Periodical Essay we find few better papers.

While Hawkesworth tried to follow in the footsteps of Johnson, Edward Moore, the projector of *The World* and its most frequent contributor, essayed rather to emulate the lighter papers of *The Spectator*; and in *The Connoisseur*, George Colman the Elder and Bonnell Thornton rarely wrote in the graver vein. Many of the papers are clever enough, but the satire is in the main a pale reflection of *The Spectator*. In *The World* Moore afforded an opportunity to a satirist of rare gifs, the misunderstood and underrated Lord Chesterfield (1694–1773). Chesterfield had written before, and written admirably, in *Fog's Journal* and *Common Sense*; but these journals are outside the canon, and on the whole the best as well as the easiest way to learn the characteristics of his satire is to turn up the articles in *The World* which were contributed by him. One of the few merits that have never been denied him is that he could write; and these papers demonstrate that he deserves all, and more than all, the credit he has received. He is a master of restrained irony; no one can give a finer point to a phrase. Though his essays are a mere handful, he sweeps the whole gamut of social satire as it was understood by Addison. He satirises pride of birth, affectation, decorum, women who paint, quacks, duellists, men of honour, men who drink when they are not thirsty, though they would think it foolish to eat when they were not hungry. His essay on duelling is more witty than any of Steele's. His man of honour, who may do anything except declining single combat and cheating at cards, is an unsurpassed satirical conception. He ridicules the language of fine ladies with great effect: "A fine woman—under this head, I comprehend all fine gentlemen too, not knowing in truth where else to place them properly—is vastly obliged, or vastly offended, vastly glad, or vastly sorry. Large objects are vastly great, small ones are vastly little; and I had lately the pleasure to hear a fine woman pronounce, by a happy metonymy, a very small gold snuff-box that was produced in company to be vastly pretty, because it was so vastly little." For vastly read awfully—*de te fabula narratur*.

The essay on the country gentleman's tour to Paris illustrates Chesterfield's happy phrasing. The gentleman tells us with regard to his son that he "passed nine years at Westminster School in learning the words of two languages, long since dead, and not yet above half revived. When I took him away from school, I resolved to send him directly abroad, having been at Oxford myself." A subsequent essay leaves the reader wondering whether the unfortunate gentleman would not have done well to let his son follow in his own steps, notwithstanding the experience so deftly hinted at here.

Chesterfield's touch is light, but the spirit which prompts it is habitually grave. They are real faults that he points out in the system of education; he is as serious in purpose as Steele in his condemnation of the morality of duelling and of the distorted fashionable conception of honour; he is perfectly sincere in his condemnation of the drinkers or "siphons," as he calls them. In spite of the ill name he has acquired through his letters to his son, he was fully conscious of the faults of his own class and of the evil example it set. Except perhaps his treatment of the man of honour, there is no better specimen of his spirit and method than the essay on decorum, with its grave approval of the subordination of the lower classes to the higher in profligacy as in other things:—

" The middle class of people of this country, though generally straining to imitate their betters, have not yet shaken off the prejudices of their education; very many of them still believe in a Supreme Being, in a future state of rewards and punishments, and retain some coarse, home-spun notions of moral good and evil. The rational system of materialism has not yet reached them; and, in my opinion, it may be full as well it never should; for as I am not of levelling principles, I am for preserving a due subordination from inferiors to superiors, which an equality of profligacy must totally destroy."

For nearly two centuries Chesterfield has stood in the pillory fashioned for him by Johnson, and for a century and a half we have known Oliver Goldsmith (1728–1774) by the well-merited encomium of the epitaph Johnson wrote, as the man who tried nearly every species of writing, and tried none that he did not adorn. He adorned satire among the rest. As humorist and satirist we know him best through *The Vicar of Wakefield*. But he is the author also of writings in which satire, instead of being merely incidental, forms the staple. He is seen at his best in *The Citizen of the World* (1762). In spite of Beau Tibbs and the Man in Black, it is less known than it deserves to be known. The plan of letters from a Chinese visitor to a friend in China (it is not, of course, Goldsmith's invention) affords limitless opportunity for the display of a satire which might easily be made corrosive. But it is tempered by Goldsmith's habitual kindliness. In the main, what he writes is not so much satire as good-natured and humorous comment. "By long travelling," says the Citizen of the World, "I am taught to laugh at folly alone, and to find nothing truly ridiculous but villainy and vice." And herein he speaks for Goldsmith; for it is folly and villainy and vice that he satirises. Differences of manners and customs were obvious themes for the

Citizen of the World; yet Goldsmith gives them not more space than Addison, but less. The Citizen is tolerant of different conceptions of beauty and of their expression in fashions strange to him. There is a cutting edge to his words only where there is something wrong; as there is in the story of the man with a wooden leg, who "was indicted, and found guilty of being poor, and sent to Newgate"; as there is too in the satire of the indecency of writers like D'Urfey, in the ironical praise of English ladies for their moderation in gambling, and in the discussion of the making and breaking of treaties and the causes of war.

In more points than one Goldsmith anticipates the great social censors of the nineteenth century. He saw before Thackeray the pettiness of snobbery, and ridicules the snob in Letter LV.; and before Dickens was born he was awake to the evil of the law's delays. Letter XCVIII. ironically urges the advantage in the administration of justice of taking plenty of time to consider the matter, and Dickens merely expanded the theme when he traced the victim of the Court of Chancery from youth to tottering age. Though he makes no serious effort to maintain consistently the Chinese point of view, it helps him occasionally to give an original turn to well-worn themes. When the Citizen of the World examines Westminster Abbey in company with the Man in Black, he is much impressed by the tombs of the illustrious dead. Surprised to learn that an especially beautiful monument commemorates neither a king, nor a warrior, nor a poet, he asks, "'What is the great man who lies here particularly remarkable for?'—'Remarkable, sir!' said my companion; 'why, sir, the gentleman that lies here is remarkable, very remarkable—for a tomb in Westminster Abbey.'" It is the foreign eye too that detects the pettiness of the demand for pay to see the monuments of the kings; and the foreigner's position brings to light the self-assurance of the ignorant. Honoured by the invitation of a great lady, the Chinaman finds that London society knows things Chinese better than he does. He is made to sit on a cushion on the floor, has a napkin pinned under his chin, and is instructed in Chinese manners and the Chinese language as they are understood by the pundits of the West.

Like the sensible man he really was (notwithstanding the "inspired idiot" theory), Goldsmith satirises especially the flaws in the things he best knows. He, a writer, turns, as his predecessors had done, again and again to literature. In his club of authors he exposes the jealousies and conceit of the craft of letters. He ridicules the phrase, "the republic of letters," as applied to a group "where every member is desirous of governing and none willing to obey." He lays bare the absurdity of pastoral elegies. He satirises the contemporary drama and the customs of the theatre, and pours ridicule upon playwrights and actors alike. In his comments upon the introduction of irrelevant considerations of wealth and rank he shows how he himself had suffered in that age of transition from the old patronage to the new system of buying and selling the heroic soul in the open market. "As soon as a piece is published, the first questions are, Who is the author? Does he keep a coach? Where lies his estate? What sort of a table does he keep?" "A man here who should write, and honestly confess that he wrote, for bread, might as well send his manuscript to fire the baker's oven; not one creature will read him."

But Goldsmith was a doctor of medicine as well as a man of letters, and there is in the excellent satire of quackery in Letter XXIV. a certain precision which betrays the man who knows. "Be the disorder never so desperate or radical, you will find numbers in every street who, by levelling a pill at the part affected, promise a certain cure, without loss of time, knowledge of a bedfellow, or hindrance of business."—"Few physicians here go through the ordinary courses of education, but receive all their knowledge of medicine by immediate inspiration from Heaven."—"If the patient lives, then has he [the doctor] one more to add to the surviving list; if he dies, then it may be justly said of the patient's disorder, that, as it was not cured, the disorder was incurable."

The satire, always happily expressed, is adorned from time to time with an inimitable felicity of phrase. What could surpass the comments on the mourning for the death of the king? The unfortunate Citizen of the World displeases one political group by the misery of the countenance he deems appropriate to the occasion, and the other by the cheerfulness he assumes on discovering this. And so he studies the fashionable air: "Something between jest and earnest: a complete virginity of face, uncontaminated with the smallest symptom of meaning."

The stream of the essay-periodicals flowed on continuously all through the eighteenth century, and social satire was always an element in it. For a few years the centre shifted from London to Edinburgh, where Henry Mackenzie (1745–1831) and a group of his friends produced first *The Mirror* (1779–80), and afterwards *The Lounger* (1785–87). They were able men and clever writers; but either the themes were exhausted or they lacked invention to discover new ones. Though the industrious Nathan Drake enumerates more than sixty collections which appeared between the date of *The Lounger* and 1809, the year in which he closed his labours, the periodical essay was dying of inanition.

Johnson's *Rambler*, as we have seen, was a revival of the more literary essay. But a few years after it politics were once more in the ascendant. The accession of George III., followed by his determined struggle to rule by favourites and to strengthen the prerogative of the Crown, gave a keen edge to the questions at issue between the parties. Smollett, a good novelist but an incompetent journalist, supported the Bute administration in *The Briton*, but was utterly overwhelmed by the far more skilful work of John Wilkes (1727–97) (assisted by Churchill) in *The North Briton* (1762). Though he does not maintain it consistently, Wilkes begins in a vein of irony, professing to be full of joy at the accomplishment of the national ambition, the planting of a Scotsman at the head of the English Treasury. This unfortunately leads to the death of Mr. John Bull, who "was choked by inadvertently swallowing a thistle, which he had placed by way of ornament on the top of his salad." The old themes of the pride and vanity of the Scots, their readiness to leave home and their disinclination to return, are handled once more. It is urged that the king should reside at least some part of the year in Scotland. True, we, the Scots, sold to his rebel subjects the last king but one who committed himself to our care. But then, "the same consideration of interest which then made us false, would now make us true."

To establish Presbytery on the ruins of Episcopacy is desirable but difficult, for "it is safer to take off the head of a layman, than to wag a finger against the beard of a priest." But it may be done. To pave the way, Scots should enter into the Church of England. Their presence will weaken opposition, and when the time comes they can change again. The charge of dissimulation and hypocrisy can be met by pleading the goodness of the cause; "and if the good of the country and countrymen was not a sufficient excuse for flattery, lying, perjury, perfidy, treason, and rebellion, what must become of every true Scot?"

Wilkes deserves rather more credit in the literary sense than he has received, but the account is more than balanced by the notoriety he won by his unsparing criticism of the king's speech in No. 45 of *The North Briton*. His highest distinction is that he "rang the bell" for the greatest of English political satirists; for the royal and ministerial persecution of Wilkes supplies a large part of the inspiration of Junius.

Stat nominis umbra. It is fortunately unnecessary here to discuss the unsolved and probably insoluble question of the identity of Junius; it must suffice to say that an extremely strong case has been made out for the view that Junius was Sir Philip Francis. Whoever he was, Junius had been writing on persons and subjects of political controversy before the series of letters which have made his name immortal began in January, 1769, in *The Public Advertiser*, a journal which made a prominent feature of letters from contributors outside the staff, and was ready to receive them indifferently from either side. It was Junius who brought the weight of the *Advertiser* down overwhelmingly on the side hostile to the Court and the Ministry.

It must be confessed that the famous *Letters*, great as is their talent, are unpleasant reading: venomous malignity and corrosive spite are qualities not beautiful to contemplate; and cold poison seems somehow to be more deadly than poison that is not so cold. Junius may have inherited the current prejudices from Wilkes, but it is more probable that he absorbed them from the atmosphere. In the phrase, "When treachery is in question, I think we should make allowances for a Scotchman," we might be reading Wilkes, except that there is a neatness in the expression that is beyond Wilkes. The rebellions, still fresh in memory, of the Jacobites, whose hopes of success rested upon Scotland, furnished materials at once for the charge of treachery which is brought against the northern people, and for sarcasms aimed at the intelligence of the king. He has had ample warning in the uniform experience of his ancestors, but "a bigoted understanding can . . . find an earnest of future loyalty in former rebellions." And his descent from the detested royal line that sprang from the hated race affords ground for a fresh gibe against the Duke of Grafton: "The mode of your descent from Charles the Second is only a bar to your pretensions to the Crown, and no way interrupts the regularity of your succession to all the virtues of the Stuarts"—virtues of such a sort that there has never been an honest man among the Stuarts.

Neatness of antithesis and pregnancy of expression are characteristic of Junius. Grafton, "a singular instance of youth without spirit," is defended by one who is "a no less remarkable example of age without the benefits of experience." He starts from one extreme to the other, "without leaving, between the weakness and fury of the passions, one moment's interval for the firmness of the understanding." In a few words Junius can convey to the king himself a melancholy truth: "The fortune, which made you a king, forbad you to have a friend"; or drop a sinister hint: "The same pretended power [that claimed by the House of Commons over Wilkes], which robs an English subject of his birthright, may rob an English king of his crown."

There is nothing finer in the *Letters of Junius* than No. XXXV., addressed to the king, from which these last quotations are taken. It is stinging satire, but it is also something far greater—truth. The statement of the effect on Wilkes of royal hostility is admirable. Wilkes has made mistakes:—

" He said more than moderate men would justify; but not enough to entitle him to the honour of your Majesty's personal resentment. The rays of Royal indignation, collected upon him, served only to illuminate, and could not consume. Animated by the favour of the people on one side, and heated by persecution on the other, his views and sentiments changed with his situation. Hardly serious at first, he is now an enthusiast. The coldest bodies warm with opposition, the hardest sparkle in collision. There is a holy mistaken zeal in politics as well as religion. By persuading others, we convince ourselves. The passions are engaged, and create a maternal affection in the mind, which forces us to love the cause, for which we suffer."

And the errors of the king have been made the graver by the folly of his ministers, who have reduced him to a situation where he can neither do wrong without ruin nor right without affliction.

Passages of this sort afford a partial excuse to those contemporaries who believed Burke to be Junius, and the excuse is strengthened by the occasional statement in the *Letters* of illuminating general principles; as when Junius points out that the man of unblemished integrity and the profligate are alike impervious to criticism: "it is the middle compound character which alone is vulnerable: the man, who, without firmness enough to avoid a dishonourable action, has feeling enough to be ashamed of it." That Burke could be sharply sarcastic is proved by the *Letter to a Noble Lord*. But the *proportion* of personality to lofty political wisdom is totally different in the two writers. In Burke lofty political wisdom is habitual; in Junius it is only occasional. And in Junius the great public question is the Middlesex election; while in Burke, even in the *Letter to a Noble Lord*, behind the Bedford estates loom the principles of the French Revolution.

It was the unhappy lot of the house of Bedford to provoke the hostility, both of the greatest of English political satirists (for Swift transcends politics) and of the greatest of English political philosophers. The former dealt with the fourth duke, and the latter with his son, the fifth duke. Junius is blighting:—

" You are indeed a very considerable man. The highest rank;—a splendid fortune; and a name, glorious till it was yours, were sufficient to have supported you with meaner abilities than I think you possess. From the first, you derived a constitutional claim to respect; from the second, a natural extensive authority;—the last created a partial expectation of hereditary virtues. The use you have made of these uncommon advantages might have been more honourable to yourself, but could not be more instructive to mankind. We may trace it in the veneration of your country, the choice of your friends, and in the accomplishment of every sanguine hope, which the public might have conceived from the illustrious name of Russell.

" The eminence of your station gave you a commanding prospect of your duty. The road which led to honour was open to your view. You could not lose it by mistake, and you had no temptation to depart from it by design. Compare the natural dignity and importance of the richest peer of England:—the noble independence, which he might have maintained in parliament, and the real interest and respect, which he might have acquired, not only in parliament, but through the whole kingdom; compare these glorious distinctions with the ambition of holding a share in government, the emoluments of a place, the sale of a borough, or the purchase of a corporation; and though you may not regret the virtues, which create respect, you may see with anguish how much real importance and authority you have lost. Consider the character of an independent, virtuous Duke of Bedford; imagine what he might be in this country, then reflect one moment upon what you are."

Would Burke ever have made the mistake of depreciating, in itself and without qualification, "the ambition of holding a share in government"? Junius goes on to mention the emoluments of office, but as an additional item, not as a qualification.

Burke is equally severe, but he is less lithe and supple. There is in him something of the clumsiness, as well as the weight, of that leviathan whose image is in his mind in a familiar passage:—

" I know not how it has happened, but it really seems that, whilst his Grace was meditating his well-considered censure upon me, he fell into a sort of sleep. Homer nods; and the Duke of Bedford may dream; and as dreams (even his golden dreams) are apt to be ill-pieced and incongruously put together, his Grace preserved his idea of reproach to *me*, but took the subject-matter from the Crown grants *to his own family*. This is ' the stuff of which his dreams are made.' In that way of putting things together his Grace is perfectly in the right. The grants to the house of Russell were so enormous, as not only to outrage economy, but even to stagger credibility. The Duke of Bedford is the Leviathan among all the creatures of the Crown. He tumbles about his un-wieldy bulk: he plays and frolics in the ocean of the royal bounty. Huge as he is, and whilst ' he lies floating many a rood,' he is still a creature. His ribs, his fins, his whalebone, his blubber, the very spiracles through which he spouts a torrent of brine against his origin, and covers me all over with the spray,— everything of him and about him is from the throne."

But what is really characteristic of Burke in the great *Letter* is the transition from the personal question to the issue between revolution on the one hand and, on the other, that public law of Europe, which is "covered with the awful hoar of innumerable ages." The Duke of Bedford will stand so long as the law of pre-scription endures; but the revolutionists "are the Duke of Bed-ford's natural hunters, and he is their natural game." And then follows the vivid picture of the pure theorist:—

" Nothing can be conceived more hard than the heart of a thoroughbred metaphysician. It comes nearer to the cold malignity of a wicked spirit than to the frailty and passion of a man. It is like that of the principle of Evil himself, incorporeal, pure, unmixed, dephlegmated, defecated evil. It is no easy operation to eradicate humanity from the human breast. What Shake-speare calls ' the compunctious visitings of nature' will sometimes knock at their hearts, and protest against their murderous speculations. But they have a means of compounding with their nature. Their humanity is not dis-solved. They only give it a long prorogation. They are ready to declare, that they do not think two thousand years too long a period for the good that they pursue. It is remarkable that they never see any way to their projected good but by the road of some evil. Their imagination is not fatigued with the con-templation of human suffering through the wild waste of centuries added to centuries of misery and desolation. Their humanity is at their horizon—and, like the horizon, it always flies before them. The geometricians and the chem-ists bring, the one from the dry bones of their diagrams, and the other from the soot of their furnaces, dispositions that make them worse than indifferent about those feelings and habitudes, which are the support of the moral world. Ambition is come upon them suddenly; they are intoxicated with it, and it has rendered them fearless of the danger, which may from thence arise to others or to themselves. These philosophers consider men in their experiments no more than they do mice in an air pump, or in a recipient of mephitic gas."

Political satire in prose never again reaches the level it attains in Burke and Junius. The Anti-Jacobins handle it, but with far less weight, and mainly in verse; and though Disraeli himself imitates Junius in the *Letters of Runnymede*, which were published in 1836, the imitation is disappointingly poor.

CHAPTER XI

VERSE SATIRE AFTER POPE

THE profound influence of Pope upon the period in which he lived and the generation following his death is seen not least clearly in the fact that nearly all the poets—minor poets at least, in whom the tendency to imitation is strongest — write satires, however small may be their share of the satiric spirit. Men like Collins and Gray avoid it almost completely. But even the amiable blind poet Dr. Blacklock must needs write satires, and, to deepen the incongruity, his *Advice to the Ladies* is coarse, and this coarseness is inscribed to a lady. Not every characteristic of Pope however proved equally imitable. Many hoped to "convey" something of his venom; but few, if any, conceived themselves capable of rivalling his airy grace. *The Rape of the Lock* still stands alone, while there were many imitations of his imitations of Horace, and the very titles of a multitude of mock-heroics attest the widespread influence of *The Dunciad*. We can trace it from *The Gymnasiad* of Paul Whitehead, through *The Scribleriad* of Richard Cambridge, *The Hilliad* of Smart, *The Rosciad* of Churchill and *The Consuliad* of Chatterton, to *The Baviad* and *The Mæviad* of Gifford.

The influence is seen no less in numerous occasional pieces in which the minor wits do their best, some in prose and some in verse, to "steal Jove's authentic fire" in order to take their revenge upon the master satirist; and not always without effect. He who deals in personal satire had better have a thick skin, which Pope had not. Though none could wield the lash so skilfully, his sensitiveness probably made his pain greater than theirs. Neither was it made easier by the fact that he was the aggressor. He pretended indeed that he had been driven to write *The Dunciad* by the attacks made on him; but the motive was certainly different, and previous to the publication of *The Dunciad* attacks upon Pope had not been numerous. It was no satire or lampoon that set Theobald in the first edition on the throne of the dunces, but the fact that in *Shakespeare Restored* he had exposed the errors in Pope's edition of the great dramatist. Neither was it any attack by Colley Cibber that caused Pope afterwards to dethrone Theobald and put Cibber in his place. Cibber had kept silence under repeated attacks; but at last he retorted in *A Letter from Mr. Cibber to Mr. Pope*—a letter without literary merit, but effective for its purpose of damaging Pope. The enginer was hoist with his own petard. John Dennis and George Ducket were also among the victims of *The Dunciad*, and *Pope Alexander's Supremacy and Infallibility Examined* is believed to be their retort. Edward Ward too struck back in *Durgen*, which he describes as "a plain satire on a pompous satirist." The verse is poor, but there is here and there a dignity in the rebuke which must have made Pope wince. Ward lays his finger on a weakness when he speaks of *The Dunciad* as a poem wherein the reader may

> " Be instructed, if untaught before,
> How to despise true merit when it's poor."

Edward Young (1683–1765), an older man than Pope, was indebted to Dryden more than to Pope, to whom, indeed, he probably gave more than he received from him. Few but students at the present day know him except as the author of *Night Thoughts*; and even that is rather famous than widely read. Those who, a little more learned, know that he devoted three books to thoughts on *The Last Day*, might be still less disposed to look for him among the comparatively flippant tribe of satirists. Yet in the age of Pope he was, after Pope himself, esteemed the foremost of satirists in verse, and his seven satires on *The Universal Passion* (1725)— *Fame*—ranked second only to the works of the master. Nor were the contemporaries of the two poets wholly wrong. Nothing will ever make those seven satires, or the subsequent *Epistle to Mr. Pope concerning the Authors of the Age* (1730), popular again; but they have very substantial merits all the same. Though few would turn to Young for models of terse wisdom, again and again he fulfils Pope's definition of wit by giving admirable expression to what has often been thought. He can state effectively a truth which only a few can know by their own experience: " None think the great unhappy, but the great"; in half a dozen words he can bring home to us the intimate relation between qualities superficially unconnected with one another—"Good breeding is the blossom of good sense." These lines illustrate what is perhaps Young's best gift, his just moral sense. The same quality which fitted him to be the poet of the *Night Thoughts* permeates his satires also. It is this which enables him to appreciate so correctly the precise worth and worthlessness of wealth:—

> " A decent competence we fully taste;
> It strikes our sense, and gives a constant feast.
> More, we perceive by dint of thought alone;
> The rich must labour to possess their own,
> To feel their great abundance; and request
> Their humble friends to help them to be blest,
> To see their treasures, hear their glories told,
> And aid the wretched impotence of gold."

Hence too springs his panegyric of good nature:—

> " Parts may be prais'd, good-nature is ador'd;
> Then draw your wit as seldom as your sword,
> And never on the weak; or you'll appear
> As there no hero, no great genius here."

The doctrine running through the seven satires is that mankind in all their activities are impelled and governed by the love of fame. This manifests itself in the most diverse ways: one seeks to gain it by following the fashion, another by affecting singularity. This makes detraction universal among women: Hortensia only is commended without reserve—and the reason is that Hortensia died last night. To express the force of the desire for eminence, Young translates into the feminine gender Cæsar's famous saying that he would rather be the first man in a village than the second man in Rome. If she cannot win the primacy for what is admirable, she will struggle for it in what is loathsome:—

> " For Harvey, the first wit she cannot be;
> Nor, cruel Richmond, the first toast for thee.
> Since full each other station of renown,
> Who would not be the greatest trapes in town? "

Occasionally time has veered round to the view of the victim in preference to that of the satirist. We of the twentieth century may be tempted to think the ladies who are ridiculed sometimes more nearly right in their theology than the divine. Punishment infinite and eternal for an offence temporal and finite no longer seems fair dealing. But we cannot deny the skill and pungency of the satire in which Young expresses his view. In the course of it he anticipated the well-known saying of the French nobleman, that God would think twice before He damned a man of the nobleman's quality:—

> " Shall pleasures of a short duration chain
> A *lady's* soul in everlasting pain? "

In that age no satirist could refrain from touching upon the theme of patronage. The frequency and the bitterness with which it is treated is the measure of the authors' sufferings. Young deals with it in the third and again in the fourth satires. The fulsome flattery which it encourages degrades, he justly insists, both him that gives and him that takes:—

> " With terms like these, how mean the tribe that close!
> Scarce meaner they who terms like these impose."

And the tribe most likely to close with them is Young's own, "the men of ink." After such a protest we reasonably hope that one author at least will be found guiltless of the vice of flattery. Alas! in the seventh satire we find the censor transmuted into a panegyrist, and giving vent to some of the most fulsome praise ever written. There is, or was, it seems, "one fam'd Alpine hill," whence burst Rhone and Po, Danube and Rhine, from whose bounty "whole kingdoms smile, a thousand harvests rise." Just such a source of blessings is that transcendent pattern of all the virtues and graces—George I.!—

> " In Brunswick such a source the Muse adores,
> Which public blessings through half Europe pours.
> When his heart burns with such a godlike aim,
> Angels and George are rivals for the Fame;
> George who in foes can soft affections raise,
> And charm envenom'd Satire into praise."

This shows poorly enough, it must be confessed, beside the irony of Pope in the Epistle to Augustus; and it makes little difference that the one poet addressed the first monarch of the name of George, and the other the second.

John Gay (1685–1732) carried a lighter armament than Young, but was all the more effective on that account. His close association with the wits of Pope's circle is well known. Swift liked him and did him kindnesses. He collaborated with Pope and Arbuthnot in *Three Hours after Marriage,* and in *The Shepherd's Week* (1714) he was used as Pope's instrument in the feud with Ambrose Philips. This lively burlesque had been preceded by *The Fan* (1713), a poem in three books, gently satirical of female fashions and vanities, which shows a good deal of real poetic fancy. At one forge the poet depicts busy Cupids forming the stiff bow and forging the fatal dart; at another forge we see female toys and trinkets fashioned:—

> " Here clouded canes 'midst heaps of toys are found,
> And inlaid tweezer-cases strow the ground;
> There stands the toilette, nursery of charms,
> Completely furnish'd with bright Beauty's arms;
> The patch, the powder-box, pulville, perfumes,
> Pins, paint, a flattering glass, and black-lead combs."

The debt to *The Rape of the Lock* is obvious; but if Gay borrows, at least he proves himself a worthy disciple.

The Shepherd's Week is a piece of higher value. Intended as a burlesque, it is so full of spirit and so redolent of the country that it rises above its type. Real rusticity is deftly set against the conventional pastoral. But Gay was too skilful and too much amused by the satire of Philips to let his fundamental purpose be forgotten. As a rule the end of each piece shows the burlesque intention. Thus, in the Wednesday eclogue, Marian is resolved on suicide, and rejects successively the knife, the cord and the pond, so that night comes on, and

> " The prudent maiden deems it now too late,
> And till to-morrow comes reserves her fate."

And so on Friday Bumkinet and Grubbinol bewail Blouzelinda, and swear to tune their lay to her for ever. But ultimately they remember that Gaffer Treadwell had said that "excessive sorrow is exceeding dry," and so

> " In ale and kisses they forget their cares
> And Susan Blouzelinda's loss repairs."

In *Trivia* we have rather a record than a satire. It recounts the scenes and customs, tricks and frauds of London in the early eighteenth century. Much of the same sort of information may be gathered from *The Tatler* and *The Spectator*, but nowhere, probably, is there a store of it so rich and so concentrated as in *Trivia*. As Gay himself says in the *Epistle to Pulteney*, *Trivia*

> " Led the draggled Muse, with pattens shod,
> Through dirty lanes."

And the draggled Muse notes the dirt and the squalor and the tricks and frauds, yet makes them not repellent and not even wholly destitute of charm. There is absolutely none of the savagery of Swift. The epitaph Gay wrote for himself embodies the spirit of the harmless, kindly, clinging man:—

> " Life is a jest and all things show it;
> I thought so once, and now I know it."

This epitaph explains the spirit of Gay's satire. It has just enough of a not unkindly malice to give pungency, but it has no trace of bitterness. He touches his highest point in *The Shepherd's Week*. There is in the *Epistles*, as well as in the *Eclogues* and *Fables*, a good deal of satire which shows the same qualities as the satire in *The Shepherd's Week*. But Gay never again succeeded quite so fully.

In the footsteps of Pope trod likewise the Wartons, Thomas and Joseph; but their capacity for satire was not great. Neither Thomas Warton's *Progress of Discontent* nor his *Newmarket*, nor Joseph Warton's *Fashion* is of any value. The Whiteheads, Paul and William, both of whom are usually dull but occasionally become interesting, are also of the school of Pope. William Whitehead (1715–85) is entertaining, for once, in *The Goat's Beard*, a spirited satirical fable whose application to the human race is sufficiently obvious. In many cases time has spoilt the flavour of these eighteenth-century fables, but in this instance it has added a new zest. Paul Whitehead (1710–74) is occasionally pungent but generally wearisome in *The State Dunces*; and *The Gymnasiad*, a short satirical epic on boxing, is poor, notwithstanding the spirit shown in the description of the gathering of the crowd. Better than either is *Manners*, a piece which led to Whitehead being summoned to the bar of the House of Lords. Apart from the offence given by the satire, Whitehead's character was not such as to stand examination, and he absconded. In *Manners* he certainly does not spare those in high places:—

> " Though strung with ribbands, yet behold his grace
> Shines but a lacquey in a higher place!
> Strip the gay liv'ry from the courtier's back,
> What makes the diff'rence 'twixt my lord and Jack?
> The same mean, supple, mercenary knave,
> The tool of power, and of state the slave:
> Alike the vassal heart in each prevails,
> And all his lordship boasts is larger vails."

Yet another follower of Pope was Soame Jenyns (1704–87), who hardly deserves the complete oblivion that has fallen upon him. His *Art of Dancing*, written in 1728, is humorously didactic, and the satire lies only in the suggestion of the trivial. But *The Modern Fine Gentleman*, written eight years later, is a really telling satire. The Fine Gentleman begins with travel:—

> " Just broke from school, pert, impudent, and raw,
> Expert in Latin, more expert in taw,
> His honour posts o'er Italy and France,
> Measures St. Peter's dome, and learns to dance."

He purchases a seat in parliament, talks nonsense, "storms at placemen, ministers and courts," plays all the night, and is so far from virtue that "not a gen'rous vice can claim a part." He impoverishes himself, "marries some jointur'd antiquated crone," squanders her money, seeks preferment, takes the minister's bribe, and at last "turns downright sharper." It is all expressed in vigorous and rapid verse. The companion piece, *The Modern Fine Lady*, has much less merit.

In *The Modern Fine Gentleman* political corruption is just an incident in a corrupt life: it is the sum and substance of the *Epistle to Curio*. Mark Akenside (1721–70), best known for *The Pleasures of Imagination*, claims a place among satirists by reason of this admirable piece. Akenside was one of those poets who cannot let their own works alone. He re-wrote *The Pleasures of Imagination* and did not improve it, and having produced a masterly satiric epistle, he must needs re-make it as an *Ode to Curio*, and ruin it. In the original form it is among the most polished and effective satires of the school of Pope. The subject of the satire is William Pulteney, once one of the most fervid of the "patriots" who denounced Walpole, and one of the most vigorous of political ballad-writers; now Earl of Bath and obedient servant of power. The bard's indignation is roused by the desertion, and he traces with rare power and skill the slow, reluctant change of his spirit from fervid admiration and unquestioning faith, first to doubt and then to the conviction of guilt. Curio has sold for "barbarous Grandeur" the powers which Reason and Truth and Virtue give, and he must find his last abode in the "fane of Infamy." There are few passages of verse more eloquent than that in which the poet summons the traitor thither:—

" But come, unhappy man! thy fates impend;
Come, quit thy friends, if yet thou hast a friend;
Turn from the poor rewards of guilt like thine,
Renounce thy titles, and thy robes resign;
For see the hand of Destiny display'd
To shut thee from the joys thou hast betray'd!
See the dire fane of Infamy arise!
Dark as the grave and spacious as the skies;
Where, from the first of time, thy kindred train,
The chiefs and princes of the unjust remain.
Eternal barriers guard the pathless road
To warn the wanderer of the curst abode;
But prone as whirlwinds scour the passive sky,
The heights surmounted, down the steep they fly.
There, black with frowns, relentless Time awaits,
And goads their footsteps to the guilty gates:
And still he asks them of their unknown aims,
Evolves their secrets, and their guilt proclaims;
And still his hands despoil them on the road
Of each vain wreath, by lying bards bestow'd,
Break their proud marbles, crush their festal cars,
And rend the lawless trophies of their wars."

Several years before Akenside wrote his *Curio* Samuel Johnson
had produced his *London*. It is an interesting fact that it
was published on the same day with Pope's *One Thousand
Seven Hundred and Thirty Eight*, "a dialogue something like
Horace." It is further interesting that in spite of Pope's great and
long-established reputation the town preferred the work of the
younger poet. Pope was then a man of fifty, and he had only six
years longer to live. The succession seemed to be assured when a
young man of twenty-nine was found able to write as well as or
even better than his literary father. Of Johnson's affiliation to
Pope there could be no doubt. Not only was his measure the heroic
couplet, but it was handled in a manner obviously based upon
Pope's. Further, *London* was, like Pope's contemporary poem, and
like many other poems of Pope that had preceded it, an imitation.
Pope had rooted firmly in English a species of composition which
was neither translation nor wholly independent verse. Here too,
then, Johnson proclaims himself Pope's follower. But his model is
Juvenal, not Horace, and he follows Juvenal much more closely
than Pope follows Horace. In this kind of work the most perfect
success is won when the model merely gives a suggestion; any
approximation to a rendering is a flaw, for it raises the thought of
Rome rather than of London. In *London* Johnson falls into this
mistake. Successful as the poem was, the reader is conscious that

in many respects it does not express the real feelings of Johnson. This may be partly due to the presence of a quasi-dramatic element, if it be true, as Hawkins asserts (though Boswell denies), that the Thales of the piece is Savage. But we may reasonably believe that there was another cause at work as well — that Johnson was not yet mature. Certainly there is an immense advance in *The Vanity of Human Wishes*. With the knowledge we now have of Johnson's opinions and likings, we are disturbed in *London* by praises of the country as a setting for life far preferable to the Strand. But in *The Vanity of Human Wishes* we feel the pulse of Johnson's thought from start to finish. These, we know, are *his* sentiments, this is *his* sombre view of life. Every line rings true, every thought comes from the heart. The philosophy of the piece is suggested in its title, and summed up in the lines at the close which bid men pray for a healthful mind, passions under strict control, and resignation of the will. Nothing else will endure. Flattery attends the great and prosperous, but deserts the unfortunate and the fallen. A Wolsey has a train of followers only so long as he can reward them. The pursuit of knowledge too ends in disappointment; and even though the student remain faithful to his task, resist the temptations of sloth and of love, and escape disease and melancholy, he must not think to enjoy a life free from grief or danger. There is the bitterness of hard experience in the famous lines:—

> " Deign on the passing world to turn thine eyes,
> And pause awhile from letters to be wise;
> There mark what ills the scholar's life assail,
> Toil, envy, want, the patron, and the jail.
> See nations, slowly wise and meanly just,
> To buried merit raise the tardy bust.
> If dreams yet flatter, once again attend,
> Hear Lydiat's life, and Galileo's end."

It is "dangerous parts" and "fatal Learning" that lead Laud to the block; dulness escapes more lightly. Therefore,

> " Around his tomb let Art and Genius weep,
> But hear his death, ye blockheads, hear and sleep."

How frail is the foundation of the warrior's hopes is shown by the story of Charles of Sweden, slain by a dubious hand before a petty fortress. The prayer for length of days is equally mistaken. It is granted, and

> " From Marlb'rough's eyes the streams of dotage flow,
> And Swift expires a driv'ler and a show."

The mother prays for beauty for her daughters:—

> " Yet Vane could tell what ills from beauty spring,
> And Sedley curs'd the form that pleas'd a king."

This great moral piece contains less than four hundred lines. How many poems are there of no greater length that yield so many lines universally known? Several of them have been quoted or referred to above, and it would be easy to add to the number. The whole poem is closely packed with a sad wisdom almost too measured and grave for satire. Except the apostrophe to the blockheads there is hardly a touch of mere smartness. In every line the moralist stands revealed—the moralist whose view of the world is coloured by poverty and disease: the experience of having to live on 4½d. a day sank into the soul of Johnson. But the conclusion shows the man with a faith unconquered yet. He can still pray

> " For love, which scarce collective man can fill;
> For patience, sov'reign o'er transmuted ill;
> For faith, that, panting for a happier seat,
> Counts death kind Nature's signal of retreat."

It is easy to understand Sir Walter Scott's fervent admiration of the poem, even though we may not share it to the full.

Very different was the chief of the satirists of the school of Pope some twenty years later. Charles Churchill (1731–64) resembled Johnson as little in moral tone as in life. His dissipations in company with the hapless Robert Lloyd (1733–64), his schoolfellow at Westminster, his fellow-poet and his unwearied panegyrist, have left their mark on his verse. Drunkenness and immorality, grave sins in any man, are peculiarly unbecoming in a clergyman. On the other hand, it must be remembered that Churchill showed fidelity and generosity in supporting Lloyd in his latter days from means none too ample.

While Johnson is measured, Churchill from the start shows the determination to say the sharpest thing he can think of. In the former, truth came first; in the latter, effect. Endowed as he was with a vigorous mind and a gift for pungent expression, while there is no evidence that he possessed any high degree of imagination, satire was his natural medium. He showed the opinion, commoner in the sixteenth and seventeenth centuries than in the eighteenth, that harshness of verse was not only permissible, but desirable, if

not even necessary, in satire. Hence he illustrates a reaction from
Pope to Dryden. "E'en excellence, unvaried, tedious grows," he
says with reference to Pope. "Perish my Muse," he exclaims,

> " If e'er her labours weaken to refine
> The gen'rous roughness of a nervous line."

And so to avoid tedium he mingles with excellence much that
is less excellent. His verse is studiously rough; but his virile
force of mind renders it effective, not because of, but in spite
of, this roughness. His earliest satire, *The Rosciad* (1761)—a kind
of *Dunciad* directed against actors—was highly successful, and
won the anonymous author fame, while it naturally provoked
attacks. It is said to have been suggested by Robert Lloyd's piece
called *The Actor*, which is rather an *Essay on Criticism* applied to
the stage than a satire; while, in so far as it is satirical, the satire
is general rather than personal. Though the two men were friends,
so different are they in tone that it is astonishing to find that Lloyd
was among the men to whom Churchill's work was ascribed. The
very insufficient reason, no doubt, was that in *The Actor* Lloyd had
handled the same theme. His admiration of Churchill led him to
admire the personal satire, and in an epistle to his friend he urges
him to pursue it farther:—

> " Fools on and off the stage are fools the same,
> And every dunce is satire's lawful game."

But it would be a mistake to suppose that this is typical of Lloyd's
own satire. He is rarely personal: in some respects the friendship
between him and Churchill was a friendship of opposites.

The Rosciad depicts a tribunal assembled on a spacious plain
to determine the question of precedency among actors. Shakespeare
sits first, and next him Jonson; and the former, in a few lines of
unstinted praise, assigns the chair to Garrick. The interest has
evaporated, for we no longer know the numerous actors at whom
Churchill aims his shafts; but the personalities had point at the
time and helped to make the piece popular. Churchill rarely makes
a serious slip, but when we read that the actor must "act from
himself, on his own bottom stand," we can only marvel at the
acrobatic agility which made such a feat possible. Sometimes the
satire, though personal, has a sufficiently wide application to be

effective still. Most frequenters of the theatre can probably apply the lines,

> " With truly tragic stalk
> He creeps, he flies—A hero should not walk";

and the good sense which inspires the satire on the critics is worthy of remembrance to this day:—

> " A servile race
> Who in mere want of fault all merit place;
> Who blind obedience pay to ancient schools,
> Bigots to Greece, and slaves to musty rules."

Churchill had attacked too many to escape attack himself. *The Critical Review* published a hostile article which Churchill believed to be by Smollett, and this evoked a second satire, *The Apology*. Though inferior in fame to *The Rosciad*, it is intrinsically a better performance. While there is still too much personality, it relies more than *The Rosciad* upon general principles. The poet condemns blind adherence to tradition in a nervous couplet:—

> " Fools that we are, like Israel's fools of yore,
> The calf ourselves have fashion'd we adore."

The success of these two pieces fixed the destiny of Churchill. He was recognised as the foremost satirist of his day, and he sustained his reputation by a remarkably rapid series of poems. Johnson, who did not love him, acknowledged his fertility: "He only produces crabs. But, Sir, a tree that produces a great many crabs is better than a tree which produces only a few." Churchill's fluency is shown by the appearance of no fewer than three considerable poems in the September before his death—and this in succession to two others in the same year. Of the three, *The Times* is merely loathsome; *The Farewell* is a vigorously argued dialogue on the love of country; and *Independence* illustrates Churchill's proud spirit and his hatred of that patronage which in those days so often threatened the independence of authors. He had already treated the same subject in *The Author*, where he laments the absence of "real spirit." Authors are

> " The slaves of booksellers or (doom'd by Fate
> To baser chains) vile pensioners of state."

And as illustrations he adduces Smollett and Johnson himself.

These pieces are much less personal than the two by which Churchill first won fame. There is still less personality in *Night*,

a fine epistle to the poet's friend Lloyd, in which he depicts himself
and his friend as creatures of the night, the season for threadbare
Merit, the season also which they naturally prefer. And, he maintains, it is the duty of men to be men, to follow their own bent,
to do what they themselves believe to be right and good, not to
bow to the opinion of the majority. In this piece Churchill shows
in some respects true self-knowledge. He is right when he depicts
himself as one

> " Too proud to flatter, too sincere to lie,
> Too plain to please, too honest to be great."

On the other hand, if he really saw himself in his renunciation of
"Prudence and the World,"

> " Whilst Mirth, with Decency his lovely bride,
> And wine's gay god, with Temp'rance by his side,
> Their welcome visit pay,"—

he was profoundly self-deceived. The sad facts of his life show that
the visits of Temperance were rare, and that Decency was only
too often absent.

The more genial tone of *Night* is however exceptional in
Churchill. *An Epistle to William Hogarth* shows a personality even
sharper and more virulent than the early pieces, while it has far
less merit. In Churchill's principal satire, *A Prophecy of Famine*
(1763), which is described as "a Scots pastoral," there are personalities enough—about Bute, who is to release Discord, imprisoned
by Pitt, and call her peace; about the Ramsays, "of whom one
paints as well as t'other wrote"; about Home, "disbanded from
the sons of prayer for loving plays"; about Macpherson, with his
"old, new, epic pastoral Fingal." But these are relieved by the
satire of a people which opens wider issues, and by ridicule of the
artificiality of the pastoral and the absurdities of poetic diction.
No one probably had hitherto so effectively dealt with this last
subject. Churchill throws up the affectations of the time by contrast with himself:—

> " Who boast no merit but mere knack of rhyme,
> Short gleams of sense, and satire out of time,
> Who cannot follow where *trim* Fancy leads
> By *prattling* stream o'er *flower-empurpl'd* meads;
> Who, often, but without success, have pray'd
> For *apt* Alliteration's *artful aid*;
> Who would, but cannot, with a master's skill,
> Coin fine new epithets, *which mean no ill*,"

The prophecy itself is prefaced with an exposure of the nakedness of a land which is safe from the plague of locusts, "for in three hours a grasshopper must die"; where there are no birds but birds of passage; and where "half-starv'd spiders prey'd on half-starv'd flies." Then, after a dialogue between two shepherds, Jockey and Sawney, the gaunt spectre Famine, who has "here fix'd her native home," speaks, prophesying that,

> " Having trod
> For the fix'd term of years ordain'd by God
> A barren desert,"

her children shall soon reap the wealth they disdained to sow, and shall win, not in the face of peril, but by cunning,

> " Dominion o'er a race
> Whose former deeds shall Time's last annals grace."

Churchill is said to have been half a Scot by blood, but there is nevertheless a venom in his satire which makes its effect wholly different from that of the growls of Johnson. We are reminded rather of Cleveland in the preceding century. Both in him and in Churchill, political causes contributed to the virulence of their abuse—in Cleveland the part the Scots had played in the great quarrel between King and Parliament; in Churchill the rise of Bute and the danger which menaced English freedom from him and the King's Friends.

Churchill's roughness of style and virulence of spirit are alike foreign to William Cowper (1731–1800), though there is a sharp edge to Cowper's satire which is surprising enough to those who, not having read him, think of him only as the pious recluse of Olney. Take for example the stinging lines on the Prude:—

> " Yon ancient prude, whose withered features show
> She might be young some forty years ago,
> Her elbows pinioned close upon her hips,
> Her head erect, her fan upon her lips,
> Her eye-brows arched, her eyes both gone astray
> To watch yon amorous couple at their play,
> With bony and unkerchiefed neck defies
> The rude inclemency of wintry skies,
> And sails with lappet-head and mincing airs
> Duly at clink of bell to morning prayers."

But though there is sometimes severity there is never venom in Cowper. He is faithful to the principle he himself proclaims, that a love of virtue should light the flame of satire, and he never "rails to gratify his spleen." It is because he is "ambitious not to sing in vain" that he becomes a satirist. But he does not exaggerate the power of the satiric pen. It may "retrench a sword-blade, or displace a patch."

> " But where are its sublimer trophies found?
> What vice has it subdued? whose heart reclaimed
> By rigour, or whom laughed into reform?"

Notwithstanding the modesty of his expectations, however, Cowper did attempt by his satire to promote reforms more serious than those of sword-blades and patches. In *Tirocinium* he launches a severe satire of the public schools of his time; and there was, and is, more ground for it than many are willing to admit. And both in *Tirocinium* and in *The Task*, with reverence for the Church and the true teacher of religion, he shows clear vision of the pretender and the hypocrite. He appeals to bishops to

> " Lay not careless hands
> On skulls, that cannot teach and will not learn";

and he draws no flattering portrait of the bishop himself, bred in the faith that "the parson knows enough who knows a duke":—

> " Behold your bishop! Well he plays his part,
> Christian in name, and infidel in heart,
> Ghostly in office, earthly in his plan,
> A slave at court, elsewhere a lady's man.
> Dumb as a senator, and as a priest
> A piece of mere church furniture at best."

In short, literature and politics, freedom and slavery, all come within the purview of the satirist, and the recluse shows himself to be in his retirement surprisingly keen-eyed and observant. Not the least interesting passage is that on duelling in *Conversation*, for there we find him at one with his pet aversion—Chesterfield.

As a satirist Cowper follows the classical tradition, and, except in *The Task*, he adopts the classical vehicle of the heroic couplet. But the classical tradition was already on the wane, and after Cowper only George Crabbe (1754–1832) followed it consistently. It is easy to trace a gradual change in Crabbe: he grows more polished and less satirical as he grows older; but there is no deviation from the tradition. As satirist he is perhaps best in *The Village* (1783). *Tales of the Hall* (1819), on the whole his best work, is satirical only here and there; most of the stories are simply moral tales, in which the bard narrates the facts he knows or imagines, and hardly criticises them. Everyone is familiar with his general outlook. His aim is to paint life, and especially the life of the poor, as it really is; and at the start he inclines to that school of realism which regards the painful and ugly as rather more real than the beautiful and pleasant. Cowper before him took the conventional view that the simple life is happy:—

> " The innocent are gay, the lark is gay.
>
> .   .   .   .
>
> The peasant too, a witness of his song,
> Himself a songster, is as gay as he."

Wordsworth after him took a profounder view, and found in his leech-gatherer's lot, if not pleasure, blessedness. But Crabbe's peasants know neither pleasure, nor happiness, nor blessedness. He ridicules the absurdities of the pastoral poets, whose

> " Shepherds' boys their amorous pains reveal,
> The only pains, alas! they never feel."

He "sought the simple life that Nature yields"; but

> " Rapine and Wrong and Fear usurp'd her place,
> And a bold, artful, surly, savage race."

But does not the labour the peasants undergo bring health?—

> " See them alternate suns and showers engage,
> And hoard up aches and anguish for their age;
> Through fens and marshy moors their steps pursue,
> When their warm pores imbibe the evening dew;
> Then own that labour may as fatal be
> To these thy slaves, as thine excess to thee."

And to describe their fare as homely and healthy is to play with truth:—

> " Homely, not wholesome, plain, not plenteous, such
> As ye who praise would never deign to touch."

Their destiny is the workhouse, where the happiest inmates are the idiot and the madman; their sick-bed is attended by the quack, "whose most tender mercy is neglect"; the physician of the spirit is a jovial youth, unfit "to raise the hope he feels not." Death closes all, "and the glad parish pays the frugal fee." Rarely, if ever, has a grimmer picture been painted. The truth of it is undeniable. But so is the truth of Wordsworth's poem, and it goes deeper, as the spiritual is always more profound than the material. When Crabbe wrote the celebrated lines in which he declared that he would tell the truth about the lives of the poor, he evidently meant, and believed it to be in his power, to tell the whole truth. Herein lay his mistake. "There is no such thing," says the wise man, "as the whole truth." The whole truth, about anything whatever, can be told only when the secret of the universe is completely solved.

In his later works Crabbe gradually grows mellower in spirit and smoother in style, but it may be doubted whether he was ever again as impressive as he is in *The Village*. In the later works, as in that, it is his own experience which supplies him with material, whether his purpose be satirical or not. Alike in *The Borough* (1810), in the miscellaneous *Tales*, and in the *Tales of the Hall*, he deals freely with his own profession, and with the attitude of the laity towards it. The picture of the vicar in *The Borough* is an admirable illustration of the power which strict adherence to truth gives. It is impressive without exaggeration, effective without straining for effect. *The Natural Death of Love*, in the introductory lines on the rector, "the Moral Preacher," satirises the laity and their expectations:—

> " ' Heathens,' they said, can tell us right from wrong,
>   But to a Christian higher points belong."

And their zeal for these higher points makes them somewhat stern judges of "the Moral Preacher":—

> " His life was pure, and him they could commend,
>   Not as their guide, indeed, but as their friend:
>   Truth, justice, pity, and a love of peace,
>   Were his—but there must approbation cease;
>   He either did not, or he would not see,
>   That if he meant a favourite priest to be
>   He must not show, but learn of them, the way
>   To truth—he must not dictate, but obey:
>   They wish'd him not to bring them further light,
>   But to convince them that they now were right,
>   And to assert that justice will condemn
>   All who presumed to disagree with them."

Another phase of the lay view is shown in *The Squire and the Priest*, where the Squire advises his nephew that while it is permissible at times to dwell on sin and frailty, it is well, except in the case of poachers and drunkards, to do so in such a way as not to pain the sinner:—

> " Let it always, for your zeal, suffice,
>   That vice you combat, in the abstract—vice."

Though Crabbe does not profess to "survey mankind from China to Peru," his range is wide; for the clergyman's flock is really an

epitome of humanity, and Crabbe embraces the whole of it, from
the habitués of clubs, whose chief end in life is eating and drinking
—"the earliest dainties, and the oldest port"—to the inmates of
the almshouse and the workhouse, who may have been brought
there by dissipation, but have the means to dissipate no longer.
In between lie professions and trades, the law-abiding and the
lawless, and on all Crabbe has something to say—always shrewd and
often pungent. On no class in *The Borough* does he comment with
more effect than on the strolling players, well fitted by Nature for
farce, but forced to play tragedy because the audience "love all
that rant and rapture as their lives":—

> " Sad happy race! soon raised and soon depress'd,
> Your days all pass'd in jeopardy and jest;
> Poor without prudence, with afflictions vain,
> Not warn'd by misery, not enrich'd by gain;
> Whom justice pitying, chides from place to place,
> A wandering, careless, wretched, merry race,
> Who cheerful looks assume, and play the parts
> Of happy rovers with repining hearts;
> Then cast off care, and in the mimic pain
> Of tragic wo, feel spirits light and vain,
> Distress and hope—the mind's, the body's wear,
> The man's affliction, and the actor's tear:
> Alternate times of fasting and excess
> Are yours, ye smiling children of distress."

The web of literature is varied even in periods when it is supposed
to be most homogeneous. We sometimes speak of a dictatorship of
letters, and we probably think of Ben Jonson as a dictator in one
age, and of Samuel Johnson as a dictator in another. Perhaps we
think of Pope as a dictator, at least in poetry, in a third. But the
divine right of kings never has been and never can be admitted in
literature; what is great in that must always be individual and
independent. The most despotic of the dictators has had among
his contemporaries men who have owned but partial allegiance to
him—if they have owned any at all. In the very heyday of Pope's
influence there were men who preferred to bow before the throne
of Spenser, and *The Castle of Indolence* is only the most conspicuous
of many evidences of the fact. What was true in the realm of the
higher poetry was true also in that of satire. While during his life,
and for more than a generation after his death, the more ambitious
and the more polished satire was modelled upon Pope and Dryden,
there was a type of satire less polished and less formal whose vehicle

was octosyllabic verse, and in which the influence of Butler blends with and modifies, even if it does not wholly overpower, that of Pope. Churchill supplies examples. *The Ghost* is a tedious piece of Hudibrastic verse in six books; and *The Duellist*, which satirises Samuel Martin on behalf of Churchill's friend Wilkes, is less tedious only because it is not quite so long.

There were others who handled the octosyllabic line with greater skill than Churchill, and their writings, quite apart from the numerous direct imitations of *Hudibras* which have been already referred to, attest the continued influence of Butler. Swift, as we have seen, wrote in this measure. So did Gay in the *Fables*. So, most commonly, did Churchill's friend, Robert Lloyd. So did Henry Brooke (1703?–83), author of *The Fool of Quality*, that curious romance beloved of Wesley in the eighteenth century, and of which Kingsley write in the nineteenth that he had learnt from it more of what was pure, sacred and eternal, than from any other book which had been published since Spenser. Brooke was a man who played many parts before he became a mystic. He wrote verse ranging from philosophical and heroic to lyrics verging on doggerel. His opera *Jack the Giant-Queller* contains some sprightly satire of the power of wealth. He is a very skilful fabulist, and while his fables are mainly moral and didactic, they contain passages of effective though kindly satire. His satire of women in *The Temple of Hymen* and *Love and Vanity* shows a curious blend of Pope with Butler. But Brooke is never venomous and rarely sharp, and with regard to women his normal tone is not satirical, but is rather that of *The Sparrow and the Dove*, a charming picture of domestic love.

In the case of Robert Lloyd too a natural kindliness gives an unusual and attractive flavour to satire. His verse, if not great, is pleasing; he is sensible and lucid; he always "deals in meanings," and the meaning is never strained. His hero-worship—with Churchill for hero—peeps out from time to time and makes him lovable. In his epistle on *The Poet*, he pays a fine and generous tribute to Churchill. His special field is that of literary criticism expressed in satiric verse. He is sensitive to the defects of the poetry of his time, and condemns

> " The see-saw Muse that flows by measur'd laws,
>   In tuneful numbers, and affected pause."

In *The Poet* he satirises authors and critics, and depicts the latter
as a malignant race. In an epistle *On Rhyme* he ridicules the padding
of lines with meaningless archaisms:—

> " *Whilom, what time, eftsoons,* and *erst,*
> (So prose is often times beverst)
> Sprinkled with quaint fantastic phrase,
> Uncouth to ears of modern days,
> Make up the metre, which they call
> Blank, classic blank, their all in all."

He satirises the magazines,

> " Which teach all things at once,
> And make a pedant coxcomb of a dunce ";

he satirises the booksellers and their suggestions for display and
advertisement in the lively dialogue entitled *The Puff*; he satirises
various forms of verse in *The Poetry Professors*, a doggerel commentary on the compositions to be expected on the birth of the
Prince of Wales. Probably no other writer of the period spent so
much pains on literary subjects.

A similar intermingling of Pope with Butler may be detected in
Richard Cambridge (1717–1802). His mock-heroic satire of the
follies of learning—*The Scribleriad*—is, it is true, to the measure of
his capacity, pure Pope. But its six books are wearisome now.
It is in the minor pieces that we find Butler flavouring Pope.
They are political, and are based on Horace. The best, *A Dialogue
between a M.P. and his Servant*, shows that the M.P. practises the
very vices which his legislation condemns in those of meaner position.
But the finest passage, and that which best illustrates the intermingling of Pope's influence with Butler's, is the following:—

> " Lady Prue,
> Who gives the morning church its due,
> At noon is painted, drest and curl'd,
> And one among the wicked world:
> Keeps her accounts exactly even
> As thus: ' Prue, creditor with Heaven,
> By sermons heard on extra days:
> Debtor: to masquerades and plays.
> Item: by Whitfield, half an hour:
> Per contra: to the colonel, four.' "

Lady Prue does not stand alone. Nor is this species of reckoning
attempted by women only. Mr. Lytton Strachey's brilliant essay
in *Eminent Victorians* shows that no less a personage than Arch-
deacon, afterwards Cardinal, Manning, kept just such an account,

and finding the balance wrong because of great sins past, of great sinfulness, and of "most shallow repentance," decided to redress it by mortifying himself and by making his "night prayers forty instead of thirty minutes."

But for the fame he won and merited as a poet, Chatterton would hardly deserve mention. His *Consuliad* has the virulence without the point of Churchill; *Resignation,* though better, is still commonplace; and *Kew Gardens* is largely unintelligible because of the multitude of asterisks. Bute and the Scots, the Princess Dowager of Wales (mother of George III.), Grafton, North and other politicians are the subjects of his attacks.

Satirical ballads and songs are to be found from the first rise of satire in English, and we have had examples of them in earlier chapters. They were a favourite weapon of political writers. The controversies of the seventeenth century produced a plentiful crop, and the stream still ran copiously through the eighteenth. Each reign, and each turn of the political wheel, produced its own themes. Laudian ritualism and Cromwellian militarism of the days of civil war give place under Charles II. to the complaints of disappointed Cavaliers; under James II. to the satire of popery; and under William III. to groans about the heavy taxation caused by war. In the reign of Queen Anne the Sacheverell case has left its mark; and the rhymers afford ample evidence of dissatisfaction with the Treaty of Utrecht. With the Hanoverians come ballads of Jacobite plots, and, a little later, of the South Sea Bubble. It would be foolish to judge Walpole's statesmanship by the ballads; but they afford no bad index to his power. Generally they are hostile to him, as is natural, for satire is the weapon of opposition, rather than of power. The detested Excise Bill of 1733, the wisdom of which is admitted by the dispassionate judgment of later times, is the theme of a group of very spirited songs, which Mr. Percival believes to be by Pulteney. In one of them the dragon Excise is thus described:—

> " Your cellars he'll range,
> Your pantry and grange,
> No bars can the monster restrain:
> Wherever he comes,
> Swords, Trumpets, and Drums,
> And Slavery march in his train.
> Horse, foot, and dragoons,
> Battalions, platoons,

> Excise, wooden shoes, and no jury;
> Then taxes increasing,
> While traffic is ceasing,
> Would put all the land in a fury."

Walpole's belief in the power of money, his ribbon of the garter, anything and everything that he had, or thought, or was, were seized upon by those of his political enemies who chanced to possess the gift of rhyme. Of course he was attacked in prose as well as in verse. The most notable of the periodicals hostile to him was *The Craftsman*, edited by Nicholas Amherst. Among its contributors were Pulteney and Bolingbroke. The Government put its printer on trial for libel. He was acquitted, and the chief balladist of the party, Pulteney, burst forth in triumphant praise of *The Honest Jury*. But Walpole had rhymers in his service too, and one of them retorts with a rollicking satire of *The Craftsman* and its contributors:—

> " To frighten the mob, all inventions they try,
> *Ribbledum, scribbledum, fribbledum, flash,*
> But money's their aim, tho' the country's the cry,
> *Satyrum, traitorum, treasondum, trash ;*
> Popery, slavery, bribery, knavery.
> Irruptions, corruptions, and Some-body's fall,
> Pensions and places, removes and disgraces,
> And something and nothing, the devil and all."

Thus, by writers like Robert Lloyd and Pulteney, and by others whose very names are lost, the tradition of satire in octosyllabics or in lyrical measures, inherited from Butler and the ballad writers of the seventeenth century, was carried on to the middle of the eighteenth, side by side with the classical tradition of the followers of Pope. Both traditions survive through the remainder of the eighteenth century and on into the nineteenth; and frequently the same writer follows now one, now the other. Both traditions were carried on by the group of Whig writers who conceived the happy idea of a criticism of a non-existent epic, *The Rolliad*, whereby they were enabled to suggest at once their political and their literary principles, to help their friends and to make heavier the burden of life upon their foes. Most of the interest however has evaporated. Neither is there much of permanent value in the *Political Eclogues* to which they turned when *The Rolliad* was exhausted; nor in the *Probationary Odes* written when the death of William Whitehead opened the question of the laureateship. Though they contain some spirited banter, political as well as literary, the workmanship is crude.

Among the writers of *The Rolliad*, he who is best known by name is George Ellis (1753–1815), the antiquary, whom we afterwards find working on the other side of politics among the far more brilliant group who wrote *The Anti-Jacobin*. But before we proceed to them it is necessary to deal briefly with the one satirist on the Whig side who is still well known by name—John Wolcot (1738–1819), who wrote under the *nom de guerre* of Peter Pindar. He must be ranked with the political writers, and also with those who wrote lyrical satire, in spite of the fact that, on the whole, he succeeds better in the comparatively few pieces in free-and-easy heroic couplets than in his numerous odes. Nowhere is he better than in *One Thousand Seven Hundred and Ninety-Six*, a satire in two dialogues, which in its very title proclaims the influence of Pope, though the writer made no attempt to emulate Pope's polish.

A satire might be written on the vanity of contemporary judgments, and it could be copiously illustrated from the fields of literature, religion, politics and commerce. It is still worth while to turn over the leaves of the five volumes of his collected works in order to see how apt an illustration is afforded by Peter Pindar. In his own day no less a person than Robert Burns speaks of him with marked respect. Peter Pindar is a tower of strength; his name will go far towards ensuring success to a collection to which he contributes; it is an honour to a Burns to be engaged in the same undertaking. When Burns attempts verses for an air Peter Pindar had used, he apologises to Thomson: "Not that I intend to enter the lists with Peter—that would be presumption indeed!" He who reads those five volumes now will probably come to the conclusion that, notwithstanding their undeniable cleverness, they are all but worthless. Such titles as *The Lousiad* indicate the vulgarity and coarseness that pervade them. The descent is as steep from the grave moral dignity of Young and Johnson as from the polished artistry of Pope. Wolcot is in danger of missing even such qualified commendation as he deserves, for "damnable iteration" undoes him. The irritation caused by this half blinds us to the fact that tales like *The Pilgrims and the Peas* are entertaining, and that Wolcot has, as Courthope has pointed out, one gift of a truly literary sort. He is very skilful in his use of similes for the purposes of satire. Thus Pitt, fascinating the nation to its destruction, is likened to a snake fascinating a bird. Another example is the simile in *Ode upon Ode*, describing Majesty looking down with surly grandeur on Sir Charles Thompson:—

> " Thus when a little fearful puppy meets
> A noble Newfoundland dog in the streets,
>   He creeps, and whines, and licks the lofty brute;
> Curls round him, falls upon his back; and then
> Springs up and gambols, frisks it back agen,
>   And crawls in dread submission t' intreat him,
> With every mark of terror, not to *eat* him."

As a rule the subjects of Peter Pindar's satire are quite legitimate. The connoisseurs who affect to worship the old but show themselves wholly blind to the merits of the new are fair game; and so are the ascetics "who starved the Body to preserve the Soul." Sir Joseph Banks as President of the Royal Society, and Thomas Warton as Poet Laureate, held public positions. Royalty stood necessarily in the public eye, and royal penuriousness, and even quarrels in the royal household, might be commented on. Still more were royal inroads on the public purse, and above all royal machinations against popular liberties, legitimate themes. But Peter Pindar wears them all threadbare, and handles them all in a manner that degrades the satirist as well as his victim.

In literary gifts the writers of *The Anti-Jacobin* towered almost as high above Peter Pindar as they did in character and in social station. Never, probably, did a group of satirists include so many men destined to reach the highest political eminence; for among them were Lord Mornington, afterwards the Marquis Wellesley and Governor-General of India; Robert Banks Jenkinson, afterwards Earl of Liverpool and Premier; and, most illustrious of them all, George Canning (1770–1827), who also became Premier. These men had great advantages of birth and station, but they had brains of the first order as well. There were others who, though less illustrious, still proved themselves able to make each a name that has lived for more than a century. George Ellis, the least celebrated, has been mentioned already. And there was also John Hookham Frere (1769–1846), in literature the most considerable person of the group. They were all highly educated, they wrote well, and, both in verse and in prose, their satire was keen and biting. It is their verse with which we have now to deal, and which is in the literary sense most memorable. The writers of it were Ellis, Frere and Canning—these in ascending order of importance, so far as *The Anti-Jacobin* is concerned; that is to say, if we may take as correct the attribution to the several writers in the edition of the works of J. H. Frere edited by W. E. Frere. The table of contents of *The Poetry of the Anti-Jacobin* differs on some points.

The Anti-Jacobin was a weekly journal which ran through thirty-six numbers between November, 1797, and July, 1798. Its editor was William Gifford (1756–1826), author of *The Baviad* (1794), to which a year afterwards he added *The Mæviad*; and his presence, as well as *New Morality*, the most weighty though not the best known of the *Anti-Jacobin* satires, shows how impossible it is to keep the thread of the lighter lyrical satire strictly separate from that of the classical satire. For *The Baviad*, to which Gifford owed his position, followed the classical tradition. Further, it was a satire of literature. Gifford, like the other writers of *The Anti-Jacobin*, was a convinced Tory, but in his life hitherto, and on the whole afterwards, politics were subordinate to literature. The brilliant young writers of *The Anti-Jacobin* were genuinely interested in literature, and wrote some very telling satire of the poetry they did not like; but in their case literature was subordinate to politics. The predominance of politics is a notable feature of satire towards the close of the eighteenth century. It could hardly be otherwise; for the world was in a blaze only less threatening than the recent conflagration.

The two writers of the time who most directly disputed that predominance were Gifford and Thomas James Mathias (1754?–1835), author of *The Pursuits of Literature*, in which the offences, literary and moral, of poets are castigated in four dialogues written in the orthodox style of the Pope school. These dialogues are pedantic and tedious; and the reader of the present day is left wondering at the popularity Mathias enjoyed in his own time. In Gifford's *Baviad* the skill is higher and the satire more pungent. *The Mæviad* is written on similar lines. Gifford had the insight to choose his dunces not indiscriminately, but with a clear end in view. A man of keen intelligence rather than imagination, he was roused to anger by the silly inanities and sentimentalities of the school of Della Crusca,

and he performed a valuable service in exposing them. We need
not lament over much that he never realised the hope that at some
future day he might "give to fancy all th' enraptured mind"; for
there is no evidence that he possessed the necessary powers. But
the castigation of the Della Cruscans was worth while; and it
was most effectively administered. Robert Merry, who had assumed
that name, and the group of sentimentalists who imitated, or at
least wrote like him, were overwhelmed with ridicule. They would,
no doubt, have died any way. But not so soon. Nonsense is like
an infectious disease that spreads in certain states of the mental
atmosphere. Gifford knew this from his own experience:—

> " I, too, my masters, ere my teeth were cast,
> Had learn'd, by rote, to rave of Delia's charms,
> To die of transports found in Chloe's arms,
> Coy Daphne with obstreperous plaints to woo,
> And curse the cruelty of God knows who."

All who have read much of the artificial and sickly love-verse of the
eighteenth century will be grateful for this satire. All who have
dipped into the Della Cruscan verse must see that Gifford's description of it is just:—

> " Abortive thoughts, that right and wrong confound,
> Truth sacrificed to letters, sense to sound,
> False glare, incongruous images, combine;
> And noise and nonsense clatter through the line."

Gifford's own conception of what verse ought to be is high and just:—

> " Verse! That's the mellow fruit of toil intense,
> Inspired by genius and inform'd by sense."

Far other is the genealogy of the verse which is not what it ought
to be:—

> " The abortive progeny of Pride,
> And Dulness, gentle pair, for aye allied;
> Begotten without thought, born without pains,
> The ropy drivel of rheumatic brains."

In several respects Gifford resembled Pope in his life and relation
to the world. He had had to struggle against disabilities physical
and social. Hence in part, perhaps, the fact that his relation to
Pope is closer than was usual when he wrote. The plan of *The
Baviad*, a "paraphrastic imitation" of the first satire of Persius,
as well as the whole tone, is Popean. Hence, still more probably, a
certain note of virulence which pervades his satire. He feels it to

be *his* business to "hunt the clamorous brood of Folly down."
He feels that he was born to the task:—

> " I was born
> To brand obtrusive ignorance with scorn;
> On bloated pedantry to pour my rage,
> And hiss preposterous fustian from the stage."

Such was the man who in 1797 became editor for the *Anti-Jacobin* band. They too, as has been said, were interested in literature, and they dealt several shrewd blows in satire of that in it
which they deemed amiss. Ellis, Canning and Frere all took part in
The Loves of the Triangles, an extremely clever and ingenious skit
at Erasmus Darwin; and they were also united in *The Rovers*,
a parody of the rant and fustian of the German stage, which was
then coming to be known and admired in England; while Gifford,
Canning and Frere, without the help of Ellis, wrote *The Progress
of Man*, a lively satire of Payne Knight's *Progress of Civil
Society*. The satirists had from their point of view an admirable
theme, and they made the best use of their opportunity. Knight
had ascribed a great part in the progress of society to the power of
love, and insisted that it sways the animal creation as well as
man. He had written that love

> " In softer notes bids Libyan lions roar,
> And warms the whale on Zembla's frozen shore."

The merciless parodists reproduce this fine sentiment. Love, they
tell us,

> " Warms, midst seas of ice, the melting whales;—
> Cools the crimpt cod, fierce pangs to perch imparts,
> Shrinks shrivell'd shrimps, but opens oysters' hearts."

The very title, however, of *The Anti-Jacobin* proclaims the predominance of the political interest. Here they had against them
heavier literary metal than Erasmus Darwin or Payne Knight;
for the man they set themselves most of all to scarify was a person
no less respectable than Southey. Southey, however, had a way
of laying himself open to ridicule, and he was destined long after
to suffer at the hands of Byron far more severely than he did from
the *Anti-Jacobin* group. But they were sufficiently cutting. Everybody knows the sudden change of tone of the Friend of Humanity
to the Needy Knife-Grinder, when he discovers that the spiritless

wretch has no complaint to make against squire or parson or lawyer, but would gladly drink the Friend of Humanity's health in beer:—

> " *I* give thee sixpence! I will see thee damn'd first—
> Wretch! whom no sense of wrongs can rouse to vengeance—
> Sordid, unfeeling, reprobate, degraded,
> Spiritless outcast! "

Indignation so unmeasured would hardly stop at words. The Friend of Humanity "kicks the Knife-Grinder, overturns his wheel, and exit in a transport of Republican enthusiasm and universal philanthropy." It is an irresistible criticism at once of Southey's political principles and of his Sapphics; as are the less widely known and less effective *Soldier's Friend* and *Soldier's Wife* of his dactylics. Both these pieces seem to have been the joint work of Canning and Frere; and so were the well-known lines on the 'Prenticecide Mrs. Browning, which travesty Southey's on the regicide Henry Marten.

New Morality also was the joint-work of the two friends; but much the larger and the better part of it was Canning's. It is so important, and its importance is so inadequately recognised, that it deserves to be examined with some care—all the more as it shows that, if he had devoted his powers to verse, Canning would have been, after the two masters, the foremost satirist in the line of Dryden and Pope. There is even evidence that he had it in him to win no mean rank among poets of a loftier type than satirists. Gifford, as we have seen, aspired to such a position, but probably lacked the power to gain it. There is no evidence that Canning aspired, but if he had done so, and had had sufficient liberty of soul from politics, he probably had the capacity. In the fervid apostrophe to Burke, then recently dead, there is a note which is rare in satire, even in the satire of the masters. There is true poetry in the prophecy that, as perfumed lamps burn for ever in the tombs of Eastern kings,

> " So, mighty Burke! in thy sepulchral urn,
> To fancy's view, the lamp of Truth shall burn."

The main business of *New Morality*, however, is not panegyric, but satire, and even in the passage from which these noble lines are taken the author immediately passes on to say that if only she had Burke's genius the Muse should

> " Tell of *what wood young Jacobins are made*;
> How the skill'd Gardener grafts with nicest rule
> The *slip* of Coxcomb on the *stock* of fool;
> Forth in bright blossom bursts the tender sprig,
> A thing to wonder at, perhaps a *Whig*."

Such is the theme of satire in this admirable piece; and it is illustrated by caustic comments upon that universal philanthropy which had already been ridiculed in *The Friend of Humanity and the Knife-Grinder*; upon the "sweet Sensibility" of Rousseau; and upon that boundless impartiality which leads to the belief that "black's not *so* black, nor white *so very* white."

Universal philanthropy of the kind Canning mocks is not that which dries the orphan's tears,

> " But *French* philanthropy;—whose boundless mind
> Glows with the general love of all mankind;
> Philanthropy,—beneath whose baneful sway
> Each patriot passion sinks, and dies away."

Shall a single island bound the love of the enlightened philanthropist?

> " No—through the extended globe his feelings run
> As broad and general as th' unbounded sun!
> No narrow bigot *he*;—*his* reason'd view,
> Thy interests, England, ranks with thine, Peru!
> France at our doors, *he* sees no danger nigh,
> But heaves for Turkey's woes the impartial sigh;
> A steady Patriot of the World alone,
> The friend of every country—but his own."

It is the prerogative of genius to write for all time. There is surely something familiar in the friend of every country but his own. We are not unacquainted with the man whose scepticism a few years ago was proof against a crushing weight of evidence of the guilt of Germany, yet whose facile credulity was ready to accept bare assertion without any evidence at all against England.

"Sweet Sensibility" is equally unsatisfactory. She has been taught by Rousseau to cherish a plentiful supply of tender tears, "and pour them in the brooks that babbled by":—

> " Taught by nice scale to mete her feelings strong,
> False by degrees, and exquisitely wrong;
> For the crush'd beetle *first*,—the widow'd dove,
> And all the warbled sorrows of the grove;
> Next for poor suff'ring *guilt*;—and *last* of all,
> For Parents, Friends, a King and Country's fall."

Her fair votaries "pour the pearly shower," like Sterne, over a dead jackass, but hear unmoved of the blood-stained Loire and of the massacres of Lyons.

Though he differed from them in politics, Thomas Moore (1779–1852) showed himself to be akin to the Anti-Jacobins in his satire.

His *Twopenny Post-Bag* (1813) is probably best known now because Lockhart quotes the satire on *Rokeby*, which represents Scott as "coming by long quarto stages to town," and meaning to "do" the gentlemen's seats by the way. There are other good strokes in it, and in particular some effective ridicule of religious bigotry. The same theme is dealt with in *Fables for the Holy Alliance* (1823)—a better work. Good sense as well as wit is shown in the satire on the connexion between Church and State, which is the theme of the fifth fable; and also in the sixth, *The Little Grand Lama*, which teaches that just as the small monarch needs a whipping, so monarchs of a larger growth are all the better for some constitutional restraint. Moore was in earnest about the Holy Alliance, and the fable in which he foreshadows its dissolution—a dream of the monarchs dancing in an ice-palace on the Neva—is a very clever play on the slippery and melting foundations of their policy. *The Fudge Family in Paris* (1818) also conceals beneath a veil of burlesque serious political views and aims. There is keen satire on the transfer by treaty of the allegiance of millions from one sovereign to another, on the doings of the Holy Alliance, and on the amusements of sovereigns. The peace was recent, and Moore seems to have found it as little satisfactory as that under which Europe groans to-day. Phil Fudge's book will prove

> " That Europe—thanks to royal swords
>   And bay'nets, and the Duke commanding—
> Enjoys a peace which, like the Lord's,
>   Passeth all human understanding."

Wherever Castlereagh is mentioned there is an underlying bitterness. The ridicule of his mixed metaphors shows that Sir Boyle Roche is not without rivals among his countrymen:—

> " Kingship, tumbled from its seat,
> ' Stood prostrate ' at the people's feet;
> Where (still to use your Lordship's tropes)
> The *level* of obedience *slopes*
> Upward and downward, as the *stream*
> Of *hydra* faction *kicks the beam*."

Before leaving Moore it may be worth mentioning that he attempted satire in the heroic couplet in *Corruption, Intolerance* and *The Sceptic*, but with very little success.

CHAPTER XII

AFTER the lapse of several generations it is easy to see that towards the close of the eighteenth century English literature stood in need of new measures, both for the purposes of the lyric and for satire. But the northern division of the island was in a different position from the southern. In Scotland no new invention or introduction was needed, but only the power to use what had long been familiar and had recently been revived. Burns found his instrument ready to his hand, and his success as a satirist was certainly in some measure due to the metres he used—partly to their inherent qualities, and partly to their history.

Scottish vernacular verse was revived by a group of writers who sprang up in Edinburgh about the beginning of the eighteenth century. Through the whole of the previous century *belles lettres* had been practically dead in Scotland. James Watson's *Choice Collection of Comic and Serious Scots Poems* was a symptom of revival. The first part appeared in 1706, and it was followed by a second in 1709 and a third in 1711. Thus, just when the union of the Parliaments brought, in Lord Belhaven's well-known phrase, "the end of an auld sang" in politics, the "auld sang" of another sort is reborn; for the *Choice Collection* included ancient pieces as well as modern, and the ancient pieces were a good deal more noteworthy than the modern. Allan Ramsay (1686–1758) was stirred up to write, and after a few years he in turn published two compilations—*The Tea-Table Miscellany* (1724–27) and *The Evergreen* (1724). It is the very depth of the preceding sleep that makes this reawakening important. English poetry had begun to suffer from convention; but there could hardly be convention in a country where for more than a century poetry had not existed. Birds had not been translated into "the plumy people," nor fish into "the finny tribe." Traditions were broken, and everything was to be made anew. If Allan Ramsay, and even writers of less ability, were leaders in the return to nature, it was not because of superiority of genius. On the contrary, there were no more abject slaves to convention than they were in the pieces they wrote in English. In the vernacular they escaped conventionality because there was no convention. Thus all the measures which Ramsay and his coadjutors found in the older poets were, so to speak, free to be used according to their intrinsic qualities. They carried with them no serious load of tradition such as, after Pope, made the English heroic couplet the vehicle of reason in rhyme, and stamped with burlesque any use of the lyrical measures for purposes of satire. There was, it is true, a "standart Habby" behind the most notable of these revived Scottish measures; but, though its influence was considerable, it was not fettering.

This measure of "standart Habby," the stave of six lines with two rhymes, came originally from the Troubadours and was well known in medieval England, but had been forgotten. For purposes of humour and satire it is the favourite of both Ramsay and his more highly-gifted successor, Robert Fergusson (1750–74). But in truth both poets are humorists rather than satirists. Ramsay's *Elegy on John Cowper*, the kirk-treasurer's man, is directed against the kirk session's jurisdiction of morals, and may be regarded as a tentative and cautious prelude to Burns's great satires. In *The last Speech of a Wretched Miser* the picture is too much that of the miser as others see him. Ramsay could not rise to the height of showing the miser as he saw himself and out of his own mouth condemning him, as Burns did with Holy Willie. In his other pieces in the same measure Ramsay is just the humorous observer; and in his occasional imitations of Pope in the heroic couplet he is contemptible.

Fergusson too is rather a keen-eyed, dispassionate, amused spectator than a critic and satirist. *The Rising of the Session* and *The Sitting of the Session* are themes which invite to satire, but the poet is not satirical. Still less is he so in *The Farmer's Ingle* and *Leith Races*. Yet at times he has a satirical note. *Hame Content* proclaims itself a satire. Its purpose is to dissuade from excessive greed of money and to inculcate contentment with the beauties

of home, instead of wandering abroad in restless search for that
which is no better. In *Braid Claith* the thesis is that fine clothing
opens the way to fame and to love. The lady will not look at the
lover unless he wears fine garments:—

> " Braid Claith lends fouk an unco heese,
> Maks mony kail-worms butterflees,
> Gies mony a doctor his degrees
> 　　For little skaith;
> In short, you may be what you please
> 　　Wi' guid Braid Claith."

This is respectable, but it would be absurd to call it great. There
have been scores of village poetasters since who have put more
pungent satire into this measure than either Ramsay or Fergusson.

It was Robert Burns (1759–96) who showed the way to do it.
He handled the two measures (this stave of six lines and another
of nine) in which the majority of his satires are written with such
skill and power as to make him one of the very foremost of British
satirists, and he wove in with the satire such pure poetic beauty
as no satirist had ever mingled with it before, and as only Byron
combined with it afterwards. It is this mingling of poetic beauty
with satiric keenness which is the special feature of the new satire.
An excellent illustration may be found in *The Holy Fair*. The
opening stanza depicts a scene of quiet natural beauty:—

> " Upon a simmer Sunday morn
> 　　When Nature's face is fair,
> I walked forth to view the corn
> 　　An' snuff the caller air.
> The risin' sun o'er Galston muirs
> 　　Wi' glorious light was glintin',
> The hares were hirplin' doon the furrs,
> 　　The lav'rocks they were chantin'
> 　　　　Fu' sweet that day."

There is not the faintest hint of satire, and clearly the piece might
go on to the end in the spirit in which it has begun. It might, but
the poet has determined otherwise, and there is nothing in the
nature or traditions of his measure to hinder him from changing
the note. Here is the description of the congregation to which his
crony Fun and Superstition and Hypocrisy, her companions for
the nonce, introduce him:—

> " Here some are thinkin' on their sins,
> 　　An' some upo' their claes;
> Ane curses feet that fyl'd his shins,
> 　　Anither sighs an' prays:

> On this hand sits a chosen swatch,
>   Wi' screwed-up, grace-proud faces;
> On that a set o' chaps, at watch,
>   Thrang winkin' on the lasses
>   To chairs that day."

In a subsequent stanza we get a picture of hell drawn with that fidelity to the teaching of the pulpit to which Burns's satires owe half their effect; and in the end, thanks to the poet, we understand, partly at least, that amazing assembly of the pious, filled "with faith and hope, and love and drink."

The six-line stave was equally flexible, and Burns used it too now in the serious vein and now in the comic. In it he wrote that touching *Bard's Epitaph* which remains to this day perhaps the justest analysis of his own character; and in it also he wrote *Death and Doctor Hornbook* and *Holy Willie's Prayer*.

Satire cannot rise to its highest point unless it has a great theme. Juvenal's was the corruption of Imperial Rome, Dryden's that of Restoration England. Burns was an actor on a narrower stage, but the theme he chose was of fundamental importance there. The Scottish Reformation had aimed at establishing a theocracy, and had succeeded in concentrating great censorial power in the hands of a very democratic ecclesiastical organisation. The way of transgressors was hard; Burns was a transgressor, and in his satires on the Kirk he was moved by the very human desire to hit back. He had to fight for his friends as well as himself. Gavin Hamilton, to whom he dedicates his first volume of poems, had been attacked by the champions of orthodoxy, and the case has left its mark on *The Twa Herds* and on *Holy Willie's Prayer*. It is on Hamilton's basket and store, kail and potatoes, that Holy Willie prays for a curse, and it is because of the acquittal of Hamilton that he invokes a curse on the Presbytery of Ayr. In Burns's time, though the old orthodoxy was still dominant, it was beginning to be challenged. The moderates were in a minority, but they included the most intellectual men in the kirk. Robertson the historian was one of them, and Carlyle of Inveresk another. The New Light therefore could not be wholly hid, but the power of the Auld Light is shown by the fact that Home, the author of *Douglas*, was induced by the ferment caused by his offence of writing a play to abandon his profession. This was a few years before the birth of Burns. In the intervening time the liberal movement had spread into country districts as well as through the cities. In the postscript to the *Epistle to William Simpson* Burns gives a grotesque explanation of the meaning of the two Lights, and indicates the spread of the heresy and the virulence of the quarrel. It is a dispute as to whether the new moon *is* a new moon, or only the old one, that has "turn'd a neuk." From argument it came to blows, and some were burned. The New Light herds were driven out, but now there is one "amaist on every knowe." The flocks and herds of the other party are disturbed:—

> " Nae doubt the Auld-Light flocks are bleatin',
>   Their zealous herds are vex'd and sweatin';
>   Mysel, I've even seen them greetin'
>   Wi' girnin' spite,
>   To hear the moon sae sadly lie'd on
>   By word an' write."

These theological disputes are the staple of most of Burns's satire. The New Light appealed to reason, and made much of the difficulty of reconciling some of the orthodox teaching with that faculty. Orthodoxy seemed to be irreconcilable with common sense. But the Auld Light claimed to have something better than common sense. Burns was too acute to miss the chance. He makes one leader of the Auld Light after another belabour Common Sense:—

> " Curst Common-sense, that imp o' hell,
>   Cam in wi' *Maggie Lauder*.[1]
>   But Oliphant aft made her yell,
>   An' Russell sair misca'd her:
>   This day Mackinlay taks the flail,
>   An' he's the boy will blaud her!
>   He'll clap a shingan on her tail,
>   An' set the bairns to daud her
>   Wi' dirt this day."

And in *The Twa Herds* (the first, he tells us, of his poems that saw the light):—

> " Then Orthodoxy yet may prance,
>   An' Learnin' in a woody dance,
>   An' that fell cur ca'd Common-sense
>   That bites say sair,
>   Be banish'd o'er the sea to France—
>   Let him bark there."

Naturally he puts no high value on the brains of those who

---

[1] A satirical ballad which had been written on the controversy.

so dread and hate the "fell cur." They are at once violent and stupid:—

> " Calvin's sons, Calvin's sons,
> Seize your sp'ritual guns,
> Ammunition you never can need;
> Your hearts are the stuff
> Will be powder enough,
> And your skulls are storehouses o' lead—
> Calvin's sons!
> Your skulls are storehouses o' lead."

Akin to this satire of the hostility of orthodoxy to common sense is that which is directed against the exaltation of Faith over Works. Though in the person of Holy Willie faith shines radiant, the torment of the "fleshly thorn" has to be confessed. But perhaps it is permitted by Supreme Wisdom lest one so gifted should turn too high and proud. Again, the herds of the New Light preach on morals, but the elect know how to spend their time better than in listening to them:—

> " Smith opens out his cauld harangues,
> On practice and on morals;
> An' aff the godly pour in thrangs,
> To gie the jars an' barrels
> A lift that day."

Burns was a man of the people, and he sang in ringing notes that

> " The rank is but the guinea's stamp,
> The man's the gowd for a' that."

His astonishing popularity in Scotland is partly due to the fact that he is felt to demonstrate in his own person the democratic doctrine of equality. But that is certainly not the doctrine of these satires of the Kirk. On the contrary, he is scornful of the "brutes," or the "hissel" (*i.e.* the flock). The question of patronage was one of the points at issue between the moderates and the orthodox. Few indeed of the former would have been allowed to minister if the matter had depended on the voice of the congregations. They were usually imposed by patrons on congregations either cold or actively hostile—sometimes so actively hostile that the patron's nominee could not be inducted. Now the democratic Burns is uniformly disrespectful to election by the "brutes" or the "hissel." He knew that if that system had prevailed through the country not a step could have been taken towards a more enlightened theology. In *The Twa Herds* the obscurantist Auld Light ministers,

who had quarrelled about the boundaries of their parishes, owed
their position to popular election, and by their quarrel they had
given the profane occasion to blaspheme:—

> " O sirs! whae'er wad hae expeckit
> Your duty ye wad sae negleckit?
> Ye wha were no by lairds respeckit
>   To wear the plaid,
> But by the brutes themselves eleckit
>   To be their guide! "

The general satire is greatly enriched by personal touches on
the chief actors whom the poet introduces—Mackinlay laying the
flail on Common Sense, Russell scrubbing the mangy sheep or
hanging the New Light herds "o'er the burning dub," Moodie
climbing the holy door "wi' tidings o' damnation" (a telling stroke
which Burns owed to Dr. Blair), or playing the faithful shepherd
by a war on vermin:—

> " The thummart, wilcat, brock, an' tod
> Weel kent his voice thro' a' the wood;
> He smell'd their ilka hole an' road,
>   Baith out and in;
> An' weel he lik'd to shed their bluid
>   An' sell their skin."

Burns is severe enough in these general satires of the Kirk, but
he is amused rather than virulent. A humour not unkindly plays
over the whole. The case is different with the great personal satire
of this group—*Holy Willie's Prayer*. Probably there is nothing else
so mercilessly severe in English, and there is nothing more masterly.
The opening stanzas are awful, but those who would condemn
Burns for them must remember that there is not a sentence there
but what expresses with the strictest accuracy doctrine which had
been preached from the pulpit hundreds of times. The difference
between the poem and the sermons lies not in meaning, but in the
terse nervous energy of the poem. And if when it is all thus brought
to a point we are disposed to ask whether it is consistent with the
reverence due to Omnipotence, surely the answer is that the real
irreverence lies in obscuring in a mist of words doctrine which is
so shocking when expressed tersely and lucidly. If Burns was
irreverent, then a hundred times more irreverent were the
Calvinist ministers from whom he drew his material.

And yet there is something to be said on the other side. The moderates began a process which is going on still. Burns with his weapon of satire fought more effectively than they all. There was need of change. But any faith is better than no faith at all, and the observer of the present day is tempted to ask whether the old rigid creed, even if it produced an occasional Holy Willie, was inferior on the whole to the cult of pleasure which for multitudes has taken its place.

Though it is still sufficiently severe, the other great personal satire, *Death and Doctor Hornbook*, is far less bitter in tone, and as the victim seems to have been harmless enough, except for such unintended mischief as he may have done by his quackery, it is pleasant to know now that Lockhart was mistaken in saying that the satire drove him from his home. Still, such satire as that about the country laird who is helped out of life by his son and Doctor Hornbook is, when pointed against an individual, unjustifiable. But this is not the normal tone of the piece. It is humorous and laughable rather than sharp and bitter. The figure of Death is ludicrous, not awful, and the conversation between him and the poet is friendly. The pharmacopœia of the Doctor is richly comic: "mite-horn shavings, filings, scrapings," "sal-alkali o' midge-tail clippings,"

> " Calces o' fossils, earth, and trees;
> True *sal-marinum* o' the seas;
> The *farina* of beans an' pease,
>   He has't in plenty;
> *Aqua fontis*, what ye please,
>   He can content ye."

This piece is the best illustration of all of that mingling of the poetic spirit with the satiric which has been mentioned as characteristic of the new satire. The picture of Death is poetic as well as ludicrous, the whole setting is poetic—the poet setting his staff to steady his uncertain steps, the rising moon glowering over the distant Cumnock hills, the eerie midnight atmosphere.

There are other pieces in Burns in which the humorous spirit so completely overpowers the satiric that they cease to be satires altogether. This is especially the case with his masterpiece *The Jolly Beggars*. There are elements of satire in it, as in the struggle between the fiddler and the caird for the frail lady whom both claim; but it is all drowned in the torrent of riotous humour. There is satire of popular superstition in *Hallowe'en*, but the same is essentially true of it; and though there are hints of satire of ecclesiastical superstition, as well as of popular, in the *Address to the Deil*, here too it is all submerged in the abounding humour. The difference is apparent if we contrast this with the picture of hell in *The Holy Fair*. In the latter we have the substance of a sermon which might well have been preached:—

> " A vast, unbottom'd, boundless pit,
>   Fill'd fou o' lowin' brimstane,
> Whase ragin' flame, an' scorchin' heat,
>   Wad melt the hardest whunstane!
> The half-asleep start up wi' fear,
>   An' think they hear it roarin';
> When presently it does appear,
>   'Twas but some neebor snorin'
>   Asleep that day."

In the *Address to the Deil* it is the poet's "reverend grannie" who has heard the fiend bumming "ayont the dyke."

Burns, then, inherited measures which enabled him to give most effective expression to his gift of satire, and to mingle with it no small measure of his gift of poetry. But in England the heroic couplet was outworn, and still more outworn was Hudibrastic verse. The hour had come for something new, and the man had come too who could supply it.

Among the poets of *The Anti-Jacobin* the primacy clearly belongs to Canning, and Ellis is the least important. It must be repeated however that in literature the greatest name of the group is that of Frere; for while Canning was soon completely wrapped in the dust of the political arena, Frere lived a life comparatively free and leisured, and continued to write works of note. Not only is his masterly translation of Aristophanes a highly important contribution to satire, but his original work *The Monks and the Giants* is at once valuable in itself, and even more valuable for the impulse it gave to a genius greater than his own; for Byron borrowed from it not only the verse, but in no small degree the satiric manner of *Beppo* and *Don Juan*. Even if it had no merit of its own, for this reason alone *The Monks and the Giants* would be memorable. But while there is no doubt about the fact that it was Frere who inspired Byron—for Byron tells us so—it must be added that the verse had been introduced into English in William Tennant's *Anster Fair* some years before Frere's poem appeared. The date of *Anster Fair* is 1812, and that of *Whistlecraft*, the first part of *The Monks and the Giants*, 1817. To Tennant therefore belongs the credit of introducing the *ottava rima*, and to Frere that of inspiring Byron and using the measure in the way most suitable to Byron's genius. For *Anster Fair* is simply a humorous piece, too good-natured to be satirical. At any rate, the service the two together did amounts to no less than this, that they made available in English perhaps the most perfect medium ever devised for satire in verse—a medium certainly more perfect than had hitherto been known to English writers. In a matter like this the final court of appeal is constituted by the satirists themselves; and it is significant that the two greatest satirists in verse subsequent to the eighteenth century—Byron and Gilbert Frankau—have both chosen the stanza which Tennant and Frere introduced.

The introduction of this measure was the prime service of Tennant and Frere to English literature—a service of far greater value than the addition either of the two made to its content, meritorious as that was. What was required was a measure of a sinuous sort, one capable of winding in and out through all the complexities of life. It was desirable that it should admit of use to an indefinite length, a quality which the lyrical measures did not possess. It must be capable of sinking, without violence to its nature, to an easy conversational tone; and it would be all the better if it were capable of rising on rare occasions to the tone of high poetry. Now the stanza Frere used in *The Monks and the Giants* possesses every one of these requisites. We might be dubious about its capacity to rise were it not that Byron has proved it. Perhaps the most convincing evidence of his greatness is that he, and he alone, succeeded in parts of *Don Juan* in imparting qualities all but the highest to the measure he used as a rule so familiarly. Frere never did this. Even Mr. Frankau, who uses the stanza for satire with a skill not greatly inferior to Byron's own, does not do it. We cannot say that he could not do it, for he simply does not try.

An originator who is followed by a successor much greater than himself runs a risk of losing the credit that is due to him. He who reads *The Monks and the Giants* now will find so much of what he will instinctively think of as Byron in it, that he must take trouble to remind himself constantly of the chronological facts if he wishes to be fair to Frere. Take for illustration a stanza descriptive of the character of Sir Tristram:—

> " From realm to realm he ran—and never staid;
>   Kingdoms and crowns he won—and gave away:
> It seem'd as if his labours were repaid
>   By the mere noise and movement of the fray:
> No conquests nor acquirements had he made:
>   His chief delight was on some festal day
> To ride triumphant, prodigal, and proud,
>   And shower his wealth amid the shouting crowd."

It is the movement of the verse here that sounds Byronic; and we have to remember that Tennant and Frere deserve the credit of that movement. But there is a more intimate Byronism in the grotesque illustration used in the case of the "anti-tintinnabularian" monk:—

> " Wise Curs, when canister'd, refuse to run;
>   They merely crawl and creep about, and whine,
> And disappoint the Boys, and spoil the fun—
>   That picture is too mean—this monk of mine
> Ennobled it, as others since have done,
>   With grace and ease, and grandeur of design;
> He neither ran nor howl'd, nor crept nor turn'd,
> But wore it as he walked, quite unconcern'd."

Byronic too are the rhymes:—

> " Adviser-general to the whole community,
> He served his friend, but watch'd his opportunity."

So is the sly turn in those lines, and in these:—

> " It often happens in the hour of need,
> From popular ideas of utility,
> People are pitch'd upon for mere ability."

So again is the satire of the great:—

> " Princes protecting Sciences and Art
>   I've often seen, in copper-plate and print;
> I never saw them elsewhere, for my part,
>   And therefore I conclude there's nothing in't."

Byronic above all, perhaps, is the opening of Canto II. with its humorous raillery: —

> " I've finish'd now three hundred lines and more;
>   And therefore I begin Canto the Second,
> Just like those wand'ring ancient Bards of Yore;
>   They never laid a plan, nor ever reckon'd
> What turning they should take the day before;
>   They follow'd where the lovely Muses beckon'd."

When it is borne in mind that all this Byronism precedes both *Beppo* and *Don Juan,* it becomes evident how considerable was

Byron's debt to Frere. It is hardly too much to say that the latter effected a revolution. Satire of the classical type survived for a time, but he had dealt it a heavy blow.

Frere had effected a revolution so far as England was concerned; but it is well known that he was in turn a borrower. The measure was Italian, and so was the spirit in which it was handled. Byron's reference to Frere in a letter to Murray, dated 12th October, 1817, leaves the impression that the Englishman was his sole model for *Beppo*; but in *Don Juan* he calls Pulci "sire of the half-serious rhyme"; and Mr. Fuess[1] has shown reason to believe that he borrowed some hints from Casti, and in particular was led by him to carry Juan to the court of Catherine II. of Russia.

But for Frere Byron (1788–1824) would in all probability have followed the classical tradition in satire. He started on that course in *English Bards and Scotch Reviewers*, where, in the heat of wounded pride, he confounded innocent with guilty, and satirised his contemporaries all round for the fault of *The Edinburgh Review*. The flavour is gone. There is too much personality, and antiquated personality is uninteresting. Once and again in after years Byron chanted his *peccavi* to men whom he had lashed in his haste—in particular to Scott and Moore, both of whom became valued friends. The piece is notable now only as a stinging retort, which might have taught critics to mend their manners, but failed to do so. Afterwards, in *Hints from Horace*, in *The Curse of Minerva*, in *The Waltz* and in *The Age of Bronze*, Byron still used the heroic couplet; and in no case with very striking success.

It is in *Beppo* that Byron first strikes his characteristic note in satire; and on that and *The Vision of Judgment* and *Don Juan* his position in satire depends. *Beppo* itself, good as it is, is little more than a prelude. The story is Italian; but, as in *Don Juan*, the story is the smallest part of the piece. It is merely a peg on which to hang the poet's humorous and satirical criticisms of life; and though the life here is mainly Italian, there are caustic observations on England as well. There is, as in all his works, much of the man Byron. He reveals himself in the good sense, here very slightly elevated by poetry, of the easy, colloquial verse; in the contempt for "the author that's all author"; in the love of the Italian climate

[1] *Byron as a Satirist in Verse.*

and the Italian language, "that soft bastard Latin," so different
from

> " Our harsh northern whistling, grunting guttural,
> Which we're obliged to hiss, and spit, and sputter all."

Characteristic too, down to the looseness of grammar, are the
lines on satire:—

> " I fear I have a little turn for Satire,
> And yet methinks, the older that one grows
> Inclines us more to laugh than scold, though laughter
> Leaves us so doubly serious shortly after."

That miracle of wit and humour *The Vision of Judgment* deals
with the death and burial of George III., and satirises Southey's
panegyric which bears the same title. The subject was an explosive
somewhat dangerous to handle, and John Hunt, the publisher,
was fined on the ground that the poem was a danger to the public
peace. Lamb considered it a poem " of the most good-natured
description "; and so it is superficially. But in real intention and in
effect it is mercilessly severe both on the king and on Southey.
Byron blamed Southey for spreading evil reports about him, and
there had been literary sword-play between the poets, in which
Byron hitherto had got the worst of it. He was determined to have
his revenge, and no reader of *The Vision of Judgment* can doubt
that he succeeded. "Put yourself in his place." Addison had felt
the lash a century before, but who would not rather be Addison,
smarting from the character of Atticus, than Southey after reading
The Vision of Judgment? It is not merely the few stanzas at the end
which deal directly with Southey; not merely that we see "the
renegado," though not yet a ghost, carried in by the devil Asmodeus
to the assembly of devils and angels, who are debating the
admission of the ghost of the king to the celestial gate. The whole
assembly is scattered when Southey begins to read *his Vision
of Judgment*:—

> " These grand heroics acted as a spell;
> The angels stopped their ears and plied their pinions;
> The devils ran howling, deafened, down to Hell;
> The ghosts fled, gibbering, for their own dominions—
> (For 'tis not yet decided where they dwell,
> And I leave every man to his opinions);
> Michael took refuge in his trump—but, lo!
> His teeth were set on edge, he could not blow!"

Southey has only got to the fourth line when this stampede occurs;

at the fifth, St. Peter knocks him down. He falls into his lake, sinks to the bottom, like his works, but rises again to the surface, like himself and all rotten things. It is all ludicrous and impossible, and therefore, Lamb seems to have held, harmless. But these lines are really more stinging than the most neatly executed epigram of Pope. It has been said that a dog would rather be beaten than laughed at, and those who know dogs well will readily believe it to be true. In this respect men are just the same; they would rather be seriously injured than made utterly ridiculous. Pope used the whip, Byron laughed. Pope inflicts "deep wounds before," Byron bestows a kick in the seat of honour; and Hudibras knew that the latter is the more painful.

But the attack on Southey is not confined to the few stanzas with which his name is directly associated. The whole poem bears on him. He has made himself the panegyrist of George III., and therefore the arraignment of the king before the powers of heaven and hell is an arraignment equally of the laureate. The king, seated in the place of power, has caused, and the panegyrist has stamped with his approval, the state of things on earth. The measure of the king's responsibility is to be found in a comparison between the beginning of the reign and the end. In Satan's plea against the king we see the beginning as it appeared to Byron:—

> " Look to the earth, I said, and say again:
>   When this old, blind, mad, helpless, weak, poor worm
> Began in youth's first bloom and flush to reign,
>   The world and he both wore a different form,
> And much of earth and all the watery plain
>   Of ocean called him king: through many a storm
> His isles had floated on the abyss of Time;
> For the rough Virtues chose them for their clime."

The difference between this beginning and the end has already been shown in the earlier part of the poem. St. Peter is sitting at the celestial gate, but he has had little trouble "since the Gallic era eighty-eight." The Recording Angel however has been busy. He has "stripped off both his wings for quills," and six angels and twelve saints have been named his clerks. There is much business every day,

> " Till at the crowning carriage, Waterloo,
> They threw their pens down in divine disgust,
> The page was so besmeared with blood and dust."

As for the king, who comes to stand his trial for admittance,

> " A better farmer ne'er brushed dew from lawn,
> A worse king never left a realm undone ! "

He has received a pompous burial, and everything has been done to preserve the body, but "all his spices but prolong decay." The poet is not without hope that the poor old king,

> " An old man
> With an old soul, and both extremely blind,"

may escape eternity of punishment. He is not without hope even of the worst of men, but thinks he may be quite alone

> " In this small hope of bettering future ill
> By circumscribing, with some slight restriction,
> The eternity of Hell's hot jurisdiction."

In the particular case the hope is more than justified, for we take leave of George "practising the hundredth psalm." But the poet knows how heterodox and how dangerous is the thought :—

> " I know this is unpopular; I know
> 'Tis blasphemous; I know one may be damned
> For hoping no one else may e'er be so;
> I know my catechism; I know we're crammed
> With the best doctrines till we quite o'erflow;
> I know that all save England's Church have shammed
> And that the other twice two hundred churches
> And synagogues have made a *damned* bad purchase."

The meeting between Satan and Michael presents the best example the piece affords of Byron's way of mingling the highest poetry with satire. The portrait of Satan in Stanza XXIV., which owes something to Milton, is magnificent, and the phrase which describes the look that passes between the two great leaders is in the loftiest strain of poetry. There is

> " A high, immortal, proud regret
> In either's eye."

But Byron well knew that to maintain this high tone long would be to pass altogether out of the realm of satire ; and so he sinks again. The meeting is not unfriendly, and

> " Though they did not kiss,
> Yet still between his Darkness and his Brightness
> There passed a mutual glance of great politeness."

And it is sound psychology which makes the defeated haughtier than the victor :—

> " Satan met his ancient friend
> With more hauteur, as might an old Castilian
> Poor Noble met a mushroom rich civilian."

The gist of Satan's plea against the king has already been given. King George has undone his realm, the blood of countless thousands is on his soul, "he ever warred with freedom and the free." This is supported by a cloud of witnesses so great that Michael grumbles:—

> " We lose
> Our Time, nay, our Eternity, between
> The accusation and defence: if we
> Hear both, 'twill stretch our immortality."

The handling of the two who are chosen to bear witness for the opposition is admirable. Wilkes refuses to oppose. With him old scores are past, and besides, he beat the king in the end. Moreover, the king merely acted after his kind:—

> " In the sky
> I don't like ripping up old stories, since
> His conduct was but natural in a prince."

Still more masterly is the treatment of Junius. Even the Devil seems puzzled to guess whose are the features. In his superb description Byron may have had in mind Milton's Death, but he has not borrowed:—

> " The shadow came—a tall, thin, grey-haired figure,
> That looked as it had been a shade on earth;
> Quick in its motions, with an air of vigour,
> But nought to mark its breeding or its birth;
> Now it waxed little, then again grew bigger,
> With now an air of gloom, or savage mirth;
> But as you gazed upon its features, they
> Changed every instant—to what, none could say."

Byron adds to the multitude of guesses the very fitting conjecture that Junius "was *really—truly*—nobody at all." For why should not letters be written without hands since we daily see them, and books too, written without heads? And it is fitting too that, while " *Nominis Umbra* " was still speaking, "away he melted in celestial smoke."

Enough has been given, in quotation and reference, to show how exhaustless is the store of wit and humour in this unsurpassed masterpiece. Byron is his own sole rival, and *Don Juan* is greater than *The Vision of Judgment* only because it is on a greater scale. And for that reason too though greater it is less perfect. The shorter poem is an almost flawless whole; *Don Juan*, at its best, is unsurpassed within the whole realm of satire; but in the later cantos it frequently sinks almost to the commonplace.

What is the plan of *Don Juan?* Murray asked the question, and Byron answered it in a letter dated 12th August, 1819: "You ask me for the plan of Donny Johnny: I *have* no plan; I *had* no plan; but I had or have materials." He says the same thing in verse:—

> " I rattle on exactly as I'd talk
> With anybody in a ride or walk."

And again:—

> " Note or text,
> I never know the word that will come next."

There is no reason to doubt his sincerity; on the contrary, this is just the impression the poem gives. Such plan as it shows arises from the fact that it gives an impression of lawless wandering and limitless confusion, like the world itself. "I sketch the world exactly as it goes," says the poet.

It is not so easy to take Byron quite literally when in the letter above quoted he goes on to say that "a playful satire, with as little poetry as could be helped," was what he meant. It is to be remembered that the letter was written soon after the publication of the first two cantos, and that these cantos contain, among other fine things, Julia's letter, the shipwreck, and the first part of the idyll of Haidée. If Byron really meant to exclude poetry he was singularly unsuccessful, and must be accorded the praise of approaching nearer his ideal as he went on; for the second half of *Don Juan* is far less poetical than the first half, and also far inferior. No previous satirist, with the possible exception of Burns, had so intermingled pure poetry with irony and satiric wit, as Byron does in these early cantos.

Don Juan is Byron's commentary on life, and it is his greatest work, not because it is the most perfect, but because it is the most complete. In other poems—in *Childe Harold*, in *Manfred*, in *Cain* —we have phases of Byron; in *Don Juan* we have the man and poet in all his complexity. The commentary is not simple or unilateral— it is at least three-fold. At one moment Byron is passionate, at another satirically critical. And occasionally he is seriously reflective. As the last quality is by far the rarest, it may be well in the first place to prove its presence. Seriousness indeed is far from rare; an undercurrent of seriousness runs through the whole poem; but usually there is levity on the surface, and often enough burlesque and buffoonery. The description of the storm and shipwreck is serious; that is proved by the fact that there is hardly a detail of it for which authority cannot be found in Byron's "Grand-dad's Narrative," or in that collection of *Shipwrecks and Disasters at Sea* which he had studied so carefully. But the seriousness is hidden by the veil of levity. Thus, just before the sinking of the ship, which is followed by the two famous stanzas which tell of "the wild farewell" and "the bubbling cry of some strong swimmer in his agony," we have Juan with his loaded pistols standing guard over the spirit-room to keep aloof the crew,

> " Who, ere they sunk,
> Thought it would be becoming to die drunk."

There are two things especially, Byron tells us, that calm the spirit —rum and true religion. Having thus treated the one he proceeds to deal with the other, and tells us of a terrified sailor

> " That begg'd Pedrillo for an absolution,
> Who told him to be damn'd—in his confusion."

Of seriousness thus rubbing shoulders with levity, there is no lack in *Don Juan*, and frequently the levity serves and is intended to deepen the seriousness. What is rare is gravity unmocked by the clown's grimace. But it occurs. Toward the close of Canto III. Byron sounds his higher strain, as he rarely fails to do when the subject of freedom crosses his mind; and we have *The Isles of Greece*. He is in the middle of the story of Haidée, and the shadow of the resuscitated Lambro—

> " The mildest manner'd man
> That ever scuttled ship or cut a throat "—

is already falling across the lovers. In the beginning of Canto IV. he pauses to reflect. He is quite serious when he tells us that he laughs to prevent his weeping, and that he would prefer apathy to either emotion:—

> " And if I laugh at any mortal thing,
>   'Tis that I may not weep; and if I weep,
> 'Tis that our nature cannot always bring
>   Itself to apathy, for we must steep
> Our hearts first in the depths of Lethe's spring,
>   Ere what we least wish to behold will sleep:
> Thetis baptised her mortal son in Styx;
> A mortal mother would on Lethe fix."

And again, in IV. xii. we have Byron's commentary on life, neither satirical, like the bulk of the poem, nor, like the Haidée episode, passionate, but grave and solemn:—

> " ' Whom the gods love die young,' was said of yore,
>   And many deaths do they escape by this:
> The death of friends, and that which slays even more—
>   The death of friendship, love, youth, all that is,
> Except mere breath; and since the silent shore
>   Awaits at last even those who longest miss
> The old archer's shafts, perhaps the early grave
> Which men weep over may be meant to save."

The later cantos of *Don Juan* are inferior to the earlier, largely because of the comparative rarity in them of the grave spirit of pure poetry. But even in them illustrations may be found—the beautiful stanzas, for instance, in which Byron enshrines his love of Newstead, and, above all, the exquisite closing stanza of Canto XV.:—

> " Between two worlds life hovers like a star,
>   'Twixt night and morn, upon the horizon's verge.
> How little do we know that which we are!
>   How less what we may be! The eternal surge
> Of time and tide rolls on, and bears afar
>   Our bubbles; as the old burst, new emerge
> Lash'd from the foam of ages; while the graves
> Of empires heave but with some passing waves."

Of the presence in *Don Juan* of passion intense, and through long passages unmingled with satire, who can doubt? The story of Haidée is here and there lightly touched with satire, but in essence it is one of the most beautiful of love idylls. The story of Julia is pungently satirical; but the letter of Julia is seriously meant and profoundly felt. It is true the modern woman has changed it all, but Byron's Julia wrote Stanza CXCIV. from her heart, and Byron himself believed her to be right—pathetically right:—

> " Man's love is of man's life a thing apart,
>   'Tis woman's whole existence; man may range
> The court, camp, church, the vessel, and the mart,
>   Sword, gown, gain, glory, offer in exchange
> Pride, fame, ambition, to fill up his heart,
>   And few there are whom these cannot estrange;
> Men have all these resources, we but one,
> To love again, and be again undone."

But we touch the very core of the spirit of *Don Juan* in Stanza CXCVIII., which follows immediately after this beautiful and heart-wringing letter:—

> " This note was written upon gilt-edged paper
> With a neat little crow-quill, slight and new;
> Her small white hand could hardly reach the taper,
> It trembled as magnetic needles do,
> And yet she did not let one tear escape her;
> The seal a sun-flower; ' *Elle vous suit partout*,'
> The motto, cut upon a white cornelian;
> The wax was superfine, its hue vermilion."

At one moment the agony of a woman's heart—at the next, the fripperies and trivialities of feminine daintiness. In the same spirit the pathos of Juan's farewell to Spain is made ridiculous by his sea-sickness. It is by such juxtapositions that Byron barbs his satire; the root of his cynicism is the doctrine that the petty, the contemptible and the base will always be found close to the heroic and the pathetic. No man is a hero to his valet, because the valet sees the pettiness. So much the worse for the valet. And so much the worse for the satirist if he imagines that the admixture of pettiness makes the heroism unreal.

A satirical and occasionally ironic review of human nature— that is the substance of *Don Juan*. If Matthew Arnold's definition of poetry as "a criticism of life" is true anywhere, it is true here. Don Juan starts in Spain, makes his way to Turkey, thence to Russia, and finally to England, in order that the special follies and vices of the several countries may be brought to light. But the differences are subordinate; they serve only to drive home the doctrine that human nature is everywhere fundamentally the same, and, alas, that everywhere it is fundamentally vile and base. Not that the good is absolutely excluded or wholly denied. Byron's design is to give both sides—good as well as bad. "I sketch the world exactly as it goes," he says; and to prove it, in the midst of the horrors of the storming of Ismail we have Juan saving the child. There are elements of humanity as well as courage in the adventurer Johnson too; and the tale of the fight of the Tartar Khan and his five sons is in the vein of the true heroic, which rises to its summit in the self-sacrifice of the deformed son, who

> " Had been neglected, ill-used, and what not,
> Because deformed, yet died all game and bottom,
> To save a sire who blush'd that he begot him."

Such things are; but in the main life is trivial. It exhales,

> " A little breath, love, wine, ambition, fame,
> Fighting, devotion, dust,—perhaps a name."

And again:—

> " When we have made our love, and gained our gaining,
>   Drest, voted, shone, and, may be, something more;
> With dandies dined; heard senators declaiming;
>   Seen beauties brought to market by the score,
> Sad rakes to sadder husbands chastely taming;
>   There's little left but to be bored or bore.
> Witness those ' *ci-devant jeunes hommes* ' who stem
> The stream, nor leave the world which leaveth them."

"Perhaps a name": is there comfort to be found here? We learn the answer in Byron's treatment of ambition; and we find that in all forms, and especially in that of military glory, it is worthless, or worse:—

> " What is the end of Fame? 'tis but to fill
>   A certain portion of uncertain paper:
> Some liken it to climbing up a hill,
>   Whose summit, like all hills, is lost in vapour;
> For this men write, speak, preach, and heroes kill,
>   And bards burn what they call ' the midnight taper,'
> To have, when the original is dust,
> A name, a wretched picture and worse bust."

The ambitions of peace are touched upon in all grades, from the county magnate and J.P., Lord Henry of Canto XVI., to the statesman Castlereagh; and on all this judgment is passed—vanity of vanities. The treatment of Castlereagh demands some notice. What Byron says of him in the fiftieth stanza of Canto IX. is not satire, but mere vulgar abuse; and in the phrase "carotid-artery-cutting Castlereagh" the poet sinks beneath the lowest level permissible to a gentleman. Nearly everything he says of the great but unhappy statesman supports the contention of those who hold that there was in Byron an ineradicable vulgarity. Besides the references in *Don Juan*, he has three epigrams and an epitaph upon Castlereagh; and there is little to choose between them: all are virulent, vulgar, indefensible. For a partial defence we must look elsewhere. If Byron could be virulent and abusive in his satire, he could also be generous in recantation. His palinodes in the cases of Scott and Moore have been mentioned already; and even the editor of the offending *Review* gets a generous acknowledgment of his merits. "I do not know you," Byron writes of Jeffrey,

> " I do not know you, and may never know
> Your face—but you have acted on the whole
> Most nobly, and I own it from my soul."

Yet once more, on the other side, the "chevalier sans peur et sans reproche" would never have written the satire on Lady Byron which Byron has hidden under the name of Donna Inez.

The principal part of Byron's discourse on the vanity of ambition is devoted to military glory, and it is most unfavourable. The "sucking hero"

> " Turns out to be a butcher in great business,
>   Afflicting young folks with a sort of dizziness."

Cantos VII. and VIII. are mainly devoted to this theme. The horrors of the siege of Ismail (in which nearly 40,000 Turks were said to have perished) stirred Byron to the depths, and he determined to "teach, if possible, the stones to rise against earth's tyrants." It gives no high conception of the justice of the cause to see the women waiting,

> " While their beloved friends began to arm,
>   To burn a town that never did them harm."

Nor is the picture attractive of

> " The greatest chief
>   That ever peopled hell with heroes slain,
>   Or plunged a province or a realm in grief."

Suwarrow in outward appearance is

> " An old man, rather wild than wise
>   In aspect, plainly clad, besmear'd with dust,
>   Stript to his waistcoat, and *that not* too clean."

In character he is

> " Hero, buffoon, half-demon, and half-dirt,
>   Praying, instructing, desolating, plundering;
>   Now Mars, now Momus; and when bent to storm
>   A fortress, Harlequin in uniform."

Such is the chief who trains the besieging army and directs the assault; and the doings of the host are in harmony with the character and figure of their leader. There is more devilry and dirt than glory; and well may the Cockneys of London and the muscadins of Paris ponder, as the poet bids them, "what a pious pastime war is." And the whole account is, like that of the shipwreck, carefully reproduced from authentic records.

In Canto IX. Byron takes leave of Ismail, but not of the theme of military glory. Wellington undergoes a criticism different from yet hardly less severe than that on Suwarrow. But it is infinitely less effective. The reader feels that it is carping and unreasonable, and the massive figure of the great Duke stands undamaged.

But vain and empty as is military glory, there is after all a reality in life. It is money. "Yes! ready money *is* Aladdin's lamp." It is cash that

> " Rules the camp, the court, the grove:
> Cash rules the grove, and fills it too besides:
> Without cash, camps were thin, and courts were none;
> Without cash, Malthus tells you, ' take no brides.' "

It rules the marriage-market as absolutely as the market for potatoes, and its possessors are the real masters of the world:—

> " Who hold the balance of the world? Who reign
> O'er congress, whether royalist or liberal?
> Who rouse the shirtless patriots of Spain?
> (That make old Europe's journals squeak and gibber all./
> Who keep the world, both old and new, in pain
> Or pleasure? Who make politics run glibber all?
> The shade of Bonaparte's noble daring?
> Jew Rothschild, and his fellow-Christian, Baring."

Byron laughed, as he has said, that he might not weep. There lies behind most of his satire a profound seriousness. And of all things he felt most deeply on liberty. To that he devoted the noblest part of his life—its close. Everybody is familiar with the thrilling stanza of *Childe Harold*, in which he depicts the torn banner of freedom streaming like a thunder-storm *against* the wind. And in *Don Juan* itself he treats it seriously in the finest of his lyrics, *The Isles of Greece*. He loves freedom so much that he resents the tyranny of mobs, as well as that of kings:—

> " I wish men to be free
> As much from mobs as kings, from you as me."

In *Childe Harold* he distinguishes between battles such as Morat and Marathon, fought in the cause of freedom, and battles such as Waterloo and Cannae, where he is less confident of the purity of the motive. He satirises Suwarrow because he sees in him the instrument of a tyrant; and he satirises Wellington because, perversely enough, he sees him in the same light: Waterloo he regards as a king-making victory. The winning of freedom is man's highest achievement, treason to it is his blackest crime, and incapacity to preserve it is proof of the worst incompetence. The later cantos of *Don Juan* are full of satire of English society and English life; but of all his criticisms none probably in Byron's own view struck so deep as that which is meant to show how imperfect is the boasted freedom of England. Having brought Don Juan to the summit of Shooter's Hill, he makes his wanderer moralise that here

> " Is Freedom's chosen station;
> Here peals the people's voice, nor can entomb it,
> Racks, prisons, inquisitions; resurrection
> Awaits it, each new meeting or election."

Here, he goes on, wives are chaste, lives pure (points which the sequel makes doubtful),

> " Here laws are all inviolate; none lay
> Traps for the traveller; every highway's clear:
> Here,—he was interrupted by a knife,
> With—' Damn your eyes, your money or your life.' "

The later cantos are largely an expansion of this, and an exposure of the imperfections of government and of life in the country which is supposed to be the freest and the best ordered. The freedom of the highway is challenged; vice permeates the society—"a microcosm on stilts"—which fills the stately home of the Lady Adeline Amundeville, though sometimes hypocrisy or fear makes it "not quite adultery, but adulteration." And above all, as the emptiness of life is its sorest trial, so it is eminently English:—

> " *Ennui* is a growth of English root,
> Though nameless in our language:—we retort
> The fact for words, and let the French translate
> That awful yawn which sleep cannot abate."

It is a commonplace of criticism that the man Byron is always present in the verse he wrote. He certainly is present in *Don Juan* —purposely and necessarily. The home of Lady Adeline Amundeville is unmistakably Byron's own stately heritage—Newstead. It expresses the pride and love of Byron's heart, with just a few satiric touches, as in the description of the picture-gallery:—

> " And here and there some high stern patriot stood,
> Who could not get the place for which he sued."

The deformed son of the Pasha reveals the suffering of the lame poet. With more questionable taste he embodies his satire of Lady Byron in the Donna Inez of the opening cantos. There is a cutting edge in the praise of the serenity with which "this best and meekest woman" bore her husband's woes:—

> " Calmly she heard each calumny that rose,
> And saw *his* agonies with such sublimity,
> That all the world exclaimed, ' What magnanimity! ' "

The Princess of Parallelograms of the Lady Melbourne letters is clearly visible in the blue-stocking Donna Inez; the education of Juan is a satire of prudery; and her choice of the vocation of teaching after the disastrous issue is a bitter gibe at her self-sufficiency:—

> " The great success of Juan's education
> Spurred her to teach another generation."

It is very effective, it is in the worst taste, and it gives reasonable ground for suspecting that the writer was bad at heart.

There are other grounds as well for the suspicion. Southey, in a letter to Landor, called *Don Juan* a "foul blot" on English literature, and "an act of high treason on English poetry." Blackwood, the founder of the great publishing house, refused to sell the poem. We may if we please discount Southey's denunciation as that of a prejudiced person; and Blackwood seems to have been uneasy in his mind as having overstepped his function as a bookseller, yet glad that his relations with Murray at the time gave him a colourable ground for the refusal. But impartial criticism must admit that their words and their action were not without excuse. *Don Juan*, though a work of high genius, is also the work of a vicious man; and the vice is not explained away or excused by pronouncing the word satire. On 10th October, 1822, Byron writes to Murray: "*Don Juan* will be known by and by, for what it is intended—a *Satire* on *abuses* of the present states of society, and not an eulogy of vice." To call a spade a spade is not a sin: on the contrary, plainness of speech is often meritorious. We must judge by the general tone, the atmosphere of the whole piece. And the atmosphere is tainted. There is much in *Don Juan* which it would be sublime simplicity to believe to be there for the purpose of reformation. In the harem cantos especially Byron simply wallows in vice; in the moral sense they are radically bad. Has art nothing to do with morality? So some think, but so Byron does not plead; perhaps has not the courage to plead in the letter to Murray quoted above. Take him on his own terms, and he stands condemned.

Compare him with the few who may without absurdity be regarded as his peers in satire. Juvenal is unsparing in his exposure of the foul sore he seeks to heal; but no one can dream that he does it from love of the sore itself. Swift becomes loathsome in his treatment of vice, and we may begin to doubt the healthiness of his mind. But we cannot for one moment conceive that he loves that which he shows to be so hideous. The difference between Byron and these two is that he is still at heart the profligate, impenitent and unreformed. Shakespeare has put into the mouth of Duke Senior in *As You Like It* what may have been his own judgment on this offence. The Duke pronounces that Jaques, himself tainted, commits "most mischievous foul sin in chiding sin." There are no water-tight compartments in human nature. Art is defiled by moral defilement. Unfortunately, this grave flaw pervades Byron's greatest achievement—for such, after all, *Don Juan* is.

CHAPTER XIII

In the latter part of the eighteenth century political satire in prose reached its highest point in Junius, and early in the nineteenth century poetical satire culminated in Byron. An observer fore-casting the future might with every show of reason have predicted that ere it ended the nineteenth century would enrich literature with satires equal, if not even superior, to those of the eighteenth. Yet the forecast would have been wholly wrong. Since the re-birth of satire in the seventeenth century there has been no period so poor in that species of literature as the century between the death of Byron and the present day. It has yielded but one satire in verse that can be called great—Mr. Gilbert Frankau's *One of Us* (for his *One of Them* is much inferior); and though there is a good deal of satire intermingled with the prose, there is no single great prose work that can without reservation be called a satire. There is much satire in *Sartor Resartus*; but that "spiritual autobiography" is far more than a satire, and the fact that the general idea was suggested by *A Tale of a Tub* does not alter its character. *Vanity Fair* is heavily charged with satire; but though the novel or the drama may embody satire, they necessarily embody much besides. Only in Peacock and Samuel Butler does the satire outweigh all else. Whatever may have been the reason, the facts show that satire was uncongenial to the age. Perhaps the age had grown more tolerant: it is certain that many themes which a century earlier would have been treated satirically are dealt with humor-ously or in the vein of sentiment. When satire is used it is generally of the lighter sort. No period is so rich in that species which finds expression in parody. But the parodies in *Rejected Addresses* and *The Bon Gaultier Ballads*, and those of Calverley and J. K. Stephen, are merely good-natured skits, and not at all satires in the sense in which *The Vision of Judgment* is a satire on Southey.

The spirit of romance is not friendly to satire, and doubtless the prevalence of romance from the close of the eighteenth century onwards had much to do with the decay of satire. It is significant that the one great satirist, Byron, was the champion of Pope in an age which had repudiated him. The influence of Byron helped to turn Shelley to satire. But *Swellfoot the Tyrant* and *Peter Bell the Third* only show how ill fitted he was for the rôle; and in *The Masque of Anarchy* there burns the fire of an aspiration more religious than satirical. Either thus, by rising to the serious lyric, as in Mrs. Browning's *Cry of the Children* and in Hood's *Song of the Shirt*, or by turning the matter into humour, the themes which might have given rise to satire are otherwise disposed of.

How romance weakens satire is well shown in Bulwer Lytton's (1803–73) *The New Timon* (1843), one of the very few long poems of the nineteenth century that is actuated by a satirical purpose. The few who know it at all now know it best by the satire on Tennyson's "darling little room so warm and bright," and the "blue fly singing in the pane." But besides literary satire it contains satire on the laws of England, satire on the social system, and above all, satire on the evils of the factory system—those evils which about the middle of the century so moved the hearts of poets like Hood and Mrs. Browning, novelists like Charles Kingsley and Mrs. Gaskell, and philanthropists like Lord Shaftesbury. They are stern themes, and should have been treated with the sternness of a Juvenal. But the sub-title of *The New Timon*, "A Romance of London," accurately describes the piece. It is sentimental and gushing, and gush and sentimentality will no more mingle with satire than oil with water.

In another way the deplorable decline in satire is illustrated by Philip James Bailey's (1816–1902) *The Age* (1858). The phrase "a colloquial satire," by which it is described on the title-page, warns the reader to expect something as far removed from the point and wit of Pope as from the grand harmonies of Milton. The interlocutors are "Critic, young Author and Mutual Friend," and the scene is an editor's room in town. The bulk of the piece is a criticism of literature, from the Greeks down to the writer's own time. But social and political subjects—the ballot, the extension of the suffrage, the abuses of the press and the evils of war—are also discussed. So is the theme, then fresh, of the great exhibition, when

> " Peace-men had their beatific vision,
>   And Art-schools were to render earth Elysian."

And it is all weary and flat and unprofitable.

It is a relief to turn from Lytton and Bailey to Thomas Hood (1799–1845), whose *Miss Kilmansegg and her Golden Leg* is the best satirical poem of the nineteenth century after Byron. It appeared originally in parts, in Colburn's *New Monthly Magazine*, in 1840–41. Much was lost to the world through the destiny which doomed Hood to jest for a living. He was a true poet who could rarely afford time for poetry. He had also the humbler gifts of the satirist. But here the loss is less serious; for *Miss Kilmansegg* does not suffer very gravely from the punning which had become habitual with Hood, and which he knew to be remunerative. The satire is with rare skill blended with humour, and the fantastic rhymes and puns rather show up than hide the depth of feeling and the seriousness of the thought.

No satire can be great unless the evils at which it is aimed are real and are prevalent. *Miss Kilmansegg* is a satire on the besetting sin of a commercial age—the love of wealth in itself and apart from its uses, of wealth not regarded as a *means* of life, but elevated to the place of the supreme *end* of life. With marvellous ingenuity Hood rings the changes on Gold. The colour floods the poem, the substance loads it, and the hapless Miss Kilmansegg is buried, intellect, heart and soul, under mountains of it. By Gold her spirit is stifled in infancy, her last sleep on earth is filled with dreams of "golden treasures and golden toys," and the crash of the Golden Leg upon her skull ends her life. Vanity of vanities!

The curse of a civilisation materialised and devoted wholly to the acquisition of wealth is that it produces misery all round. Hood leaves us under no illusion as to the impotence of gold to buy happiness, but he knew too well the hardships of poverty to idealise that. A roof "neither wind nor water-proof—that's the prose of Love in a Cottage." And if the gilded Miss Kilmansegg lives and dies miserable, her poor sister is wretched too:—

> " Whilst Margaret, charm'd by the Bulbul rare,
>   In a garden of Gul reposes—
> Poor Peggy hawks nosegays from street to street
> Till—think of that, who find life so sweet!—
>   She hates the smell of roses!"

Has anyone ever found a more poignant expression for misery than this—"she hates the smell of roses"?

It is part of the privilege, which is the curse, of wealth, that it makes its own code of morals. Miss Kilmansegg appears at her fancy ball as Diana, with a crescent "that should be silver, but would be gold":—

> " And her jewelled Garter! Oh Sin, oh Shame!
> Let Pride and Vanity bear the blame,
> That brings such blots on female fame!
>   But to be a true recorder,
> Besides its thin transparent stuff,
> The tunic was loop'd quite high enough
>   To give a glimpse of the Order!
>
> But what have sin or shame to do
> With a Golden Leg—and a stout one too?
>   Away with all Prudery's panics!
> That the precious metal, by thick and thin,
> Will cover square acres of land or sin,
>   Is a fact made plain
>   Again and again,
> In Morals as well as Mechanics."

The true poet is something of a prophet, and surely Hood proves the validity of his title to Parnassus by an interpretation of the Kilmansegg pedigree whose soundness the Great War demonstrated anew:—

> " That the Golden Ass, or Golden Bull,
> Was English John, with his pockets full,
>   Then at war by land and water:
> While beef, and mutton, and other meat,
> Were almost as dear as money to eat,
> And farmers reaped Golden Harvests of wheat
>   At the Lord knows what per quarter!"

In Hood's satire there is not the faintest political note. The author of *Miss Kilmansegg* and of *The Song of the Shirt* is awake to the grave social evils inseparable from a system in which greed of gain is the chief motive to action, but whether he is Whig or Tory cannot be determined from the poems. But there are other writers contemporary with or a little later than Hood in whom the political note rings clear and loud. No mistake is possible as to the political sympathies of Ebenezer Elliott (1781–1849): they are proclaimed in the very title of his most famous and greatest work—*Corn-Law*

Rhymes (1831). In the best of them there is a lyrical fervour which transcends satire; but regarded as a whole they are a fierce condemnation of the fiscal system as it then was. The doctrine of Hood is that the evil lies in the pursuit of wealth for its own sake, and it can be cured only by the substitution of some nobler end of life. Elliott advances no objection against the pursuit of wealth, nor does he even condemn all the wealthy. There are two species of the genus rich man; one, the landlord, plunders the poor; the other, the employer, enriches them. When Elliott wrote the industrial system was still comparatively young; and Elliott's own position as an employer no doubt helped to blind him to the evidence which already existed as to the evils inherent in the wages system. In the three generations which have passed since then the Corn Laws have been repealed, food has been cheapened, the people have drifted from the country to the towns, and countless miles of mean streets have been built to house them. If landlordism still exists, it has ceased to be the controlling power, while Elliott's beneficent capitalism has grown enormously in importance. And yet the millennium seems no nearer. Hood saw deeper than Elliott.

The group of writers who supported the Chartist movement saw deeper too, though they show less poetic power in support of their views. Capell Lofft (1806–1873), the author of the Chartist epic *Ernest, or Political Regeneration* (1839), was rather a Utopian visionary than a satirist, and Ebenezer Jones (1820–1860), the author of *Studies of Sensation and Event*, is only now and then satirical. But he is so frequently enough to show his sympathy with the Chartist point of view, and he makes it plain that he would draw no such distinction as Elliott draws between different sections of the rich.

Neither would Ernest Charles Jones (1819–1869) or Robert Barnabas Brough (1828–1860). The former, though an able as well as a high-minded and most disinterested man, was a somewhat feeble poet. The satire in *The Cost of Glory* (included in *The Battle-Day*) shows violence without strength. But in the verse of a later collection —*The Songs of Democracy* (1856–57)—there is sometimes a fairly effective swing; as, for example, in *The Song of the Lower Classes*:—

> " Our place we know—we're so very low,
> 'Tis down at the landlord's feet:
> We're not too low—the bread to grow,
> But too low the bread to eat."

Brough reaches a higher level in his *Songs of the Governing Classes* (1855) which he dedicated to his friend E. M. Whitty, himself the author of a collection of skilful satirical portraits in prose of political leaders, under the title of *The Governing Classes of Great Britain.* Want of intelligence, want of principle, want of morals—these are the characteristics of the governing classes as Brough sees them. My Lord Tomnoddy is a fool:—

> " His Lordship's brow is far from wide,
> But there's plenty of room for the brains inside."

The Marquis of Carabas, though he is old, has an unwrinkled brow, for "brows keep so that have not got to think." It is however *Lady Godiva* that most clearly reveals what moves Brough to satire —a keen sense of the "something rotten" in the industrial system. Godiva, loving all things beneath the sun, is saddened by the excessive deference and self-abasement of the rustics, and puzzled by the churlish bitterness of the workmen in the town. "What had she done to wrong them?"

> " For wrong'd they were, she felt it sore—
> Else, whence such faces wan and gloomy?
> In smoke, and filth, and discontent,
> Why thousands, thus in alleys pent,
> And earth so rich and roomy? "

This is far from the standpoint of Ebenezer Elliott. It is the factory system rather than private ownership of the land that produces the smoke and filth, and, in Brough's mind, it must be condemned as well as the landlord.

In the nineteenth century the lyric became more and more the predominant form of poetry. The drama passed into prose, and the epic was obsolescent. It is noticeable that most of the satire just touched upon is in lyrical measures. Neither Byron's stanzaic form nor the heroic couplet has held its ground; for Lytton and Bailey fail in the latter. Robert Browning (1812–1889) however, an exception to most rules, most frequently used blank verse. His satirical pieces, though not numerous, are highly characteristic. His satire is neither satire of human nature, like Swift's, nor of some feature of an age, like Hood's satire of Mammon, or Burns's of Scottish orthodoxy; nor is it personal in the sense in which Dryden attacked the man Shaftesbury and the man Shadwell and Pope satirised Addison. No doubt the features of Cardinal Wiseman can be detected in Bishop Blougram, and those of the medium

Home in Sludge; but nevertheless Blougram and Sludge are types rather than individuals *Sludge the Medium* satirises that spiritualism which Browning conceived to be false, fraudulent and degrading; and in embodying it in a *persona dramatis* he was simply following the bent of his genius. The individuality of Home is a matter altogether secondary. So it is too in the case of *Bishop Blougram's Apology*. Browning himself was a man of a faith profound though not orthodox; and in this poem he emboaies his detestation of a faith anything but profound, though it professes to be orthodox. Blougram knows that the profession of faith pays. It has brought him honour among men, high position, the luxuries that wealth can buy; while Gigadibs, the sceptic, is poor, unknown, insignificant. Moreover, the creeds *may* be true; men are no longer certain on the point as they were in the previous century; and if they *do* chance to be true, dark is the outlook for the sceptic. If the sceptic is right, he gains nothing, while if he is wrong, he loses immeasurably. But what a faith, and what a religion that has such a faith for its foundation! In one respect Blougram's faith reaches the sublime. He has attained the point of believing that the "Grand Perhaps" he worships may be deluded as to the nature of the adoration he offers. This has to be suggested through the lips of Blougram himself, for Gigadibs is merely a listener. It is done with inimitable subtlety. The whole argument is in favour of Blougram, and the whole atmosphere supports the argument; and yet, without the slightest violation of dramatic propriety, we are made aware that the argument is sophistical, and that a faith such as Blougram's is no faith at all.

Subjects of a religious or semi-religious sort were Browning's favourite material for satire. The contrast between the faith professed and the spirit displayed gives a satiric force to *Holy-Cross Day*, and the effect of asceticism upon a nature to which it is alien is vividly shown in *A Soliloquy of the Spanish Cloister*. In that strange poem, *Caliban upon Setebos*, the satire is as subtle and penetrating as it is in *Bishop Blougram's Apology*. The sub-title, "Natural Theology in the Island," reveals the purpose of the piece. It was published among the *Dramatis Personæ* in 1864, and we have to think back towards the theological conceptions of sixty years ago in order fully to comprehend the satire embodied in this theology of the brute Caliban. He fashions a God in his own image—a God impelled to creation chiefly by spite, utterly capricious, dealing out reward and punishment (but mainly punishment) without principle, "loving not, hating not, just choosing so." As Setebos has no motive better than caprice, his ways are "past finding out," and it is dangerous to try to understand them. Reason is no guide, for reason implies a binding principle, and where then is omnipotence? "'Doth as he likes, or wherefore Lord?" Even when *Caliban upon Setebos* was written, theology of the sort which is covertly satirised was already on the wane, and it has since died out so completely that the younger generation may easily mistake the satiric purpose. But some who still live have heard from the pulpit conceptions of the Deity and His ways on which Caliban's words are a perfectly fair satiric commentary. It is strange that Browning felt impelled more than once to lash the absurdities of this moribund theology. He does so once more in *The Inn Album*, where the creed of the heroine's bigoted husband is carefully expounded and his conception of hell in particular is given in detail. It is a powerful exposure of evangelicalism as held by a mind naturally small and narrow. But why did Browning think it worth while? Burns wrote for an earlier generation, and his readers were men to whom the dogmas he satirised were matters of the deepest moment. Of Browning's readers scarcely a handful could have been in serious doubt as to the doctrine of eternal punishment.

In the dramatic monologues there are frequent satiric points, but the delineation is rarely satirical throughout; and Browning is so absorbed in the study of human character that he has hardly ever leisure or inclination for satire, unless it can be expressed through that. There is however one exception so masterly that it deserves to be quoted at length. Formally, indeed, it is part of a dramatic monologue, but it has no true relation to the character speaking. It is an interpolation, and exhibits Browning in the unwonted guise of a satirist of literature. In *Prince Hohenstiel-Schwangau* the prince thus satirises the famous apostrophe to the ocean, which is one of the purple patches of *Childe Harold*:—

> " How did the foolish ever pass for wise
> By calling life a burden, man a fly,
> Or worm or what's most insignificant?
> ' O littleness of man!' deplores the bard;

And then, for fear the Powers should punish him,
' O grandeur of the visible universe
Our human littleness contrasts withal!
O sun, O moon, ye mountains and thou sea,
Thou emblem of immensity, thou this,
That, and the other,—what impertinence
In man to eat and drink and walk about
And have his little notions of his own,
The while some wave sheds foam upon the shore!'
First of all, 'tis a lie some three-times thick:
The bard,—this sort of speech being poetry,—
The bard puts mankind well outside himself
And then begins instructing them: ' This way
I and my friend the sea conceive of you!
What would you give to think such thoughts as ours
Of you and the sea together?' Down they go
On the humbled knees of them: at once they draw
Distinction, recognise no mate of theirs
In one, despite his mock humility,
So plain a match for what he plays with. Next,
The turn of the great ocean-playfellow,
When the bard, leaving Bond Street very far
From ear-shot, cares not to ventriloquize,
But tells the sea its home-truths: ' You, my match?
You, all this terror and immensity
And what not? Shall I tell you what you are?
Just fit to hitch into a stanza, so
Wake up and set in motion who's asleep
O' the other side of you in England, else
Unaware, as folk pace their Bond Street now,
Somebody here despises them so much!
Between us,—they are the ultimate! to them
And their perception go these lordly thoughts:
Since what were ocean—mane and tail, to boot—
Mused I not here, how make thoughts thinkable?
Start forth my stanza and astound the world!
Back, billows, to your insignificance!
Deep, you are done with!' "

In prose too, as has been said already, satire in the nineteenth
century is generally a subordinate ingredient; but there are two or
three writers of distinction in whom it is predominant, and through
whom satire in prose is raised to a higher level than the contemporary satire in verse ever reaches, except in Hood. Thackeray,
like Fielding, in the major novels stands in the class of students
of human nature, rather than in that of censors of its vices. *Vanity
Fair* perhaps trembles on the verge, but even Becky Sharp does
not make it simply a satire. Thackeray however has his *Barry
Lyndon*, as Fielding has his *Jonathan Wild*, and *The Book of Snobs*
is more than equivalent to Fielding's journalistic satires. Thomas
Love Peacock is in a different category. If *Gryll Grange* were typical
of his work, he too must be classed as a writer of fiction with

pronounced satirical tendencies, yet hardly a satirist. But *Gryll Grange* is not typical, and from *Headlong Hall* to *Crotchet Castle* it is clear that satire is the substance and staple of Peacock. The same holds true of Samuel Butler. The author of *Erewhon* and of *The Way of all Flesh* is, no doubt, other things as well, but he is first and foremost a satirist. These three are the chief prose satirists of the nineteenth century.

In the case of Thomas Love Peacock (1785–1866) it is largely the satiric spirit and purpose that has prevented the attainment of any wide popularity. Though he adopted the form of prose fiction, Peacock used it in a fashion all his own—a fashion which made small appeal to the public. Compare *Nightmare Abbey* or *Crotchet Castle* with even *Vanity Fair*. In Peacock's volumes story counts for nothing and character for very little. Flosky and Mr. Cypress are merely lay figures at which the shafts of literary satire are shot; Squire Crotchet and Sir Simon Steeltrap serve the same purpose for satire of another sort; as do Mr. MacQuedy and even Mr. Chainmail for yet other species of satire. Only Dr. Folliott becomes a living being, almost in his creator's despite. But in Thackeray's work all the characters are much more than so many butts for satiric wit, and though *Vanity Fair* is "a novel without a hero," it has a story—it *is* a novel, while the other two are works of fiction, but not really novels.

Peacock's first work of prose fiction was *Headlong Hall*, published in 1816. But he had made his début as a satirist two years before with the ballad of *Sir Proteus*, in which he deals with a number of contemporary writers. In rapid succession after *Headlong Hall* came *Melincourt*, *Nightmare Abbey* and *Maid Marian*; then, after an interval of seven years, *The Misfortunes of Elphin*, and in 1831 *Crotchet Castle*; and finally *Gryll Grange* in 1861. *Maid Marian* and *The Misfortunes of Elphin* stand apart from the other five, because they have a historic foundation of a sort, and they are laid in the far past. The rest are the somewhat fantastic creations of Peacock's fancy, and they belong to his own time. But all alike are fundamentally satirical. When *Headlong Hall* appeared Peacock was twenty-nine — sufficiently mature in years, though still young. But he was not yet mature in literary art. *Headlong Hall* is a little crude, and if he had not afterwards improved the author would soon have been forgotten. When *Gryll Grange* was published he was over seventy-five, but was far from being in his dotage. It is the fruit of an old age, "frosty, but kindly"; the work of a master of style who has not forgotten his cunning, of a man to whom long experience has given insight into character.

If the question were asked, where can be found the best compendium of Peacock's satire, the answer would be, in the admirable sixth chapter of *The Misfortunes of Elphin*, which describes the education of Taliesin. But even that does not cover the whole ground. Peacock's range is wide. His satire is social, political, literary, academical and educational, military, racial. The War Song of Dinas Vawr, we are told, is "put upon record as being the quintessence of all the war-songs that ever were written, and the sum and substance of all the appetencies, tendencies, and consequences of military glory." And these appetencies and tendencies lead to the carrying off the valley sheep because they are fatter, though the mountain sheep are sweeter—the title of the raider to either being precisely the same, that is to say, no title at all. The manner in which the transference of property is achieved affords opportunity for satire of another type. The raiders, we are told, "limited their aggressions to coming quietly in the night, and vanishing before morning with cattle; an heroic operation, in which the pre-eminent glory of Scotland renders the similar exploits of other nations not worth recording." For Peacock was one of the line of satirists, unbroken from Cleveland to his time, to whom the Scot was anathema. Peacock's dislike is manifested in characters like Mr. MacQuedy, the "learned friend" (Brougham), with his Steam Intellect Society, and in the pedigree of Squire Crotchet, the descendant of Ebenezer MacCrotchet, Esquire.

Satire of this sort is however incidental: what Peacock really spends himself upon is what relates to the structure and life of society, and politics, and literature.

Peacock's opinions with regard to social and political conditions changed considerably in the course of his life. As to the changing follies of society he probably held much the same view from first to last, and would at any time have satirised the whim of the hour as he satirises taste in *Melincourt*. There is always, we are told, a fashionable taste, "but no gentleman would be so rash as to have a taste of his own, or his last winter's taste, or any taste but a fashionable taste." With respect to deeper matters and to politics, there is, as Mr. Saintsbury points out in his introductions, a consistent movement along a definite line. In *Headlong Hall* Peacock lashes the Tories and leaves an impression of radicalism; in *Gryll Grange* he is essentially conservative. As late as *Crotchet Castle* he is very severe on the landed aristocracy; but he would hardly have repeated the satire in *Gryll Grange*. In the former work Squire Crotchet is led to cultivate the leaders of "the march of intellect," because he cannot find occupation for his mind in the pursuits of his class:—

" He could not become, like a true-born English squire, part and parcel of the barley-giving earth; he could not find in game-bagging, poacher-shooting, trespasser-pounding, footpath-stopping, common-enclosing, rack-renting, and all the other liberal pursuits and pastimes which make a country gentleman an ornament to the world, and a blessing to the poor; he could not find in these valuable and amiable occupations, and in a corresponding range of ideas, nearly commensurate with that of the great King Nebuchadnezzar, when he was turned out to grass; he could not find in this great variety of useful action and vast field of comprehensive thought, modes of filling up his time that accorded with his Caledonian instinct."

Squire Crotchet is not such a man, but we are introduced to one in whom the characteristics of the class are incarnate:—

" Sir Simon Steeltrap, of Steeltrap Lodge, member for Crouching-Curtown, Justice of Peace for the county, and Lord of the United Manors of Spring-gun and Treadmill; a great preserver of game and public morals. By administering the laws which he assists in making, he disposes, at his pleasure, of the land and its live stock, including all the two-legged varieties, with and without feathers, in a circumference of several miles round Steeltrap Lodge. He has enclosed commons and woodlands; abolished cottage-gardens; taken the village cricket-ground into his own park, out of pure regard to the sanctity of Sunday; shut up footpaths and alehouses (all but those which belong to his electioneering friend, Mr. Quassia, the brewer); put down fairs and fiddlers; committed many poachers; shot a few; convicted one third of the peasantry; suspected the rest; and passed nearly the whole of them through a wholesome course of prison discipline, which has finished their education at the expense of the country."

Within a few years of the same time Carlyle penned a criticism in much the same spirit, summing it up in a famous epitaph, which states the number of partridges the deceased has slain; and Carlyle, as well as Peacock, lived to modify his opinion of the class satirised.

If the landed aristocracy is handled severely, the magnates of commerce are not spared. To them, "respectable means rich, and decent means poor." Mr. Crotchet the younger makes a fortune in the loan-jobbing firm of Catchflat and Company. "Here, in the days of paper prosperity, he applied his science-illumined genius to the blowing of bubbles, the bursting of which sent many a poor devil to the jail, the workhouse, or the bottom of the river, but left young Crotchet rolling in riches." Mr. Touchandgo, the great banker, disappears one morning with the contents of his till, with the help of which he once more becomes a respectable man by making a new fortune through the agency of paper-money in the state of Apodidraskiana. "The people here knew very well that I ran away from London, but the most of them have run away from some place or other; and they have a great respect for me, because they think I ran away with something worth taking, which few of them had the luck or the wit to do." There are few more scathing satires of commercial morality than the letter of Mr. Touchandgo to his daughter, from which the quotation is taken.

In short, it seems to have been Peacock's view, for at least the first half of his life, that position and wealth are sure to be used only for the advantage of the possessor and to the oppression of those below. Such is the view indicated in *Maid Marian*, where we are told that in the days of Robin Hood what was called social order was "the preservation of the privileges of the few who happened to have any, at the expense of the swinish multitude who had none, except that of working and being shot at for the benefit of their betters, which is obviously not the meaning of social order in our more enlightened times."

Perhaps then political justice and social welfare are to be attained by levelling inequalities. Both *Melincourt* and *Maid Marian* give ground for the belief that Peacock expected at least considerable amelioration from a reform of the franchise. In the former he aims his satire at political abuses through his pictures of the city of Novote with 50,000 inhabitants and no member, and over against that, "Mr. Christopher Corporate, the free, fat, and dependent burgess of the ancient and honourable borough of Onevote," returning by his own voice two members—one of whom proves to be Sir Oran Haut-ton. But if such were Peacock's original opinions, they seem to have changed considerably before he wrote *Gryll Grange*. There we find Mr. MacBorrowdale discoursing on the power of public opinion, which is symbolised for him by a piece of granite, which had broken his father's window by way of emphasising that opinion, and making remarks not over-laudatory on extensions of the franchise. Peacock was "contented wi' little" in the way of franchise reform. In 1861 there was still a long road to travel towards democratic equality.

There was nothing that more stirred Peacock's wrath than the self-satisfaction of the nineteenth century and the boasts of progress so loudly and confidently made all through his life. The Steam Intellect Society of *Crotchet Castle* and of the Pantopragmatics of *Gryll Grange* are targets for his keenest shafts of satire. Mr. Gryll proposes to invoke spirits, and to ask the illustrious of former days "what they think of us and our doings? Of our astounding progress of intellect? Our march of mind? Our higher tone of morality? Our vast diffusion of education? Our art of choosing the most unfit man by competitive examination?" In not one of these things did Peacock believe, and while he changed in his views of politics, in respect of the boasts of progress he remained firm from beginning to end. Already in *Headlong Hall* Mr. Escot insists with no mean force on the evils that accompany the developments of machinery, and when Gryllus is called up in *Gryll Grange*, he finds everything not better but worse than of old:—

> " Bigotry, whose chief employ
> Is embittering earthly joy;
> Chaos, throned in pedant state,
> Teaching echo how to prate;
> And ' Ignorance, with looks profound,'
> Not ' with eye that sweeps the ground.' "

Among the things of which the nineteenth century was specially proud was the development of education. Peacock did not live to see its later phases, but we may confidently infer what his view would have been. The ridicule of competitive examinations in *Gryll Grange* is in the same spirit as the ridicule of the Steam Intellect Society and the March of Mind in *Crotchet Castle*. By their admirable system of demanding what is irrelevant the examiners reject Hannibal, Cromwell and Cœur-de-Lion as candidates for a military life; and Dr. Folliott's opinion of the March of Mind is tersely expressed in a conversation with Mr. MacQuedy:—

" *The Rev. Dr. Folliott:* It has marched into my rick-yard and set my stacks on fire with chemical materials most scientifically compounded. It

has marched up to the door of my vicarage, a hundred and fifty stron;
ordered me to surrender half my tithes; consumed all the provisions I ha
provided for my audit feast, and drunk up my old October. It has marche
in through my back-parlour shutters, and out again with my silver spoon
in the dead of night. The policeman, who was sent down to examine, sa·
my house has been broken open on the most scientific principles. All th
comes of education.

" *Mr. MacQuedy:* I rather think it comes of poverty.

" *The Rev. Dr. Folliott:* No, sir. Robbery, perhaps, comes of poverty, b·
scientific principles of robbery come of education. I suppose the learned frien
has written a sixpenny treatise on mechanics, and the rascals who robbed n
have been reading it."

" What was Jacquerie in the dark ages is the march of mind i
this very enlightened one—very enlightened one," he repeats.

Elementary education then has its dangers. The training o
intellect, without training of character may produce results a
undesirable as they are unforeseen. The higher education is a
fault too, not so much for what it imparts, as because it impart·
little or nothing. Oxford is "a Babylon of buried literature." Dr
Folliott, visiting it with Mr. Crotchet, laid a wager "that in al
their perlustrations they would not find a man reading," and wo·
it. Peacock, who had acquired scholarship without the help of an·
university, loses no chance of throwing scorn on the institution
he had found to be, at any rate, not indispensable.

A subtler point with regard to the things studied is made i·
Dr. Opimian's speech on science: "Science is an edged tool, wit·
which men play like children, and cut their own fingers." Few sa·
the possibility fifty years ago, but the Great War has made i
plain to many. Within the last century or two man's mastery ove·
matter has grown a hundred-fold; his moral progress is doubtful
and has been at the best small. Is he fit to be entrusted with th·
appalling power which science may put into his hands to-morrow
Or even with that which he already possesses?

In some respects the literary is the most interesting of all th·
phases of satire in Peacock. A man of his type of intellect, bor·
when he was born, was predestined to be a satirist of literature
Coleridge, Wordsworth, Southey, Scott, Byron and Shelley wer·
colouring literature richly with romance. Peacock himself begin·
with romance, and gives a romantic setting to his *Maid Maria·*
and *The Misfortunes of Elphin.* But he could never fully accep·
the cult. The reason why he could not becomes clearest perhap·
in his satire of Coleridge. Something akin to mysticism underlie·

all romance; it is "the renascence of wonder"; it rests upon the conviction that "there are more things in heaven and earth than are dreamed of in our philosophy." And it is just this element of mysticism, the insistence upon that which transcends understanding and refuses to be expressed in a logical proposition, that constitutes the offence of Mr. Mystic of Cimmerian Lodge, and of Mr. Flosky (both of whom are Coleridge). "Exquisitely dusky and fuliginous," we are told of the former, is Coleridgean praise, as "*bright thoughts* and *luminous ideas* are the praise of common people." And of Mr. Flosky it is written that he "plunged into the central opacity of Kantian metaphysics, and lay *perdu* several years in transcendental darkness, till the common daylight of common sense became intolerable in his eyes." To him, "the great evil is that there is too much commonplace light in our moral and political literature; and light is a great enemy to mystery, and mystery is a great friend to enthusiasm." But fuliginous Kantian principles have exercised probably more influence upon thought during the last three or four generations than anything else, and now that the solid atom has been resolved into a group of electrons in eternal movement round a nucleus, "the common daylight of common sense" becomes a little dubious. The Germany that ruled an empire in the clouds was a blessing to humanity; the Germany of "realpolitik," guided by "the common daylight of common sense," was its greatest curse. The poet usually sees clearer and sees farther than the satirist.

Wordsworth as Mr. Paperstamp of Mainchance Villa, and in *Crotchet Castle* as Mr. Wilful Wontsee, is satirised on other grounds. In *Melincourt* we are introduced to servants who are relations of Lucy Grey and Alice Fell, and who make journeys, "philosophising all the way in the usual poetical style of a Cumberland peasant." Satire of Wordsworth's trivialities and of his attribution of philosophy to the Cumberland peasant is quite legitimate. So is satire of Coleridge's obscurities. But Peacock clearly went too far when in *Mainchance Villa* and elsewhere he represented the three Lake Poets (Southey especially, under the name of Mr. Feathernest) as selling their souls for lucre. He came to feel so himself. The references to the three poets in *Gryll Grange* are all respectful, and seem to be dictated by a desire to make amends.

Not so in the case of Byron: the satire aimed at him under the name of Mr. Cypress in *Nightmare Abbey* is never retracted, and it is effective. The Byronic "gesture" (to borrow the blessed word of the politicians) is made ridiculous in a sentence: "Sir, I have quarrelled with my wife, and a man who has quarrelled with his wife is absolved from all duty to his country." Two stanzas of *Childe Harold* are admirably "transprosed" in a speech put into the mouth of Mr. Cypress, and in Mr. Flosky's speech which follows the satire is skilfully widened to cover everything that Peacock abominated:—

" *Mr. Cypress:* I have no hope for myself or for others. Our life is a false nature; it is not in the harmony of things; it is an all-blasting upas, whose root is earth, and whose leaves are the skies which rain their poison-dues upon mankind. We wither from our youth; we gasp with unslaked thirst for un-attainable good; lured from the first to the last by phantoms—love, fame, ambition, avarice—all idle, and all ill—one meteor of many names, that vanishes in the smoke of death.

" *Mr. Flosky:* A most delightful speech, Mr. Cypress. A most amiable and instructive philosophy. You have only to impress its truth on the minds of all living men, and life will then, indeed, be the desert and the solitude; and I must do you, myself, and our mutual friends, the justice to observe, that let society only give fair play at one and the same time, as I flatter myself it is inclined to do, to your system of morals, and my system of metaphysics, and Scythrop's system of politics, and Mr. Listless's system of manners, and Mr. Toobad's system of religion, and the result will be as fine a mental chaos as even the immortal Kant himself could ever have hoped to see; in the prospect of which I rejoice."

Mr. Cypress's speech is pure Byron, except that metre is eliminated and the atmosphere is different. There could be no more striking demonstration of the power of atmosphere. The song too, "There is a fever of the spirit," has so much of Byron in it that it almost ceases to be a parody. And yet it is ridiculous. Mr. Glowry's "Let us all be unhappy together" seems to sum up the spirit of the morbid school, and to pronounce the final condemnation upon it. Peacock, as has been said, never retracted this satire on Byron, as he partially at least retracted that on the Lake Poets. Why? Probably because he had come to the conclusion that the Lake Poets were sincere, while Byron in *Childe Harold* was posing. But he had a high opinion of *Cain*, of *Sardanapalus*, and above all of *Don Juan*.

Peacock's satire on Shelley stands on a different footing, for Shelley was his friend, while the others were not. Some have held that in painting Scythrop Peacock was unfaithful to the friendship. And it is true that he aims some keen shafts at his friend. But at any rate Shelley did not feel it necessary to break the friendship, and Peacock remained one of the wisest and truest of his helpers. The man who felt as we have seen Peacock felt about Coleridge and his principles could not but be sharply critical of much in Shelley. But it must be remembered in the first place that though there is a good deal of Shelley in Scythrop, Scythrop is so wild a caricature that nobody could mistake it for a portrait; and in the second place, if Scythrop is sometimes made ridiculous and is implicitly condemned, he is sometimes represented as eminently right and wise. What could be better than his retort upon his father Mr. Glowry, who, to comfort him for the desertion of the beautiful Emily Gironette, has read him a commentary on Ecclesiastes, insisting particularly on the text, "One man among a thousand have I found, but a woman among all those have I not found." "How could he expect it," said Scythrop, "when the whole thousand were locked up in his seraglio? His experience is no precedent for a free state of society like that in which we live."

There is something of Shelley in Mr. Foster the perfectibilian of *Headlong Hall* as well as in Scythrop. The critical and sceptical Peacock could not refrain from poking fun at Mr. Foster's eager optimism, and he sums up this side of his criticism in the title of a treatise of which Scythrop is the author: *Philosophical Gas, or, a Project for a General Illumination of the Human Mind*. It is amusing and harmless. There are other gibes which are not quite so harmless in the opinion of the devotees of Shelley. Scythrop, "in love, at the same time, with two damsels with minds and habits as remote as the antipodes," comes uncomfortably close to the Shelley who was the husband of Harriet and the lover of Mary, and reminds us that Peacock took the side of Harriet, firmly refused to believe the stories that were told to blacken her character, and disliked Mary. Shelley's position was at any rate sufficiently dubious to entitle Peacock to his own opinion. The farcical satire of Scythrop is essentially good-natured, only part of it can be connected with the man Shelley, and the fair conclusion seems to be that Peacock remained a true, though not an uncritical, friend.

As has already been said, William Makepeace Thackeray (1811–63) as novelist stands in the main outside the scope of this book;

but as miscellaneous writer, as contributor to *Fraser's Magazine* and to *Punch,* he is among the great satirists of the nineteenth century. His connexion with the former periodical had been formed at least as early as 1835; with *Punch* it began in 1842, and lasted till 1850. To both his contributions were numerous and were prevailingly satirical; and in each case there is one work which stands out conspicuous and overshadows all the rest. *Barry Lyndon,* which was published serially in 1844, ranks among the works which shed lustre on *Fraser's Magazine*; and *The Book of Snobs,* of which the parts appeared in *Punch* in 1846-7, conferred honour upon even that most attractive of comic journals. These two books are indubitably Thackeray's greatest contributions to satire; but in minor collections there is enough to have made no mean reputation. In the *Memoirs of Mr. C. J. Yellowplush* and the *Diary of C. Jeames de la Pluche,* Thackeray set the example of systematic misspelling, afterwards followed with more fun though with less satire by the American Artemus Ward. In both books the satire is highly effective, but it is essentially of the same type as that which we find later and better in *The Book of Snobs.* It is the satire of flunkeyism, here written by the flunkey, but showing the prevalence of the same mean spirit in all ranks of society. The *Diary* however devotes itself especially to gambling on the Stock Exchange at the time of the railway mania; and the meanness of society is shown up by the treatment of the flunkey when Mr. Plush announces that he has made £30,000 by speculating in railroads:—

" Sir George, who was at breakfast, instantly rose, and shook Mr. P. by the hand; Lady Flimsy begged him to be seated, and partake of the breakfast which he had laid on the table; and has subsequently invited him to her grand *dejeûner* at Richmond, where it was observed that Miss Emily Flimsy, her beautiful and accomplished seventh daughter, paid the lucky gentleman *marked attention.*"

The same spirit reigns through the *Diary.* A certain justification of the toadying to Jeames is given in the end when fortune deserts him, and he is again reduced to poverty. He bears his losses not without dignity, and proves himself worthier of prosperity than the Sir Georges and high financiers with whom the freaks of chance bring him for a time into contact.

Less characteristic of Thackeray is the satire of literature, of which there is a strain in the Yellowplush Papers, and which forms the substance of *Novels by Eminent Hands*, and of the admirable *Rebecca and Rowena*, where real admiration of the original and its author takes all sting from the parody. Some sting remains in the parodies of the "eminent hands" of the day. *Codlingsby* shows disdain of the weaknesses of Disraeli, who, many years afterwards, repaid the compliment in the St. Barbe of Endymion. In *Barbazure* and *George de Barnwell* Thackeray looks down from a height on authors whom he felt, rightly, to be his inferiors. Bulwer Lytton, who is satirised in the latter, was a writer of whose faults both of style and substance Thackeray was peculiarly impatient, and whom he satirised more than once with a keenness bordering on virulence, which he afterwards regretted. In *George de Barnwell* the themes of satire are the bombast of Lytton's style and the unwholesome sentimentality of the morals underlying the novel of crime. The style is ridiculed in the description of the grocer's shop:—

" Among the many brilliant shops whose casements shone upon Chepe, there stood one a century back (about which period our tale opens) devoted to the sale of Colonial produce. A rudely carved image of a negro, with a fantastic plume and apron of variegated feathers, decorated the lintel. The east and west had sent their contributions to replenish the windows. The poor slave had toiled, died perhaps, to produce yon pyramid of swarthy sugar marked ' ONLY 6½d.'—That catty box, on which was the epigraph ' STRONG FAMILY CONGO ONLY 3s. 9d.,' was from the country of Confutzee—that heap of dark produce bore the legend ' TRY OUR REAL NUT '—'Twas Cocoa—and that nut the cocoa-nut, whose milk has refreshed the traveller and perplexed the natural philosopher. The shop in question was, in a word, a grocer's."

Bombast was despicable to Thackeray, but he would not have spent much time and strength in ridiculing that alone. What roused him to indignation was the moral rottenness of the novel of crime, and upon that his lash fell most fiercely, both in the rapid sketch *George de Barnwell* and in the more extended satire *Catherine*. He leaves no room for mistakes as to the special object of his satire. When George de Barnwell falls in love, "his genius breaks out prodigiously. He talks about the Good, the Beautiful, the Ideal, etc., in and out of all season, and is virtuous and eloquent almost beyond belief—in fact, like Devereux, or P. Clifford, or E. Aram, Esquires." And in the end, when Barnwell is about to be hanged after a career in which he "outdoes all the dandies, all the wits, all the scholars, and all the voluptuaries of the age," he describes the murder of his uncle as "the ridding the world of a sordid worm"; and the footnote admits that the sentiment is plagiarised, and has been "expressed much more eloquently in the ingenious romance of *Eugene Aram*."

Catherine, which appeared in *Fraser's Magazine* in 1839–40, like *George de Barnwell*, satirises the novel of crime, but does so on a much larger scale. Less emphasis is laid on style. Like its greater successor *Barry Lyndon*, it is profoundly influenced by Fielding's *Jonathan Wild*, and, like that, aims at producing disgust of those crimes which writers like Lytton and Ainsworth had treated as if they were things to be admired. Thackeray loathes the sort of life he has to depict too much to conceal himself altogether behind the veil of the impartial narrator; and in the last chapter of all—"Another Last Chapter"—he comes into the open and avows the hidden purpose he has set before himself:—

" It has been the writer's object carefully to exclude from his drama (except in two very insignificant instances—mere walking-gentlemen parts), any characters but those of scoundrels of the very highest degree. That he has not altogether failed in the object he had in view, is evident from some newspaper critiques which he has had the good fortune to see; and which abuse the tale of *Catherine* as one of the dullest, most vulgar, and immoral works extant. It is highly gratifying to the author to find that such opinions are abroad, as they convince him that the taste for Newgate literature is on the wane, and that when the public critic has right-down undisguised immorality set before him, the honest creature is shocked at it, as he should be, and can declare his indignation in good round terms of abuse. The characters of the tale *are* immoral, and no doubt of it; but the writer humbly hopes the end is not so. The public was, in our notion, dosed and poisoned by the prevailing style of literary practice, and it was necessary to administer some medicine that would produce a wholesome nausea, and afterwards bring about a more healthy habit."

The story of *Catherine* embodies the main facts of the life of a woman, Catherine Hayes, who murdered her husband, and was burned for the crime at Tyburn in 1726. She was Irish, and one of her countrymen took such offence at the story as to threaten Thackeray, who first informed the police, and afterwards reasoned his enemy into a sober frame of mind.

Barry Lyndon follows *Jonathan Wild* in a manner somewhat different from that adopted in *Catherine*. The latter is a narrative in the third person, the former is an autobiography—the autobiography of an unprincipled scoundrel. It is a masterpiece; but it shares with *Catherine* a characteristic which, it has been argued, puts it artistically below *Jonathan Wild*. Thackeray, we have seen, does not, in *Catherine*, entirely conceal himself. He specifically avows his purpose in the end; and through the book here and there may be found indications of the views of the writer. The same is true of *Barry Lyndon*. It is not the heartless rascal Barry, it is Thackeray, who utters the reflections on the ingredients of military glory with which Chapter IV. closes. The adventurer moralises on the incidents of the Battle of Minden:—

> " It is well for gentlemen to talk of the age of chivalry; but remember the starving brutes whom they lead—men nursed in poverty, entirely ignorant, made to take a pride in deeds of blood—men who can have no amusement but in drunkenness, debauch, and plunder. It is with these shocking instruments that your great warriors and kings have been doing their murderous work in the world; and while, for instance, we are at the present moment admiring the ' Great Frederick,' as we call him, and his philosophy, and his liberality, and his military genius, I, who have served him, and been, as it were, behind the scenes of which that great spectacle is composed, can only look at it with horror. What a number of items of human crime, misery, slavery, go to form that sum-total of glory! "

Unquestionably there is here a violation of dramatic propriety: Barry Lyndon was not capable of such reflections. *Jonathan Wild* is free from such inconsistencies, and is so far, it would seem, the better book. And yet the reader who refuses to judge by abstract principles when his deepest feelings cry aloud against the conclusion they suggest, knows that it is far inferior to Thackeray's work. The sordid squalor of *Jonathan Wild* makes it almost unreadable, while *Barry Lyndon*, the autobiography of a scoundrel as base as Wild himself, can be read with a grim pleasure. The eighteenth century was somewhat given to wallowing in filth— witness Swift and Smollett, as well as Fielding. The nineteenth century denied writers that privilege; and Thackeray imagined that the restraint was bad for his art. He was mistaken. There is plenty of filth in the world, and only the coward ignores it. To clear it away is a man's job, and if he gets soiled in the process, the stain can be washed off. If he wallows, it gets beneath the skin, and then not all great Neptune's ocean will ever wash him clean. Thackeray's heart pierced deeper than his head. He was stronger, not weaker, greater, not less, by reason of the restraints which the age laid upon him. *Jonathan Wild* would have been a far finer book than it is if Fielding had felt himself to be under similar restraints. Inconsistencies such as we see in the passage quoted above are the protest of Thackeray's heart that the work he was engaged upon was not the highest kind of art. If they are failings, they are failings that lean to virtue's side. Artistically, they do not stand on the same level with those scenes like the porter scene in *Macbeth* and the grave-diggers scene in *Hamlet*, whereby Shakespeare relieves the tragic tension; but though they cannot be defended on the same grounds, they subserve a similar purpose. They are a relief to the reader—and he needs it, as well as the spectator of *Macbeth*. It is *not* the business of art to depict impartially the ugly and the beautiful, whether the ugliness be physical or moral. Its function is to interpret the beautiful to men, and it may legitimately deal with the ugly only by way of showing up its opposite by contrast.

Barry Lyndon, as delineated by himself, is the most callous and heartless of scoundrels. In his view, mothers exist for their sons, and without scruple or remorse he trades upon that maternal love which is the one redeeming feature of his own mother. Of course wives exist for their husbands; and he brutally ill-treats Lady Lyndon, after having followed the advice of that far from admirable lady's former husband: "Get a friend, sir, and that friend a woman —a good household drudge, who loves you. *That* is the most precious sort of friendship, for the expense of it is all on the woman's side." He is for ever scheming in the spirit of this advice. After a particularly base plot, this "gentleman" justifies himself, and puts his philosophy of life into a few sentences: "I say that anything is fair in love, and that men so poor as myself can't afford to be squeamish about their means of getting on in life. The great and rich are welcomed, smiling, up the grand staircase of the world; the poor but aspiring must clamber up the wall, or push and struggle up the back stair, or, *pardi*, crawl through any of the conduits of the house, never mind how foul and narrow, that lead to the top."

Just so Barry Lyndon thinks, and just so Barry Lyndon acts all through life and not merely in affairs of love. He is a gambler and a cheat, and according to him all who gamble cheat also. It is true he repudiates the word, but the uninitiated may be pardoned if they fail to see the moral difference between his methods and those of the cheat. He knows that the ignorant will be shocked: "Some prudish persons may affect indignation at the frankness of these confessions, but heaven pity them! Do you suppose that any man who has lost or won a hundred thousand pounds at play will not take the advantages his neighbour enjoys? They are all the same. But it is only the clumsy fool who *cheats*, who resorts to the clumsy expedients of cogged dice and cut cards."

Thackeray never lets the scoundrel have the best of it to the close. Catherine ends her life at Tyburn, and Barry Lyndon is outwitted and becomes the pensioner of his ill-used wife, until she dies and her successor sternly cuts off the annuity, devoting the sum to charities.

It was in 1844 that *Barry Lyndon* ran its course in *Fraser's Magazine*. Two years later the articles which ultimately made *The Book of Snobs* began to appear in *Punch*. Thackeray thus lifted the word " snob " from slang and gave it a place in literary English. He had used it already at Cambridge in an ephemeral paper *The Snob*, but that has long been forgotten. *The Book of Snobs* is unquestionably Thackeray's most characteristic contribution to satire. He was a close student of the eighteenth century, and he was certainly influenced by the essayists in his choice of a domain of satire. The Queen Anne essayists dealt with the minor morals, and Thackeray fixed upon, not the seven deadly sins, but the forty odd meannesses, which he seemed to regard as scarcely less deadly. "He who meanly admires mean things is a snob," he says; and in forty-five successive papers he deals with so many groups or types of snobbery. To admire is natural to man, and admiration may be either noble or base, according to the nature of the thing admired. Six years earlier Carlyle had treated the tendency as a virtue in *Heroes and Hero-Worship*, where the heroes are men like Luther and Knox, Dante and Shakespeare, Johnson and Burns. The derided Boswell is worthy of respect, not ridicule, for his hero-worship, because that which he admires is truly admirable. Thackeray looks at the subject from the side of the corresponding vice. We are still dealing with men in an attitude of admiration, only that which they admire is not great, but contemptible. Carlyle knew the saying that no man is a hero to his valet; and he retorts in effect—so much the worse for the valet if he does not reverence the heroic when he encounters it. Thackeray's position is, so much the worse for both valet and master, if they admire or claim admiration for that which is not admirable.

Sometimes it is better to be casual and unsystematic than to have a definite plan. *The Book of Snobs* suffers because it is too carefully

planned. The method of the Queen Anne essayists was the sounder.
They set out to

> " Eye nature's walks, shoot folly as it flies,
> And catch the manners living as they rise."

Their range was in consequence wider and their satire more varied
than Thackeray's. It was only from one point of view that he
treated follies and manners; they dealt with them literally as they
rose. Hence a monotony which in the long run makes *The Book of
Snobs* somewhat tedious. The suspicion arises too that the snob
is dealt with more severely than he deserves. He certainly deserves
ridicule. It is mean and ridiculous of Muggins to become De Mogyns,
and it is far from admirable on the part of Lady Susan Scraper to
manage her charities so that "there is no respectable lady in all
London who gets her name more often printed for such a sum of
money." It is further true that the evils engendered by snobbery
are sometimes very grave. Thus Major Ponto, "a good-natured,
kindly English gentleman" with a thousand pounds a year, is
reduced to hopeless penury and has his nature all twisted and distorted by the pretentiousness of the life he is induced to live:—

"What tenant can look for *his* forbearance? What poor man can hope for
his charity? 'Master's the best of men,' honest Stripes says, 'and when we
was in the ridgment a more free-handed chap didn't live. But the way in
which the Missis *du* scryou, I wonder the young ladies is alive, that I du!'
"They live upon a fine governess and fine masters, and have clothes made
by Lady Carabas's own milliner; and their brother rides with earls to cover;
and only the best people in the county visit at the Evergreens, and Mrs. Ponto
thinks herself a paragon of wives and mothers, and a wonder of the world,
for doing all this misery and humbug, and snobbishness, on a thousand a year."

Here is mean admiration of mean things; this is fair game for
the satirist. It may be feared too that Thackeray is not wrong
when he insists that this kind of meanness is peculiarly prevalent
in England—or rather in Britain; for if the smaller peoples insist
upon the more comprehensive name when praise is awarded, they
must accept it for blame as well. And certainly Thackeray had no
intention of drawing a distinction in their favour. In Britain, then,
Thackeray insists, everybody is a snob; and his admission that a
snob walked about under his own hat is well known. There is a
singularly neat instance of the art of suggesting such universality
in the paper on the snobbery of Gorgius IV., King of Brentford:
"If you want to moralise upon the mutability of human affairs,
go and see the figure of Gorgius in his real identical robes, at the

waxwork.—Admittance one shilling. Children and flunkeys sixpence. Go, and pay sixpence."

Only a syllogism in Barbara will prove the conclusion, All Englishmen are snobs; and therefore we may reasonably doubt Thackeray's universal. Not all admiration is mean; if the flunkey cannot admire the hero—so much the worse for the flunkey: his failure does not disprove the existence of the hero; rather it proves the existence of a flunkey soul in a flunkey body. The ambition for distinction is legitimate, and the ambition for social distinction is not less legitimate than other forms of ambition. Thackeray of course knew this, but the very plan of his book tended to throw the knowledge into the background of his mind, and to turn him from the straight path which leads to truth. It also tempted him to exaggerate. He exaggerates, for example, about the *Court Circular*: "As long as the *Court Circular* exists, how the deuce are people whose names are chronicled in it ever to believe themselves the equals of the cringing race which daily reads that abominable trash?" Granted the despicable meanness of the *Court Circular*, still it is not so important as all that. Among those whose names appeared in it from time to time, while Thackeray was writing, was the Duke of Wellington, who had assuredly kept his head fairly level through many years of *Court Circulars*. It is not proved that *all* Englishmen are snobs. Unfortunately Thackeray does not keep *his* head level on this subject. He sees on Mrs. Ponto's drawing-room table "the inevitable, abominable, maniacal, absurd, disgusting *Peerage*." Though Mrs. Ponto is a snob, it is this language, not the *Peerage*, that is absurd. "The rank is but the guinea's stamp"—true; but if the metal stamped be real gold, the stamp is very useful. Thackeray declared himself to be "not a Chartist, only a republican," and a strong opponent of aristocratic government. If, as he smilingly feared, he was a snob at all, the snobbery is to be found here, and not in his inability to walk without elation down Piccadilly arm-in-arm with two dukes. He does not wholly escape the lash of Shirley Brooks, who became editor of *Punch* soon after Thackeray cut his connexion with that journal:—

> " A prince can make a belted knight,
> A marquis, duke, and a' that,
> And if the title's earned, all right,
> Old England's fond of a' that.

> For a' that, and a' that,
>> *Their* balderdash and a' that,
> A name that tells of service done
> Is worth the wear for a' that."

Burns himself, as well as Old England, was fond "of a' that," and he records in verse the pride he felt when he dined with the Earl of Glencairn.

There is much satire scattered through the other miscellaneous works of Thackeray—in *Sketches and Travels in London*, in *The Kickleburys on the Rhine* and the *Essay on Thunder and Small Beer*, prefixed to the second edition and satirising the critic of it. Perhaps the most noteworthy of these miscellaneous writings is *The Second Funeral of Napoleon*, with its companion piece in verse—*The Chronicle of the Drum*. Writing some thirty years after the close of what was then the greatest of wars, he repeats and expands in these pieces that philosophy of military glory which he had adumbrated already in *Barry Lyndon*, and to which recent events have given a fresh poignancy. The most perfect expression of it is in the closing verses of *The Chronicle of the Drum*, and these afford perhaps the most revealing light that is anywhere shed upon that compound of severity and tenderness which was the soul of Thackeray:—

> " He captured many thousand guns;
>> He wrote ' The Great ' before his name;
> And dying, only left his sons
>> The recollection of his shame.
>
> Though more than half the world was his,
>> He died without a rood his own;
> And borrowed from his enemies
>> Six foot of ground to lie upon.
>
> He fought a thousand glorious wars,
>> And more than half the world was his,
> And somewhere now, in yonder stars,
>> Can tell, mayhap, what goodness is."

After Thackeray a considerable time passed before any noteworthy satire in prose appeared. There is much satire buried in the pages of various journals and magazines, especially in those of *Punch*. But in that kindly periodical humour as a rule predominates over satire, and it seldom shows either the power or the seriousness of purpose that mark *The Book of Snobs*. In the main the work of Douglas Jerrold and other contributors was ephemeral, and much of it was laughable burlesque rather than satire. Not till we come to

Matthew Arnold (1822–88) do we find a worthy successor to Thackeray. Arnold was only some eleven years junior to Thackeray by date of birth; but his earlier writings were poetical, and when he began to issue volumes of prose they were either not at all or only here and there satirical. He comes within the scope of this book only as the author of *Friendship's Garland*, one of the wisest, and also one of the least appreciated of satires. No book better illustrates the difference between the satire of the eighteenth and that of the nineteenth centuries. The latter is far more urbane. It relies less on mere keenness of wit and more upon humour. In the essayists, if anywhere, we find something akin in the eighteenth century, not either in Pope or in Swift. In *Friendship's Garland* Arnold is serious enough, but he throws a veil of playfulness over his deeper purpose, and contents himself with raillery.

Arnold was never a widely popular writer, and *Friendship's Garland* was one of the least popular even of his books. The occasion was the war between France and Germany, and Arnold's purpose was to awaken his countrymen to a sense of the folly and danger of the self-laudation with which they were fed. Arnold had already shown his power as a satirical critic of English institutions and the English character. The war with the Philistines was already begun. In the preface to the first series of *Essays in Criticism*, dated 1865, the noble apostrophe to Oxford singles out as the special glory of the great university the fact that she had never given herself to the Philistines; while in the first of the essays which follow this preface we find Arnold quoting the boast of one politician that "the race we ourselves represent, the men and women, the old Anglo-Saxon race, are the best breed in the whole world"; and the prayer of another that "our unrivalled happiness may last." In juxtaposition with this the satirist puts the newspaper report of a shocking child-murder by a wretched girl, reiterating "the final touch—short, bleak, and inhuman: *Wragg is in custody.* The sex lost in the confusion of one unrivalled happiness; or (shall I say?) the superfluous Christian name lopped off by the straightforward vigour of our old Anglo-Saxon breed."

When Arnold wrote the Philistine middle class was England. Matters have doubtless improved greatly in these days when the middle class is swamped in the vast masses of the lower class, but in 1871 the exhortation addressed to the ruling Philistines through the mouth of the imaginary Arminius was very pertinent: "To search and not rest till it sees things more as they really are, and how little of a power over things as they really are is its money-making, or its unrestricted independence, or its newspaper publicity, or its Dissent, or any of the things with which it is now most taken." The idea of clap-trap is dominant, and the cure for it is to "get Geist"—intelligence. Clap-trap teaches that liberty and publicity can be a substitute for thought, study and seriousness; but it is false. Clap-trap insists that material wealth is the be-all and the end-all. "'Yes; war,' I said, 'interrupts business, and brings intolerable inconvenience with it; whereas people have only to persist steadily in the manufacture of bottles, railways, banks, and finance companies, and all good things will come to them of their own accord.'" "Business as usual." *Laissez faire.* Our incomparable civilisation rests firmly on solid matter, and our incomparable and truly British qualities "have just triumphed over every obstacle and given us the Atlantic telegraph." "'Pshaw!' replied Arminius, contemptuously; 'that great rope, with a Philistine at each end of it talking inutilities!'"

Arnold was an educationist, and English education is duly satirised. Lord Lumpington, the Rev. Esau Hittall and Bottles Esquire are magistrates, on qualifications which look strange to Arminius. The two former have been educated at public schools, where they followed "the grand, old, fortifying, classical curriculum," and at Oxford, where, however, "they were so much occupied with Bullingdon and hunting that there was no great opportunity to judge" how much their minds were braced by their mental gymnastics. "There are our young barbarians, all at play." As to Mr. Bottles, the representative of commerce, his antecedents are different. He has been educated at the Lycurgus House Academy under Archimedes Silverpump, Ph.D., a man of modern views: "'We must be men of our age,' he used to say. 'Useful knowledge, living languages, and the forming of the mind through observation and experiment, these are the fundamental articles of my educational creed.' Or, as I have heard his pupil Bottles put it in his expansive moments after dinner: 'Original man, Silverpump! fine mind! fine system! None of your antiquated rubbish—all practical work—latest discoveries in science—lots of interesting experiments—lights of all colours—fizz! fizz! bang! bang! That's what I call forming a man.'"

It is however the social and political conceptions (of which education is an expression) prevalent in England that Arnold most insists upon. He refuses to accept the current view that they are good absolutely and in themselves. His view of liberty might still do good, if people would take the trouble to understand it. Arminius has been explaining himself, and his friend comments:—

" The truth is, he cannot rise to an Englishman's conception of liberty, and understand how liberty, like virtue, is its own reward. ' We go for self-government,' I am always saying to him. ' All right,' he says, ' if it is government by your better self.' ' Fiddlesticks about our better self!' answer I. ' Who is to be the judge? No, the self every man chooses.' ' And what is the self every man will choose,' cries he, ' when they are not told there is a better and a worse self, and shown what the better is like? ' ' They will choose the worst, very likely,' say I, ' but that is just liberty.' ' And what is to bring good out of such liberty as that? ' he asks. ' The glorious and sanative qualities of our matchless Constitution,' I reply; and that is always a stopper for him."

Only a few years after the publication of *Friendship's Garland* Arnold himself was the subject of satirical banter, clever and diverting, in *The New Republic* (1877), by William Hurrell Mallock. Mr. Luke, who represents Arnold, is marked by that Olympian superiority and aloofness which were supposed to characterise the great critic and poet. The satire however is of a wholly different and far less important sort than that of *Friendship's Garland*. Arnold's book is really a veiled appeal, profoundly serious, to the better spirit of England. Mallock's satire is purely personal, taking off other prominent persons, particularly Jowett and Ruskin, as well as Arnold, and Jowett even more than Arnold.

Last in time among the prose satirists of the nineteenth century stands Samuel Butler (1835–1902). His *Erewhon*, published anonymously in 1872, was warmly praised and promised to achieve a wide popularity, so long as it was thought to be by Lytton, whose modern Utopia *The Coming Race* had appeared in the previous year. As soon as *Erewhon* was found to be by a nobody the interest in it faded away, and Butler passed the rest of his life with scanty recognition. The note he made in 1899 on sales of his books shows a loss on every one except *Erewhon* and *Life and Habit*; and except *Erewhon* not one even approaches a sale of a thousand. But amends have been made since, and by one or two critics praises have been showered upon *The Way of all Flesh* which seem to imply that Butler's place is in the foremost rank of human greatness. His true position is a good deal humbler.

The gist of Butler's satire is contained in four books, and these, in the order of publication, are: *Erewhon*, *The Fair Haven* (1873), *Erewhon Revisited* (1901), and *The Way of all Flesh* (1903). It should however be noted that *The Way of all Flesh* was begun in 1873, and was finished in 1884. Though there is satire also here and there in the miscellaneous essays and papers, and in the interesting and suggestive, though over-rated, *Note-Books*, little of moment is added to what we find in the four books just named. But because Butler was no poet, as well as for their great intrinsic merit, it is worth noting two pieces written in free verse—*The Righteous Man*, which compresses into twenty or thirty stingingly severe lines the quintessence of Butler's satire of human nature, and the wholly admirable *Psalm of Montreal*, Butler's protest against the blindness of a commercial age to beauty and the prudery of the Puritan:—

> " The Discobolus is put here because he is vulgar—
> He has neither vest nor pants to cover his limbs;
> I, Sir, am a person of most respectable connections—
> My brother-in-law is haberdasher to Mr. Spurgeon.
> O God! O Montreal! "

Butler's satire is so profoundly influenced by his own experiences that it is essential to bear constantly in mind a few of the facts of his early life. He reads the universe in the light of his own history; no satirist is more autobiographical. He was the son of a clergyman, and the grandson of another clergyman who became Headmaster of Shrewsbury School and afterwards Bishop of Lichfield. He was educated at Shrewsbury under Dr. Kennedy, and at St. John's College, Cambridge, where he took a first class in the classical tripos. He was designed for the Church, and began in London to prepare for ordination, but became so shaken as to the faith he had been taught that he gave up this intention. Instead, he started sheep-farming in New Zealand in 1859. There he began his literary career as a writer for the *Press* of Christchurch. When he sold his sheep-run in 1864 and returned to England his character was completely formed, and the facts of his subsequent life have little bearing upon his satire.

The kinship in circumstance between Butler and Ernest Pontifex, the hero of *The Way of all Flesh,* is manifest at once. Ernest too is the son of a clergyman, he is educated at a public school and at Cambridge, and he is designed for the Church. Of course Butler does not adhere to fact in every detail: Ernest is ordained, and he himself was never ordained. But all the experiences that were really formative of character were Butler's as well as Ernest's. Not only was Ernest the son of a clergyman, but his father Theobald is drawn from the life, and is a picture of Butler's father as his son saw him. So is Christina a picture of Butler's mother. His father and mother reappear (or rather they had appeared before) in old Mr. Owen and Mrs. Owen of *The Fair Haven*—the former, as Mr. Festing Jones tells us, by contraries; and experiences of Butler's own are embodied in the imaginary John Pickard Owen of the Memoir prefixed to the book, whose defence of the dogmas of Christianity is just Butler's ironical attack upon them.

Practically the whole of Butler's satire is aimed at two institutions—the family and the Church. And of these the family is fundamental; for it is his early experiences that ultimately shape Butler's views of religion as well as of society. That there is much to be said in excuse of him is obvious; but equally obvious is it that excuse is needed. A son who had a father so extremely disagreeable as Theobald of *The Way of all Flesh* could not be expected to be enthusiastic about his home; but he might reasonably be expected to refrain from drawing a universal conclusion from a single instance; and in spite of the happy family of Yram in *Erewhon Revisited* and of the happy relations between George and his newly-discovered father, that is substantially what he does. In the *Note-Books* he writes that Melchizedec "was a really happy man. He was without father, without mother, and without descent. He was an incarnate bachelor. He was a born orphan." That is to say, the family relations are a curse, and happy would man be could they be dispensed with. Yet surely human history proves that the establishment of the family on the basis of monogamy is the greatest step forward ever taken by man. But perhaps Butler did not mean what he said in the note. If he did not, the note seems pointless; and that he meant it seems to be the fair conclusion from *The Way of all Flesh*. The children with whom Ernest Pontifex is provided are left in the care of people who are not their parents; the "cash nexus" is the only tie with their father that is not wholly severed.

If then we may take the account of the family relations given in *The Way of all Flesh* as something more than a particular case, it is most depressing and unpleasant. Satire and cynicism run through the whole of it. The love-making, engagement and marriage of Theobald and Christina are satirised. Theobald felt magnanimous when he refused to be released from his engagement. "True, at the moment of magnanimity the actual cash payment, so to speak, was still distant; when his father gave formal consent to his marriage things began to look more serious; when the college living had fallen vacant they looked more serious still; but when Christina actually named the day, then Theobald's heart fainted within him." The view of the relations between parents and children is cynical:—

" To parents who wish to lead a quiet life I would say: Tell your children that they are very naughty—much naughtier than most children. Point to the young people of some acquaintances as models of perfection, and impress your own children with a deep sense of their own inferiority. You carry so many more guns than they do that they cannot fight you. This is called moral influence, and it will enable you to bounce them as much as you please. They think you know, and they will not have yet caught you lying often enough to suspect that you are not the unworldly and scrupulously truthful person which you represent yourself to be; nor yet will they know how great a coward you are, nor how soon you will run away, if they fight you with persistency and judgment. You keep the dice and throw them both for your children and yourself."

This passage occurs in the account of the family of which Theobald's father was head; and yet of that family we are told that "there would be ten families of young people worse off for one better." The spirit here outlined runs through *The Way of all Flesh* from beginning to end. Butler pays not the slightest regard to the pieties of the family; evidently he believed that the fifth commandment had been abrogated. But the fifth commandment expresses the judgment of one of the greatest races of humanity on the family relations. The story of Orestes buttresses the judgment of the Hebrew by the judgment of the Greek. It teaches that the retribution would be just were it inflicted by another hand. But nothing can justify the son who slays the mother.

Almost any man would shrink from stripping his mother naked, even if she were a bad mother; and to strip the soul is an incomparably graver offence than to strip the body. But Butler never hesitates: the letter of Christina printed in C. XXV. is the actual letter written by Butler's mother on an occasion similar to that described in the novel, and preserved by her as by Christina. Butler has ingenious but wholly unconvincing reasons for printing the letter. We know Wordsworth's opinion of the man who "would peep and botanise upon his mother's grave." Which is the wiser and the grander—the poet or the satirist?

It is evident that Butler considered himself, and he is considered by many others, to be one of the greatest and most original of recent philosophers. It is the business of philosophy to rise above prejudice, and he who cannot do so has but little title to the name. Try Butler by this test. In C. XXVI. he writes: "It is matter of common observation in England that the sons of clergymen are frequently unsatisfactory"; and for this reason he thinks the Church of Rome wise in enforcing celibacy upon the priesthood. It is matter of common observation that the sons of any class of men are frequently unsatisfactory; that only means that human nature leaves a good deal to be desired. The implication obviously is that the sons of clergymen are unsatisfactory in a larger proportion of cases than the sons of lawyers or doctors or mechanics. So understood, the statement, though often repeated, is sheer prejudice. There are thoughtful and able men who maintain that it would be worth the while of the State to pay the salaries of all the parsons, just that they might bring up those "unsatisfactory" sons. And it is not a case merely of opinion against opinion. Mr. Havelock Ellis investigated the antecedents of 829 distinguished men and women. He found that 139 of them, or 16·7 per cent., had clergymen or ministers for fathers, while only 21, or 2·5 per cent., sprang from the class of "artisans or unskilled labourers." Now, an Anthropological Committee of the British Association quoted by Mr. Ellis estimated the professional classes (including law, medicine, education, the army, etc.) to include only 4·46 per cent. of the population of Britain. Probably the clergy and ministers were less than one-fourth in number of the professional classes—say, one per cent. of the population. Artisans numbered, according to this committee, 26·82 per cent. of the population, and labourers 47·46 per cent.—together, over 74 per cent. Apparently, therefore, one per cent. of the population produced more than six times as many children who achieved distinction as the 74 per cent. of artisans and labourers. Put it in another way: Choose by lot one child from the group of clerical families, and one from the group of working-class families, and the one from the former group will have nearly five hundred times as much chance of attaining distinction as the one from the other group. Evidently there is more to be said for those who regard the clerical home as an inestimable source of intellectual and moral wealth to the State than for Butler. Such is the wisdom with which satire is written.

The connexion between the satire of the family and the satire of religion is obvious; both are Butler's reaction against the experiences of his childhood and youth. Religion as it was presented by Theobald and Christina was not very attractive, and Butler's intellect was far too keen to remain long unaffected by the criticism to which Victorian orthodoxy was being subjected. But it was not the criticism of others that first shook Butler's orthodoxy: it was reasoning from his own experience; and the fact shows that his mind had remained in a singularly naïve condition until after he had passed through the university. How deep was the impression made by the discovery that the sacrament of baptism produced no apparent effect upon character is shown by the fact that it has left its mark on *Erewhon* and on *The Fair Haven*, as well as on *The Way of all Flesh*. In the former there is the incident of the baptising of Chowbok, and the uneasiness of the administrant afterwards, because "on the evening of the same day on which I baptised him he tried for the twentieth time to steal the brandy, which made me rather unhappy as to whether I could have baptised him rightly." There is also all the satire of godfathers in the chapter on Birth Formulæ. In the memoir prefixed to *The Fair Haven* there is narrated of the imaginary John Pickard Owen precisely the discovery which in Butler's own experience in London gave rise to the doubts which prevented him from being ordained, and in the end made him what he professed to be till the end of his life—"a member of the more advanced wing of the English Broad Church." A very advanced wing indeed, as any one will agree who has studied

Butler's opinions. The discovery in question, as narrated in the memoir of Owen, is made while performing the duty of a Sunday School teacher:—

"When he was explaining the effect of baptism to one of his favourite pupils, he discovered to his great surprise that the boy had never been baptised. He pushed his enquiries further, and found that out of the fifteen boys in his class only five had been baptised, and, not only so, but that no difference in disposition or conduct could be discovered between the regenerate boys and the unregenerate. The good and bad boys were distributed in proportions equal to the respective numbers of the baptised and the unbaptised.

When the basis of investigation is widened the result is still the same. Owen attributed the mischief to the institution of sponsors and of infant baptism. But doubt has been started, and it even spreads to other dogmas. Finally he reaches the conclusion that Christianity is true, not in spite of the discrepancies and inconsistencies of the Gospels, but because of those very discrepancies.

It is this position that furnishes the basis on which the ironical *Fair Haven* is constructed. Many failed to detect the irony, and the presentation is sufficiently subtle to give some excuse for the misapprehension. But the true meaning is clear enough if we consider the strength of the chapters on "certain ill-judged methods of defence," and contrast with it the exceeding weakness of the conclusion, which professes to pass in review the arguments of the sceptics. If this be defence, we may well pray to be delivered from our defenders.

Butler stands on firmer ground in his satire of the dogmas of the orthodox than in his satire of the family. The futility, and even the dishonesty, of much of the defence affords far too much ground for the irony of *The Fair Haven*, and the analogy between supernatural Christianity and the Sunchildism of *Erewhon Revisited* is skilfully indicated. Many will reject the views insinuated by Butler and think the whole subject unpleasant. But the impartial mind must admit the legitimacy of the satire. Keen as it is, even those whose withers are wrung must find it entertaining. The pictures of Professors Hanky and Panky and Mr. Balmy in *Erewhon Revisited* are things profitable for the soul to dwell upon. The Sabbatarian would be all the better for remembering the interpretation put by the Erewhonians on the stranger's observance of the Sabbath. They ascribed it to "a fit of sulkiness, which they remarked as coming over me every seventh day." The missionary might do well to ponder the reflections of the adventurer with regard to his efforts for the conversion of Chowbok: "He was, indeed, stony ground, but by digging about him I might have, at any rate, deprived him of all faith in the religion of his tribe, which would have been half-way towards making him a sincere Christian"; and the satire on those who devote themselves to "saving souls, and filling their own pocket at one and the same moment" is also well worth laying to heart. So too the neat way in which Arowhena turns round upon the conception of God the argument that the idea of the personality of justice and hope was quite without influence is calculated to give rise to profitable thought; and the conclusion very deftly insinuates the weakness of some of the arguments that were current when *Erewhon* was written: "I did wince a little," says the adventurer; "but I recovered myself immediately, and pointed out to her that the case was entirely different, because we had books whose genuineness was beyond all possibility of doubt, as they were certainly none of them less than 1800 years old; that in these there were the most authentic accounts of men who had been spoken to by the Deity Himself, and of one prophet who had been allowed to see the back parts of God through the hand that was laid over his face. This was conclusive."

But the core of Butler's satire of dogmatic Christianity is contained in the chapter on the Musical Banks, an unsparing exposure of the difference between the professions of the Church and the actual beliefs of laity and clergy alike. The currency of these banks was not current. All who wished to be respectable must have some of it; but what they really trusted was the money of the other banks. Even the managers and cashiers of the musical banks were not paid in their own currency. It was the ladies mostly who frequented the musical banks, but even they with little real conviction. Butler's own experience peeps out again in the closing sentences of the chapter, where he condemns the conduct of parents who "bought the right of presenting to the office of cashier at one of these banks, with the fixed determination that some one of their sons (perhaps a mere child) should fill it."

At the same time, we may find in this chapter the explanation of the fact that Butler's satire of religion is much sounder than his satire of the family. In the latter case his unfortunate experiences in childhood and youth distorted permanently his conception of the family; in the former, he was completely alienated from orthodoxy, but his sympathy with that of which orthodoxy is only one expression was never killed. This is clearly shown in his description of the building to which the ladies carry the adventurer when they visit their musical bank:—

" It was an epic in stone and marble; neither had I ever seen anything in the land comparable to it. I was completely charmed and melted. I felt more conscious of the existence of a remote past. One knows of this always, but the knowledge is never so living as in the actual presence of some witness to the life of bygone ages. I felt how short a space of human life was the period of our own existence. I was more impressed with my own littleness, and much more inclinable to believe that the people whose sense of the fitness of things was equal to the uplifting of so serene a handiwork, were hardly likely to be wrong in the conclusion they might come to upon any subject. My feeling certainly was that the currency of this bank must be the right one."

The Fair Haven and *Erewhon Revisited* would hardly exist except to fulfil the function of satires of religion. *Erewhon* and *The Way of all Flesh* have a broader basis. The treatment of the family in the latter has already been dealt with; the general satire of the former must now be briefly touched upon. The Erewhonian war against machinery, lest it should come to dominate man, is a skit at evolution. The colleges of unreason and their study of hypothetics satirise the system of education in England. But above all, the whimsical conception of ill-health as a thing to be punished by law, while embezzlement and theft and intemperance and ill-temper were met with the kindest sympathy, is made to throw a revealing light upon society. The trial of the prisoner for the crime of being consumptive suggests doubts as to the injunctions sometimes addressed to prisoners in our own country. The Erewhonian is enjoined to reform the constitution of his whole body; which may, after all, be as easy as to reform the constitution of the soul. On the other hand, "the people were the healthiest and comeliest imaginable, owing to the severity with which ill-health was treated"; which gives ground to hope that if only we treat moral offences with sufficient severity we shall become the best and most moral people imaginable.

In all that Butler has written there is nothing worthy of closer attention than the chapter of *Erewhon* on Ydgrun and the

Ydgrunites, nothing that more clearly reveals his inner thought. No one else probably has so sanely estimated both the worth and the worthlessness of Mrs. Grundy, a goddess whom it is easy to overwhelm with ridicule, yet whom common sense perceives to be indispensable. Had Butler always kept his balance as he does here, his reputation for wit might have been less, but he would have shown a higher wisdom. His finding is that the High Ydgrunites [gentlemen] "in the matter of human conduct and the affairs of life appeared to me to have got about as far as it is in the right nature of man to go. . . . They were more like Englishmen who had been educated at such a school as Winchester (if there be such another), and sent thence to one of the best colleges at Oxford or Cambridge, than any whom I have seen in other countries."

Butler stands clearly at the head of the satire of the later nineteenth century; but not in the first rank of satire, and still less in the first rank of literature. Swift, with whom his affinities are most obvious, is far superior in breadth of range, in force of thought, and in keenness of wit. On the other hand, Butler is much more humane; but this unfortunately is an advantage which diminished with time. *The Way of all Flesh* is far less pleasant and humane than *Erewhon*.

More than five centuries of English satire have been passed in review. At the beginning stands *Piers Plowman*, and the fundamental theme of his satire is religion; at the end stands Samuel Butler the Second, and the fundamental theme is still religion. In between we have men like the earlier Samuel Butler and Swift absorbed in it likewise. In essentials, human nature is invariable; and so long as men are men the same problems will remain unsolved, and the lash of criticism will fall from age to age on what seem to be absurdities in the way of handling them.

FINIS

INDEX

THE END